2/10/97

Design by Motley

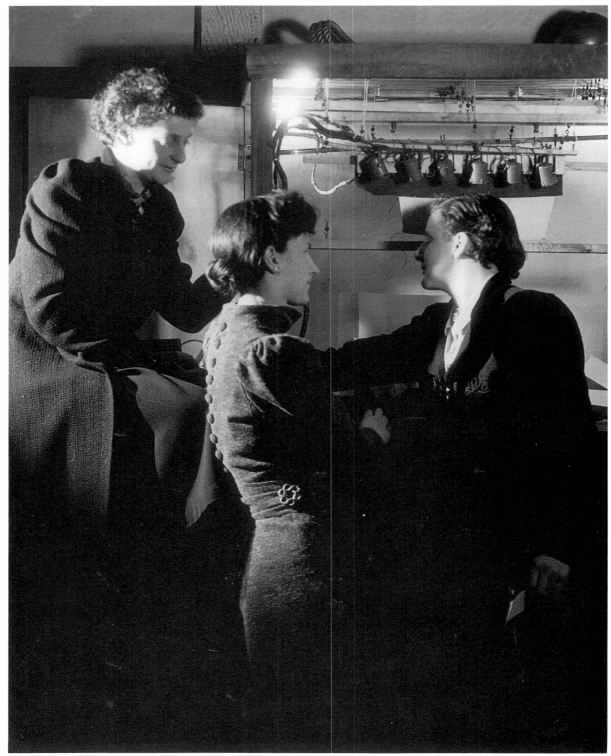

"Motley," publicity photograph by Howard Coster. Sophia Harris is on the left, Elizabeth Montgomery is center, and Margaret Harris is on the right. The photograph comes from Motley's files; it was later published in Terence Pepper's Howard Coster's Celebrity Portraits *(National Portrait Gallery, London, in association with Dover Publications, Inc.).*

Design by Motley

MICHAEL MULLIN

Foreword by Sir John Gielgud

DELAWARE

Newark: University of Delaware Press
London: Associated University Presses

Associated University Presses
440 Forsgate Drive
Cranbury, NJ 08512

Associated University Presses
25 Sicilian Avenue
London WC1A 2QH, England

Associated University Presses
P.O. Box 338, Port Credit
Mississauga, Ontario
Canada L5G 4L8

The paper used in this publication meets the requirements of the American National Standard for Permanence of Paper for Printed Library Materials Z39.48-1984.

Library of Congress Cataloging-in-Publication Data

Mullin, Michael.
    Design by Motley / Michael Mullin; foreword by Sir John Gielgud.
        p.   cm.
    Includes bibliographical references and index.
    ISBN 0-87413-569-9 (alk. paper)
        1. Motley, pseud.   2. Costume designers—Great Britain—Biography.
    3. Costume design—Great Britain—History—20th century.   I. Title.
    TT505.M68M85   1996
    792′.026′0922—dc20
    [B]
                                                                94-42667
                                                                CIP

PRINTED IN THE UNITED STATES OF AMERICA

For Catie, Bridie, Meggie, and Betsy

Sine qua non

Contents

Foreword
  SIR JOHN GIELGUD   9
Preface   13
Acknowledgments   15

  1. Childhood and Youth (1900–1930)   19
  2. Foundations and Beginnings (1927–1932)   25
  3. An Emergent Style (1932–1935)   33
  4. Motley's the Only Wear (1936–1940)   55
  5. Motley Takes the Town: New York (1940–1945)   76
  6. Elizabeth Montgomery in New York (1946–1966)   86
  7. Motley in London (1940–1947)   108
  8. The Old Vic, the Young Vic, and the Old Vic School
     (1947–1953)   114
  9. The English Stage Company and The Royal Court
     Theatre (1954–1966)   124
10. The Shakespeare Memorial Theatre (1948–1958)   135
11. The Sadler's Wells Opera and the English National
     Opera (1952–1978)   155
12. In the West End (1946–1975)   173
13. Film (1933–1966)   195
14. The Motley Legacy: The Design Course (1966–   )   206

Appendix: Motley's Students   212
Chronology: Motley Productions and Credits (1927–1976)   216
Notes   235
List of Works Consulted   240
Index   247

Foreword

SIR JOHN GIELGUD

I can hardly believe that it is sixty years since I first made the acquaintance of Sophie and Percy Harris and Elizabeth Montgomery, three shy young women living together in a flat off Church Street, Kensington, where I visited them to thank them for some drawings of myself which they had brought me when I was acting at the Old Vic in a succession of great Shakespearean parts.

We became friends immediately, and I was greatly taken with the work that they showed me. When I was asked to direct for the Oxford University Dramatic Society a production of *Romeo and Juliet,* I suggested that my new friends should design the costumes, which were an outstanding success and proved to be the foundation stone of their long and distinguished careers. This was in 1932. A year later I was able to recommend that the girls should design both the scenery and the costumes for a new play, *Richard of Bordeaux,* which was mounted for a few performances at the Arts Theatre in London. Not long afterwards, the same play was produced at the New Theatre (now the Albery) and was a huge success. The Motleys were given permission to employ a somewhat larger budget, allowing them to display their brilliant work, and they were immediately established as original and versatile designers. They seemed able to create remarkable results at a comparatively modest cost, using and adapting economical materials with superb effect.

We worked together in most of the productions which I directed until the beginning of the Second War, notably *Hamlet, Romeo and Juliet, Strange Orchestra, The Old Ladies,* and the four plays which I

presented at the Queen's Theatre in 1937 and 1938—*Richard II, The School for Scandal, Three Sisters,* and *The Merchant of Venice.*

A big studio at the top of St. Martin's Lane had now become their workshop. Once said to have belonged to Chippendale, it was destined to be destroyed in the Blitz of 1941, and, the morning after the raid, I found the buildings wrecked with only my kingly cloak from *Richard II,* spread soaking and disconsolate over the pavement below. But for many years before, the Motleys had made it a delightfully memorable rendezvous for a number of actors and artists who were friends of both of us. George Devine, who had met the girls in my Oxford *Romeo,* became their faithful devotee and business manager when Sophie Harris opened a boutique for private customers in addition to her stage work.

When Michel Saint-Denis arrived in London to direct an English production of Obey's *Noah,* which he had already successfully created and acted in with his own French Compagnie des Quinze, I was able to introduce him to the girls. That meeting was to develop into an enthusiastic friendship and cooperation for them all, which was to last until the deaths of George and Michel, both of whom were determined to teach and influence young stage aspirants in all the different departments of the theatre as well as pursuing their professional careers. The Motleys worked with them in planning productions, schools, and other ambitious schemes, some of which, of course, were cut short by the War; but they continued to work unceasingly, though Devine enlisted and Michel be-

John Gielgud as Richard in Richard of Bordeaux. *In this production Gielgud emerged as a producer and director with Motley as his designers. The glamorous production dazzled London audiences. The photograph appears in a clipping in Motley's files.*

came an important officer in the French Resistance. In 1939 Laurence Olivier persuaded the girls to go to America, but the production there of *Romeo and Juliet,* in which he appeared on Broadway with Vivien Leigh, was a disappointing failure. Nevertheless, Motley-designed productions that followed met with great success. Percy returned to England after the War, though Elizabeth Montgomery married an American and stayed in the United States for many years, achieving considerable success on her own with stage work of many different kinds.

Tragically, Sophie Harris died in 1966. With Elizabeth's absence in America, the trio had become sadly separated. Percy managed to survive indomitably. Her energy, craftsmanship, and sweet nature have combined to enable her to develop throughout the long years which have seen such extraordinary changes in the English theatre. She has never submitted to any deviation from her capacity to learn, teach, and remain a dedicated artist of the highest diligence and expertise. She has never made money an important considera-tion, except for the necessity of finding funds to enable her to pursue her talents in adequate sur-roundings. I feel very privileged to have been so lucky in being one of the first to recognize the remarkable gifts of these three accomplished art-ists, whose record is such a shining example of their outstanding careers. The influence they have had will surely be recorded, as it is in this book, by all who have been fortunate enough to share their enthusiasms and triumphs in the challenging theatre of their day.

John Gielgud
August 1992

Preface

In 1932 there appeared in the program for *Romeo and Juliet* at Oxford University, "Costumes designed by Motley," the name taken from Jaques's quip "Motley's the only wear" in *As You Like It*. Three young women were behind the name. Margaret Harris (b. 1904) and her sister Sophie (1900–1966) had come from their family home in Hayes, Kent, to study art in London. At art school they met Elizabeth Montgomery (1902–1993). The three developed a friendship that was to endure for decades as their careers in the theatre moved from triumph to triumph. In the course of time both Sophie and Elizabeth married—Sophie to George Devine, the English actor-director and founder of the English Stage Company at the Royal Court Theatre; Elizabeth to the American writer Patrick Wilmot—and the married Motleys each had families. World War II swept through the 1940s, and a profoundly different sensibility emerged. In New York during the 1940s, 1950s, and 1960s Elizabeth made historic changes in the designing of costumes for Broadway musicals and for opera at the Met, also painting portraits of opera stars. In London at the same time, Sophia Harris designed for the avant-garde Royal Court Theatre, for the West End, and for films. After the War, Margaret Harris worked chiefly at the Shakespeare Memorial Theatre, Stratford-upon-Avon, and at the English National Opera, London. Through it all, "Design by Motley" continued to appear among the credits for so many plays, operas, and ballets that the phrase became a watchword for style, elegance, and excellence in London, New York, and theatre capitals around the world. For audiences numbering millions in both England and America, Motley's sets and costumes created a rich legacy of dramatic interpretation.

In one sense, that legacy has vanished, as all theatrical performance vanishes once the lights go out in the theatre. Yet Motley's influence remains through the memories of those millions of playgoers. It remains also through Motley's training of hundreds of new designers and through their effect on other designers. Having been preserved by great good fortune, the designs themselves provide a record of achievement that invites investigation. In reconstructing that record in the pages that follow, I have been able to draw upon not only the designs and the public record, but also upon Margaret Harris's and Elizabeth Montgomery's recorded accounts, from which I often quote.

In September 1981, the University of Illinois Library received two large steamer trunks from Motley, the English set and costume designers. In the trunks were found costume designs, set sketches, notes, photographs, prop lists, story boards, and even swatches of fabric—everything belonging to Motley from their work in the English and American theatre: 5,500 items that represented 160 of Motley's 300+ productions. The contents of these two trunks took more than two years to sort and catalogue. In 1984 the Motley Collection at the University of Illinois Library was opened for research.

It is indeed remarkable that so much of Motley's work has survived. That it did is owing to the designers' foresight in preserving many of their drawings. Rather than discarding them once the show had opened, they tucked the designs away, in no particular order. The designs first came to light in 1976 in the course of the author's research on Shakespeare. In the years following, the surviving designs were collected, sorted, and preserved by the University of Illinois Library. During the years 1986–1991, with the aid of grants from the National Endowment for the Humanities and the University of Illinois Foundation the author conceived, wrote, and directed a major exhibition on Motley's work. Entitled "Design by Motley," it featured reconstructed Motley costumes and the original costume worn by Peggy Ashcroft as Cleopatra, set models for a dozen Motley productions, a video interview produced by the BBC, and original set and costume drawings. The exhibition was on display in the United States at the Los Angeles Theatre Centre, the Ashland, Oregon, Shakespeare Festival, the Seattle Public Library, the Boston Public Library, the University of Texas at Austin, the Kennedy Center in Washington, D.C., Lincoln Center in New York, the Broward County Public Library in Fort Lauderdale, and the 1800 North Clybourn Gallery in Chicago. It subsequently transferred to the Royal National Theatre in London.

This book extends and completes the research on which the exhibition was based.

During the nineteen years that have elapsed since I first encountered Motley—in the person of Margaret Harris in 1976—my primary sources have been the Motley designs and Margaret Harris's clear recollections, supplemented by those of Elizabeth Montgomery. To extend their recollections, I have also interviewed Sophia Harris's daughter Harriet Jump as well as theatre artists who worked with Motley: Dame Peggy Ashcroft, Maxine Audley, Maurice Daniels, Andrew Eaton, Peter Gill, David Gothard, Hayden Griffin, Roger Howells, Carol Lawrence, Mitsuru Ishii, and Glen Byam Shaw, among many others. Central, of course, are the set and costume designs, renderings, storyboards, and sketches in the Motley Collection of the University of Illinois at Urbana-Champaign. For reviews of productions that Motley designed I turned to the Manders and Mitchenson Theatre Collection and the Theatre Museum in London, as well as to the Shakespeare Centre Library, Stratford-upon-Avon, and the University of Illinois Library. Besides these sources, the bibliography at the end of this book lists published works consulted. An audio recording of Margaret Harris's recollections (1992) may be consulted in the British Institute of Recorded Sound, London.

Acknowledgments

So many people have contributed to this book that it is impossible to thank them all individually. To Margaret Harris and Elizabeth Montgomery, the Motley women who contributed to every stage of this book's preparation, I owe the most. Without their interest and unstinting encouragement, this wide-ranging research could not have been undertaken or completed. Thanks too to Sir John Gielgud, whose foreword graces this volume, and to the many theatre artists whose encouragement sustained my research efforts: Dame Peggy Ashcroft, John Boundy, Maurice Daniels, Andrew Eaton, Peter Gill, Hayden Griffin, Reg Hanson, John Langley, Joanna Morgan, Chris Rodgers, and Glen Byam Shaw. Dr. Harriet Jump, Sophia Harris's daughter, helped throughout, especially in reconstructing her mother's contributions to Motley.

Utmost appreciation is extended to the faculty and staff of the University of Illinois, whose generous help has been unfaltering and to the University of Illinois Library Friends, whose private gifts turned the dream of acquiring the Motley Collection into reality. Timely assistance in the acquisition came from former Chancellor John E. Cribbet, the late University Librarian Hugh C. Atkinson, Deans Jack H. McKenzie and William F. Prokasy of the colleges of Fine and Applied Arts and Liberal Arts and Sciences, respectively.

At the University Library many helped: In the Rare Book Library, Mary S. Ceibert, N. Frederick Nash, Gene K. Rinkel, and Nancy L. Romero made it possible to use the Motley Collection. In Collection Development and Preservation, Norman B. Brown, William T. Henderson, and William H. Huff assisted in the cataloguing and storing of the materials. For this arduous task, many thanks are also due to Associate Professor of Theatre Paul J. Brady and graduate assistants Ananda Lal and Ann E. Timmons. Ron Terragrossa made the slide copies. Carl Deal, Michael Gorman, Deloris Holiman, and Dale Montanelli each lent their special expertise without stint. Joan M. Hood, development director, was everywhere instrumental in securing needed private funding.

For helping with the research upon which this document rests, special thanks go to Professor Charles T. Garey of Santa Barbara City College and to the able research assistants called the "Motley Crew": Jonathan Brown, Dan Bruzzini, Mary Frances Budig, Darin Collier, Wendy Dodson, Kristi Esgar, Maria Finatri, Stephen Huh, Joann Jacoby, Ronnie Johnston, Lisa Kernek, Nelie Keinenan, Carol Kostka, Mark Lackner, Nancy A. Marck, David McGuire, Betsy Mullin, Bridie Mullin, Catie Mullin, Meggie Mullin, Lisa Quayne, Michael Roeschlein, Sarah Schmidt, Martin Siemer, Kathryn Socha, Melissa Staats, Monica Tibbitts, Michael Trizna, and Jennifer Vodvarka.

Marian Pringle, Senior Librarian at the Shakespeare Centre Library, Stratford-upon-Avon, assisted in every phase of the research. Invaluable expert help came from Richard Mangan, Director of the Manders and Mitchenson Theatre Collection. Professor Dale Harris of the Tisch School of the Arts, New York University, contributed his expertise in ballet, opera, and theatre. Edmund Tracey, former opera critic and retired director of the English National Opera, scrutinized the chapter on opera, as did my colleague Thomas Schleis of the University of Illinois School of Music. Catherine Suroweic, researcher at the British Film

Institute, provided expertise on Motley's costume designs for film. My friend John T. Phipps provided expert legal counsel.

This book's final form owes much to the sharp editorial eye of my wife, Margaret Mary Mullin. For her skills and good judgment as a writer, no less than her understanding and encouragement, I remain profoundly thankful.

To these and to the many others who helped are owed deep gratitude, more than I can pay. Theirs the virtues, mine the faults.

Design by Motley

1

Childhood and Youth
1900–1930

The world in which the Motley women grew up was very different from ours today. Britain ruled over a relatively peaceful empire that was full of opportunity overseas for the young men of the middle classes, among whom could be counted the restless young William Harris, the Harris sisters' father. Reportedly a scamp when he was at Oxford University, he settled down only after spreading his wings in South Africa as a prospector and sometime amateur actor. When he returned from abroad, work as an insurance broker for Lloyds provided him a stable income and subsequently supported his wife and family.

Life was comfortably middle class for the Harris sisters in the distant London suburb of Hayes, Kent. Their mother Kathleen was an unconventional woman, who enjoyed making costumes for her girls and dressing them up to take photographs. One of her designs for them—the "romp-suit," as Margaret Harris called it—expressed a nonconformist view of young girls' dress, unusual for the time. Their casual schooling was overseen by governesses.

With World War I came tragedy for the family. Margaret and Sophia's brother was killed in the War, and their mother succumbed to tuberculosis not long afterwards. Disconsolate at the double loss, their father moved his small family into London, where the girls were enrolled in formal schools. He moved back to Hayes several years later, but their brief acquaintance with London made the Harris girls quite comfortable with the city. Their subsequent enrollment in art school in fashionable Chelsea was a happy change for them.

Although Margaret Harris did not allude to it directly, the freedom she and her sister experienced as children must have been extended by their mother's death in 1916, when the girls were in their teens, and by their father's subsequent withdrawal into grief and early death in 1924, when they were still in their twenties. They found themselves on their own, but not destitute, for they had a small inheritance that they could eke out by work as illustrators and, occasionally, by selling some of the family silver.

In art school they met Elizabeth Montgomery, who had moved with her family to Fulham, London, from Cambridge. The Montgomerys were also a middle-class family, very different from the Harrises in that Mr. Montgomery was a somewhat disaffected cleric; his wife, an Irishwoman renowned for her fiery temperament. World War I drew upon Montgomery's unusual skills as a linguist and cryptographer—skills that enabled him to decode the "Zimmerman telegram" that brought the United States into the War. Unlike the Harris girls, who were informally educated and who had not studied art before coming to London, Elizabeth had been trained in art from a very young age.

In talking with Margaret Harris and Elizabeth Montgomery about their upbringing, one is struck

Margaret and Sophia Harris dressed and posed by their mother as if "on safari" in Africa. Their mother made the costumes for the two girls and took the photograph.

by how different their experience was from that of today's young middle-class women, who face a wider range of career choices. Yet the Motleys' twenties also seem to have been very free, with a rather happy-go-lucky nonchalance about making one's way in the world. Perhaps made rosy by nostalgia when remembered from the vantage point of the 1980s, the picture they evoke of three young women enjoying art school, the theatre, and London of the 1920s reveals how energetic and undirected were their early years there. With hindsight, of course, it is clear that their immersion in the theatre and culture of London was exactly the right preparation for their work as designers. They had learned the taste of the town and were ready to put their ideas to the test.

Unlike many successful theatre people then and now in England and America, neither the Harris sisters nor Elizabeth Montgomery came from "theatrical" families. Theatre designer Edward Gordon Craig, for instance, had unusual entrée through his mother, Ellen Terry, as had John Gielgud, through a connection to the Terry family. The actor and director Glen Byam Shaw, with whom Motley worked extensively, benefited from having a father who was a famous and well-connected London artist. Lacking any loyalties to theatrical traditions, the Motley women brought to the London theatre scene the fresh eyes of those for whom theatrical convention lay open to question.

None of the Motley women had grown up in the capital, and none had had any special educational advantages. They succeeded not only because of their talent as artists, but also for their ability to sense how sets and costumes would be interpreted by people like themselves, who came from the larger society, outside the world of the theatre. In telling their family histories, both Margaret Harris and Elizabeth Montgomery emphasize the comparative "ordinariness" of their background. Not false modesty, their insistence that they came from families representative of the middle class underlies an attitude towards work and style in the theatre that was both practical and humble, without affectation.

However "ordinary" their background may have been in the context of a society that routinely dispatched its young men to far distant posts in the British Empire, the Harris sisters could lay claim to an adventuresome father, an artistic mother, and an eventful upbringing.

Margaret Harris

Our father was called William Birbeck Harris (1867–1924) and was born in or near Bradford. His father was a businessman, a Yorkshire Quaker. Both his parents died when he was three. He and his elder sister, our Aunt Katie, were brought up by Uncle Ben and Aunt Mary in Warlingham, near Croyden.

I don't know at all whether his childhood was happy or unhappy; he didn't ever say anything about that. But he used to visit his uncle and aunt fairly regularly when we were very small, and sometimes we accompanied him. They too must have been Quakers; they were certainly very strict people. Aunt Mary, I remember, wore a black dress and a white cap, and she used to use the pronouns "thee" and "thou."

Will was sent to school in Shrewsbury. Whether he was successful there, he never vouchsafed. After he spent a short time in Germany, presumably learning German, he went to Hertford College, an Oxford University college, where he seems to have been extremely wild. The family used to tell stories of his misbehavior: Of his being chased by the proctors, scrambling up the steps of a horsebus onto the top, jumping off, landing on his feet, and running away; of using a saddle to climb over the college walls late at night; of following the lamplighter round Oxford on the shoulders of a tall friend, who had the nickname of "Seven Foot of Damnation," putting out the lamps that the lamplighter had just lighted; of driving four horses at full gallop down the High Street and straight into the stable without easing up; and of taking the reins from the driver and himself driving the London-to-Oxford coach. After this, rather understandably, he was sent down [expelled]. His story always was that he next borrowed all his sister's money and returned to Oxford and stayed at the Randolph Hotel, taking with him the girls from the Gaiety Chorus. His uncle, naturally, was extremely displeased about this. To avoid his uncle's wrath, Will seems to have run away, but was pursued round England by his uncle. They eventually met on some small railway platform, whereupon he was dispatched to South Africa—presumably to learn how to behave himself.

In South Africa, my father did a little bit of gold prospecting, but he found a very small amount of gold, apparently only enough to make a signet ring for himself, which I now wear, and a wedding ring for my mother. He fought in the Matabele War and was wounded. He rode in steeplechases and said that he won the first steeplechase to be run in South Africa. He met up with a company of actors there who, because he had some very interesting clothes, asked him to be their leading man. Although he'd never been trained in any way to act, he toured with them for some time playing various important parts. When he returned to England he became a Lloyds Insurance broker and married in 1895.

Our mother was a Miss Kathleen Carey (1873–1916). Her parents lived in Shortlands, Kent. Her father must have died when she was quite young because one never heard anything about his presence. Her mother was somewhat of an invalid and died when I was so small that I don't remember her at all, although I think Sophie had a faint recollection. She had three older brothers: Uncle Arthur, Uncle Harold, and Uncle Wilfred. Uncle Arthur died very young, having married, but not having had any children.

My mother was obviously quite an athletic character. She played tennis and other games. Her mother's house seems to have been a collecting place for all the young men in the area, among whom my father featured very large. She was also very skillful at sewing, and she drew very well. She had a strong artistic leaning. When we were small she used to go to the smart London shops

William Harris and Kathleen Harris, parents of Margaret and Sophia.

and look at the children's clothes and make drawings of them on the sly. Then at home she would cut and sew adaptations of them for Sophie and me. She was also a keen amateur photographer, and she used to enjoy posing us, sometimes in costume.

When they married, they took a house on Hayes Common, in Kent. It was then really in the country, with the common land in front, woods and fields at the back, and about an acre of ground. It was a small Regency farmhouse. Their eldest son Teddy was born in 1896; he got diphtheria and died in 1899. The second son, Norman, was born in 1898, just before the older one died. Then Sophie was born eighteen months after that in 1900, and then after another four years, I was born. I think we had a very happy childhood, but we were not very much accepted by the mothers of the other little girls in the area because we were dressed in a kind of romp-suit, which was a combination of a dress and knickerbockers. We were allowed to run very free in the woods and fields around the house.

Rather than attending a school, Sophie and I had governesses, some of whom were very nice and some not very nice. There were the usual family difficulties like whooping cough and chickenpox, and things like that. One rather dramatic thing was when Sophie fell forty feet out of a tree. She didn't seem to hurt herself, but it was quite an alarming occasion. I remember very well seeing it happen. When he was eleven my brother went to Osborne Royal Naval Junior College. Until World War I things seemed to go pretty smoothly, except that my father was always a very heavy drinker, which made Sundays rather a problem. I remember very well when the telegram arrived from my brother at the beginning of the War, saying, "We are mobilized." He was then at the Royal Naval Colleges of Dartmouth. They were short of naval officers, so they took the last year or so of boys from Dartmouth to turn them into midshipmen. In the very first few months of the War, the ship to which he was posted was sunk and he was lost. This I think was the last straw for my mother, because two years afterwards in 1916 she died of tuberculosis of the lungs.

My father then took a house in London for a

Elizabeth Montgomery as a child, and at age eighteen.

couple of years, to get away from Hayes, where he must have been fairly miserable and where we certainly were not very happy. We had our first experience of going to school then. We went to a day school in South Audley Street, designed for young ladies of the upper class, which I can't say we enjoyed very much. When we came back to Hayes from London, it was decided that I should be sent to boarding school. So I went to Down House, a school in the house where Darwin had lived in Down, Kent. After three or four rather undistinguished years there, I left.

Sophie and I then started to go to art school, first to the Queen Anne Studios, run by a lady called Miss McMunn, and later to the Chelsea Illustrators, run by Mrs. Goulden. Both were in Chelsea. At the Chelsea Illustrators we met Elizabeth.

Elizabeth Montgomery

My father, William Montgomery was born in Liverpool of Scottish-Irish parents. He was one of four brothers. His father worked for the shipping company, The White Star Line. When he was of college age, his father having died, there wasn't any money to send him to Cambridge or Oxford, so he came up to London—I think to London University. After studying there, he joined the Presbyterian Church.

My mother, Marta Corbett, was born in Northern Ireland at Fahan on Loch Swilley, not far from Londonderry. She was the eldest of a family of two brothers and three sisters. One of the sisters died quite young, and Marta had to help bring up the rest of the family. Marta's mother was a very ferocious little lady, I believe, who went through the Troubles [the uprisings for the Irish Free State]. She used to sleep with a revolver under her pillow.

When we lived in Fulham my mother used to rush out of our house, which backed onto the football field, waving an empty revolver at the football crowds, who swarmed over the garden wall to get in without paying. "You needn't laugh; you wouldn't be the first man I'd shot," she used to say. She used to tell me that she remembered as a child holding onto her own mother's skirt while

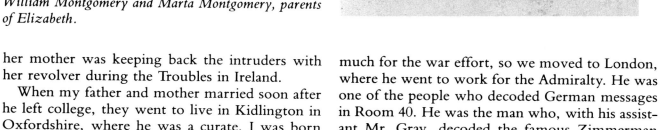

William Montgomery and Marta Montgomery, parents of Elizabeth.

her mother was keeping back the intruders with her revolver during the Troubles in Ireland.

When my father and mother married soon after he left college, they went to live in Kidlington in Oxfordshire, where he was a curate. I was born there. After about three years, he decided that he didn't really agree with everything he had to preach about and talk about in the Church. So he left and moved to Cambridge, where he became a lecturer in theology at St. John's College. He was a member of the Society for the Study of All Religions. I was therefore brought up in Cambridge from the age of three until World War I, when I was about twelve. My father was a great friend of Albert Schweitzer, and he translated nearly all his books. He also wrote a well-known book about St. Augustine. His hobby was sailing, which he taught me.

After the War broke out, my father moved us for a year or two to Malvern, where he taught in the public school. But he didn't feel he was doing much for the war effort, so we moved to London, where he went to work for the Admiralty. He was one of the people who decoded German messages in Room 40. He was the man who, with his assistant Mr. Gray, decoded the famous Zimmerman telegram, which brought America into the War.

During all this time in London, we lived in Westminster. A little later on, about the time the Harris sisters started going to art school, the Montgomery family moved to Fulham in London. We all went to the same art school in Chelsea, and there we met. I started going to a children's art school when I was six. It must have been in Cambridge. It was run by Graham Greene's sister. Then I went to Westminster Art School when we came to London. Walter Sickert was a lecturer there, quite a famous nineteenth-century painter. When I was nineteen I had a picture entitled "A Tibetan Goatherd" in the Royal Academy summer exhibition.[1]

2
Foundations and Beginnings
1927–1932

Having finished art school, the three young women looked for opportunities to apply their training commercially. They occasionally designed fancy dress costumes; they painted one-of-a-kind furniture; sometimes they designed street clothes for private customers. Elizabeth Montgomery illustrated children's books and magazines, among them the children's page in *Good Housekeeping* and the Christmas pages for *The Tatler* and *The Illustrated London News*.

At the same time, they developed an active interest in the theatre. The three would collect at the Montgomery house in Fulham, "usually with a good many other people—various young men," said Margaret Harris. "We would then drive out to the Lyric Hammersmith, with our little car absolutely crammed with people. The car, being a Morris, was called 'Nine men's Morris, muddied all without' [from Shakespeare's *Midsummer Night's Dream*]. We could get in for something like one shilling and sixpence [about thirty-five cents]."

Their initially casual connection with the theatre in the late 1920s edged toward the professional. "During the time we were going to the Old Vic," said Margaret Harris, "we used to do sketches of the cast in various roles and sell them to the actors for ten shillings and sixpence each [$2.75 at the 1930 exchange rate]. That was how we first met John Gielgud, who used to say, 'Well, if I can wait until Friday [payday] to pay for them, and if I can

have three for the price of two, I'll have them all.'"

Motley's first commission as theatrical designers, however, was in amateur theatre. For the Christmas season of 1927, the Reverend "Pat" McCormack, well-known vicar of St. Martin-in-the-Fields and uncle of an art school friend, asked them to design and make costumes for the church's annual Nativity Play. Despite its amateur status, a Nativity Play in a church facing Trafalgar Square could hardly be called an obscure venue for their first costumes.

The visual inspiration for the designs came from paintings of the Italian Renaissance, which Elizabeth Montgomery had seen when she visited Florence in 1923. For the Virgin, Joseph, and the other principals, the designers used very strong color; the angels' costumes were all white. Kings' and attendant's costumes were made in clear colors of a cheap cotton fabric called "casement cloth," purchased from Burnett's, a shop that stocked material for theatrical costumiers. Appliqués of gold or silver "American cloth," a heavy, coated fabric, distinguished the costumes of the Magi. The three women made all these costumes themselves with the help of the family at the vicarage. "We were quite pleased with the result. Everybody rather liked it," said Margaret Harris.

The Nativity production sparked their inventiveness. The angels' cellophane haloes were decorated with a rim of foil or completely wrapped in foil—then fastened to caps of fine wire. The Vir-

Elizabeth Montgomery's 1929 sketch of John Gielgud as Richard II at the Old Vic Theatre. Her sketches of actors in costume paved the way for Motley's entry into professional theatre, her other sketches from this period have vanished. The sketch was published as a souvenir postcard and was later reproduced in The Ages of Gielgud, *edited by Ronald Harwood (London: Hoddard and Stoughton, 1984).*

gin's halo was larger than the rest and was covered with foil stars. For the Angel Gabriel, the women applied gold foil to a very large pair of plywood wings and placed them in the west window, where the young man who portrayed Gabriel merely stood in front of them. The angels' gowns were made of cheap white rubber sheeting, which had the advantage of hanging in sculptural folds but was extremely difficult to keep together—the stitching tore through the fabric. Tape on the seams kept the costumes intact long enough for the one or two performances. "We had a certain amount of trouble because the little boys who played the attendants refused to take their shorts and stockings off underneath their tights," Margaret Harris laughed. "They felt that it was indecent not to wear shorts and stockings, as there were ladies about. They looked rather strange."

In order to have working space in central London, the three women rented a room in the house of Miss McMunn, who had been their teacher at the Queen Anne Art School. They had worked previously out of the Harris house in Hayes, sometimes using the Montgomery residence in Fulham, London, as a pied à terre. In their new "studio," in Warwick Square, Westminster, they designed and made costumes for a Chinese ballet performed by children in "Miss Vacani's" society dancing class. They constructed these costumes of cotton-backed satin, a stiff and shiny fabric with the quality of old-fashioned "silk satin." For this production they sought professional assistance from the niece of the village dressmaker from Hayes, Hilda Reader, who showed the three women how to cut fabric and piece costumes together. This established a pattern for the designers of both designing and making their costumes—a practice that continued throughout their careers.

It is significant that these neophytes did not follow the custom of going to established costumiers—who usually dressed London theatre productions with new clothes or adaptations from their stocks. Instead, the three beginning designers invented their own designs and turned to a skilled seamstress for help in making them. Mass manufacturing of men's and women's clothing was then beginning to be a feature of the new department stores. As a result, many talented but poorly paid seamstresses were dependent upon the patronage of the middle classes, who still commonly had their clothes made to order. For Motley, it was natural to call upon a seamstress they knew personally. Later in their careers, they could easily find skilled seamstresses eager to help them execute their theatrical designs, but Hilda Reader always remained their head cutter.

To attract more attention to their creations, in 1928 the three women took a stall at the Agricultural Hall in Vincent Square, Westminster, where there was an exhibition of women's work. They wore the fancy dresses they had made for themselves and otherwise exhibited their creations, which by now included street clothes for sale to private buyers. "We were brave enough to telephone John Gielgud and ask him if we could borrow some of the drawings that we had done of him to show there," remembered Margaret Harris. "And he said, 'Yes, certainly.' I remember very well going to fetch them, up the stairs at 7 Upper St. Martin's Lane, where he lived at that time. He had had them framed. In the stall next to ours was 'Flower Decorations,' run by Constance Spry. John Perry, her assistant who looked after the stall, was a great friend of John Gielgud. So John Gielgud used to come to the exhibition to see his friend. He looked at our work at the same time and evinced a certain amount of interest in it."[1]

In the late 1920s the Harris sisters and Elizabeth Montgomery began going to the Old Vic costume balls. For the annual fund raising festivity, they would assemble a large party and make the clothes for all of them. John Gielgud judged the competition for the best costumes and in 1930 and 1932 the three women won those prizes. Through the combination of the theatre sketches, the exhibition, and the Old Vic balls, they came to Gielgud's attention repeatedly. After he had awarded them first prize for the Old Vic ball costumes in 1930, he asked them to design two costumes for a production of *Much Ado About Nothing* at the Old Vic. (In 1928 Elizabeth Montgomery had designed the costumes for Terence Gray's *Romeo and Juliet* at the experimental Cambridge Festival Theatre. The work was of no particular consequence itself, except for what followed afterwards.) For *Much Ado,* they designed a "domino"—a hooded cloak—for Gielgud as Benedick and a dress for Dorothy Green as Beatrice. His voluminous domino was black sateen and silver American cloth sewed together in wide stripes. Her dress was made of a peach-colored, cotton-backed satin, appliquéed with a pineapple pattern in gold American cloth. They were the first Motley-made costumes to ap-

pear in a professional performance.

The success of these costumes gave the three women the confidence to pursue a career as professional designers, calling themselves "Motley." The designers' interests and ambitions spanned both theatre and fashion. "We thought perhaps we might be able to make some money out of the fancy dresses that we'd made and perhaps get some orders," Margaret Harris explained. "So we took them round, very early in the morning, to some of the stores. We had to go into the store before it opened, meet the buyer, and put on the costumes so the buyer could see them being worn. At Peter Jones's they bought one or two. We also got orders apart from that from people who somehow knew about us. We made just a little bit of money out of making fancy dresses." None of the women had much money at this point in their careers. Elizabeth lived with her parents and earned some income from her illustrations of children's stories. The Harris sisters had a small private income, but extra money was necessary.

In 1932, after the three had for the second time won the Old Vic costume ball competition, they accepted with surprise and delight Gielgud's invitation to design the costumes for his production of *Romeo and Juliet* in Oxford. This production would be the springboard from which their career as theatre designers was launched.

In the world of the London theatre that the three young women entered as professionals, lasting changes were in process—changes that the Motley women absorbed as part of the aesthetic values of their generation.[2] They would be both innovators and implementers, finding ways to satisfy the new theatrical taste for artistic coherence in theatre design and the new, scaled-down production methods. The influences on their art were personal, rather than societal or economic.

For an older generation "the theatre" had meant beautiful, Romantic *tableaux vivants,* picturesque scenes enhanced by dim lighting and crowds of supers who framed the extravagant acting of the actor-manager and his leading lady. Colors were muted, costumes were heavy and sometimes awkward. Massive settings, built in three dimensions, required the audience's patience while stagehands changed sets behind the tableau curtains.

The last practitioner of this illustrative approach was the actor-manager Sir Herbert Beerbohm

Tree, whose extravagant Shakespeare productions appeared as a kind of annual spectacle at His Majesty's Theatre. As a precedent for realistic representation of the play's period in both sets and costumes, Tree could look back to such distinguished precursors as Sir Henry Irving at the Lyceum and, earlier, Charles Kean at Drury Lane. Every year from 1888 to 1914, Tree staged a Shakespeare play. In these spectacular productions he tried to outdo his predecessor Irving with yet more grandiose sets—live rabbits and a running brook for the *Dream* (1900)—and with large crowds of well-drilled supers in historically accurate dress. The actor-manager himself played the leading parts. Tree washed everything in a romantic idealism that prettified and melodramatized the plays. Huge sets and elaborate stage business impeded the pace of the plays with "waits" between set changes that could add an hour or more to the performances. His 1911 *Macbeth* stretched over more than four hours with one-third of the text cut. Critics, George Bernard Shaw among them, complained that the audiences were not getting Shakespeare's plays, but romanticized adaptations.

In Europe, new ideas were connecting theatre with the artistic vision and social consciousness of the times. Compared to Chekhov and Ibsen, England's West End plays seemed thin and inconsequential, a point driven home tirelessly by George Bernard Shaw in his reviews and in his plays. Often Harley Granville-Barker, a playwright and director of whom Bernard Shaw approved, attempted to serve up plays of substance—the British equivalent of Continental social drama. But these attempts never outshone their European inspiration. They did succeed, however, in putting Granville-Barker's and Shaw's concerns onstage at the Royal Court Theatre in Sloane Square and in the West End.

Indeed, new approaches to Shakespeare and the English classics began to appear even before the War in Granville-Barker's productions of *The Winter's Tale* (1912) and *A Midsummer Night's Dream* (1914) at the Savoy Theatre. Instead of romantic, gauzy fairies, for instance, Granville-Barker's fairies were inspired by Balinese dancers. "Barker was one of the first directors," Margaret Harris recalled, "to use designers in the way we now understand designing." The Lyric Theatre in Hammersmith also offered a stage hospitable to

experiment—notably the innovative *Beggars' Opera* and *As You Like It* (1920 both) by designer Claude Lovat Fraser. He too, Motley acknowledged as a major influence. "We became tremendously excited by Claude Lovat Fraser's designs for *The Beggar's Opera*," said Margaret Harris. "He was the first theatre designer we saw who got away from the traditional stuffiness and fustiness. He used clear color, and he really tried to get the style right. No trimming: cut right, but no trimming." Other influential designers at the Lyric Hammersmith were James Sherringham, with whom Sophia Harris later worked in films, and Doris Zinkeisen, with whom Motley would work on Cochran's Revues at the Trocadero. Nigel Playfair, who directed the Lyric, took over the theatre late in 1918. In the decade following, under his direction, it became a mecca for the best in new theatre in London.

Outside the West End, on the South Bank near Waterloo Station, the Old Vic Theatre had long provided its own kind of Shakespeare. It opened in 1818 as the Royal Coburg Theatre, a replacement for the theatre pulled down to build Waterloo Bridge. During the middle decades of the century it degenerated into a brawling house of melodrama, only to be redeemed after 1880 by Emma Cons and her niece Lilian Baylis. The women took charge of the theatre and transformed it into the respectable "Old Vic," specializing in wholesome entertainment and almost exclusively in Shakespeare from 1914 onwards. Actors and directors in the 1920s were drawn to the Old Vic by its reputation for the best in new talent and its dedication to excellence. Among them were Robert Atkins, Tyrone Guthrie, John Gielgud, Laurence Olivier, Ralph Richardson, and Alec Guinness, all of whom Motley would work with. Before Motley, the Old Vic Shakespeare was noted for its emphasis on fine acting (not always Tree's strong suit) and its meager sets and costumes, assembled from stock scenery and a threadbare wardrobe.[3]

"During the 1920s, when we went to the Old Vic where John Gielgud was playing, we were tremendously excited by the Shakespeare performances," remembered Margaret Harris. "But we were so distressed by the very unattractive and dull decor, that we became keen to try and do something different ourselves. For costumes, the Vic had old furnishing brocades in dark rusty colors, with bits of rabbit-fur trimming, tinselly chains, and artificial jewelry. Because the Vic had no money, it became the tradition for actors to dress like that. They, not the designer, often chose the costumes out of the wardrobe stock. Many times the designer would do only the sets, and we thought these were wrong too. What we wanted to get rid of was the way that they tried to represent a whole place, a whole bit of a castle, for instance. You can't do that because the scale is all wrong, and the texture is all wrong, and it's very dreary. What we wanted to do was to put on the stage something that represented and evoked a place rather than trying to imitate it."

In Warwickshire the Shakespeare Memorial Theatre had nurtured another Shakespeare tradition. Under the long tenure of director Frank Benson, the Stratford-upon-Avon Shakespeare company became known for its vigorous, athletic acting and its somewhat moth-eaten stock sets and costumes. Beginning in 1879 with a season lasting only a few weeks in April and early summer, the Stratford season grew into a summer-long festival with four or more plays in repertory. It drew somewhat grudging attention from the London critics as a principal provincial event. When the old Victorian-era theatre burned in 1926, a massive international campaign to rebuild it resulted in a new theatre opening in 1932. As with the Old Vic, the Stratford tradition favored stock costumes and sets. The story is told of how audiences recognized and applauded a stuffed deer, borrowed from nearby Charlecote Manor, when it was trundled out once again for *As You Like It*.[4]

In addition to these theatre practitioners came the prophetic voice of Edward Gordon Craig, who drew his inspiration from European theatre and his authority from membership in the theatrical aristocracy. Well before World War I Craig had argued for a theatre in which all elements of production were controlled and interrelated by the artistic vision of the director. Not good enough for Craig were the costumes pulled from stock wardrobes or the stock "castle" set. Rather, he believed that settings and costumes should be designed to express the mood and place of the drama. Because of his standing as Ellen Terry's son and because he was making an argument that coincided with changing tastes in art, Craig's influence greatly exceeded his actual production experience. He produced a famous *Hamlet* at the Moscow Art Theatre in 1912, some shows for his mother, and a handful of other productions. Yet his writing on the theatre and his designs, which were published and exhibited in England and Europe, helped to give stage designers much more power in shaping productions than the "scene painters" had ever had.[5]

Post-War actors, directors, and theatregoers wanted to move beyond the fussy, heavy-handed, and needlessly expensive practices of the past. They wanted ensemble performances, not star turns by an actor-manager, graced by crowds of supers. Like Craig, they wanted to "restore" the full text of classic plays that had for centuries been cut ruthlessly to make room for time-consuming set changes. They wanted a theatre that gave them productions that were artistically integrated—the acting, the sets, and the costumes all forming a dramatic unity.

Craig and his supporters notwithstanding, the practicalities of a post-War economy provided other reasons for integrating and unifying the visual and spatial in theatrical productions. Before World War I labor was cheap and the economic organization of the theatre assumed that there would be plenty of stage carpenters and stagehands to build and move the sets, plenty of actors for hire as supers, and an ample budget for renting or making costumes. The system encouraged a dispersal of production tasks. After the War, especially in the straitened circumstances of Lilian Baylis's Old Vic or the Oxford University Drama Society where Motley got their start, large, expensive settings were out of the question.

Motley had no special training in stage production methods. The women approached their new craft with fresh ideas, yet they did not start from scratch. Like others of their generation, they knew of and applauded not only the innovations of Lovat Fraser in his designs for plays at the Lyric, Hammersmith, but also the work of Leon Bakst and Alexandre Benois for Diaghilev's Ballet Russe. Diaghilev is generally credited with raising the ballet from entertainment to an art form in its own right, insisting that each of his productions form an artistic whole, integrating dance, music, and design for sets and costumes. His Ballet Russe, based in Monaco after the Russian Revolution, toured Europe and played regularly in London from 1911 onwards. Even before the Harris sisters had met

Elizabeth Montgomery, all three had gone on their own to the Russian Ballet. Later they went together and came away thrilled by its power and beauty. "All the great Russian designers were designing for the Ballet Russe, and it was where we really began to think and talk about what was in the theatre—the awful brocades and bits of rabbit fur! 'The only way to design for the theatre,' we said, 'is the way these Russians do.' Their clarity of color, their strength, their gaiety—everything about it we thought was so beautiful, and so exciting," reported Margaret Harris. During the 1920s the Ballet Russe's lavish color, exotic costumes, and sensuality thrilled audiences. From these productions came several strong influences on Motley: unity of sets and costumes and a "painterly" style that applied ideas from past and present art to theatrical decor.

The three women also came to know the work of Theodore Komisarjevsky, a director and designer who astounded audiences with his radical inventiveness.[6] "Komis," as his English friends called him, had fled to England from the Russian Revolution in 1919. During the 1920s his innovative productions of Chekhov at the Barnes Theatre fascinated theatre people, who regarded him as an exotic and mysterious character—an image he cultivated. His 1933 *Macbeth,* for example, broke Stratford-upon-Avon's comfortable provincialism. The production featured a set constructed of giant scrolls of aluminum placed on end, costumes reminiscent of the military garb of World War I, a screen onto which were projected the apparitions as Macbeth intoned their words, and, for Lady Macbeth, a crown fashioned out of barbed wire and metal scouring pads. As director and designer, Komisarjevsky's vision dominated the acting and the audience's response. "By the time we were starting he had come to England," Margaret Harris remembered, "and we had seen his work, which we were very much interested in, although we thought it a bit constructivist." His influence on Motley would come through George Devine, whom the Russian cast in several productions in the West End after seeing him in the amateur production of *Romeo* in 1932.

Modern-dress Shakespeare provided a different sort of innovation. It was begun by Barry Jackson, the founder of the Birmingham Repertory Theatre, who staged a modern-dress *Hamlet* in 1925.

The fad rested on a kind of skewed logic that argued history backwards. If, as the scholars were insisting, one ought to see Shakespeare staged as he had originally done it, then one ought to recognize also that his costumes and theatre were "contemporary," not of any historical period but the present. Hence, this reasoning continued, modern dress and modern furnishings were a good way to remain "faithful" to Shakespeare's intentions. As an antidote to the reverential spectacles of Tree or the scruffy efforts at the Old Vic or Stratford, Barry Jackson had a point. His *Hamlet* seems to have reawakened audiences to the power of the play itself. The same formula faltered disastrously, however, when applied to plays set in a definite period. His 1928 *Macbeth,* for instance, played as a drawing-room tragedy of Scots royals, drew howls of laughter by the last act. Barry Jackson's experiments demonstrated, if demonstrations were necessary, a modernism that Motley rejected completely.[7]

Quite the opposite were the "Globe restored" ideas of William Poel and his Elizabethan Stage Society, founded in 1899 and active until World War I. Poel argued fervidly that the authentic Shakespeare must adhere as nearly as possible to the conditions of performance for which he wrote: Elizabethan dress, a reconstructed Globe stage, and "Shakespearean" speech patterns that Poel somewhat mystifyingly called "the tunes." Only he seems to have been able to hear them, according to actors frustrated by his monomaniacal insistence on strange intonations. His ideas gained widespread currency as principles that ought to underlie Shakespearean production, even if their literal implementation was usually modified to suit contemporary taste. Although they never saw Barry Jackson's modern-dress experiments—or the "Shakespearean-dress" experiments of William Poel and the Elizabethan Stage Society (1898–1905)—the Motley women were aware of them and knew that they wished to avoid such excesses and anachronisms in their own work.

Among those who had a positive influence on Motley's work, Margaret Harris named contemporary directors—Harley Granville-Barker, Nigel Playfair, Tyrone ("Tony") Guthrie, and American designer Robert Edmond Jones. Through *Theatre Arts Monthly* and through Theatre Guild productions that transferred from New York to London, they had a clear understanding of American theatre design and its realism. They did not admire innovators in design uncritically, however, objecting strongly to the work of Oliver Messel, which they found overly decorative.[8] Most of all, they admired the work of John Gielgud and his impeccable artistic taste.

By the time Motley came to design Gielgud's 1932 production of *Romeo and Juliet* at Oxford, they assumed that Shakespeare should be played in a contemporary theatre idiom, with as few scene changes as possible in a space that approximated the acting areas of the Globe theatre, even if it looked nothing like Shakespeare's Globe. They had formed strong ideas about how they thought plays, Shakespeare in particular, should be designed. Tree and his traditional spectacle they rejected as old hat and far too expensive. Rather, Motley accepted Gordon Craig's insistence that a production ought to express the play, even if they did not agree that the powerfully shaping hand of the director-designer should control everything in the production. What Motley looked for was what Margaret Harris calls "simplicity," or what modern theatre designers might call a "design concept." "Without Craig," she says, "neither Motley nor, more generally, modern theatre design would be as it is. He was not generally accepted here in London, but he really got at the basis of simplification." Motley believed in expressing the values of the play, rather than pushing a program—such as Poel's "Globe restored"—or a theory—such as Craig's or Barry Jackson's—or indulging an egoist's impulse to shock—such as Komisarjevsky's. They did not, in short, come to design in the theatre as unreflective innocents: For years they had discussed among themselves and with their friends what they thought the theatre designer should and should not do. What Motley wanted to create were costumes and settings that would be economical, practical for the actors to move in, and beautifully expressive of the play. To do so they turned to clear colors, new materials and fabrics, and settings that suggested, rather than reconstructed, the architecture and environment of a period and place.

In 1932, as it is today, the Oxford University Dramatic Society, or the O.U.D.S., was an opening into the professional theatre for undergraduate actors and directors.[9] Lacking women members, the O.U.D.S. turned to professional actresses for

the women's roles and to professionals to direct the show. The *Romeo and Juliet* directed by John Gielgud and starring Peggy Ashcroft as Juliet and Edith Evans as the Nurse, also established the undergraduate O.U.D.S. president George Devine's credentials as an actor and producer. An undergraduate at Wadham College, Devine had become president of the O.U.D.S. after some heavy politicking for the office. As was customary in those days, he invited a professional director to produce their major play, *Romeo and Juliet*. At once, Devine scored a coup when Gielgud accepted his invitation. The young O.U.D.S. president had snared one of the best Shakespearean actors by offering him something he too wanted very much: a chance to direct. "John accepted the idea and was very excited by it," Margaret Harris recalled. For Gielgud, its success anticipated his 1935 triumph with the same play in London. For Motley, it was the debut that established them as part of the Gielgud company.

For his set designer, Gielgud turned to the established Molly McArthur. His invitations to her and the Motley women provoked Devine, remembered Margaret Harris. Learning of Gielgud's fait accompli, Devine shouted angrily, "We never have outside designers. We always have everything designed by a member of the O.U.D.S.!" Gielgud contacted the Motleys and said, "I'm afraid Devine won't have it. I don't think it's going to come off, but let me have the sketches, and I'll take them up and show them to him." So, Margaret Harris recalled, "We gave him the sketches, he took them up, and George accepted them. He was really rather delighted with them. John rang us again, and said, 'It's all right. He's given in. You can do it!' We were wildly excited of course, after the disappointment of thinking that it wasn't going to happen." Molly McArthur's set was also accepted, apparently without any fuss.

"We stayed in Oxford during most of the time of rehearsals," said Margaret Harris. "Two ladies there, the Misses Heron, were going to make the costumes. Naturally, we wanted to be there for the fittings and to supervise what was going on. We also planned to make quite a lot of the props ourselves. We had our sewing machine in the O.U.D.S. clubroom. A lot of the cast came in and helped us, among them George himself. They got pretty good at using the sewing machine. The costumes were based on the Italian Renaissance, in particular the fifteenth-century painters Botticelli and Carpaccio. We used mainly plain colors. Most of the costumes were wool, with only a few of them painted. Some of Juliet's had a painted design on them. The color scheme was less developed than in later productions. George Devine's costume was mainly red, but we made no very clear decision about how it should look as a whole.

"The cast was interesting because quite a lot of them have made a considerable name in the theatre and as writers since then. Christopher Hassel played Romeo, and George Devine played Mercutio. William Devlin played Tybalt. Hugh Hunt played the Friar. Terry Rattigan played a very small part; he was one of the musicians—the one that says, 'Put up your pipes and begone.'"[10] Edith Evans and Peggy Ashcroft gave wonderful performances that foreshadowed those that they would later give in Gielgud's 1935 production.

The play ran for about a week at the New Theatre in Oxford, drawing theatre devotees from London—in part because Gielgud was directing for the first time. After the Oxford run, theatre producer Bronson Albery engaged the company to come to London for a weekend and play at the New Theatre for a Sunday performance to benefit the Old Vic and Sadler's Wells. The right people saw their work, and Motley were off to a flying start.

"We went to a very splendid party at the O.U.D.S. after the first night, where we were introduced to drinking Black Velvet—champagne and stout mixed," remembered Margaret Harris. "Lord David Cecil, who was an ex-member of the O.U.D.S., made a speech. John couldn't come to the first night, because he was playing at His Majesty's in *The Good Companions*."[11]

Reviews culled from John Gielgud's scrapbooks attest not only to the production's success, but also to the impression Motley's costumes made. "The costumes," wrote one reviewer, "have the double virtue of being separately delightful and of resolving themselves continually, under the influence of Mr. Gielgud's grouping, into pictures glowing with a composed richness of color." "The figure

of Tybalt in his red and black was unforgettable," wrote another, and the design for that costume shows a menacing, graceful and dangerous figure, who might have been drawn by Erté. Although the reviewers also praised Molly McArthur's sets, essentially three arches with the balcony to one side, the Motley women had not been happy with them. They resolved that the next time—and they were sure there would be a next time—Motley would design sets as well as costumes.

In the O.U.D.S. *Romeo*, Motley set an enduring pattern for themselves in several ways. They approached the text fresh, unbound by traditions or conventions, but devoted to making the author's intentions work. They collaborated closely with director and actors to achieve artistic and practical coherence. And they looked to the art of the period, in this case the Italian Renaissance, for a consistency of color, line, and style.

"It was in every sense, a momentous production," wrote Michael Billington, "one that forged vital links between a group of people whose professional lives were to be interconnected over the next three decades. If there was a sense of family in the upper echelons of British theatre, it had its origins in this production."[12] As that "family" formed, Motley were an essential part of it, working with the others to shape the way in which English and American audiences conceived of drama in that decade and those to follow.

As the three women returned to London from Oxford in the late spring of 1932, they were on the brink of great success. Modest about their accomplishments, they nevertheless knew their own minds artistically. While it is beyond the scope of this book to enter their personal lives, it is clear that during the stay in Oxford, they were forming deep personal friendships. From that company, George Devine, the president of the O.U.D.S., who played Mercutio, would come to marry Sophia Harris and, himself an actor, to serve as the Motley's first business manager. The artistic friendship with John Gielgud would deepen as they worked closely with him through the 1930s. Peggy Ashcroft, then an up-and-coming young actress, would become a lifelong friend.

3
An Emergent Style
1932–1935

From the very first Gielgud's ideals had inspired Motley. No slavish devotees, they found in him a collaborator whose values they shared, an inspiration who enabled them to realize their dreams of the theatre. What in modesty they omit to say, however, was that the relationship was symbiotic. From that partnership sprang Gielgud's career as a director no less than Motley's as designers. "The Motleys," he wrote, "have been associated with me in nearly all my productions, and any success I have had as a director I gladly share with them, for they are at all times the ideal collaborators."[1]

From 1932 to 1935, Motley emerged with Gielgud as a dominant force in the English theatre. Looking back at the sixteen productions they designed in those three years, one is amazed at the diversity. True, not all were especially notable and some are best forgotten. Many, however, left their mark in establishing the New Stagecraft. Particularly significant were the 1934 *Hamlet* with Gielgud, *Noah* in 1935 with Michel Saint-Denis, and *Romeo,* in the same year, with Gielgud and Olivier.

Motley's success with *Romeo and Juliet* at Oxford led to an engagement later that spring to design sets and costumes for *Men About the House* at the Globe Theatre in London. The play was a vapid comedy by Robert York, revolving around the romantic intrigues of an aristocratic actress in the imaginary duchy of "Kondesburgh." Directed by Andre Charlot, an established director known for revues—Noel Coward's *London Calling,* for in-

stance—the play was of no great consequence in itself. Motley's part in the production was significant, however, because it marked their acceptance as professionals. "It was not a very good play," wrote Mary Grigs in the *Evening News* (16 November 1932), but she did like the set design. "All the action took place in one room, and this room was a *real* room. . . . It was there between the acts, and not instantly dissolved into the stuff of fancy by the dropping of a curtain." In keeping with its up-to-date sophistication, Motley followed a contemporary fashion fad and created an all-white set.

Later that spring came a major breakthrough for Motley as designers and for Gielgud as a director-actor. He invited Motley to design both costumes and sets for *Richard of Bordeaux,* a history play by the woman playwright "Gordon Daviot," the nom de plume of Elizabeth Mackintosh. "John said, 'I thought I'd ask Molly [McArthur] to do the sets again,'" remembered Margaret Harris. "And we said, 'We want to do the sets too.' We wanted the whole design to hold together. 'But do you know how?' he asked. We said, 'We'll find out.' And he finally gave in."

Gielgud had guessed rightly that audiences would flock to this romantic treatment of Richard II's reign—"a capital Shakespeare-without-tears chronicle," as J. C. Trewin called it—and that Motley's pictorial, "painterly" style was right for the script.[2] "I showed the script to the Motleys, who were enthusiastic, and full of ingenious schemes for saving time and money over the de-cor," Gielgud recalled.[3] Backed by Bronson Al-bery, Gielgud first produced the play for two special performances at the Arts Theatre in June 1932, then transferred it for a regular run at the New Theatre, opening on 3 February 1933. "The cost of the whole production was extraordinarily little," Gielgud continued, saying that, to his taste, "the final result was beautiful, even spectacular." The Motleys established themselves by their ex-quisitely graded color scheme and simple but bril-liantly suggestive scenery. "In Motley," commented the actor and director Anthony Quayle, who was in the production as a walk-on,

Gielgud "had discovered a young innovative de-sign team whose work was as fresh as a spring breeze, and he had shown that romantic costume drama could once again be brought to life in the West End—and made to pay."[4] Among the critics and at the box office *Richard of Bordeaux* proved to be an enormous hit, playing for an eighteen-month run in London, then touring. Harold Hobson re-membered "queues round the New Theatre from dawn until the evening performance."[5] "*Richard of Bordeaux*," wrote Audrey Williamson, "sealed Gielgud's success with the West End public."[6]

For *Richard of Bordeaux* Motley set up their own workshops in Duke's Lane, Church Street, Ken-

Richard of Bordeaux, *New Theatre, 1933. Gordon Daviot's play about Richard II sparked a fad for glamorous costume drama. Richard II (John Gielgud) and Queen Isabella (Gwen Ffrangcon-Davies) with Robert de Vere (Francis Lister) and a lady-in-waiting (Barbara Dillon). The photograph comes from Motley's files.*

sington. They wanted to be there when the costumes were being made, which would not have been possible had they hired a commercial costumier. The three women cut and made all of the costumes themselves for the first *Richard of Bordeaux* in 1932. When it transferred for a West End run, Motley had to strengthen and remake the costumes. "John's sleeves flew off at the dress rehearsal," said Margaret Harris. "He shot his arms out, and the stitching gave."

Motley's insistence that they design both costumes and sets, and the resultant unity of style and concept, marked a significant increase in the designers' artistic control. They based costumes and sets on medieval miniatures in manuscripts and on the fifteenth-century *Milles Fleurs* tapestries at the Victoria and Albert Museum. They took the color scheme from them, using wool, instead of silk, with velvet trimming. By simplifying the shapes, Motley got a feeling of the silhouette without the detail.

The set was simplicity itself. They began with cut plywood and built up details in bas relief. "We had a very strong feeling that we didn't want to try to represent reality by painting the scenery," explained Margaret Harris. "Yet we didn't want to overbuild. So we had simple arches and some curtains that could have a pattern painted on them, to look like tapestries." "Motley's sets evoked striped garden pavilions and cloisters through a strict range of three colors, indigo, cream and rust red, taken from tapestries in the South Kensington Museum," reported Irving Wardle.[7] Surrounding the stage picture was a false proscenium with entrances on either side, and a border, or "header," across the top to form a three-sided design, with a wide center opening and two side arches. To change the scene, the curtain in the center closed; the action continued downstage; and the new scene was set up behind the curtain.

"For the first scene," said Margaret Harris, "we had a little representation of a town, which appeared as the backing to one of the arches in the false proscenium." Instead of using a flat, painted backdrop, the designers made a bas-relief "town" out of tin, which was bent or curved to represent the buildings. Angus McBean, who later became a famous theatre photographer, built the tin backdrop. "It was an enormous job," he recalled, "a medieval townscape with a kind of false perspec-

tive like the drawings in the Duc de Berry's *Book of Hours.* . . . I built it of wood and tin, then Motley painted it."[8] McBean also made all the shoes for the production, which he formed from canvas, with leather soles. He followed Motley's designs, giving the shoes the right period shape by not using a modern last. "Angus used to wear a kilt and he had a red beard in those days," remembered Margaret Harris with amusement.

"Working with the Motleys," recalled Gielgud, "I planned out rough ideas for every scene. . . . The scenery throughout the play gave an admirable suggestion of the size and bareness of the medieval palaces of those days, with their high roofs and narrow corridors, steep steps, and embrasured windows. There was just the right amount of detail—a few very simple pieces of furniture, rich hangings and table appointments, luxurious materials used for the lovely clothes, but nothing distracting or overdone. . . . I was helped enormously by my costumes, which expressed exactly the development and gradual aging of the character as I had conceived it."[9]

The transfer to the West End was not without its trauma for the young designers. "There was a terrible disaster when we came into the theatre just before the play opened," Margaret Harris said. "We went onto the stage, and the set had been changed. The center part, with three suspended arches had had a pediment with a fleur-de-lys on the end of each center drop. When we came into the theatre, the fleur-de-lys had been sawed off! We accosted the carpenter: 'What's happened?' And he said, 'Mr. Gielgud said that they must be cut off.' We flew into a fury. John was in his dressing room, and he called out, 'I'm sorry, girls, when I was sitting on the throne at the beginning, they couldn't see me from the gallery.' Nothing could be done at that stage, so it sadly remained as it was."

Reviewing *Richard of Bordeaux* after its transfer to the New Theatre from the New Arts Theatre, the London *Times* (3 February 1933) pronounced the play, "an uncommonly firm piece of dramatic storytelling"; the acting, "exceptionally high level"; and the Motley design, "beauty of color and form." James Agate wrote: "The piece was beautifully mounted, and its appeal to the eye continuous. In fact, I am not sure that the exquisiteness of the production flowing like music did not give this work greater quality than it actually possesses."[10] The box office returns confirmed the rave reviews. *"Richard of Bordeaux* was the success of the season,"* Gielgud recalled. "From the window of my flat, I could look down St. Martin's Lane and see the queues coiled like serpents round the theatre." He gave a party in Motley's studio to celebrate the play's success. And, in turn, the show's "runaway success," states Michael Billington, "led to [Gielgud's] extended contract from Bronson Albery and the chance to do classic plays in the commercial heartland."[11]

By this time the three women had made a name for themselves as "Motley." It expressed their sense of group identity. On the one hand, no single individual would take the credit; on the other, they set themselves apart from other, more individualistic designers. The name annoyed John Gielgud, remembered Margaret Harris. "He used to say, 'Couldn't I just say it was by Elizabeth Montgomery? Motley sounds so arty.' But we wouldn't let him." Shortly after *Bordeaux,* B. J. Simmonds's, the big costume firm, wanted to buy up the newcomers' young enterprise. When Simmonds's representative found the women crawling on the studio floor cutting out enormous cloaks, "he was rather horrified," laughed Margaret Harris, "and he never came back."

With a long-running hit to their credit less than two years after they designed their first production for the O.U.D.S., Motley had become known for beauty and excellence in set and costume design. "Their work was full of light and air," recalled designer Jocelyn Herbert. "Where others were over-decorated and stiff, their simple costumes were graceful; their sets were simple architectural forms; and their colors were very beautiful."[12] Writing about *Bordeaux* fifty years later, critic Richard Findlater stated simply: "The design for Gielgud's production established the supremacy of the Motley team."[13]

Although it is their early and ongoing connection with John Gielgud that everyone remembers, in their first professional season (1932–1933) they also had a play in Regent's Park, another in the West End, and yet another at the Old Vic. That summer, following a precedent set by the German director Max Reinhardt at Oxford, director Robert Atkins staged an open-air *Midsummer Night's Dream* in Regent's Park. The first of many such open-air productions there, it was an immediate success, if one could allow for the occasional shower and the intermittent cooing of wood pigeons when they landed near the microphones hidden in the trees. Motley designed the costumes. Enthusiastic reviews in the London *Times* (6 July, 16 August 1932) especially praised Phyllis Nielson-Terry as Oberon, Robert Atkins as Bottom, and Jessica Tandy as Titania. Motley's costumes pleased the critics with their "general charm." Although the designs were pronounced "extremely successful with the fairies," said Margaret Harris, the critics also commented that the costumes were "a little freakish in the matter of ladies' trousers," meaning that the women did not wear dresses or skirts. Although Motley would later design and redesign the *Dream,* their decision to set the play in Shakespeare's time, rather than in the traditional "Athens," early marked them as innovators willing to break with tradition. The designers themselves, however, were not as enthusiastic as the public. "It looked horrid, and we weren't pleased with it," said Margaret Harris flatly.

September 1932 found Motley in the West End designing *Strange Orchestra,* a situation comedy directed by Gielgud in which the set helped to create the comedy by allowing the audience to see comic disasters on a staircase that projected towards the stalls. In a boarding house run by a scatty landlady played by Laura Cowie, eccentric lodgers Hugh Williams and Jean Forbes-Robinson collided physically and emotionally.[14]

Motley ended 1932 with *The Merchant of Venice,* directed by John Gielgud at the Old Vic. As described earlier, the Old Vic was notoriously short of funds and staged Shakespeare productions less noted for sets and costumes than for fine acting by such established names as Gielgud himself or such up-and-coming actresses as Peggy Ashcroft. Its dowdy wardrobe and tired sets usually escaped censure by virtue of the Vic's poverty. Motley were able to create lively costumes and sets for this production with ingeniously cheap innovations. Acting on Gielgud's suggestions, they covered the sets in unpainted burlap. The artistic director, Harcourt Williams, remembered the sets as being "a rich gold under the stage lighting."[15] (Williams played Aragon and filled in as director when Gielgud was called away for filming.) It was a design success. "The *Merchant* [was the] first play I was

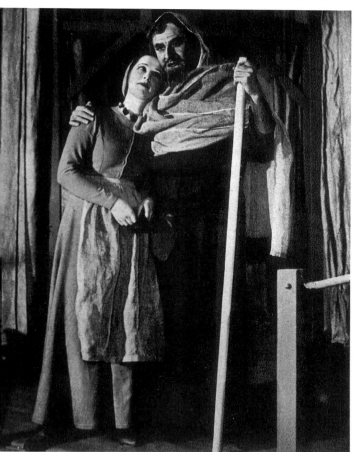

The Merchant of Venice, *Old Vic Theatre, 1932.*
Malcolm Kean as Shylock. Motley's innovative and in-
expensive costumes dressed Shylock in the cheap mate-
rial used for dishrags, to the astonishment of critics. The
press photograph in Motley's files was later reproduced
in Harcourt Williams's The Old Vic Saga *(London:*
Winchester Publications, 1949).

rifying £80 (about $400 in those days) spent on decor. "The effect, on those used to the Vic's patchwork drabness, was stunning."[18] Motley became known as the inventive designers who had made, as the reviewer for the *Evening News* (16 November 1934) remembered years later, "a small revolution in that dishcloth–clad Shylock." The innovative materials used in the costumes, in fact, and the "three girls" who had designed them had become a story in itself, as one reviewer after another sought out Motley in "a Queen Anne cottage in Kensington." "'We realized,'" they were quoted

in at the Old Vic that was designed," said Anthony Quayle. "Behind everything there was a brain."[16] "Each costume had been designed and actually made to fit each individual actor. We actors could not believe what had befallen us; the whole company took wing and soared;" he recalled in his memoirs.[17]

As Shylock, Malcolm Keen drew the critics' attention because Motley had fashioned his costume from dyed dishcloths. "All the costumes were a bit camp, over decorative in a silly sort of way," Margaret Harris recalled. Despite a simple setting and costumes of cheap materials, the doughty Lilian Baylis, who ran the Vic, balked at the hor-

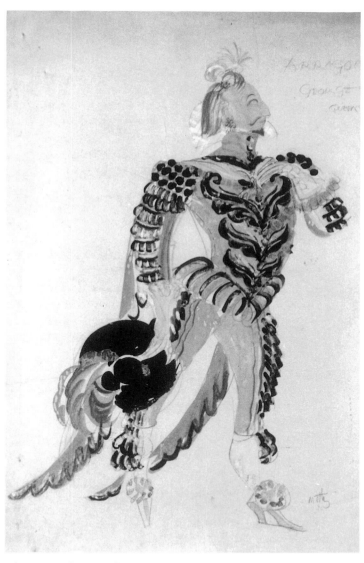

The Merchant of Venice, *Old Vic Theatre, 1932.*
The particolored costume for the Prince of Aragon
brought a light and fantastical tone to Portia's Belmont.

in a piece in *The Star* (no date, 1932), "'that extraordinarily rich effects could be obtained with striking color and good folds—and that rich velvet of the best possible quality looks nothing at all on the stage."

"The costumes are inspired by many periods, but are actually of no known historical fashion," Gielgud wrote in the program. "They are conceived in relation to the characters . . . and to the general scheme of color and design. The entire pictorial and musical side of the production is frankly decorative and unrealistic. I believe this treatment to be a good one, preserving the fantasy of the Portia story and throwing into strong relief the realism of the character of Shylock."[19] The London *Observer* (14 December 1932) praised the production for "clearing away the litter of tiresome 'business' and setting Shakespeare free." To the reviewer, the production was "strongly influenced by ballet and the striking, but economical color scheme of the best kind of revue." Motley's set made Belmont a "fantastication, a Never-Never land whose air is nimble, a kingdom where anything may happen, even the idiocy of metal-divining as a means to matrimony."

"Money apart," said Irving Wardle, "they were genuinely in revolt against what they saw as the clichés of their craft. 'We were determined to avoid the use of tinsel, bright gilt braid, and other elaborate . . . trappings which had bedecked costumes for many years.' Instead of silks and velvets, they went in for upholstery cloth, huckaback toweling and unbleached calico. For leather, they used thick felt treated with kitchen soap and paint. For lace, they used pipecleaners."[20] At a time when Oliver Messel was making a name for his elaborate, spectacular costumes and sets à la Hollywood, Motley had marked out a radically different course.

By February 1933, when Motley remounted *Richard of Bordeaux,* they had to expand their workshops and move from Duke's Lane, Kensington, to the West End. Their studio was across the street from the New Theatre, where many of Gielgud's productions were staged. Long before, Chippendale had used the premises for his workshops. It was his custom to keep tea on hand for actors who might drop in for conversation. Motley revived the custom. Around the corner, the famous Garrick Club, founded by David Garrick and his friends, served as a respectable setting for theatre

luminaries to meet with writers, statesmen, attorneys, and others with an interest in the theatre. It was then and still remains an exclusive club for those who have made their mark. Tea in the Motley workshop offered a similar opportunity for younger members of the profession to meet. "In the heart of the theatre district, just off St Martin's Lane, is a centuries-old yard where at almost any hour of the day or night you may see famous actresses, actors, producers and managers picking their way over the ancient kidney cobbles. It is to Chippendale's workrooms in the seventeenth-century granary they come, to visit the present inhabitants, those equally hard-working artists, the Motleys," wrote the *News Chronicle* (December 1936). The actor and director Harcourt Williams remembered it as a place "to sip a cup and hear the passing gossip of the theatre, not tittle-tattle, but workman-like news. There one may meet stars of both firmaments: poets, artists, and at least one cheerful, enthusiastic Motley." Or, to cite another habitué, Anthony Quayle, "The 'Motleys' became an unofficial and unique club—a sort of eighteenth-century 'Coffee House.' It was the most haphazard coffee house in London; the people who dropped in from time to time—Peggy Ashcroft, Edith Evans, Gwen Ffrangcon-Davies, Jack Hawkins and Jessica Tandy, Robert Donat, the Redgraves, the Byam Shaws, Michel Saint-Denis; younger actors like Alec and Merula Guinness, Steven Haggard—were all friends who enjoyed each other's company, shared each other's aims, and were to a greater or lesser extent under John Gielgud's patronage. At its center was John himself, lord of the London stage—but never lording over it, always generous to young actors, and always blithely tactless."[21] "Everybody used to come over," Margaret Harris remembered. "We couldn't afford to give them drinks, so we used to give them tea. It cost us £200 a year in tea and cakes!" For Motley, of course, it meant that their work was conceived and executed in close collaboration with the performers and directors.[22]

Motley's business mushroomed. From its modest beginnings, the operation grew to fill two houses in St. Martin's Lane. The site of Chippendale's workshop in St Martin's Lane had degenerated into a rather dingy nightclub before the Motley women took it over, spruced it up, and turned it into their design studio. By 1936, Number 66 St. Martin's Lane, or "Sixty-Six" as Motley called it, had become the workshop that turned out Motley's costumes. "We had to earn £200 a week to meet the payroll, before *we* got anything. That seemed a terrible lot of money," recalled Margaret Harris. When their own work was slow, under the name of "Dix" they produced costumes for other designers, thereby keeping some sixty employees in continual work.

The Motley design studio was no small enterprise. Margaret Watts supervised, standing over the cutter Mrs. Batten. The head cutter was Hilda Reader, the dressmaker from the Motley's hometown of Hayes, who stood over thirty seamstresses. The three Motley women lived at various addresses nearby. For a time the actor and director George Devine, who also lived with them, helped them to manage their modern dress house accounts.[23] At his urging, they incorporated themselves legally as "Motley, Ltd." Sophia Harris, who would later marry Devine, ran the household. Besides theatre costumes, she also designed fashionable dresses for "Motley Couturier," a boutique designed by Bauhaus architect Marcel Breuer. It was located around the corner in Garrick Street.

Initially, the three women did everything together. All three had an art school training, but their talents differed. As time went on, an informal division of labor evolved. "Elizabeth was the most talented in painting and drawing," said Margaret Harris. "She had a highly developed sense of color and decoration. She was often the instigator of the visual conception, often making the preliminary sketches of sets and costumes. Sophie contributed humanity and humor, confining herself mostly to costume designs of great delicacy. Later in the 1930s she ran the modern dress house most of the time, helping Elizabeth and myself with theatrical costumes as needed. Only much later, during and after the War, did she really come into her own as a costume designer for the theatre and films. My contributions were in the realm of the practical and ingenious. I developed the group's ideas into actuality, making the sets and costumes take shape in space. I made the models and coped with the stage technicians."

After the second *Bordeaux* in 1933 there came a hiatus, with little work for Motley until a re-staging of the *Dream* in Regent's Park that summer. It was followed in autumn by *The Ball at the Savoy,*

Oscar Hammerstein's adaptation of the libretto by Alfred Grunwald and Fritz Lohner-Beda with music composed by Paul Abraham. Set at the Savoy Hotel in Nice, this musical comedy required dozens of costumes. The London *Times* (6 September 1933) judged them "not beautiful, but an entertainment in themselves," suggesting that they captured the play's lighthearted spirit, as did the scenery—which Motley did not design—"elaborately gorgeous in the manner of gilt and pink roses." The *Evening News* (16 November 1934) said of Natalie Hall's costume that it "must have been the first time on record that a dress had been given a 'hand' on its own account in a London production." Although the show itself failed, it was successful as a vehicle for Motley's work. The three women eked out the year by making streetwear, fancy dress, and theatre costumes for other designers.

In 1934, with their studio and workshops organized, Motley went into full swing as established West End designers, taking on the design of historical costume dramas, popular revues, West End commercial plays, ballet, and Shakespeare. Early in the year came *Spring 1600* by Emlyn Williams, a costume drama about Richard Burbage and Shakespeare's company. Having failed to interest Bronson Albery in producing the play, John Gielgud took it on himself. As revision followed revision, Gielgud reported, "my suggested additions overweighted the production side of the play. The slender plot sank gradually deeper and deeper in to a morass of atmosphere and detail. The Motleys designed elaborate sets, I engaged madrigal singers, a large orchestra, and a crowd of supers. . . . By the time the curtain rose on the first night we had spent £4,000."[24] "Isabel Jeans played a lady with a great black servant, whom we dressed in a dusty pink Elizabethan costume," Margaret Harris recalled. "Her servant had to carry a monkey that was supposed to belong to her. It bit everybody; they were all terrified of it."

To represent the inside of an Elizabethan theatre, showing an audience present, Motley set plywood flats in a semicircle around the back and sides of the stage. Gielgud could not afford to hire extras to represent the "Globe" audience onstage, so Motley made padded, bas-relief figures out of the hairy felt used under carpets. Complete with masks and costumes, the figures were glued and nailed to the plywood. "It was a very strange effect," commented Margaret Harris, "Extraordinary." "Mr. Gielgud's production," said the London *Times* (1 February 1934), "combined with richly decorative designs by Motley, keeps the evening fresh to eye and ear." James Agate, however, found the production too pretty, lacking the earthiness of Elizabethan England.[25]

During the 1920s and 1930s a form of popular entertainment was "Cochran's Revues"—song-and-dance numbers with showgirls and their partners, produced by the impresario Charles B. Cochran. These ephemeral productions were rarely featured in the newspapers, leaving behind little permanent record.[26] For Cochran's annual revues at the Trocadero nightclub in the early 1930s, Motley created dazzling effects with ordinary materials on a small budget.[27] Most of the costumes for the Trocadero shows were created by Doris Zinkeisen, a successful designer who had made her mark in the 1920s. Motley's contributions were only occasional. Margaret Harris remembered best the "Samoiloff number," so-called because of the Samoiloff lighting, which could cut out certain colors.[28] "We had a lot of girls with a special make-up and very bright-colored clothes," she continued. "At first, they looked European. When the lighting changed, they turned into African girls with other-colored clothes. In another number, the girls were entirely dressed, covered in black, their faces and all, with a black background. This special light effect came on and all you saw was the white knickers, bras, gloves and shoes. They had little frilly pants, and little white bras, pink gloves, and headdresses. The white pieces stayed white. You couldn't see the girls at all. You could only see these dancing little pants and things."

The Haunted Ballroom, a new ballet by composer Geoffrey Toye for Lilian Baylis of the Vic-Wells Ballet, was choreographed by Ninette de Valois, whose company was later renamed the Sadler's Wells Ballet, and still later the Royal Ballet. In 1934, the Vic-Wells Ballet was in its second season; London audiences were supporting the beginnings of a national "English" ballet company, distinct from Continental imports. In his first leading part, Robert Helpmann danced as the Master of Tregennis in a plot that had him "danced to death" by wraiths—among them Alicia Markova, who had begun her career as a child dancer with Diaghilev

in the Ballet Russe. After the premier Margot Fonteyn, dancing in her first feature role in London, replaced Freda Bamford as Young Tregennis. The ballet received a standing ovation on opening night, "exceptional in this theatre," the London *Times* (4 April 1934) reported. The *corps de ballet* were a mixture of English and Continental talent. Motley's set and costume designs represented the capabilities of English talent in a field hitherto dominated by such famous foreigners as Leon Bakst. The *Times'* reviewer credited Motley's beautiful set and costume designs for keeping the "macabre" from becoming "grotesque and ludicrous." Motley created an "atmosphere of mystery and foreboding that extended their scope and their audience."[29]

In the next Motley-designed production, *Queen of Scots* by Gordon Daviot, Gielgud sought to repeat the success of Daviot's *Bordeaux*. He directed a cast that starred Gwen Ffrangcon-Davies, Margaret Webster, Glen Byam Shaw, Laurence Olivier, and some carry-overs from the earlier cast. Motley were not pleased when the director-actor asked them to share the design with McKnight Kauffer, a well-known designer of posters. "We were very upset because John had asked McKnight to do the sets and men's costumes and only asked us to do the ladies' costumes," Margaret Harris said. "Probably McKnight had said that he didn't know how to do ladies' costumes." The rehearsals were not without their amusing moments. Margaret Harris remembered Glen Byam Shaw, who would later distinguish himself as a director, playing Darnley to Ffrangcon-Davies's Queen. "He had a wonderful death scene with Gwen Ffrangcon-Davies. He was in the bed there, dying, and Gwen kept wanting to change things. She kept saying, 'Well, don't you think, if he was at the other end of the bed, then I could be there, or don't you think if we turn the bed sideways, and then I could be there.' She was trying to get a better position for herself onstage, but the set just simply didn't allow her to. Whatever she tried to do, there *he* was. He had it all his own way, and it was very difficult for her to play the scene at all." *Queen of Scots* was moderately successful at the box office. But, as Olivier attested in his memoirs, it cemented lifelong artistic friendships among himself, Gwen Ffrangcon-Davies, Glen Byam Shaw, Margaret Webster, the manager Bronson Albery, and, of course, John Gielgud and the Motleys.[30]

Sweet Aloes, for which Motley designed the costumes, linked them with two more strands in theatre history—the innovative director Tyrone Guthrie and the serious "social" drama à la Ibsen. A new play by Jay Mallory, *Sweet Aloes* explored the conflicts that arise from an unwanted pregnancy. Diana Wynyard drew praise from the critics as the distressed mother-to-be. Guthrie, who would later become famous as the visionary founder of theatres in Stratford, Ontario, and Minneapolis, earned Motley's admiration for his quirky production concepts, even if, as others did, they thought him eccentric.

The year closed with John Gielgud's acclaimed *Hamlet* at the New Theatre. Besides Gielgud, the cast included Anthony Quayle, George Devine, Jessica Tandy, and Glen Byam Shaw, a group of actors who might now be considered an acting company in their own right. Broadcast by BBC radio, the production came to be seen as the "ideal" *Hamlet* of the 1930s. "All the costumes were made of scenery canvas, painted with dyes and metallic pigments in gold, silver, and copper—sometimes sprayed on around a masked-out design. The trimming used was velveteen, which contrasted well with the flat canvas."[31]

"Gielgud's *Hamlet,*" wrote Audrey Williamson, "began the series of classical productions which were to revolutionize West End taste before the War."[32] The New Theatre *Hamlet* set a standard of quality that was to hold until the 1958 production at the Royal Shakespeare Theatre starring Michael Redgrave, which Motley also designed. Comfortable period costumes evoked medieval Denmark while allowing the actors to move easily. The setting at once sustained the play's dark atmosphere and permitted the scenes to flow one into the next

Hamlet, *New Theatre, 1934. Motley's sumptuous sets and costumes combined with their ingenious and efficient use of the theatre space. The photograph shows Claudius (Frank Vosper) holding court. It comes from Motley's files and has been published in Hallam Fordham's* John Gielgud: An Actor's Biography in Pictures *(London: John Lehman, 1952).*

with a minimum of delay for set changes. Not only was Gielgud's performance recognized as definitive for its time, but the acclaim for the design and the staging was equally rapturous. "An ideal performance . . . free of physical impediment," reported the London *Times* (15 November 1934), continuing: "Motley's setting is, in most scenes, beautiful if examined, and has the supreme virtue of submitting itself to the play." The production's success with the critics and at the box office confirmed the talents of the entire company, the designers no less than the actors. Surviving are many of Motley's costume sketches, some working drawings of the sets, a storyboard showing Claudius at prayer, and their copy of the New Temple edition of the play with the cuts marked. Taken together these record a fully successful realization of the play.

For inspiration, Motley turned to the paintings of Lucas Cranach. The costume colors associated with Claudius and his court were dark and muted. "It's a dark play," Margaret Harris insisted. "It's not young and passionate; it's a play of procrastination, nervous tension, neurosis, and evil." In sharp contrast to the Depression-weary styles of the mid 1930s, the period costumes suggested an almost foppish extravagance, with elaborate tailoring, slashed sleeves and legs, and hand-sprayed fabrics. For Claudius, Motley stressed power and wealth, designing for Frank Vosper—"a big heavy man"— a rich-looking costume that was "very ornate, with little slits in the fabric, black and reddish brown." For the Queen, "a big, stout woman," Motley chose a "warm, turgid brown color, [mixing] gold, black, and a reddish, russet brown." Completing the picture, Polonius appeared in gray; Rosencrantz, in a dark wine-red; Guildenstern, in a rusty-red; and Laertes, "in black, wore a bearskin cloak to suggest the cold, damp, Northern climate." Motley dressed the Players in ordinary, simple, clothes, with costumes for the Mousetrap scene that avoided any resemblances to Claudius or Gertrude. Offsetting the rest of the court were the "good" characters: Horatio in blue-gray, Fortinbras in "slatey-blue," and Ophelia in blue and silver. Motley thus separated the people surrounding Hamlet into two groups by color— Claudius, the Queen, and the rest in dark shades; Horatio, Ophelia, and Fortinbras in lighter tones.

For Hamlet himself the script clearly requires four costumes: black mourning dress for the beginning ("a suit of sables"), the same costume disheveled until he leaves for England ("his doublet all unbraced"), outdoor or traveling dress for the graveyard ("my seagown scarfed about me"), and clothes suitable for dueling in the last scene ("the readiness is all"). Motley followed these requirements, interpreting them in terms of the romantic traditions of the role—"a fitted black suit, a tousled wig of light-brown hair, a gold necklace, and other clothes in brown, roan colors," thereby enhancing Gielgud's romantic performance.

Motley's costume designs for *Hamlet* formed part of a larger interpretation of the play, at times suggesting individual points of character interpretation, at other times helping to set the atmosphere of the scene, and at each turn providing the actors with expressive and elegant dress. Their visualization of Claudius at prayer is depicted in the only surviving storyboard from the 1934 production. Garbed in white, Claudius kneels in prayer, the intimate interior suggested by a vast tapestry hanging just to stage left of center and by a shuttered screen and a tall candlestand upstage right. Unseen by Claudius, Hamlet stands downstage, the better to speak to the audience. Here the point of interpretation would seem to be Claudius's sincerity in his attempt to repent—the white gown—and Hamlet's understandable mistake about its efficacy. By such powerful images, Motley created the environment in which the play came to life. Where costumes provided the close-up of individual characterization and general atmosphere, the sets provided the physical structure—a dynamic space that, with lighting, completed the stage pictures with which Motley interpreted the play.

In designing a set, Motley sought not only to convey the play's locale and atmosphere, "a feeling of darkness, decay, and evil," Margaret Harris said, but also to create a spatial structure that would permit scene changes without interrupting the action. They turned to Cranach's paintings for details—the colors and patterns for tapestries and the design of the thrones. They looked for clues in the text as to the space needed to stage each scene effectively. The battlements, Claudius's court, rooms within the palace, the graveyard— action had to move quickly and easily from one scene to the next. Motley's solution was a multilevelled revolving drum, overhung with tapestries

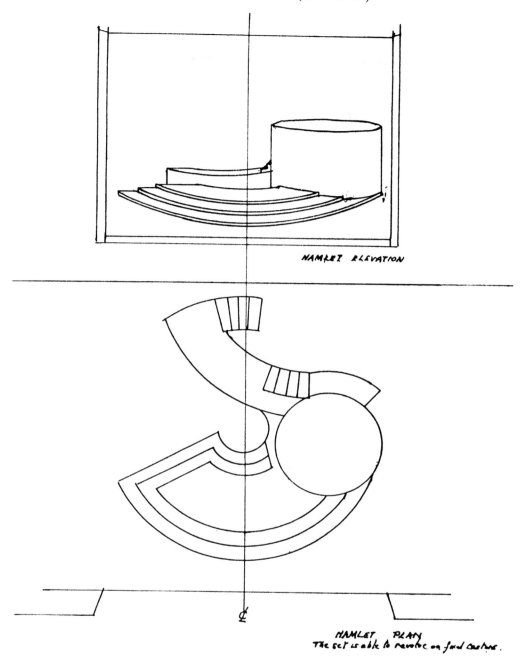

Plan for the stage set of Hamlet. *The set was able to revolve on fixed castors.*

that could be swagged this way and that to indicate a change in scene quickly. The revolving stage in the 1934 *Hamlet* drew praise for the swiftness of its scene changes and for its beauty. As can be seen in the sketches, the essential set structure was a low circular platform on which a drum-shaped rostrum, reached by stairs, created upper acting areas. The sketch (mislabeled "Macbeth Old Vic") shows the stage as it was set for the court scene (I, ii). Motley partially masked the upper areas by hanging tapestries and screens, with a bench and two thrones brought on. When the hangings were flown out and the lighting changed, the upper areas became battlements on which the Ghost appeared. For the mad scene (IV, v), the set was rotated ninety degrees, and different hangings were dropped in to mask it, thereby creating the effect of another place in the castle. In the graveyard scene (V, i; not shown), which began the third part of the play in Gielgud's division, the orientation of the set remained the same but without hangings and with some ornate crosses upstage to suggest tombstones.

The set thus satisfied both Shakespeare's original requirements for speed and for different acting areas. Even if the text does not absolutely require it, the performance benefits from an upper space for the battlements, a public and perhaps several private interiors, and the graveyard. The rich tapestries and costumes (themselves part of the setting, in a way) created a sense of the play's atmosphere and period, without burdening the production with the elaborate, three-dimensional settings that an earlier era would have thought necessary to evoke gothic Elsinore. Critic J. C. Trewin wrote that it was "the key Shakespearean revival of its period . . . the work of a player-producer who had learnt from modern masters, Craig here, Barker there. . . . It ran for 155 performances, a record exceeded only by Henry Irving's original Lyceum production."[33] As the then very junior Alec Guinness recalled, "the production evolved in a spirit of inspired improvisation." Delighted at Guinness's Osric, the director cried, "Motleys! Motleys! You should give him a hat with a feather like the Duchess of Devonshire." And they did.[34]

With the huge success of *Hamlet* just before Christmas, Motley could no longer be regarded as "up-and-coming." They had arrived. Financially insured against thin times in the theatre by the dress shop and the steady business of making costumes for others, central to new developments in the theatre through their well-attended teas in the St. Martin's Lane workshops, and increasingly well known for their innovative work in theatre, ballet, and cabaret, they had become fixed stars. They were part of the "New Stagecraft" that was redefining theatre production in Great Britain, America, and Europe.

With two exceptions, Motley's 1935 productions rate only brief mention. *The Old Ladies,* a play about three women living in a boarding house, required a set that would permit the audience to see into each woman's room simultaneously. Motley's ingenious design placed one room downstage right, the others upstage center and

right. Not only did the setting work physically, but the London *Times* (14 April 1935) praised it as well for skillfully delineating the characters. "Each room describes its inhabitant." It was a pleasing melodrama, but not of special note compared to what was to come: *Noah* with Michel Saint-Denis and *Romeo* starring Gielgud and Olivier. These two shows marked a watershed after which ensemble production and acting became the ideal that would inspire English theatre.

In 1927 and again in 1931 Michel Saint-Denis and his Compagnie des Quinze had played in London. The son-in-law of Jaques Copeau, Saint-Denis and the Compagnie he established were sensational innovators. The Compagnie lived and worked together, everyone sharing in the creation and fabrication of the sets and costumes. Director, designers, actors, acrobats, mimes, and musicians, the Compagnie and their stylized production fascinated the Motley women and George Devine. Possibly their best known production was *Noé (Noah)* by Andre Obey (with whom Saint-Denis had worked to develop the script). In the story of the animals coming together to the ark they found a powerful allegory about humanity's relationship with God and nature.[35]

The French company made a deep impression on the Motley women, who knew them from their two earlier visits to London. In the designs of Madeline Gautier, the mother of Michel's youngest son Blaise, Motley saw a revelation of color and style. In the Compagnie des Quinze itself George Devine saw an enticing model for an ideal theatre company. "What we found marvelous was how the Compagnie were able to give the most extraordinary theatrical effect without ever being false," Margaret Harris stated. "Their design and acting had a truth. They worked with important subjects, such as in *Noah,* the relationship of man and God, the creation of the different races, and the preservation of the animals—rather fundamental subjects, all of them, which they made very dramatic and very exciting. The acting had such depth and such reality to it. Although representational and realistic, the productions were never naturalistic. They always had a point of view, a crafted, studied beauty and truth, without ever becoming superficial."

Bronson Albery had seen their work in Paris and brought them over to play in London first at the New Theatre, later at the Arts Theatre. When Michel Saint-Denis subsequently came over to talk to Albery about directing *Noah* with John Gielgud in English, he made a point of seeing Gielgud's acclaimed *Hamlet* and sought out the rest of the company who had created it. Tom Harrison, the semi-professional amateur director who had done the Nativity Plays at St. Martin-in-the-Fields with Motley brought Saint-Denis over to their studio. Saint-Denis discovered that he shared a remarkable rapport with George Devine, then Motley's business manager. To Saint-Denis's relief—his English was then only "reasonable," said Margaret Harris—Devine spoke perfect French. That meeting resulted in a collaboration, for, not long afterwards, the French director appeared at Motley's studio to read *Noah* to them in French. He asked them to design the London production.

At first, Saint-Denis wanted Motley to design the sets only, preferring for the costumes to use Susan Salaman, an English woman who had designed them for the production in France. Motley were firm: "'No,' we said. 'If we do the sets, we want to do it all.' We had a tremendous battle. Then Liz did sketches of the set. Michel looked at them and said, 'That I know I shall have.' And Liz said, 'Not unless we do the costumes.' How we had the audacity, I don't know, because we were very, very anxious to work with him. Finally he said, 'Well, do sketches for the costumes.' And we did them," said Margaret Harris, making it all sound much easier than it must have been.

Motley found the costumes for the animals a special challenge. At the director's suggestion they strove to create designs for the English audiences that were more realistic than the stylized costumes of the Compagnie. The Motley costumes turned out to be more ponderous and less delicate than the original French ones. To achieve their effect, they had to be elaborate, heavily padded, and thick, much to the actors' discomfort. "George Devine got boils all over because of getting hot in the padding of the Bear," said Margaret Harris. "John Gielgud fainted at dress rehearsal. His costume as Noah was very heavily padded. His mother came and asked if we could think of a way to make his padding out of wicker, so that it was light and he didn't get so hot. We could never get the costumes dry between the matinee and the evening performances. It was a very hot summer, and they sweated so much."[36]

The differences between French and English notions of what an animal should look like also created problems. "For the cow we tried forty different designs. Michel said that the cow should be *méchante*, 'rather wicked.' We simply couldn't understand, because English cows are not *méchante*. We kept doing these cows, sort of good old English cows, very placid. Finally, Michel had to accept one, because we couldn't get what he wanted. Later, when we went to France, we saw that French cows are quite different. They have curly hair and wicked little faces. That was what he wanted, but we didn't understand because we didn't know what French cows looked like."

Motley did not work without help from the French; Madeline Gautier came over from Paris to contribute her services. She and Margaret Harris

Noah, *New Theatre, 1935. Costume sketch for Harry Andrews as the Lion. Motley Collection.*

made all the masks for the animals. Some of them—the elephant for instance—were enormous and had to be made in several parts. "I never could have made them without her," Margaret Harris recalled. "And Michel was always there to see that the clay masks were as he imagined them." Making the masks wearable posed problems. Most of them were bigger than life size, so a structure to hold them firmly in place was required underneath. The elephant's mask, for instance, had to be worn right above the actor's head. He had to have a large support mounted on his head and shoulders to carry it.

Just before the opening in early July, Motley painted the set on the New Theatre stage all though the night. "We'd been up nights and nights and nights, and finally we went to sleep on Mount Ararat," remembered Margaret Harris. The three women were found there sound asleep the next morning by the head stage carpenter, Harry Henby. They still had not finished the set painting. "He was a wonderful old carpenter at the New," Margaret Harris continued, "who wore a bowler hat and spats, one of those smart gray suits, a very high starched collar and a tie. He used to be very terrible to the stagehands. He frightened the wits out of us too. 'Call that a model?' he used to say ferociously. But he taught us a great deal."

Mr. Henby's fierceness put an edge on a mishap during the final preparations. The first scene depicted Noah building the ark. It featured several large trees, some made out of costers' baskets, the round baskets that market vendors traditionally carried on their heads. At the end of the scene, the trees were flown out and were to remain suspended in the flies for the rest of the evening. During the fit-up, one of them dropped suddenly out of the flies, narrowly missing Mr. Henby. "We wondered if it could be revenge for his ferocity with the flymen," laughed Margaret Harris.

She remembered the rehearsals fondly. "There was a very narrow ladder leading up to the ark. All the animals had to come onstage and climb the ladder. When the elephant reached it, he couldn't climb, because his feet were so big they wouldn't fit on the rungs of the ladder. Michel Saint-Denis got absolutely furious with him. He said, 'I will put on the costume and do it myself. It is perfectly easy.' And he couldn't. Eventually, they had to make the ladder wider. Saint-Denis's English

wasn't altogether good. As he was directing, he said, 'The monkey must jump under the tiger.' So the poor tiger sort of raised herself up in an arch, and the monkey kept trying to get underneath. 'No, no, *under* the tiger,' Michel kept insisting. And all the time he meant 'over.' It took hours to get that sorted out."

The play was a huge success. Reviewers could not say enough in praise of Gielgud as Noah, Alec Guinness as the Wolf, Merula Salaman as the Tiger, Barbara Seymour as the *"méchante"* Cow, Harry Andrews as the Lion, and George Devine as the Bear. The London *Times* (3 July 1935) wrote, "There is poetry, both in the unspeaking animals and in Motley's beautiful decor." "The designs for the animals," said Geoffrey Whitworth, "were an attempt to give the actors a real impression of the animals they represented, without being naturalistic."[37] Audrey Williamson wrote that "its masked animals achieved a simple pathos, and the scene in which, grouped sympathetically round Noah, they sniffed the wind that marks the return of God, attained a quality of breathless beauty."[38] *Theatre World* (August 1935) proclaimed *Noah* its "Play of the Moment," in which "Motley's clever costumes and settings merit the utmost praise." Motley extended their range from the best of the mainstream to the newest avant-garde in designing *Noah*. With Michel Saint-Denis, Motley found further affirmation for their approach independent of their mentor Gielgud. Whatever the period, costumes must express character, the set must establish atmosphere, and both must help to form a unified production.

The collaboration on *Noah* later led the group to form their own "company"—the London Theatre Studio. For Michel Saint-Denis, ideal theatre was created by a "company" of artists dedicated to their art and to training future artists. Saint-Denis's theatre differed radically from the English theatre of the actor-manager-director who hired designers and actors to realize his vision of the play, a model which John Gielgud himself followed, albeit with great camaraderie and consideration. Saint Denis's ideals represented a new kind of theatre—not only for Motley but for the profession at large. The idea that theatre artists worked as collaborators and in a rough way as equals now included the director who coordinated, the designer who helped make the production visually and spatially coherent, and

Romeo and Juliet, *New Theatre, 1935. Costume designs for the Nurse's servant, Peter (George Devine). His tights are a vivid red. Motley Collection.*

the actors whose performances brought the play to life. Traditionally, reviewers and audiences paid attention first to individual actors; as the new approach took hold, the contributions of the director and the designer came to be recognized. Today, of course, the name of such directors as Peter Brook or such designers as Ming Cho Lee often attaches itself to a production, overshadowing the contributions of individual actors. To account for the importance of director and designer in today's theatre, it is necessary to look back to this time, when these new functions in the production of plays were being defined.

From starring in *Noah,* Gielgud moved to a fresh triumph in *Romeo.* The 1935 production at the New Theatre came to stand as the benchmark pro-

duction of the play. Theatre critics would refer to it for decades to come. On his second three-year contract with Bronson Albery at the New Theatre, Gielgud had, in effect, formed a "company" of actors with himself at the head and Motley as the company designers. It loosely resembled Saint Denis's ideal. Laurence Olivier joined them, scrubbing his own plan for a *Romeo* that season. "That *Romeo* was the first classical play that Larry did," recalled Margaret Harris. "He was very, very good—marvelous! He looked so beautiful. He had a yellow hat, and he insisted on having a yellow hat when we did it in New York with him [in 1940]."

Renowned for its alternating of Olivier and Gielgud in the roles of Romeo and Mercutio, the production carried over from the O.U.D.S. production Edith Evans as the Nurse, Peggy Ashcroft as Juliet, and George Devine as Peter. Glen Byam Shaw as Benvolio, Geoffrey Toone as Tybalt, George Howe as Friar Lawrence, and young Alec Guinness as the Apothecary rounded out the cast. The production enjoyed an unusually long run for a Shakespeare play and then transferred to the provinces.[39] It was taken for granted that Motley again would design both costumes and sets, aiming at the visual unity in production that had become their trademark.

Infusing the production with glamorous costumes and exciting, swiftly changing sets, Motley drew unusual praise from the critics, who were especially struck by the elegance and grace of the settings. London critics echoed the praise of *Play Pictorial* (November 1935, 26–33): "John Gielgud and Motley have combined to make *Romeo and Juliet* a feast for ear and eye. . . . The permanent set is so artfully contrived that it has always something fresh and lovely to offer. The eye lends wings to the production, and this is the swiftest Shakespeare the West End has seen." Each scene appeared to be quite different from the others. Production photographs suggest, even in black-and-white, how rich and varied was the scenery's visual appeal. The secret of their swift scene changes is easier to grasp diagrammatically than from the pictures.

In keeping with their technique of suggesting rather than representing the period of the play, Motley turned for inspiration to the paintings of the Italian Renaissance. In 1932, they had looked to Botticelli; in 1935 inspiration also came from Carpaccio for the color scheme, the cut of the costumes, and the architectural forms and details.

Motley and Gielgud's seminal inspiration was to place the balcony center stage as a tower on columns, making it hollow underneath, and to work the scene changes around it. A two-level square structure, its arches and surface decoration were reminiscent of the Italian Renaissance. Its inner spaces could be opened or closed by a curtain or by shutters. Running to it diagonally across the stage from each wing was a set of black velvet curtains. When the play began, the Prologue spoke in front of the downstage black curtain, which opened to reveal the permanent set with all the curtains open for a street scene. As the action unfolded, the side curtains could be opened and closed, and furnishings changed behind the closed

curtains. When the curtains were opened again, the inner spaces behind them could be revealed in turn as Juliet's bedroom, the Friar's cell, or the tomb. For the Capulets' ball, all four curtains were opened, and from above Motley flew in a large horizontal hoop hung with streamers, giving the stage a festive air and transforming the space. A change of lighting, the closing of curtains, and the setting was transformed into Capulets' garden. Following Michel Saint-Denis's advice, they lightened the atmosphere with a strip of sky at the back to indicate sunlight and heat.

As in the 1932 production, costume changes indicated alterations in a character's state of mind or circumstances. For example, Juliet's costumes marked the progression from the young girl at the ball to the young wife bidding her husband farewell, to the corpse on the catafalque. Motley did not merely copy from fifteenth-century paintings—they used the paintings to interpret the text. "We wanted to keep the play young, to have the freshness of the colors of spring," Margaret Harris stated. Juliet's party gown was bright red with gold stars, her everyday dress a pale gown inspired by Flora in Botticelli's "La Primavera." The red and gold gown emphasized Juliet's passion and youth—rather than her innocence, say, or her naiveté, a design choice that suited Peggy Ashcroft's beauty and stage presence. The concept of a passionate Juliet was firmly grounded in the text. Her self-confidence and self assertion enable Juliet to propose marriage to Romeo and to stage manage their wedding night.

While each costume interpreted an individual character, it also formed part of a larger pattern that distinguished the two households from each other and from the other Veronese. Motley decided that the Capulets and Montagues, although "both alike in dignity," as the Prologue states, were distinct in social status. Each group had its appropriate colors. Party-givers and bon vivants, the Capulets were sensitive about their honor because they were nouveau riche merchants. Accordingly, Motley dressed the Capulets somewhat ostentatiously in bright reds, blacks, whites, and greens. The Montagues Motley saw as an older, aristocratic family—witness Benvolio calling Romeo's father "noble" and the Prince sparing Romeo's life. Accordingly, this family appeared in darker, conservative colors—blacks, browns, and

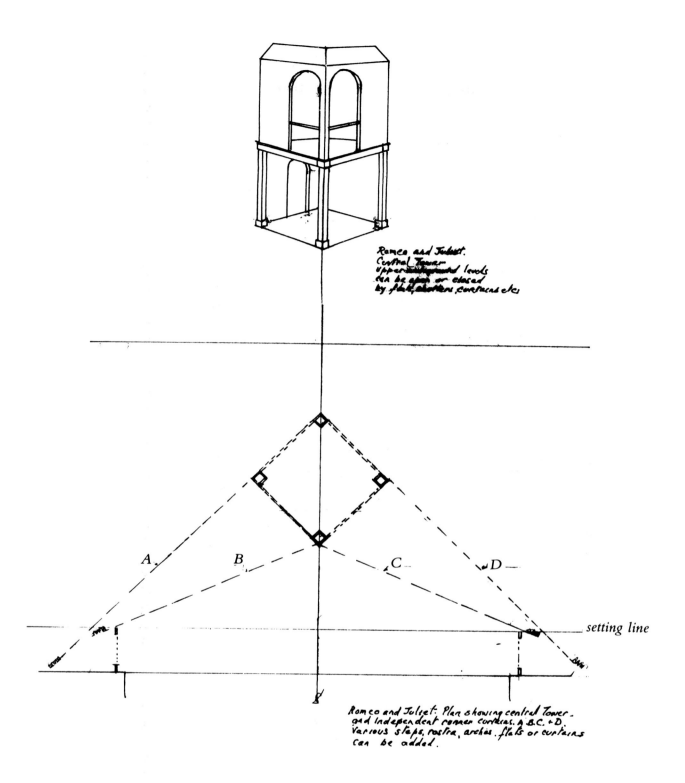

Romeo and Juliet.
Central Tower.
Upper and ground levels
can be open or closed
by flats, shutters, curtains etc.

setting line

Romeo and Juliet: Plan showing central Tower.
and Independent runner curtains. A. B.C. + D.
Various steps, rostra, arches, flats or curtains
can be added.

Stage setting for Romeo and Juliet. *Top: the central tower. The upper and ground levels can be opened or closed by flats, shutters, curtains, and so on. Bottom: the plan showing the central tower and the independent runner curtains A, B, C, and D. Various steps, rostra, arches, flats, or curtains can be added.*

Romeo and Juliet, *New Theatre, 1935. Production photograph, the ball scene. Pictured center stage are Juliet (Peggy Ashcroft) greeting Romeo (John Gielgud). The others have not been identified. The photograph comes from a press cutting in Motley's files.*

grays. The Prince, Paris, Mercutio, Benvolio, and the others wore muted shades of gray, green, mauve, and off-white—completing the stage picture.

Simple and effective, the costume designs were also dynamic. The script calls for several costume changes. For the ball scene Romeo and his friends appeared in masks and party attire: Capulet's guests were dressed lavishly. With changes in mood came costume changes, until, by the end of the play, the entire color scheme had gone to black—mourning wear for the deaths of Tybalt, Juliet, and Romeo—subconsciously but powerfully underlining the tragedy as a communal loss.

The colors themselves came from the paintings: deep reds, greens, grays, and blacks that made a dark palette against which the young lovers' lighter-colored garments stood out. Having found a color scheme that differentiated the two households from each other and from the rest of the townsfolk, the designers distinguished individual characters within the two groups by the style and cut of their costumes. Tybalt's costume—particolored tights and dashing red hat—suggested his ar-

rogant, impetuous nature. The Nurse—in bulky dark red and white—seemed less a figure of comic fun than a peasant, fat and slow, but shrewd and cunning. The Motley sketches make her look almost sinister, as indeed she may seem to Juliet when she counsels the young girl to betray Romeo in favor of Paris. In contrast to Tybalt, Romeo was dressed simply, conservatively, and romantically, with a loose, flowing white shirt for the scene in Juliet's bedroom.

Behind the scenes some dramas of another sort unfolded. The men's tights were sent out to be dyed—a tricky job because they were particolored: one leg one color and one another. In some pairs the legs were divided into stripes, in others there were different patterns on each leg, reflecting the dress in the Italian paintings that inspired Motley. The tights failed to turn up by the dress rehearsal, so the actors made do with black cotton tights. An hour before the curtain on opening night, the dyed tights arrived, still damp. "The actors were in an absolute frenzy," remembered Margaret Harris, "but nobody got pneumonia."

Sharing a dressing room during that production

Romeo and Juliet, *New Theatre, 1935. Photograph of Margaret Harris on the set. Photograph by Angus McBean, from Margaret Harris's personal files.*

and Gielgud drew raves. "For Peggy Ashcroft," wrote Michael Billington, "Juliet was a major turning point. It made her into a star."[41] In that production Motley created fresh, beautiful costumes that combined the excitement of a new "modern" play with the grace and eloquence of Shakespeare.

Following their success with *Romeo,* Motley completed the year 1935 with *Aucassin and Nicolette,* a romantic ballet choreographed by Wendy Toye for the famous dancers Anton Dolin and Alicia Markova. It was one of a series of ballets the two dancers performed at the Duke of York's Theatre during the Christmas holidays. Designs from this production and from *The Haunted Ballroom* (1934) were included in a special, book-length edition of *The Studio* (Winter, 1937). Entitled *Design for the Ballet* and edited by Cyril W. Beaumont, it put Motley among such well-known designers as Bakst, Benois, Dali, and Picasso.

"Looking back on those days," said Margaret Harris, "it is evident that the biggest influence on us was John Gielgud. He was making such a name in London, and Motley went with him. He is the man who put the English theatre on its feet. There is no doubt about it. It wasn't Larry [Olivier]. It wasn't anybody but John. Almost any actor you can think of now who started in that period and who has succeeded, John found. He even found Olivier as a classical actor. He fostered and developed so many of the others too—Alec Guinness, Glen Byam Shaw, Peggy Ashcroft, whom he got into the classical theatre. He also brought in Jessica Tandy, who played Ophelia with him. Above all, he dared. He used to say, 'If you really want to do it, and believe in it, the audience will like it.'

"John was amazing. He was so adventurous! He dared to use us when nobody had ever heard of us. And he dared to let us do really what we liked. He encouraged us and helped us. As a boy he had done a lot of designing himself, and he knew very well what he wanted. But he somehow managed to be very flexible and helpful. He was really extraordinary. It was a terribly exciting time.

"We tried to make the costumes give a real feeling of style. We thought we were doing period style, but in fact, our costumes were tremendously influenced by our own period. Unconsciously, they were expressions of the present. The same period portrayed in the theatre now wouldn't be

were George Devine, Glen Byam Shaw, and Laurence Olivier, young men fond of a joke, often resulting in their shrieking and shouting with laughter. "The dresser used to come up," said Margaret Harris, who tells the story. "He would plead with them. 'Mr. Gielgud says you can be heard on the stage,' and that would quiet them down for a bit. They were very rowdy boys."

One can imagine the audience's delight at the production's swift pace and visual beauty. It was a hands-down box office and critical success. "There used to be queues outside the theatre," Margaret Harris remembered. "We had a percentage of the profit for the first time. We used to say, 'Each one of those people on the queue is a farthing to us.'" Besting Gielgud's 1934 *Hamlet's* run of 155 performances, *Romeo* ran for 186 performances, as reported by Trewin.[40] Already preeminent, Olivier the way we had done it then. For the 1930s, for instance, the clear, light color we used was very typical of the period. People had white rooms, white furniture, white carpets. They simplified everything.

"Naturally, as we got more experience, we understood better how to make actors look their best, how to be more interesting with color, and how to get more variety and more detail. And especially to work on the appearance of the actors' heads, so that they gave the impression of the period rather than being a sort of hotchpotch, a modernized version of an idea of the medieval.

"At that time, it was considered to be absolutely the only thing to do to take an ideal view, and to make everybody look as ideally perfect as possible. Nowadays, designers are much more inclined to let the personality of the actor come through. But then, everything had to look very beautiful. Unless the character was obviously intended to be unpleasant, or ugly, or something like that, the designer did everything possible to idealize the appearance. With the men, one had to take great care about what their legs looked like. In those days one could get woolen tights that had much more body, and were more bulky, than the modern lycra, nylon ones that are so very sleek, slim, and close-fitting. One could get what were called leg pads, or, as the Americans called them, 'symmetricals,' which were made of lambswool. They were like footless tights, and they came very woolly all over, and could be trimmed to pad the part of the leg that wasn't ideal. Many actors in those days used them, and everybody thought that actors always grew wonderful legs.

"Shoes, hats, jewelry—all those things had to be very carefully thought out. For the shirts we used a kind of soft crepe. It must have been washable I think, because the actors would perspire and the costumes needed to be laundered. Rather than the stiffness of the cotton shirts that had usually been used for those sorts of things, we had materials which made very beautiful folds and looked like the Renaissance paintings. Again, the costumes stressed beauty and elegance. When we were trying to keep this beauty, we hoped we didn't lose the character. We felt very strongly that the character was vitally important, and everything that we did was considered from that point of view, especially in color, and form, and detail.

"We didn't light our shows ourselves. At first

John Gielgud lit them with the electrician [the stagehand in charge of running the lights, or "electrics," in stage parlance]. When we were getting started, there weren't lighting designers as such. The first one that we worked with was Joe Davis; he was the father of lighting designers. Later in the century, in conjunction with the designer, the lighting designer came to have great influence on how a production looks. He decides on the rig, the color and direction of the light, and the timing and settings for lighting changes, a demanding task that requires many hours of planning and experimentation to get it right."

The critics not only responded to Motley's designs in the theatre, they also knew and reported on their work methods. The studio where Chippendale once had his workshop, the visits there by theatre people, and their beginnings in art school, later in the West End—all this had become part of the theatre lore, as reported in the *News Chronicle* in 1935. "They are in the van of a small group of young workers who are developing the new technique of composite stage design, the beginnings of which are now observable in productions of all types, from classical tragedy to cabaret. These young designers have made stage history by their vividly contemporary awareness of the logical and imaginative relation between play, setting and costume. They have rid the stage of a mass of minor conventions that were clogging the flow of its development—the convention, for example, that onstage even a maid on her afternoon off should be 'dressed' by one of the great dressmakers instead of wearing clothes according to her character." By the 1935–1936 season, Motley were recognized by the theatre community, their advice and talents sought out, and their story widely known among the theatre-going public.

In Motley's early years, amidst all the diversity there appears a consistent style, a Motley "approach." Never trying to follow an abstract theory and always practical, they nevertheless based their work on certain theoretical assumptions. Motley took as axiomatic the primacy of the text as the guide to the play's meaning. To determine the period, setting, character, and emotional coloring of a play or a scene, they looked to the words of the script, then they sought in the art and fashions of the period inspiration for the lines, colors, and shapes of the costumes and settings, thereby giving each production a consistency of style and tone.

Overall, their bent was to suggest the period, not to illustrate it, and by careful attention to detail to emphasize visual beauty. In this they shared their audience's expectation that theatre would provide a beautiful, even glamorous, vision of the world. Although not "academic" in their approach, they were naturally still aware of the profound need to create an idealized world in the theatre.

In the decades to come, although the colors and lines would change with the fashions of the times, Motley's underlying approach remained the same. A Motley production from the 1930s had a different feeling than one from the 1950s or 1960s. Yet, early in their collaboration they adopted essential principles that would underlie all their work:

1. The designer must serve the play, seeking to express its meaning in costumes and sets.

2. Costumes should help the actors, allowing freedom of movement and adding to the actors' interpretation of character. "When designing a character costume," advised Margaret Harris, "think of it first in terms of modern dress, then connect it with the period." Costumes should never be merely "decorative," expressing *only* the play's historical period.

3. Sets should provide an atmosphere, a period, and a space for the action to happen, using architectural or natural forms consistent in emotional tone with the play.

4. Costumes and sets must compliment each other. An important dimension to Motley's work was their mastery of both costume and set design, two functions often allocated to different designers. Whenever possible, they united the two in a single vision of the play.

5. The production should have visual unity. To achieve it, Motley usually turned for inspiration to paintings by artists from the period of the play's action. They sought to distill a period's essentials, not to recreate it in minute detail. For settings, they adapted the spaces depicted in paintings to suit the play's action and mood. For costumes, they adapted period dress as depicted in paintings of the period.[42]

6. The designers must integrate their work with the director's and actors' ensemble creation. For Motley, designing a production meant much more than creation of costume and set renderings and the supervision of seamstresses and set builders. Working with the director, they attempted to visu-

alize the major moments in a play with roughly sketched "storyboards." They adjusted and modified their designs during the course of the rehearsal process. In the end, "Sets and costumes by Motley" often meant the ideas not only of the designers themselves but also of the director and the actors, an ideal of theatrical collaboration that later found its natural expression in the formation of such companies as the London Theatre Studio, the Old Vic, the Shakespeare Memorial Theatre, and later still, the Royal Shakespeare Company and the Royal National Theatre.

7. The designer must always strive to communicate the meaning of the play to the audience. Motley aimed at clarifying the play and the acting for the audience, not preaching to them, or discomforting them, or bewildering them—as designers in later decades often did. Surprise and ingenuity they enjoyed, but not puzzlements that left the audience wondering what was supposed to be going on.

Even as one states Motley's principles, one is aware of how basic they seem to today's theatre. They do, in large part, because Motley and their contemporaries made these principles the standard that everyone accepted. As these principles gained acceptance in the theatre, literary criticism, particularly of Shakespeare's plays, came to accept that the script "orchestrates" theatrical complexities of speech and spectacle. It is useful to remember that, when Motley were initiating the "New Stagecraft," scholars still thought of Shakespeare's plays more in terms of character and literary technique than of dramatic structure.[43]

Gradually, the Motley approach moved from being an innovation to becoming the mainstream tradition. By the 1960s Peter Brook, a director not usually associated with upholding traditional theatre methods, could state the goal of creating costumes and settings that were true to the spirit of the play, rather than to the archaeology of the period as "a kind of law" governing historical setting: "The more deeply you plunge into a distant or unknown past, the more you must deliberately simplify and reduce the number of unaccustomed objects that appear at the same moment in your field of vision. If you want any historical period— say the tenth century—to appear absolutely true to the spectator of the twentieth century, you must be aware that such a spectator is incapable of tolerating more than a hundredth or a thousandth of the visual details of the period and still retaining the same impression of reality as though it were a question of his own period. For it is not reality that exists . . . but only, and solely, the *impression* of reality."[44]

Today, as the theatre has evolved there remains some continuity with Motley's work, but discontinuity with other aspects, especially with their comfortable engagement with audience, playwright, and performers. As Motley readily concede, by the 1990s designers have evolved further. When Motley began, theirs were the ideals of the avant-garde; they were followers of Craig, of Diaghilev, of Lovat Fraser, and the rest—all coming together under John Gielgud's direction and soon to form an independent "company" with Michel Saint-Denis and George Devine: the London Theatre Studio.

4
Motley's the Only Wear
1936–1940

Motley were in demand. In addition to John Gielgud, other important new directors turned to them: Michel Saint-Denis, Tyrone Guthrie, Irene Hentschel, and Glen Byam Shaw. During this period, too, Michel Saint-Denis's London Theatre Studio came into being, providing another important venue for Motley's talent. Through it all, their studio continued to be a meeting place for theatre people and their couturier kept Motley fashions in the public eye.

The first Motley show to open that year was *Bitter Harvest,* a play about the travails and amours of the poet Byron. It opened on 29 January 1936. Motley did the women's dresses only. The scenery was designed by Molly McArthur, the designer with whom Motley had worked on their first *Romeo* in Oxford. Apart from some beautiful period gowns for the various ladies in Byron's life, Motley's connection with this sensational play—the censor had originally banned it—seems to have been minimal. It enjoyed a good run at the Arts Theatre before transferring to St. Martin's Theatre on 12 May 1936.

When Motley returned to the Oxford University Dramatic Society (O.U.D.S.) late in 1935 to design *Richard II,* directed by John Gielgud with Glen Byam Shaw as his deputy, they came as accomplished and successful designers. Gielgud's London engagements kept him away and gave Byam Shaw what amounted to his first solo directing experience. Margaret Harris's collaboration

with him as Shakespeare director anticipated a decade of working together successfully at the Shakespeare Memorial Theatre where Byam Shaw would be artistic director in the 1950s. As they had for *Romeo* in 1932, for *Richard II* the O.U.D.S. brought in two well-known women actors—Vivien Leigh and Florence Kahn (Max Beerbohm's wife). The rest of the cast were Oxford undergraduates of no particular note, then or later. Motley designed a permanent, wooden set, which they modeled after a stone structure illustrated in a book about the period. Approximating the acting spaces of Shakespeare's Globe, the set had a central acting area with a balcony above. On the front of the balcony were "stone" shields, actually made of wood in bas relief. A staircase led down each side to a small platform and then turned and came down to the stage level. Motley wanted the set to be left unpainted so that it had the sheen of untreated wood, but it was built in Oxford when they were elsewhere, and theatrical convention prevailed. The set builder painted it all in watered-down scene color, very gray and dull. Margaret Harris expressed her disappointment, only to be told, she recalled, "Oh well, all the bits of wood were different colors, and we didn't think it would do, so we pulled them all together." The costumes came out of storage from *Richard of Bordeaux. Richard II* opened 17 February 1936 to modest praise from the Oxford critics for Vivien Leigh and little notice of the design.

The Happy Hypocrite, *His Majesty's Theatre, 1936. Costume sketch for Ivor Novello as Lord George Hell. Max Beerbohm's play, starring Novello, Isabel Jeans, Marius Goring, and Vivien Leigh burnished Motley's reputation for sophisticated glamour. Motley Collection.*

In early 1936 Motley went back and forth from Oxford, where *Richard II* was in rehearsal, to the Arts Theatre in Cambridge, where they designed an "Ibsen Cycle"—*A Doll's House, Rosmersholm, Hedda Gabler,* and *The Master Builder.* The productions were initiated and backed by the Cambridge economist Maynard Keynes as a vehicle for his wife, the dancer Lydia Lopokova, who played Nora Helmer and Hilda Wangel. The plays also starred Jean Forbes-Robertson, Esme Church, and John Laurie. Irene Hentschel, the critic Ivor Brown's wife, directed. She asked Motley to make

the sets for all the plays out of two sets of double-sided flats. *A Doll's House* has only one set; *Hedda* has one; *Master Builder* has two or three, *Rosmersholm* has two. "It was a feat to try to make them all work," recalled Margaret Harris. "We used the same doors and windows in all of them." Critics praised the productions, which later transferred to the Criterion Theatre, London.

After the *Richard II* at Oxford and the Ibsen Cycle at Cambridge, Motley designed the set and costumes for *The Happy Hypocrite,* a play adapted by Clemence Dane from Max Beerbohm's story. Maurice Colbourne directed. Wearing a pleasant mask that disguises his hideous degeneracy, the Regency rake, Lord George Hell (Ivor Novello), woos the innocent dancer, Jenny (Vivien Leigh). They fall in love and flee the degrading "Garples Open Air Theatre" where Jenny dances. The couple find refuge in a pastoral fairy-tale landscape presided over by the God of Love: Marius Goring in a copper-colored costume and holding a bow and arrow. In the end, the rake reveals the deception and removes the mask, showing that his face and his character have both changed. Since the mask was made from a cast of Novello's face, it seemed that his visage had been transformed to match it. Margaret Harris concentrated on the set for this production. Elizabeth Montgomery did some exquisite designs for the scenery. Sophia Harris did most of the costumes.

Motley's fanciful backdrop for the pastoral scenes contrasted sharply with the elegant foppery of the Regency scene. Both required elaborate scene painting—including painted backcloths. For the pastoral scenes Motley created a false proscenium with an oval opening decorated with flowers and trees, like a large wreath. "Scene-painters came to us from Alec Johnstone's studio: a little Japanese man and a little Chinese man. Matsi and Iko, they were called," Margaret Harris said. "They used to say, 'What color is this?' And we would say 'It's black.' And they would write B-R-A-C-K. Then, 'What's this?' 'That's gray.' G-L-A-Y. But they were very, very good scene painters. It was very well done."

"We had terrible disagreements with Clemence Dane! She was like a galleon, a full-rigged ship. She used to come sailing in, bossing everybody—even Ivor Novello and Vivien Leigh," said Margaret Harris. "Max Beerbohm came to the show. He sat in a box, a tiny little white gentleman, white hair, white face, and white collar and tie. He seemed to be quite happy." Because Max Beerbohm had written the story, a newspaper review was headlined "Max and Motley." "Ivor Novello was very upset because it didn't say anything about him." Critics delighted in the production's visual beauty.

For *Parnell,* a play centered on the Irish patriot's love affair with Kitty O'Shea, Motley did the women's costumes and the costume for Willie O'Shea, played by their friend Glen Byam Shaw. The play provided Motley an opportunity to indulge their affection for showy period gowns, which appear stunning in production photographs. Not especially important in itself, the production re-confirmed Motley's reputation for glamour and elegance. The critics loved it, in part, perhaps, because it had at first been banned by the Lord Chamberlain at the request of the O'Shea family.

Continuing a line of lavish costume dramas, Motley's set and costumes for *Charles the King,* starring Barry Jones as Charles I and Gwen Ffrangcon-Davies as the Queen, drew fervid praise from critic William A. Darlington for "great magnificence" in "this Autumn's best play." Photographs show the "Royal martyr" bedecked in white silk, with a rich cape, lavish epaulettes, and white shoes. Darlington praised the clash of ideas in the plot, which took shape for Motley as a clash of images—the white-suited King set off by the plain tartans of the Scots, the black cassocks and white surplices of the clergy, and the dull armor of the army. As far as Motley were concerned, "It was not a very good show. We had terrible disagreements with the producer, Hugh 'Binkie' Beaumont. An experiment with a tree didn't really quite work, and he disapproved. And there was also a lot of trouble about Barry Jones's costumes. The management thought we'd messed up the costumes for the King. So we had to have them remade by Simmons's, a costumier, at our expense. We lost a lot of money, and we could ill afford it at that time."

As Gielgud was making Shakespeare popular in the West End, across the river at the Old Vic where the Shakespearean revival had begun, Motley found themselves working with Michel Saint-Denis on Thomas Dekker's *Witch of Edmonton* (1936). It was a production of an old play outside

The Witch of Edmonton, *Old Vic Theatre, 1936. Costume sketch for Edith Evans as the Witch. Motley Collection.*

the standard repertory of Shakespeare and the classics. Margaret Harris recalled no great conceptual challenge in translating the old play to a modern stage, but rather the practical challenge to produce it with the materials at hand.

"That was the production in which the set fell down because a stage carpenter had put everything together with wiggly nails," laughed Margaret Harris. "We made a village, with a building in the middle that had a sliding shutter in front of it. Marius Goring was in bed in it, inside. The shutter was supposed to open and reveal the scene. At the dress rehearsal the hut fell down on top of Marius.

It didn't hurt him, but it collapsed. Lilian Baylis and Michel Saint-Denis were sitting on the wreckage, discussing the problem. She said to him, 'There's a little hut in *Pagliaci* we might be able to use.' The hut they had in stock was absolutely and completely different in style. Luckily, however, the original hut was put back together and it worked on the first night. At the same dress rehearsal, looking at the set, Michel suddenly said, 'But it's a village. Something is missing. What is it?' He knew what, but he wouldn't say. He went on and on until we said, 'Well, a church, I suppose.' And he said, 'Yes, there should be a church.' And so, we built a church in the scene dock behind the stage at the Old Vic, and set it up. Like the rest of the scenery, it was covered with very thick felt, painted felt instead of canvas. It was grotesque." Edith Evans played the Witch and Hedley Briggs, the devil disguised as a poodle, in "nightmarish settings that suggest the Brothers Grimm," as Stephen Williams described it (*Evening Standard*, 9 December). The play drew praise as an interesting, albeit antiquarian piece.

In addition to designing costumes and sets for theatrical productions, Motley became involved in 1936 with Michel Saint-Denis's newly founded London Theatre Studio. The "L.T.S.," as it came to be known, flourished for four years as a training ground for young actors, directors, and designers. It was revolutionary for its time in London in that it formed a "company" of artists who all participated in every phase of production much like Saint-Denis's Compagnie des Quinze. Jocelyn Herbert, who came to the L.T.S. from a painting course at the Slade, recalled Michel Saint-Denis's emphasis on the text—not a designer's personal concept—as the basis for design: "We all went to the talks Michel gave about the interpretation of text and what the idea of the theatre really was—everyone who works on a production is part of a team who are there to communicate the author's play to the audience. Nobody's there to sing their own song if it intrudes on the play."[1]

The Witch of Edmonton, *Old Vic Theatre, 1936. Edith Evans as the Witch. The photograph, which first appeared in* The Star, *10 December 1936, comes from a press cutting in Motley's files.*

L'Occasion, *London Theatre Studio, 1937. The set sketch and costume sketch display Motley's style, simplified for this student production. Motley Collection.*

The L. T. S. had its beginnings in discussions at Motley's workshops in St. Martin's Lane during the 1935 production of *Noah.* "Michel used to spend a great deal of time in our studio in those days," said Margaret Harris. "I remember long, long discussions between him and George, usually in French, but very often mixed up in different languages. I think Michel used to forget what language he was talking. He would talk to me in French and George in English. It all got very bilingual."

The group who frequented the studio in St. Martin's Lane were already close friends and collaborators. They worked together and they recreated together. "We went for a holiday together—Michel and Vera Poliakoff and George and the three of us on the river [Thames] somewhere not very far from Stains, where we borrowed a cottage from Emlyn Williams," remembered Margaret Harris. The idea of formalizing their collaboration and extending it in the configuration of a school appealed to Devine, Motley, and others who had worked closely with them. By the completion of *Noah,* Saint-Denis was ready to bring the idea of

Collage of five London Theatre Studio sketches, 1936–1939. These sketches demonstrate the adaptability of Motley's "basic costume" for L.T.S. productions. Illustrated (clockwise from upper left) are the costumes for the title role and a servant in Electra, *the Minotaur in* Ariadne, *and for Clarissa and an old woman in* The Confederacy. *Motley Collection.*

the London Theatre Studio into reality. "Where he got the money, I don't know, perhaps with Tony Guthrie's help," recalled Margaret Harris. "When he started the London Theatre Studio, he asked George Devine to work with him. We then had to get somebody else as business manager; an Oxford friend of George's called Peter Bayne stepped in."

In a single practice room in Beak Street, the L.T.S. at first had room only for actors, without designers. Later in 1936 they moved into an old Methodist chapel in Providence Place in Upper Street, Islington, where, as part of their training, the students would produce annual "programmes" for the general public. Motley joined them there as the company designers. The L.T.S. eventually would list on its technical staff a dozen theatre professionals who would come in to teach special classes on voice, movement, costume, scenery, make-up, and the like. Michel Saint-Denis held master classes for young actors. Alec Guinness and Glen Byam Shaw worked with him. Marcel Breuer, a disciple of Walter Gropius and part of the Bauhaus, designed and built the stage and the auditorium. The offices and all the office furniture were also his design. "He was the first person to do molded plywood furniture," said Margaret Harris.[2] "Breuer had made this chair, all in plywood. 'It's the strongest thing in the world. You can't break it,' he said. George Devine asked, 'Can I sit in it?' And Breuer said, 'Yes.' George was a very big man then, and he hesitated, saying, 'I don't think I'd better.' 'Oh yes, go ahead, it's perfectly all right,' said Breuer. George sat down, and the whole thing exploded. It went off with a most dreadful big bang. Breuer was terribly upset. There must have been a fault in it somewhere."

For the student actors in the L.T.S. Motley designed a basic costume. The girls' skirts were a semicircle, with a drawstring waistband. Down the seams were press-studs, or snaps. If one skirt was worn, the waistband fitted the waist. To give the effect of a full skirt with petticoats, several could be press-studded together down the seams and gathered by the drawstrings at the waist. Thus, they could be very big, for Elizabethan plays, or they could be draped back to make a bustle. The basic costumes were valuable and adaptable in other ways too. The "skirts" could also be cloaks for the men. They were mostly dark colors—blues, blacks, grays, and browns. Suria

Magito, who was part of the L.T.S. teaching staff, later introduced them at the Julliard acting school in New York. "It was a good invention," Margaret Harris concluded, allowing that a similar attempt for a basic men's costume failed. "Adaptable trousers for the men were fastened down the outsides with press-studs, so you could put a piece in to make full trousers or trim them to make breeches. But they were messy and didn't really work."[3]

Many of the L.T.S. students became well-known: Yvonne Mitchell, Peter Ustinov, and Noel Willman. Motley worked with the students to design both scenery and costumes for *L'Occasion* (1937), *Ariadne* (1938), *Electra* (1938), *Judith and Holofernes* (1938), and *The Confederacy* (1939). Although the London Theatre Studio disbanded due to the outbreak of World War II, the idea of a training program for young theatre artists would be revived by Saint-Denis, Devine, and Byam Shaw as part of the Old Vic School after the War (1949–1951) and, later, as the Motley Design Course (1966—) under Margaret Harris.[4]

During the same period, Tyrone "Tony" Guthrie emerged as an important theatrical experimentalist and visionary. That Motley agreed to design *Henry V* at the Old Vic for Guthrie reflected their moving out on their own, away from Gielgud's aegis, but not in disagreement with his approach. When Gielgud was engaged in a long run, as he often was, Motley naturally worked with other directors. Collaborating with the innovative Guthrie, whom they knew slightly from *Sweet Aloes* in 1934, was an exciting prospect for them. His brash experimentation contrasted with Gielgud's aesthetic and lyric approach as much as it did with Glen Byam Shaw's logical blend of poetry and matter-of-fact realism. Their first contact with the director, however, was a disappointment, although the production was not. "When we took the designs to Guthrie, he was rehearsing Alec Guinness in a modern-dress *Hamlet*," Margaret Harris recalled ruefully. "He took the packet of designs from us, flipped through them saying, 'Lovely, lovely, lovely, lovely, lovely, lovely, lovely. All right, carry on.' We had been expecting a real discussion of them. He was busy. He just thought they were all right and saw no need to talk about it."

Henry V presented the designers with problems—changes of scene from the English to the French court, to the battlements of Harfleur, to the

Henry V, *Old Vic Theatre, 1937. The set sketches for the battle scene and for the tavern show Motley's swift, impressionistic techniques. Motley Collection.*

English–French—could pivot in and out. For an English scene, the English flags would drop in. When it was a French scene, the French flags would. For the battle scenes, which took place after the interval, the banners appeared ragged. Audrey Williamson remembered the "imaginative use of banners, dipped or held aloft in glowing masses of red, blue, and silver (that) kept the stage pictures continually mobile and striking to the eye."[5]

"In the end it was very exciting," said Margaret

field of Agincourt, the tavern where Fluellen meets Pistol, and the palace of the Duke of Burgundy. From the apologies of the Chorus for "this wooden O," the bare stage of the Globe that must hold the "vasty fields of France," it is evident that even the playwright seems to have recognized the challenge his script presented to the imagination of the audience. Motley solved the shift from England to France and back again by using sets with huge, canvas banners on eighteen-foot poles on either side of the stage, slightly in false perspective. The pairs—English–French, English–French,

Henry V, *Old Vic Theatre, 1937. The costume sketch for the Dauphin. His blue and white garments identified him as part of the French contingent. Motley Collection.*

Harris. "Larry Olivier played Henry and Jessica Tandy, all in white, played the Princess. He was so beautiful; he really was the most wonderful looking young man—terribly attractive and raffish looking." For the "Once more into the breach" scene, Guthrie wanted crowds of soldiers, so he pulled together the whole cast plus three or four electricians in cloaks. Onto the bare stage Guthrie had them bring a short set of stairs, about six steps. In full armor—heavy, real armor made of metal—Laurence Olivier ran, clanking onto the stage, up the steps with a banner in one hand and a sword in the other, and stood on the top step to do the speech. The electricians came on in their cloaks, which disguised yards of electrical cord that trailed behind them. Carrying big spotlights, they knelt down and trained the lamps up onto Olivier's face. "It was an amazing, extraordinary effect," Margaret Harris recalled. "It was completely Guthrie, completely illogical, because it was just a set of steps brought on in order to get the actor in the right position, not for any logical reason—a cannon or something, as Glen Byam Shaw would have done."

Another Guthrie innovation that pleased Motley came in the tricky scene (III, iv) with the Princess of France. It falls between the Harfleur scene (III, iii), in which the English capture the city, and the French council scene (III, v), in which the King and court digest the news of the English victory. The Princess and her maid entered on a sort of palanquin, sitting on cushions atop a tall platform with a tiny canopy. Eight men put the platform on their shoulders, brought it on, stood it down on its long legs until the scene was over, and carried it off again. The Princess and her maid were on it the entire time.

The fad for historical plays slacked off. Gielgud took on *He Was Born Gay*, a play about the Dauphin in hiding written by the actor and director Emlyn Williams—part of Gielgud and Motley's circle. "We thought it was an awful play. It pandered to all John's tricks," remembered Margaret Harris. "We tried to tell him, but he didn't take any notice of what we said, and he still did it anyhow." Gielgud played the Dauphin, who had escaped the Revolution and become a tutor to a French family, who wondered at his devil-may-care demeanor. Despite praise from the critics, the play failed to draw audiences and was withdrawn after ten days.

April 28, 1937—*Sketch*—167

Henry V, *Old Vic Theatre, 1937. In the "Once more into the breach" scene, Tyrone Guthrie created a striking moment by dramatic lighting. The photograph, which first appeared in* The Sketch, *28 April 1937, appears in Motley's files.*

Motley's work on this production and on *The Great Romancer*, a play about Alexander Dumas, continued their long line of costume designs for period plays. "It was a marvelous period to do, the 1830s! We thought the ladies' dresses were wonderfully exciting. We made the set red, with some red costumes," said Margaret Harris. Matthew Norgate in *Plays and Players* remembered, "The central portrait owed much to the joy and gusto brought to it by Robert Morley," who played Dumas.

In late November 1937 came a disastrous *Macbeth*, directed by Michel Saint-Denis and starring Laurence Olivier and Judith Anderson. Renowned

Macbeth, *Old Vic Theatre, 1937. This sketch shows Motley's conception for the apparitions of kings shown to Macbeth at the end of the cauldron scene. The masks continue a device the designers used for their Witches. They may have reflected the director Michel Saint-Denis's penchant for masks as a means of stylizing a production. Motley Collection.*

for its difficulty in the theatre, *Macbeth* presents special problems to designers. The special effects used to depict its supposedly terrifying Witches, the Ghost of Banquo, and the cauldron scene, to say nothing of the final gore, are likely to produce titters—not horror. Knowing this, early twentieth-century directors and designers sought special approaches. Attempting to substitute stylized beauty for horror, in 1911 Herbert Beerbohm Tree treated the play as a series of romantic-gothic

tableaux, cutting the text drastically to make stage time to assemble elaborate, spectacular settings. It was lambasted for un-Shakespearean slowness and grandiloquent acting. Barry Jackson's 1928 modern-dress Macbeth, with Lady Macbeth as a flapper in a shingle-bob haircut and Macbeth as a tippling Scots nobleman, had its powerful moments—especially for Lady Macbeth. But the unscary Witches and the "Lay on Macduff" as they pulled down swords from over the mantelpiece provoked laughter and ridicule. Komisarjevsky's 1933 Stratford-upon-Avon production, with its surreal setting suggested a world of horror and nightmare, but human sympathy and deep tragedy were missing.[6]

Aware of these difficulties, Michel Saint-Denis and Motley attempted to stylize the play, presenting it in modified period costumes, heavy make-up, and masks for the witches. The unit set contained three black towers linked with a false beam across the top for the first half of the play. The same towers were surrounded by circular rostrums for the second. Actors in the production called them "the three privies." Some of the towers had steps circling around on the outside, leading to doors through which the actors could enter and exit for Duncan's murder and for the sleepwalking scene. "Judith Anderson, who played Lady Macbeth, failed to tell anyone that she suffered from vertigo," said Margaret Harris. "To reach Duncan's room, she had go up a little staircase without a handrail around the edge of the tower. Judith became panic-stricken during the scene, and later said it destroyed her performance."

Although Laurence Olivier and Judith Anderson failed to ignite dramatic interest in the two leading parts, the production had its good moments. Darius Milhaud composed the score, based on early Scottish bagpipe music. "The critics hated it, but it was rather marvelous," said Margaret Harris. "Darius came over from France to do it." Michel Saint-Denis used three actors to play the Ghost of Banquo—all in the same masks and the same costumes. The ghost could appear and re-appear mysteriously one place and then another over the set. "With stage lighting, he seemed to be disembodied," said Margaret Harris. For the set change from the first to second half, George Devine came to the rescue, cutting the time from the forty minutes it took in dress rehearsal to ten minutes on opening night. "George and I planned the change," said Margaret Harris. "He knew exactly what to do. It had all been wrongly packed, with the wrong things on top, and the stage hands didn't know where anything was."

Casting a long shadow over the production, whose opening night was postponed three days after a disastrous dress rehearsal, was the sudden death of Lilian Baylis, the Old Vic's enthusiastic manager. The Vic had never postponed an opening night before. "Everyone, including me," said Laurence Olivier, whose Macbeth was one of his rare failures, "thought that [the postponement] was really what killed Lilian Baylis."[7] Having played such a large part in the transformation of the Old Vic from a well-intentioned "temperance theatre" before World War I into a beacon across the Thames for the best in classical acting after the War, Lilian Baylis had virtually come to epitomize the enterprise. She was a spirited and parsimonious woman who never failed to express her strong opinions about the Vic's productions. She responded positively more to Motley's frugality than to their artistic innovation. Her death came as a great shock and loss to the cast and audiences, even as it eerily confirmed Macbeth's reputation as a jinxed play.

"It was a strange and frightening production," recalled Robert Speaight," with all the macabre phantasmagoria a foreign mind (Saint-Denis's) may bring to Shakespearean tragedy. . . . The treatment yielded results: The decor and costumes [with] some suggestive lighting did succeed in giving to the play what Bradley described as 'the impression of a black night broken by flashes of light and color.' The lighting was too dim; the costumes, too mannered; Motley's barbaric masks helped neither the witches nor Banquo's ghost; and Olivier's makeup . . . did not assist his humanity . . . 'Well,' quipped Vivien Leigh, 'you hear Macbeth's first line, then Larry's make-up comes on, then Larry comes on.'"[8]

"Everything had to suggest god-like proportions," Olivier recalled, with "deliberately mask-like make-up, but appearances, sets, costumes, and props were none of them wholeheartedly abstract. . . . A strange thing; it played to the best houses ever known to date."[9] Despite its failure with the critics, this production made a theatrical statement about the play as open to surrealism and abstraction—a statement that refined Komisarjevsky's 1933 production. Like a rough sketch, it also anticipated the design of the best Macbeth of mid-century, designed by Roger Furse in collaboration with Olivier, and directed by Glen Byam Shaw in 1955 at Stratford-upon-Avon.[10]

Gielgud's eight-month "Queen's Season," as the productions at the Queen's Theatre, 1937–1938 were called, seems to have been the high water mark for the directors, designers, and actors who had come into their own together during the 1930s. For the Queen's Season, Gielgud joined Binkie Beaumont in the management of the Queen's Theatre and there formed a company that presented a season of productions—Richard II, The School for Scandal, The Three Sisters, and The Merchant of Venice. This was a continuation of his earlier work at the New Theatre and a forerunner in its own way of the company spirit that would later inform the Royal Shakespeare Company and the Royal National Theatre. "It is not too much to say that this classic experiment of Gielgud's revived—in a more scholarly though no less theatrically exciting form—the traditions of Irving and Tree at the Lyceum and His Majesty's, and paved the way for the Old Vic Company in the West End," wrote Audrey Williamson.[11] Although the same group continued to work together in loose affiliation, in the next two years there began a dispersal that the outbreak of World War II made permanent. After the War, the friends would work together from time to time, but the entire company never returned to its original state.

In Richard II, the first of the plays in the Queen's Season, Gielgud in the leading role returned to the Shakespearean Richard he had first played in 1929, as distinct from his famous Richard of Bordeaux. Motley were the designers. The rest of the company included Michael Redgrave (Bolingbroke), Leon Quartermaine (Gaunt), Glen Byam Shaw (Mowbray), Anthony Quayle (Welsh Captain, Duke of Surrey), and Peggy Ashcroft (Queen Isabel). Searching for variety after their other Richards, Motley admitted that they were "a bit overelaborate in design," and Audrey Williamson remembered a "baroque elaboration in the costumes that tended to make the actors seem stiff and inflexible. The coloring was dark and at times beautiful, but infinitely the most successful scene, pictorially, was the 'tourney,' in which they set

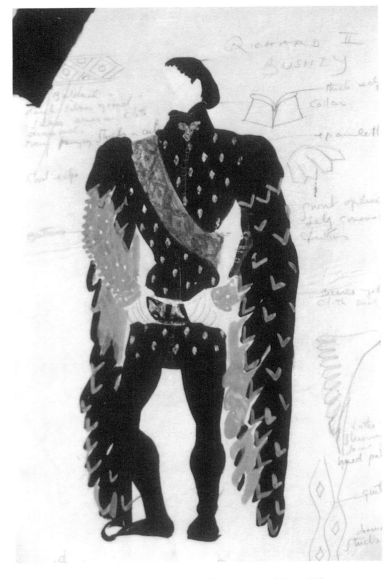

Richard II, *Queen's Theatre, 1937. The costume sketch for Bushy, its flowing lines and rich fabrics epitomizing the extravagance of Richard's court. Motley Collection.*

the King and Queen, in a splash of white and gold, like two superb jewels against the pallid azure of the sky. Only one fluttering pennant broke the expanse of egg-shell blue." James Agate (Sunday Times, 9 September 1937) also complained about the costumes, but others did not. Stephen Williams (*Evening Standard*, September 1937) admired "Motley's ingenious designs."

As with *Richard II,* Motley's decor for *The School for Scandal* came in for criticism as "over-elaborate." Sophia Harris designed lavish costumes. Elizabeth Montgomery painted sets with cloths and wing-and-shutter scene changes remi-

niscent of eighteenth-century stagecraft. The design suggests luxuriant, baroque excess. Director Tyrone Guthrie encouraged the actors to shift from "realistic" comedy acting to comic stereotypes, turning the play into a mixture of "freaks among a set of otherwise realistic characters."[12] "The scenery is billowy and impressionistic," reported the *Sunday Times* (28 November 1937), "so that the spectator is made to look at the year 1777 through the patronizing, self-conscious eyes of 1937. Curtains and candelabra are painted, and, where the setting is realistic, it has the color of dust on a skeleton. Finally, the majority of the costumes are of an unexpected hideousness." Yet for Darlington, the *Daily Telegraph* (26 November, 1937) critic, "Motley's dresses are delightful."

The Three Sisters, directed by Michel Saint-Denis, was an unqualified triumph. Saint-Denis's decision to treat the play as comedy followed the author's light-hearted intention.[13] This departed from the Moscow Art Theatre's serious and tragic approach, which Chekhov himself had derided, saying that they had made his plays into "crybabies." For the scene in their bedroom where the sisters sit during the fire outside, Saint-Denis directed them to be somewhat hysterical, not dour. Instead of melancholic brooding, their mood was nervous and giggling, because of the fire and the late hour. "Michel Saint-Denis gets into the play a quality as light, as sad, as gay as Mozart," Farjeon wrote (*The Bystander,* January 1938). That Saint-Denis saw comedy in a play that others thought somber and melodramatic may have been as much his own mordant wit as it was the Moscow Art Theatre's production style. In any case, his treatment of *The Three Sisters* drew together a stellar cast and created a fresh appreciation in England for Chekhov's artistry. For many Londoners, such as A. E. Wilson of *The Sun,* Komisarjevsky's serious production of the play in 1926 served as a reference point, and the Saint-Denis production came off as "a masterpiece." Summing it all up, Farjeon proclaimed it "a production of the very first order of one of the masterpieces of dramatic literature."

Although realistic, the costumes helped establish the characters' personalities. "We were very fortunate," Margaret Harris remembered. "When we went to Maurice Angel's, the costumier, for the uniforms, they had a considerable number of uniforms that had belonged to the Archduke Michael,

Richard II, *Queen's Theatre, 1937. From left to right are Harry Andrews (Bushy) Glen Byam Shaw (Mowbray), John Gielgud (Richard), Pardoe Woodman (Bagot), and Michael Redgrave (Bolingbroke). The production photograph from Motley's files was published in* Theatre World, *December 1937.*

who had escaped from the Russian revolution. When he came to London he'd sold them. So we had the absolutely exactly right color. Some of the cast actually wore the Archduke's uniforms, and the others wore exact copies. We had to have the cloth dyed to match." Differences in the uniforms came from small touches—higher and lower collars, the fit and condition of the uniform. Michael Redgrave, Baron Tusenbach, had a very low collar and too-short sleeves, to make him look awkward. Glen Byam Shaw's collar was stiff and his uniform was absolutely perfect, as Solyony's should be.

The School for Scandal, *Queen's Theatre, 1937. Lady Sneerwell's ochre gown and purple, fur-trimmed cape evokes the over-ripe decadence of this Restoration comedy directed by Tyrone Guthrie. Motley Collection.*

Three Sisters, *Queen's Theatre, 1938. The climax in the first act, when Andrey Prozorov (George Devine) plights his troth to Natasha (Angela Baddeley) and kisses her, to the amusement and surprise of the rest of the company. Looking on are, from left: Irina (Peggy Ashcroft), Anfisa (Marie Wright), Vershinin (John Gielgud), Kuligin (Leon Quartermaine)—raising his glass, Solyony (Glen Byam Shaw)—and seated, a maid (Barbara Dillon), Olga (Gwen Ffrangcon-Davies), Masha (Carol Goodner), Tusenbach (Michael Redgrave), Chebutykin (Frederick Lloyd), Roddey (Harry Andrews), and Fedotik (Alec Guinness). The production photograph comes from Motley's files.*

The Doctor's costume was dirty and shabby. As Vershinen, John Gielgud's uniform was fussily correct.[14] "Gielgud," wrote Audrey Williamson, "inspired perhaps by pictures of Stanislavsky in the part, devised an elaborate 'character' makeup including corded pince-nez and a carefully curled military mustache and beard."[15] In order to mark her changing states of mind, Motley gave Peggy Ashcroft as Irina a white cotton dress with *broiderie*

anglais for her name-day party and a heavy coat for the night of the fire. At the end of the play she was dressed in a shirt and blouse, working clothes that seemed to seal her fate.

Chekhov's elaborate, realistic interiors presented Margaret Harris with some difficult stage logistics. In the party scene, for instance, the challenge to the designer and director was to manage many points of focus. The set design allowed the audience to shift attention from one individual to another within a crowded scene. It was full of the ambience of the period. The four-sided dining room that opened out into the theatre was raised a little to show the supper party at the back, the drawing room in front, and the hall to one side. "Most of the scenes were played downstage and near the audience," she said. "The scene between Irina and the Baron played downstage. But there was never any worry about it being close enough to the audience; whatever the distance, the acting carried."

The critics were extravagant with their praise: "Beautifully produced and performed," wrote St.

Three Sisters, *Queen's Theatre, 1938. Costume sketches for Irina (Peggy Ashcroft) reflect her changing moods and social status in the course of the drama. Motley Collection.*

John Irvine (*Observer*, 29 January). "One of those theatrical events I shall remember all my life," said Darlington (*Daily Telegraph*, 29 January). "The Motley interiors are Motley once more at their best. The lighting of the scene when morning fills the room will not soon be forgotten," concluded Farjeon (*The Bystander*). "The whole mood of this play is established and underlined by the most cunning and subtle devices in setting, lighting, and grouping," said Wilson (*Sun*, 29 January). Peggy Ashcroft recalled years later, "I have never seen a production of *The Three Sisters* where you sensed so vividly the change of the seasons. The first act had the gaiety of Easter and Springtime. Then it was Winter in Act Two. Then it was a blazing hot summer night in Act Three. We spent hours rehearsing things like just how hot it would be. I can still see Gwen clapping her hands to show the mosquitoes were biting. It was this rapt attention to detail that made it a great production."[16] As a

final touch, Saint-Denis imagined the streets the band passed through during the last scene, the music fading as they went around a corner, and then coming up louder as they came around again.

The Queen's Season came to an end with *The Merchant of Venice,* directed by Gielgud and Glen Byam Shaw. Gielgud played Shylock as "a dingy, rancorous, fawning creature of the ghetto, gaily redolent of the slum and the usurer's attic," Audrey Williamson remembered. Yet Motley were everywhere ingenious in lightening the tone of the production: Aragon, for example, became a fantastico—perhaps within Shakespeare's lexicon of stereotypes, but almost a parody of the self-important exotic aristocrat. In the same slightly burlesque spirit, Williamson added, George Devine was "a fine ripe Gobbo, with a padded, swag belly, thanks to Motley. Motley dressed Peggy Ashcroft as Portia and Angela Baddely as Nerissa in romantic gowns."[17] "As we did for *Hamlet,*" recalled Margaret Harris, "we sprayed the costumes with dye and shaded from light in the center to dark at the edges; we made people look the right shape by shading the bits we didn't want to stand out."

All was not tranquillity during rehearsals, however, because of a silly misunderstanding about the costumes, which were fitted before they were dyed and painted. Alec Guinness, who was playing Lorenzo, came to Motley for his fitting. The costume was still white, undyed calico. "In a panic, he went back to the theatre," said Margaret Harris, "and told John Gielgud and Glen Byam Shaw—'The costumes are going to be an absolute disaster.' Of course, the costumes *did* look eccentric and unattractive in white calico." Glen Byam Shaw attacked the designers in a grand backstage row. "Once dyed and painted, the costumes were perfectly good, finally, and everyone was happy again."

The play alternates between Venice and Belmont. For this, their second *Merchant,* Motley created a white canvas dome for the unit set with a compass rose painted on the floor, to give the set a nautical feeling. A semicircle of columns, which one might imagine fronted on a canal, held up the dome-like canopy. The columns distinguished the two settings, emphasizing Venice's association with ships and canals and Belmont's romantic and pastoral feeling. For Venice, Motley turned to Canaletto, suggesting with "pastel semi-permanent

setting and costumes . . . all the color, luxury, and romantic exuberance of Venice at the height of its power," wrote Audrey Williamson.[18] When it came to Belmont, they designed a very delicate painted gauze for the cyclorama, a curved cloth representing the garden surrounding the back and sides of the stage. Columns and canopy remained throughout. The courtroom scene was played using the columns as the prisoner's dock and a platform for the judge, who sat in front of dark curtains. "Motley's settings," reported *The Tatler,* "are as attractive as they are simple and serviceable." "Motley's design for the production," added J. C. Trewin *(The Lady),* "contrives with a few slender columns, a staircase, and a variety of splendid curtains to give the effect of light and gaiety, which, with the splendor of the dresses, makes it all a fairy tale in which the machinations of the Jew are bound to be confounded."

Michael Billington wrote with keen hindsight that by the close of the Queen's Season, the Gielgud company "showed that the classics could be a box-office draw, that an identifiable team of actors could be held together in a free lance world, and that great plays repaid minute examination. Gielgud had erected a signpost to the future. It pointed ultimately towards the Royal Shakespeare Company and the National."[19] Although Gielgud stepped back after the Queen's Season, the company spirit lived on. Michel Saint-Denis and George Devine attempted to continue the "Queen's" company around London Theatre Studio productions of *The Cherry Orchard, Uncle Vanya, The Wild Duck, Twelfth Night,* and *Le Bourgeoise Gentilhomme* at the Phoenix. Peggy Ashcroft, Michael Redgrave, Glen Byam Shaw, George Devine, and Marius Goring were committed to the company, reports Michael Billington, with "cloudier expressions of support from Laurence Olivier and Ralph Richardson."[20] Noticing that many of them seemed to be in productions at the Globe Theatre, some critics spoke of a "Globe Season." But such hopes fell apart by January 1939, as much a victim of uncertainties about events in Europe as of the lack of Gielgud and a fully first-rate cast.

Parallel with their involvement in the classics of the Queen's Season, Motley continued to do commercial plays in the West End. The designers knew well their audience's longing for glamour and elegance, which they satisfied in such plays as

Dear Octopus, Queen's Theatre, 1938. John Gielgud (Nicholas) is proposing a toast "to the Family—that dear octopus from whose tentacles we never quite escape, nor in our inmost hearts, ever quite wish to." Seated to his right is Marie Tempest (Dora). The others have not been identified. The production photograph comes from Theatre World, October 1938.

Dodie Smith's *Dear Octopus,* about a quintessential middle-class English family. It was a tremendous commercial success, but not an interesting play. The glamorous cast included Marie Tempest and John Gielgud. Margaret Harris admired Byam Shaw's directing but cheerfully admitted that "Dodie really pandered to all the tastes of the audience of that period—and they did love it."

The costumes and sets were contemporary and straightforward, depicting clothes the audience might actually be wearing and interiors very like those to which they returned after the theatre. For the opening scene in a child's nursery Motley used wallpaper designed with a poem about John Gilpin. It was a common wallpaper pattern of the

time for children's rooms. Margaret Harris remembered the production without much pleasure. She especially deplored the actions of Marie Tempest, whom she characterized as a prima donna: "She used to make the girls put on their dresses half an hour before the curtain went up, and come down and stand on a white sheet before they went onto the stage; because, she said, they mustn't get the hems dirty, and they mustn't hurry. She was very ferocious with them, and she used to do the same thing herself. There was a great drama about the sofa. She had to sit in a typical stage position on the sofa. So it had to have the cushion taken off, and a plywood seat put on, and then the cushion put on top, so that it didn't give at all. Then when she sat down, it was absolutely rigid. In that uncomfortable position, as usual, she had to pour out tea gracefully from a silver teapot." J. C. Trewin dismissed the production as the well-known English playwright Dodie Smith's "cozy corner on the domestic-sentimental."[21] Yet no less a critic than James Agate deemed it "Chekhovian," and it enjoyed a long run.

As the decade moved to a close, Motley continued to work on diverse projects. As described in chapter 13, they designed costumes for films, beginning with *The Red Wagon* in 1933. They were still involved with the London Theatre Studio, working with Michel Saint-Denis, Glen Byam Shaw, and George Devine to train dozens of student designers, actors, and directors. They continued their collaboration with Gielgud, doing sets and costumes for his *Hamlet* at Elsinore and costumes for *Scandal in Assyria* in the spring of 1939. An obliquely anti-Nazi play, it criticized the Germans' persecution of Jews. The play had a brief run at the Globe under the aegis of the "London International Theatre Club," where experimental plays could be staged for one or two performances. Favorable notices do not mention Motley's costumes, although the program does.

In March 1939 Michel Saint-Denis directed Garcia Lorca's *Marriage of Blood,* now commonly referred to as *Blood Wedding,* at the Savoy Theatre in a Sunday performance in aid of the Spanish Writers' Relief Agency. L.T.S. students assisted in the production, which opened out another foreign dimension to Motley's work. The play was done on a shoestring, the designers and their students scouring flea markets for bits of embroidered material for the peasant costumes. They found black velvet Victorian capes embroidered with jet, and made aprons of them for the Spanish women. Conforming with Spanish custom, even the bride wore black. The students from the London Theatre Studio played the peasants. "It was a very simple set," said Margaret Harris. "It's a beautiful play."

For their Stratford-upon-Avon debut in 1939, at the suggestion of the director Irene Hentschel, Motley shifted *Twelfth Night* from Renaissance "Illyria" to Victorian England. Harley Granville-Barker, Barry Jackson, and Theodore Komisarjevsky had set ample precedent for experimenting with the period and setting for Shakespeare. Heretofore Motley had kept to the period of the play's action. In the first scene all the players were dressed in black, and Olivia was in mourning. Sir Toby wore a deer-stalker hat and plus-fours. The *Times* (14 April) praised the director for her fresh approach in contemporizing the play, admiring

Olivia's elegant Edwardian mourning; Malvolio "walked out of a page of Cruickshank in *Pickwick Papers.*" With the updated costumes came updated humor. To the reviewer, Maria appeared as a "saucy baggage who frisked on the borderland of French farce."

By the late 1930s, Glen Byam Shaw, who had been an actor in Gielgud's company and then his assistant director, was directing in his own right. Remnants of the "Queen's Season company" staged *Rhondda Roundabout,* as part of the so-called "Globe Season" in 1938–1939. The new play was written by member of Parliament Jack Jones about the Rhondda Valley in Wales. Motley went "on location" to Wales for inspiration, the first of many such trips for design ideas. "Glen held auditions there," Margaret Harris recalled. "The cast were nearly all amateurs from Wales, except that it had that little Welsh actor Mervyn Johns in the lead. The only other professionals in the cast were Raymond Huntley and George Devine. The Welsh actors were a bit uncontrollable. Glen would put them in a scene and they would cooperate. Then as soon as they were let loose on their own with an audience, they did what they felt like doing, and it went a bit mad." Although the critics liked the play for its compassionate treatment of the suffering miners—with a shell-shocked Englishman thrown in to boot—its run was only modestly successful.

The Importance of Being Earnest was directed by Gielgud, who also starred. Motley designed sets and costumes. By now Motley could conjure up the period set and costumes as if they had a magic wand. Critics could find no fault. As an expression of British elegance, *Earnest* became a touchstone for British patriotism during the War, a nostalgic affirmation of that world for which the Battle of Britain was being fought. To prepare for the production, Gielgud sent the Motley women to a house in Holland Park near Kensington Gardens, where an aunt of his had lived when he was a boy. He said the house with its verandah and garden was exactly right as a model for the house in the play. Motley used it as inspiration for the garden scene. For the interiors, they primarily made box sets with ceilings. They painted on a William-Morris type of wallpaper. "It was a very successful production," remembered Margaret Harris fondly. "It ran and ran." One of the most popular plays in

The Importance of Being Earnest, *Globe Theatre, 1939. John Worthing (John Gielgud) kneels to the Hon. Gwendolyn Fairfax (Gwen Ffrangcon-Davies) as Lady Bracknell (Edith Evans) looks on. This stylish production was revived again and again during World War II, and was eventually one of the first to transfer from London to New York after the war ended. The production photograph from Motley's files also appears in* John Gielgud: An Actor's Biography in Pictures *(London: John Lehman, 1952).*

London, it would be revived at least four times during the course of the War.

For some time Alec Guinness had been working on an adaptation of Dickens's *Great Expectations* for the stage. Even as the War broke out in Europe, he and George Devine produced it in Rudolph Steiner Hall, where it opened on 7 December 1939. The play was produced by the Actors' Company, directed by George Devine. An outgrowth of the

L.T.S., the Actors Company embodied Devine's ideal of a non-commercial company, something like Joint Stock fifty years later. Starring were Alec Guinness (Herbert Pocket), Martita Hunt (Miss Havisham), Vera Lindsay (Estella as a woman), Yvonne Mitchell (Estella as a girl), Marius Goring (Pip as a Man), Frank Tickle (Mr. Bumble). After a run of six weeks in Rudolph Steiner Hall, the play did not transfer as planned to the Shaftsbury Theatre, which had been destroyed by bombing. Nevertheless, film producers David Lean and Ronald Neame saw it, remembered, and after the War made the film *Great Expectations* with many of the same actors, including Guinness and Hunt.[22]

Not surprisingly, in the face of the uncertainties of wartime, rehearsals and performances were tumultuous. Margaret Harris recalled that although they knew each other well, the cast contained "quite a lot of quite cantankerous people—Martita was certainly cantankerous. They would not agree and make decisions. George kept pulling back, and saying, 'I am not making the decisions. You have to make them.' Everybody quarreled, and there were terrible scenes. In the end George had to make the decisions after all." To make matters worse, the actor who played Pip as a boy was not allowed to play on opening night because he didn't turn twelve until the day afterwards, and children under twelve weren't allowed to play on the stage at that time. "The government authorities forbade him playing, so the understudy had to play, who wasn't nearly as good," reported Margaret Harris.

Before *Earnest* and *Great Expectations*, Gielgud and company were invited to stage *Hamlet* in Kronborg Castle, Elsinore, the play's notional setting. After six performances at the Lyceum, the last before it closed as a theatre, the production went to Denmark. This was Motley's first production to be staged abroad. In many ways, it became a recap of their earlier triumph. Motley used the same costumes, based on Lucas Cranach, that they had used in London in 1934. In the courtyard of Kronborg Castle, they designed a similar structure with huge banners down each side to enclose the stage and hide the castle itself, which they found ugly. "We thought it would be dead still in the courtyard," said Margaret Harris, "but these banners flapped! 'Flap, flap, flap, flap, flap, flap, flap,' against the flagpoles. Eventually we had to strap them all down against the flagpoles so that they looked like nothing. And you could hear the ferries constantly hooting across the harbor, going across from Elsinore to Sweden."

This would be the last time that Gielgud's circle would work together. Even as they played *Hamlet* in Elsinore, the company found themselves confronted with the emotional chauvinism that ignited World War II. Two German destroyers lay moored by the quay. In the dining room of their hotel, among flags of all nations were displayed Nazi swastika flags. The actor Marius Goring removed and destroyed them, bringing on an uneasy confrontation with the authorities. As the brief run drew to a close, the troupe started playing outrageous practical jokes on each other—live chickens under the bedclothes. The company celebrated after the last performance with a champagne dinner-dance in formal dress. As the night wore on, they went down to the sea and, as Ronald Hayman reported, the evening came to an unexpected ending: "It was the Motley girls who started it. They threw one of the actresses, still in her beautiful evening gown, into the sea. Then ceremoniously, systematically, one by one, each of the actors was thrown in. Dripping figures scrambled out of the sea and stripped down to their underclothes to assist with throwing the next one in. John watched until everyone else had been thrown. Then, just as it all seemed to be coming to an end, 'Isn't anyone going to throw me?' . . . he took off his tail coat before he was thrown. . . . They must have sensed this was the last time they would be together before the war sent them off in different directions and the practical jokes were probably a kind of farewell to their youth."[23] An era was indeed passing. Gielgud's company was about to be dispersed.

With World War II afire just over the horizon and the end of Motley's first decade together as designers drawing near, they completed their theatrical range by adding opera to a spectrum that already included contemporary drama, modern classics, Restoration plays, Shakespeare, and ballet. A new production of *The Beggar's Opera* with the prestigious Glyndebourne Opera Company fittingly roused national spirits as it toured the country and then came in to London. Having received early inspiration from Lovat Fraser's 1920 designs for this English classic at the Lyric, Hammersmith, Gielgud and Motley paid him the tribute of avoiding comparison by changing the period from the late eighteenth century to the early nineteenth, a shift to Dickensian London that *Punch* appreciated. Michael Redgrave played Macheath, and Audrey Mildmay, who was married to Glyndebourne's director John Christie, played Polly. Motley dressed the women in flashy satins; Macheath, in a glamorous and dashing top hat and tails. His crew were dressed in outfits that could have been inspired by the caricatures of Dickens's "Boz," an inspiration both Motley and Gielgud acknowledged. Amazingly, the production cost a mere £1,000 sterling. It opened in Brighton and came into London, but was not much of a success. In the same newspaper in which Giles Playfair and other critics assessed the new production, there also appeared photographs of people huddled in shelters preparing for the bombardment. *The Beggar's Opera* was the last production that all three Motleys would work on with Gielgud.

It is perhaps a measure of the theatre's vitality before the War—or a general naiveté about the War's gravity—that plans in spring 1940 for a production of *The Cherry Orchard* went forward in London. Even after *The Importance of Being Earnest,* directed by Gielgud, shifted to the provinces after the outbreak of the War in August, Motley and the theatre community continued to plan productions. But *The Cherry Orchard* prepared for staging in 1940 was never staged. Motley had designed nearly the entire production. "Michel wanted uneven ground in the outdoor scene, and we were having a big struggle over this, as of course it interfered with the interiors," said Margaret Harris. Glen Byam Shaw was to play Firs. Ronald Squires was to play Gayev. Edith Evans, Peggy Ashcroft, and George Devine rounded out the excellent cast. Then its director Michel Saint-Denis was called to France because of the War, and the production was abandoned.

Summoned by Laurence Olivier, Margaret Harris and Elizabeth Montgomery sailed for the United States before the sea lanes closed. Olivier wanted Motley to design "his" *Romeo,* starring himself and Vivien Leigh. In London, as their friends in the theatre joined the war effort, everyone scattering, George Devine and Sophie Harris formalized their long-standing relationship by marrying. George Devine joined the Army. A pregnant Sophia Harris remained at home in London. She was thirty-nine. Her sister Margaret was thirty-five. Elizabeth Montgomery was thirty-seven. In seven years they had risen from earnest, talented theatre amateurs to leaders in the profession.

5

Motley Takes the Town:
New York
1940–1945

Sailing for New York in January of 1940, Margaret Harris and Elizabeth Montgomery were about to enter a new theatre world. Despite the distance between London and New York, since the early nineteenth century the two cities had shared common, overlapping theatre traditions. Each cross-pollinated the other, as productions with English actor-managers, actors, and scene painters transferred from London to the United States and American productions came over to London from New York. Inevitably the two groups merged into an international community of artists who created theatre that was Anglo-American, a process given further dimension with the rise of Hollywood filmmakers who found the glamour of English actors hard to resist. When Motley left London for New York, they were looking forward to working with people they knew personally or by reputation, among them Robert Edmond Jones, the famous American designer who was to light the show. He had written them a fan letter about their 1937 *Henry V* and was eager to work with them on Olivier's latest production.

Motley's wartime years coincided with a period in American theatre sometimes thought of as inconsequential when considered with the great events happening outside the country. "The period just before and during active American involvement in World War II emphasized escapism in the

theatre," wrote Ethan Mordden, because "daily life had grown so serious that the stage didn't dare put on much that was not comic or sentimental or patriotic."[1] For both Motley women it meant mastering a distinctly different theatrical milieu and, for Elizabeth Montgomery especially, the opportunity to extend her range from Shakespeare and straight plays to the new ballets of Agnes de Mille, to grand opera at the Metropolitan Opera House and musicals on Broadway. Margaret Harris stayed in America for the duration of the War. Elizabeth Montgomery remained until 1966. These developments were far in the future when they responded to Olivier's call to design *Romeo and Juliet*.

When the two Motley women landed in New York, they made arrangements to fly to Hollywood to join Olivier and the *Romeo* company, eager to link up with the prestige of America and their friend who had made his mark there. For his part, Olivier looked to his stylish English designers for glamour and expertise. Now an American film star, Laurence Olivier wanted to direct and star in *Romeo and Juliet* with Vivien Leigh, his new leading lady. He had joined the ranks of many talented English actors who had been wooed and won by Hollywood. Late in 1939 Olivier was making a Hollywood film. Director George Cukor suggested that Olivier and Vivien Leigh produce and star in *Romeo* on Broadway to make some "quick money." Crediting Motley with "a quite ravishing lightning job on sets and costumes," in his memoirs Olivier recalled how he "planned the production on the film set in between making shots for *Pride and Prejudice.*"[2]

"Larry and Vivien were busy filming, so the *Romeo* rehearsals were rather disrupted," remembered Margaret Harris. "A man called Bob Ross, Larry's assistant, tried to direct it. Then Larry would come in and change everything." Olivier insisted on a revolving stage which, his production note announced, "will move the scenes in perfect sequence. . . . In the first scene on the street, the exterior of the Capulet house is visible. Then the stage swings to reveal the next scene: the interior of the Capulet house. Its walls are the same walls which were visible in the first scene." Perhaps it was inspired by the quick cuts of cinema, but Olivier's idea was a set designer's nightmare. It crammed each setting onto a small wedge-shaped space like the slice of a pie cut into fifths. "Juliet's bedroom was two feet, six inches across," recalled Margaret Harris. "We somehow worked it out so that we got the street, the ballroom, Juliet's bedroom, and the Friar's cell all on the revolve—and the garden, with the balcony!" What might have been feasible in a less literally realistic design simply did not make good acting space.

The production was plagued with troubles from the start. At the opening in San Francisco, Olivier was too exhausted to make his leap up onto Juliet's balcony. Instead, he leapt, caught hold, and dangled in full sight of the audience, unable to ascend further. In Chicago, *Romeo* played in the Auditorium Theatre, "an absolutely vast theatre," said Margaret Harris. "When you were in the upper gallery, the actors looked like midgets." The Chicago reviews were tepid. When the play opened in New York the show flopped miserably. The New York critics were savage. "Much production, little play," sneered Brooks Atkinson in the New York *Times* (10 May 1940). Hampering the serious business of performance in New York were newspaper reporters more interested in the progress of the offstage romance than in the play. Alluding to Olivier and Leigh's film roles, Richard Watts, Jr., in the New York *Herald-Tribune* (10 May 1940) dubbed them "Heathcliff Romeo" and "Scarlett Juliet," at the same time faulting Olivier for his

hubris in directing and acting in his own production. "The costumes were very much the same sort of thing we'd done in the 1935 *Romeo and Juliet.* The fifteenth-century period and the colors were different from those we had used before. Larry insisted on having his yellow hat!" Margaret Harris remembered with a smile. "The production was rather elaborate and decorative. It wasn't popular, because the critics disapproved of the fact that Larry and Vivien weren't married at the time. Cars waited outside the theatre to follow their car to see if they went home together or if they went to separate places. It was really awful. A lot of tittle-tattle."

Despite their obvious qualifications as set and costume designers, Motley had been allowed to work on *Romeo* only because it was viewed as an import. War made it impossible for them to return to London. To design any future shows in America, they had to face the fact that they needed to become accredited members of the theatre unions. During the summer of 1940, they stayed with friends in Toronto while they tried to make plans for working in New York. They were able to obtain their "costume card" in New York by taking an examination. The scene designer's card, however, seemed impossible in New York—the union local there had no places available. "Somebody tipped us a wink that we could get it in California," recalled Margaret Harris. Borrowing a car from Hume Cronyn, the two women left for California, where work in residence, rather than a written exam or available space in the union local, could secure membership. In California they brought their design talent to the film musical *I Married an Angel,* thereby qualifying for their union cards. Although it had nothing to do with establishing themselves professionally, while in California they also collaborated with the designers Charles and Ray Eames, the husband-and-wife team who would become renowned for the "Eames's chair." That concept grew out of the project Motley collaborated on—splints made out of molded plywood for use on the European battlefields. Their credentials established, they were able to qualify for work in the New York theatre.

However much American and English theatre people might have had in common, there were major differences between the two nations' theatre traditions.[3] American plays and musicals differed from English not only in subject matter, but in their treatment of it. In London during the 1930s, with the possible exceptions of the plays of Bernard Shaw, Chekhov, Ibsen, and Shakespeare, the West End favored garden and drawing-room comedies and tragedies of manners. For innovation in playwriting, one could look to Gordon Daviot and Emlyn Williams, who had collaborated with Motley on glamorous, romanticized historical dramas. The theatrical spectrum was broader in New York. Serious plays by Eugene O'Neill, Lillian Hellman, Maxwell Anderson, and Clifford Odets explored harsh, even gritty realms of American experience unfamiliar to middle-class audiences. The comedies and musicals of George Kaufman and Moss Hart sustained traditions of theatre as entertainment. The Federal Theatre Project, the Theatre Union, the Theatre Guild, and the Group Theatre followed radically experimental agendas.

Theatre in London made money, but it ran almost by the rules of a private club: One spoke more of aesthetics and good fellowship than of box-office "take." Theatre artists virtually donated their talents to the Old Vic in the interests of art. The producer Hugh (Binkie) Beaumont of the management firm H. M. Tennents acted as a lordly benefactor of the enterprise.[4]

In America, on the other hand, theatre was treated as big business. The earlier nationwide monopolies of the Shuberts and Klaw-Erlanger had waned, their power sapped by the popularity of the movies. Especially in New York, however, the business of theatre dictated that the strongest motivation was often not artistic, but financial—to secure a good return on the "angels'" money. It was "management" versus "the unions." Management hired the directors, designers, actors, and stagehands, each belonging to unions whose work rules were enforced stringently. Practices were employed that dated back to vigorous "closed shop" agitation during the early 1920s. Directors had to follow strict rules governing actors' hours in rehearsal. To be cast in a show, actors were required to possess an Equity card. All scene and costume designers had to belong to the appropriate union if they were to work in the New York theatre, and entry to the unions was jealously guarded by long examinations and quotas. Designs from union designers needed a union stamp before they could be sent to the costume or the scene shop. Once inside

the theatre, what designers could—or rather could not—do was strictly regulated. They could speak and point, but they could not touch the set.[5] Only a stagehand could move a prop onstage during rehearsal. Only a stage electrician could adjust lighting—or turn it on.[6]

Nor were the powers of the costume designer as great in New York as in London. The overall look of the production was dictated by the set designer: Boris Aronson, Norman Bel Geddes, Robert Edmond Jones, Jo Mielziner, Donald Oenslager, and Oliver Smith each had strong ideas. Costumes—usually designed by women—came second, after the director and designer had made major artistic decisions. "We didn't find much collaboration between the set designer and the costume designer," Margaret Harris said.

Late in the summer of 1940, armed with union credentials, the two women set out in their borrowed car from California back to New York. There they were engaged almost at once to design sets and costumes for *Three Virgins and a Devil* by Agnes de Mille, the dancer and choreographer. A native New Yorker, de Mille had trained in London before World War I, working as a dancer and a choreographer in New York and London during the 1930s. There she came to know of Motley, if not to know them personally. Using steps that she invented herself, with Lucia Chase as collaborator, Agnes de Mille created a ballet in which three virgins—one priggish, one greedy, one lustful—flirted with a devil. It was an immediate success and became a staple of the American Ballet Theatre's repertoire. The ballet was staged "without scenery or props [but] with decor by Motley of London," remembered de Mille.[7] "The decor is a delightful theatrical adaptation of a Flemish painting," reported Grace Roberts. "The costumes are in keeping with the period, though it is difficult to reconcile the Priggish One's prim character with the gay red of her dress. Surely the modest gray worn by the Lusty One would be more appropriate. The Youth's crimson costume, with its preposterous hat and fluttering ribbons, is one of the most hilariously funny getups ever seen on the New York stage."[8] With this production, the Motley women began a fruitful collaboration with the powerful and innovative de Mille that would extend from productions of experimental ballet to the more popular Broadway musicals. Dance

The Doctor's Dilemma, *Shubert Theatre, New York, 1942. Costume sketch for Katharine Cornell as Jennifer Dubeda. Her gown is a pale lavender, with a deeper shade of the same color for the artificial bouquet at her waist. Motley Collection.*

numbers had become an integral part of American musicals following Balanchine's innovations in *On Your Toes* in 1936, and de Mille extended their popularity with her novel musical choreography.

Motley's first play on Broadway was George Bernard Shaw's *The Doctor's Dilemma,* directed and produced by the American director-actor team of Guthrie McClintic and Katharine Cornell. Sets by Donald Oenslager showcased Motley's talent for elegant and evocative period costumes. After

New York, the show played on tour. Critics lavished great praise on the production, never mentioning the war. One even blithely suggested that the aged playwright ought to take a "Clipper plane" from London to see the stellar New York production. Whatever the horrors overseas, Elizabeth Montgomery and Margaret Harris quickly established themselves within the world of Broadway. A photographic spread in the New York *Times* magazine (9 March 1941) shortly before the opening of *The Doctor's Dilemma* speculated (albeit inaccurately) that the costumes in the production, inspired by Charles Dana Gibson's "Gibson Girl" and by Boldoni's portraits of society women at the turn of the century, would lead to a fashion revival of that style.

Then came *Rodeo,* or, as it was also called, *The Courting at Burnt Ranch.* De Mille teamed up with composer Aaron Copland. This production came as a revelation to audiences and critics, who proclaimed the invention of a new and thoroughly American art form. The ballet began with improvisations on the theme that de Mille had first developed in London—a cowboy's courtship. She had revised and perfected the piece in rehearsals with the Ballet Russe de Monte Carlo during a West Coast tour. The American ballet would become a competitive response to the rival Ballet Russe, who were then creating new work in Mexico.

Motley's role in the design is somewhat mysterious. Sets were done by Oliver Smith, who had designed de Mille's *Saratoga* for performance by the Ballet Russe de Monte Carlo in 1941. In published sources, Kermit Love is credited with the costumes. Yet a Motley costume design, clearly labeled "Rodeo" and stamped with the union seal makes it plain that they did design costumes for that ballet. In an interview with the author shortly before her death in 1993, Agnes de Mille recalled that Elizabeth Montgomery did the costume designs, working with Kermit Love, who was given public credit as an established union member. In any case, *Rodeo* made ballet history, and Motley were a part of it. The new ballet was a great hit. Its combination of cowboy choreography and the Wild West setting contributed to the integration of dance into the American musical comedy, most notable in the dream sequence in a later de Mille piece—*Oklahoma!* (The idea of a dream sequence danced as ballet within a musical first appeared in

Rodeo, *Metropolitan Opera House, New York, 1942. Costume sketches for two dancers. The dress is deep red, the shirt is dark purple, and the trousers are black. Motley's costume designs often had swatches of fabric attached, as this one does. Motley Collection.*

Babes in Arms, choreographed by Balanchine in 1937.) Motley's costumes were carefree variations on Western outfits, made of lighter fabrics and cut for ease of movement. The unity of costume, setting, music, and dance within a distinctly American context opened a rich lode of material which writers of ballets and musical comedies would mine again and again. The collaboration between Elizabeth Montgomery as costume designer and Agnes de Mille as choreographer would endure through several more ballets as well as musicals.

At the same time, Motley's partnership with McClintic and Cornell continued successfully. For a Christmas week opening in 1942, Motley designed sets and costumes for *The Three Sisters.* In the credits New Yorkers read "settings and costumes by Motley of London," a qualification that would later become unnecessary. Since they had designed the play for Michel Saint-Denis's well-received production in 1938, it is hardly surprising that this version of *The Three Sisters* produced a similar outcome for the designers. The New York critics outdid each other in praising the production. The *Sun* (22 December 1942) deemed it "*The Three Sisters* at its best." "A rare experience in playgoing," said the *Herald-Tribune;* "the best American production of the play I have seen," echoed John Anderson in the *Journal-American.* Expanding on others' acclaim, the *World-Telegram* (22 December 1942) called it "without a doubt, an artistic event in the history of the theatre. . . . The settings and costumes were so unobtrusively right that you were hardly aware that they were costumes and settings." No longer able to ignore what was happening in Europe, however, the reviewer went on to argue that "with Russian women in the trenches and many of our American women in war work . . . even though expertly played, [the three sisters] seem to be three completely uninteresting females whose aspirations are trivial and whose fate is unimportant." Such cold-eyed qualifications notwithstanding, the play offered deeply moving and effective theatre as an alternative to some of the superficial entertainment that producers thought appropriate for a nation at war.

Critics had little good to say about the next play Motley designed—*Richard III*, directed by and starring George Coulouris. "It was a ghastly fiasco. George Coulouris put it on with his own money. He wanted to do something interesting, and he simply couldn't cope with trying to direct, act, and produce all at once. We didn't do too well either," admitted Margaret Harris. The *Times* (27 March 1943) remembered Barrymore's earlier performance to Coulouris's great disadvantage. Another critic, who recalled Coulouris's successes as a stage villain, could take comfort even in a weak performance: "It is something at least, in a theatre out at its spiritual elbows, to have the Bard at all" (*Journal American*, 27 March 1943). Similarly grateful for a taste of Shakespeare, *New York PM* (28 March 1943) nonetheless dismissed the production as "merely dull." The same critic found Motley's two-level unit set "a trifle monotonous."

Motley completed the 1942–1943 season with the set and costume designs for *Dim Lustre*, a ballet conceived and choreographed by Anthony Tudor. Tudor was an English dancer, who, like Motley, had come to the United States in 1940. His ballet featured two pairs of dancers moving as if mirror images of each other. Where they had shared design credit for *Rodeo*, for *Dim Lustre* Motley received full credit for both sets and costumes.

The following season *Lovers and Friends* continued Motley's association with McClintic and Cornell. A new play by the English playwright Dodie Smith, whose *Dear Octopus* Motley had designed in London, it drew somewhat faint praise as light-hearted "good theatre," "polite comedy," or "sophisticated fluff" to entertain the war-weary. Motley's settings and costumes seem to have escaped the critics' notice except for Lewis Nichols in the New York *Times* (30 November 1943), who said they were "so good that, while evening audiences may not care so much, the matinees probably will find a certain amount of envy over the dresses," indicating that Motley had not lost their eye for glamour that would appeal to sophisticated women. Not long afterward, McClintic and Cor-

nell departed for a U.S.O. tour of *The Barretts of Wimpole Street*.

Like McClintic and Cornell, Margaret Webster and Eva Le Gallienne, the director-actor team with whom Motley worked next, were well regarded as serious theatre artists dedicated to drama—rather than to mere entertainment. Margaret Webster, according to New York critics, had proved herself the American director who could make Shakespeare palatable to Americans. Her book *Shakespeare Without Tears* had been published in 1942, and her 1943 production of *Othello* had broken box office records for an American Shakespeare production, with 295 performances. Eva Le Gallienne had come over to New York from London during World War I, and quickly had established her credentials as a serious actor in the plays of Chekhov, Ibsen, and other serious drama. Her partnership with Margaret Webster was both professional and personal.

The Cherry Orchard, critics were quick to note, was Webster's first Chekhov. Motley probably seemed a natural choice to design the sets and costumes, in view of their success in London and in New York the season before with McClintic's *The Three Sisters*. Eva Le Gallienne played Andreyevna Lyubov and Joseph Schildkraut, her brother Leonid. The production got into trouble with some critics by interpolating slapstick into the Chekhovian melancholia. But most critics echoed Howard Barnes in the *Herald-Tribune* (26 June 1944) who proclaimed, "Every facet of the drama is revealed in its full splendor." Motley's settings, the *Daily News* (16 January 1944) said, "are not stunning, but they fit. They do not intrude upon the play."

Building on the success of her earlier ballets, Agnes de Mille and her dancers staged a new piece in April, towards the end of the 1943–1944 season. *Tally-Ho*, or *The Frail Quarry*, was a comic modern dance piece featuring Anton Dolin. Motley designed both sets and costumes. A Watteauesque, romantic piece, it was backed by the impresario Sol Hurok, whose support ensured good box office and further recognition for the company, the choreographer, and the designers. It departed for an American tour after a run at the Metropolitan Opera.[9]

By the mid-1940s, Motley were no longer regarded as "English" designers, suitable mainly for classical drama or period pieces. They moved further into mainstream Broadway with *Highland Fling,* a comedy farce by the actress Margaret Curtis. The play revolved around the efforts of the ghost of a Scots laird to reform a notorious local drunkard and rake. An unimportant piece in itself, it was directed by George Abbott, a distinguished playwright and director best known for his fast-paced musicals and farce—*The Boys from Syracuse, Three Men on a Horse,* and *Pal Joey.* Abbott's hiring of Motley to do the costumes for *Highland Fling* signaled their acceptance by the Broadway establishment. The play opened in the Plymouth Theatre at the end of April. Besides appreciating the play as thin entertainment in which "everyone talked like Sir Harry Lauder," as the *Daily News* reported (29 April 1944), the critics did not mention Motley's costumes.

As if to confirm their status as Broadway designers, Motley's next venture was designing costumes for *Sadie Thompson* by Howard Dietz and Rouben Mamoulian with music by Vernon Duke. This production marked Motley's first costume design for American musical theatre. Set in Pago-Pago and in the jungle, the play was based loosely on Somerset Maugham's "Rain." June Havoc played the title role. The play is probably less important in itself than as a precursor of *South Pacific,* for which Motley would also design the costumes. It ran a little over six weeks.

At the end of 1944, midway through the Broadway season, Motley designed their first war play, *A Bell for Adano.* It was adapted by Paul Osborn from John Hersey's novel about the transformation of a small Sicilian town from fascism to democracy under American forces and the restoration of the town's bell by Major Victor Joppolo. "A vibrant war drama," proclaimed the *Sun* (7 December 1944). Summing up the New York critics' consensus, the *Post* (6 December 1944) stated simply: "H. C. Potter's direction and Motley's setting help to make a superior production of a literate and timely play." It enjoyed a long run and was widely produced off-Broadway in theatres across the country.

When Margaret Webster returned to Shakespeare early in 1945 with *The Tempest,* she made news by casting the black actor Canada Lee as Caliban and the ballerina Vera Zorina as Ariel in a much-shortened text. It was not a happy production backstage. "It was directed by Margaret Webster *and* Eva Le Gallienne," recalled Margaret Harris. "Eva was on tour for part of the time, and Peggy really did it. But Eva interfered, if that's the word. She wanted the set done like stalactites. We had to go and look at some strange jewels in a cave somewhere to see how she wanted it." Rarely staged, the play surprised critics with its theatrical vitality. Original music by David Diamond, an excellent cast, and an innovative set and costumes by Motley, resulted in a solid hit that ran for three months at the Alvin Theatre.

Costumes made Ariel a glamorous dancer, Caliban a deformed ogre. Trinculo looked like a variation on Lou Costello—stout, black-suited, and sporting a fedora. Amidst the clown's antics, Motley created an atmosphere of "magic enchantment" and "pure spectacle," as the *Herald Tribune* (26 January 1945) put it. On a turntable center stage they mounted a unit set of steps and crags that allowed instant scene changes, while still permitting use of the full stage—thereby avoiding the cramped interiors experienced in Olivier's *Romeo-on-a-revolve.* Silhouetted against a blue cyclorama, the set evoked the desolate, shape-shifting island setting. "The principal scenic element was mounted on a revolve," reported Robert Speaight, "and changes of location were indicated by light and color and surface texture; a soft gray for Prospero's cave, smooth edges for cliffs under which Caliban, Stephano, and Trinculo weave their abortive conspiracy. . . . The medley of accents among the actors matched the intricacies of rocks, stairways, aisles, angles, and planes. For the shipwreck scene, Motley had taken the print of a caravel with bellying sails from Burnacini and painted it on a curtain. Through a scrim in the center of it the passengers and crew could be seen huddled aboard."[10]

Among general praise for the costume design, critics especially liked Prospero's brilliant red robe and Caliban's grotesque get-up—"like Ringling Brothers' Gargantua," said the *World-Telegram* (26 January 1945). However much the critics enjoyed the show, Margaret Harris remembered best an opening-night disaster. "We did really a very objectionable set. It was on a revolve, like an island. It had all the lights plugged in the center of the revolve. We planned a big effect for when Ariel came on and stood on the island to do the speech

'You are three men of sin.' [The stage direction in the text is "*Thunder and lightning. Enter Ariel, like a harpy; claps his wings upon the table; and with a quaint device the banquet vanishes.*"] On the opening night the cue for the special effects came. There was a blackout, but nothing more happened. No lights! Complete blackness! The operator had gone to sleep, sitting there in the middle of the revolve. No stage manager could get to him without being seen, and nothing could be done. The operator had had a few too many, and he had fallen asleep. It was absolutely horrible, absolutely disastrous!"

In *Hope for the Best,* quipped Burton Rascoe in the *World-Telegram* (8 February 1945), "you're due for the worst." Despite lukewarm to bad reviews, this new comedy had a good run, closing in mid-May. A contemporary play about the agonizing of a syndicated political columnist (Franchot Tone), supported by his mistress (Jane Wyatt), and distracted by a nutty professor (Leo Bulgakov) who designs "dramagrams" for television—its action consumed a weekend in a Connecticut living room; "a solid Connecticut farmhouse in the modern manner—like being pressed between the pages of *House Beautiful,*" said the *Post* (8 February 1945).

On 8 May 1945 the German army had capitulated, and by August World War II was over. The theatre kept on as before, but for theatre people, it marked a time to think of new projects, reunions, and continuations to careers that had been redirected by the war. One of the first American theatre artists to go over to London was Agnes de Mille, who vividly remembered the bombed-out city, the shortages, and the undertow of artistic resentment of American theatrical achievement by some British theatre people.[11]

You Touched Me!, Tennessee Williams's first play on Broadway, rounded out Motley's work with Guthrie McClintic during the war years. Adapted by Tennessee Williams and Donald Windham from D. H. Lawrence's short story, it starred Montgomery Clift. Following soon after Williams's New York debut with *The Glass Menagerie,* both the play and the production were, as Lewis Nichols said in the *Times* (26 September 1945), "a step down." Critics were about evenly divided between those who thought it "a first-rate comedy" (*World-Telegram,* 26 September 1945) and those who panned it as "a wobbly bit of symbolism" (*New York PM,* 26 September 1945) or "tenuous and

fragmentary comedy" (*Sun,* 26 September 1945). When they were noticed, Motley's costumes were praised, and the settings—"a house in rural England"—were, Louis Kronenberger (*New York PM*) said, "a problem in architecture, well solved."

Carib Song by William Archibald, with music by Baldwin Bergersen, attempted to capitalize on the popularity of the exotic Caribbean, in this case Trinidad. Caught between being a musical play and a collection of song-and-dance numbers, it featured the Katherine Dunham dancers. A thin plot line hurt the show, which closed within a month. Significantly for Motley's future, Elizabeth Montgomery designed costumes and Jo Mielziner designed the sets, extending a good working relationship with New York set designers that would endure when Elizabeth Montgomery became the sole representative of Motley in the United States. *New York PM* (28 September 1945) probably summed up the production best: "Dull goings-on in the Tropics." Elizabeth Montgomery designed the costumes without Margaret Harris, who was away sketching the interiors of a bomber for the sets for their next play.

If *A Bell for Adano* was a war play that could not go wrong, *Skydrift* never came right. It suffered from a flawed script by the novice playwright Harry Kliner. In the first half of the play seven paratroopers bail out somewhere over the Pacific and die in enemy fire. In the second half, in a series of dream adventures, one by one the men's ghosts attempt the futile task of reconciling their loved ones to loss and to going on with life. "It was directed by Roy Hargrave, who stepped back, fell off the stage into the orchestra pit, and broke his leg," said Margaret Harris. "He was very lucky that that was all he did."

"To design the airplane," recalled Harris, "I had to go to an airfield. I had to do detail sketches of everything. It had to be absolutely accurate, because I knew that there would be a lot of servicemen in the audience who would know. So I was taken into a plane by a young officer, who sat there while I measured and checked everything. Then we reproduced it completely on the stage. We had the fuselage cut through, so there was one half of an airplane on a rostrum. We got the most amazing notices for it. The critics just loved it. It's silly, because any fool can do that, you know. It's just copying." After roundly berating the author, critics praised the acting and Motley's authentic costumes and settings. John Chapman of the *Daily News* (14 November 1945) particularly appreciated their work. "The interior of a transport in flight is quite wonderful. . . . The settings for the return of the dead paratroopers to the living world are simple and beautiful . . . a blue backdrop laced with shroud lines, a billowing fragment of a 'chute and whatever setting they want to put beneath, like a house, or . . . a booth of a nightclub," he wrote.

The last production that Motley designed together in New York was a revival of Bernard Shaw's *Pygmalion*. It was directed by Cedric Hardwicke, starring Raymond Massey as Professor Higgins, Gertrude Lawrence as the Cockney, Eliza Doolittle, and Melville Cooper as her father. The production by "Theatre Incorporated," a new non-profit repertory group dedicated to the production of "important plays," was set to run for six weeks only. In the end it set a world record run of the play—181 performances, to be outdone only years later by *My Fair Lady,* the musical version of the same play. Donald Oenslager's settings were effective. "Motley's costumes," reported the *World-Telegram* (27 December 1945), "are exclusively pictorial of the period, and a couple of the dresses for Miss Lawrence could not be surpassed for setting off her grace." "I remember Gertie Lawrence in an enormous, beautiful white hat, with pink roses on it, and a white dress, which is now in the costume collection of the Museum of the City of New York," recalled Elizabeth Montgomery. "She looked so elegant!"

Looking back years later on their work in America, Margaret Harris was struck by the great contrasts they encountered in the New York theatre: "The American way hampered us. It is very important for designers to be able to create objects and handle them themselves. If you want something made in a special way, it's very valuable to be able to do it yourself. You can't always convey the feeling you want to others, except sometimes when working with somebody you're very used to working with. In New York for *Second Best Bed,* for instance, we were trying to do a rockery in Anne Hathaway's garden. I went onto the stage and moved a flower. The union said, 'If you don't stop doing that, we'll stop the show.' That was particularly difficult. It was a whole garden, full

of rockery and flowers. You weren't allowed on the stage; you had to stand in the stalls and say to the property man, who was not skilled, just a man who looked after props, 'That flower goes—you see that little bit of rock that sticks up there? Well there's a flat bit there and then there's another rock; well it goes there—no, not there!—six inches further!' It was mad, chaotic, and all it needed was the designer to go on the stage and drop the things into place and allow the property staff to fix them.

"We were mostly disappointed in directors; they didn't seem to care much about design. Guthrie McClintic cared, up to a point, but he really wanted to do what was best for Kit, his wife Katharine Cornell. So everything was centered around that. He was a real director, and we did a lot with him. He always used to change things in the middle of the production. In America, designers use technology supremely well. But they are still more decorative than we are.

"In England at that time, the prop man and all the people on the stage were craftsmen. The Americans were businessmen who organized it all outside the theatre. In England, the theatre was still at the stage where the craftsmen were working in the theatre itself. The propertymen could make anything. In America, even for things like hanging pictures, the propertyman would go out to get a craftsman to do it. So one used to say to the props man, 'Can you make a frame for that picture?' and he would say, 'I can get it done.' But he couldn't or didn't do it himself. That arrangement shook us a bit. We had to learn how to manage all that. We were also upset not to be able to use props at rehearsal unless the entire stage crew was on. I'm sure if one had been brought up in that tradition, it would have been all right, but we found it difficult.

"Even as late as 1961 when we were doing a realistic play, *The Complaisant Lover,* we weren't able to have props for rehearsals. We could use cardboard cups for a tea party, if we wanted to, but none of the furniture! That frightened us because we had to go round and choose the furniture. In England you can hire furniture, and if you don't like it you send it back and get something else. But in America you had to *buy* it all. It was absolutely terrifying. We had to go and buy the things and then they couldn't come into the theatre because there was no stage crew on the set. That show opened in Boston. The furniture had to stay in the shop until the pickup to take it all to Boston. We were horrified to learn that it was our responsibility to arrange for pickup at these different shops to collect the furniture. We thought that the management would do that. The director had never seen the pieces until they appeared on the stage. We had never seen them all together. In America, we got to learn how to deal with that.

"In England one felt the production was a team effort with everyone working together. In America, we found it was more the coordination of specialists, each of whom had an exact role. They do what they're supposed to do and no more. That made the artistic effort more diffuse in America than in England. It was difficult to deal with. We're not meaning to pan the American theatre, that's not the point. It's just a different convention. The American conventions of mounting plays hadn't hurt the finished productions we saw here. *Life With Father* and *Flare Path,* for instance, were super. The technical work was always very good. We *were* a bit surprised at first that they painted the scenery on the floor the continental way, instead of using a vertical paint frame. It's very difficult to see it on the floor. You have to go up on the gallery and look down at it.

"It could be agony! When we were redoing *Tally Ho!* for Agnes de Mille the set designer Oliver Smith absolutely ignored the fact that all the costumes were in muted colors. He made all the set colors brilliant greens and blues, which wrecked it. Of course, the same thing could happen in England: it did with *The Mastersingers,* when we did only the scenery and David Walker did the costumes. When the set designer and the costume designer are two people who are entirely unconnected, it's very difficult to make the whole work properly. It shouldn't be. Two artists should be able to merge. But some artists have such tremendously different color range and color sense."

In the six years that Margaret Harris and Elizabeth Montgomery had spent in America during the War, the name "Motley" had become a synonym on Broadway for polished elegance in theatre design. Now in their early forties, they were financially comfortable—while hardly well to do. During the course of those years Elizabeth Montgomery fell in love and married her husband, the writer Patrick Wilmot. Margaret Harris remained single, which left her free—and eager—to return to London and to her sister Sophia, now the mother of a young daughter, as soon as she could book passage.

6
Elizabeth Montgomery in New York 1946–1966

With Margaret Harris's departure for London, Elizabeth Montgomery found herself the embodiment of Motley on Broadway. At first, she and her husband Patrick Wilmot (1904–1968) lived in a Manhattan apartment just off Central Park South. Later, the couple moved with their family to a country house. He wrote mysteries, popular fiction, and plays, one of which, *The Truce of the Bear*, was produced off-Broadway. He also wrote for the *Saturday Evening Post*.

During the New York years Elizabeth Montgomery was mother to her own son and three step-children. Wherever she lived, she continued to design three or four shows a year—mostly costumes, but sometimes sets as well—for Broadway, for the Metropolitan Opera, and, later, for the American Shakespeare Festival in Stratford, Connecticut. She thrived despite union work-rules and the American custom of relegating costume design to one firm, usually run by a woman, and set design to another, usually supervised by a man. She continued to work in areas that she and Margaret Harris had begun during the War.

Elizabeth Montgomery's credits as a solo designer in the United States include such smash musicals as *South Pacific, Peter Pan, Can-Can, The Most Happy Fella,* and *110 in the Shade*. She designed *Il Trovatore, Simon Boccanegra,* and *Martha* for the Metropolitan Opera. Intermixed were plays—An-

ouilh's *Mademoiselle Colombe* and O'Neill's *Long Day's Journey into Night*. Her designs for productions on Broadway, at the Met, and at the American Shakespeare Theatre reached an astounding total of seventy-nine productions in twenty years. Spin-off work included designing fabric and women's fashions—Mary Martin's costumes for *South Pacific* were especially popular.

During the New York period of her career, Elizabeth Montgomery collaborated with set designers Ralph Alswang, Boris Aronson, Ben Edwards, Eldon Elder, Peter Larkin, Jo Mielziner, Donald Oenslager, Robert O'Hearn, Rouben Ter-Arutunian, and Oliver Smith. Throughout, the Motley women kept in touch with each other by telephone and letter, even if they were seldom able to work together. Occasional visits back and forth across the Atlantic allowed them to collaborate from time to time. In 1966, Elizabeth moved back to London to work with Margaret Harris and with the Motley Design Course until her death in 1993.

Reticent and retiring when interviewed, Elizabeth Montgomery had less to say about Motley's work than did Margaret Harris. In part, this was simply because it is often difficult to say as much about costumes as about sets, which more obviously embody a production concept. Sets pose certain problems in three-dimensional space and atmosphere that invite explanation. Costumes present problems of period design, color coordination, and characterization—problems that often boil down to specifics about fabric, line, and fitting that pertain more to the immediate situation than to the rest of the production. As Margaret Harris put it simply, "When you're just working on the costumes, you don't get as involved in the whole production, and so you don't remember as much about it." In any case, "Liz," as she was known to her friends, had always preferred to let her costumes speak for themselves. Reluctant or even unable to explain her reasons for doing what she did, she left it to others to assess the results.

"I didn't see many shows while I was in New York," she explained. "I was generally working on my own shows, and I also had a huge family to look after. In New York we had a flat just opposite the side of the Plaza Hotel, a strange old flat. It was lovely, with huge great rooms and two fireplaces; delightful. Later, about 1959, when Patrick's three grandchildren joined us, we moved to a lovely old home in Wilton, Connecticut, that was built in 1750. When my husband Patrick was finishing something on order, I took over the housework, and when I was doing a show, he did. He was a far better cook than I am. I painted the inside of our house white throughout, except for the kitchen–dining room, which had lilac walls. Pat made high-backed dining room chairs, which we stained ink-blue. They had vermilion and purple cushions."

The differences between American and English theatre practices became especially burdensome after the end of the war. Competition from television and the movies as well as work-rules worried American theatre people. "The New York theatre today is like a man who is feeling fine but is losing weight every day and cannot arrest the process," wrote Beverly Baxter in the London *Evening Standard* (11 January 1953). "The trade unions have made the cost of production so heavy that if a new play receives bad notices it is taken off at once. . . . When you add to that deficit the fact that the successful musicals play for two and three years, you will realize the shrinking opportunities for the American dramatist and the American actor."[1]

Post-War American musical comedy knit together drama, song, and dance more tightly than had its forerunners, in which the show could liter-

ally stop when it was time for a song or a dance number.[2] The operetta is generally credited with beginning the phenomenon around the turn of the century. During the 1920s, drawing upon the spectacle of burlesque, Sigmund Romberg's *The Student Prince* and Jerome Kern and Oscar Hammerstein's *Showboat* added a stronger story line and spectacular dancing. In the 1940s Rodgers and Hammerstein integrated drama, music, song, and professional dance by adapting such "straight plays" as *Green Grow the Lilacs* and *Liliom* into *Oklahoma!* and *Carousel.*

After World War II, the "New York musical" became a mainstay of Broadway and the West End, spinning profits upon profits from the original cast recording, the film version, and fashion products inspired by the show. Elizabeth Montgomery as Motley continued to be sought after for her dedication to designing costumes that blended into the overall "look" of the production. "In musical productions the costumes are extremely important for setting moods—far more so perhaps than in straight dramatic plays. . . . Ballets are almost always included in such productions, and these may require exceptionally fantastic costumes," she later wrote.[3] Indeed, Motley and the choreographer Agnes de Mille helped make the splashy dance numbers a trademark of American musicals. Elizabeth Montgomery's recollections of two decades at the center of New York theatre reflect a self-effacing modesty amidst a theatrical milieu that contained some of the larger egos in New York.

Preparation for her success in designing costumes for musicals came through Elizabeth Montgomery's earlier collaborations with Agnes de Mille. Beginning with *Three Virgins and a Devil* and *Rodeo* during the War, Agnes de Mille's ballets at the Metropolitan Opera House were often costumed by Motley. When the Loring ballet *Billy the Kid* was re-staged at the Met in 1949, Elizabeth Montgomery designed the costumes. In 1953, she also designed costumes for a series of impressionistic modern dance pieces choreographed by Agnes de Mille for the Agnes de Mille Ballet Theatre. This company toured the United States, playing in one hundred and twenty-six theatres. It was a "gut-buster of a tour," de Mille said, that included *Ballad, Conversations Pleasant and Unpleasant, Dances of Elegance, Hell on Wheels,* and *Legends.*[4] Along with her contemporaries Martha Graham,

South Pacific, *Majestic Theatre, New York, 1949.*
Costume sketch for two nurses. Motley Collection.

George Balanchine, and Jerome Robbins, Agnes
de Mille's modern dance pieces were important
both in their own right as ballets and as experiments extending her popular choreography for
Broadway musicals. For Elizabeth Montgomery
the ballet design projects provided an artistic alternative to the musicals, whose huge casts and bud-
gets were to absorb much of her energy during
her years in New York.

Although, like Agnes de Mille's ballet, the
Motley-designed musicals were interspersed with
other theatrical fare, they deserve separate treatment. "*South Pacific* in 1949 was my first real musi-

cal," Elizabeth Montgomery said, dismissing *Sadie
Thompson* (1944) and *Carib Song* (1945) as early
attempts. "We had tremendous difficulties in finding material for Mary Martin to wear. She had to
wash her hair every night for the number 'I'm
gonna wash that man right out of my hair.' We
had to get blue denim specially water-proofed. It
took ages to get something practical." Basing it
loosely on James Michener's *Tales of the South Pacific,* Joshua Logan, Richard Rodgers, and Oscar
Hammerstein used the war in the Pacific and
American sailors' high jinx as a background for
romance and racial conflict. Elizabeth Montgomery as Motley came into the show as the costume
designer through her agent Leland Hayward, co-
producer with Joshua Logan.

Already known for *Carousel* and *Oklahoma!,*
Rodgers and Hammerstein now added to their repertoire such enduring songs as "A Cock-Eyed Op-
timist," "There Is Nothing Like a Dame," "Honey
Bun," "Bali Ha'i," "I'm Gonna Wash That Man
Right Out of My Hair," "I'm in Love with a Wonderful Guy," "Younger Than Springtime," and
"You've Got to be Taught." Mary Martin and Ezio
Pinza were a great popular success as the Navy
nurse from Arkansas and the French planter who
fall in love during a lull in the fighting. Critics
found nothing in the production to fault, everything to praise. They were especially keen to point
out the show's success in integrating acting, song,
and dance to form a coherent dramatic whole,
which was in part realized through Mielziner's sets
and Motley's costumes. Even the hard-to-please
Wolcott Gibbs of the *New Yorker* (16 April 1949,
54–55), admitted, "Altogether, it is a fine show,
and I wouldn't be surprised if it were still at the
Majestic when another Presidential election rolls
around." As he predicted, the show ran and ran,
with road companies, a transfer to London, and
revivals on Broadway extending its audiences to a
million or more.[5]

So intense was interest in the play—and so enthusiastic was response to it—that Mary Martin
was featured on the covers of *Life* and the *Herald-
Tribune*'s Sunday magazine, along with sketches of
Montgomery's designs. Brooks Atkinson of the
Times (17 April 1949) claimed that business in the
city stopped and his paper revised their printing
schedule to carry his review one edition earlier
than normal.

South Pacific, *Majestic Theatre, New York, 1949. Ensign Nellie Forbush (Mary Martin) sings "I'm in Love with a Wonderful Guy" to the other Navy nurses (actors unidentified). The production photograph comes from Motley's files; it was also published in* Theatre Arts, *June 1949.*

"In *South Pacific,* we bought many of the garments worn by actors from a war surplus store, and literally beat, kicked, and dragged them into a fine state of disrepair,"[6] wrote Montgomery. The design problem, reported an anonymous newspaper clipping in the Motley files, "was getting variety and color into the costumes. With all those sailors and Seabees in dungarees, the prospect looked pretty drab to Elizabeth Montgomery at first, till the authors told her about the play-within-a-play—the show that the service men put

on. The costumes for it demanded ingenuity, as they had to be made from odds and ends available on that island. These improvised effects get plenty of laughs from the audience. There are costumes draped with camouflage netting and others trimmed with rope, tropical flowers or vines. It was Leland Hayward who suggested dressing up somebody in colored comic sections from newspapers from home. 'At our New Haven opening, the skirt was really paper,' said Elizabeth Montgomery. 'But in Boston the *Globe* helped us to get comics printed on white cotton cloth. Then we pasted it on crinoline to stiffen it.'" She did fifty-eight costume designs for the show, the same article reported, though only one survives. Not long afterwards, *Vogue* featured a photo of a Mary Martin look-alike modeling the newspaper-comics skirt that Martin had worn for the "Thanksgiving

South Pacific, *Majestic Theatre, New York, 1949.*
Mary Martin sings "One Hundred and One Pounds
of Fun," a number that "always stops the show," said
Theatre Arts, *May 1949, which published the produc-*
tion photograph.

Frolics" number in the show. Soon knock-offs of
Mary Martin's denim top, the "comic strip" skirt,
and the oversized sailor suit were for sale in the
New York stores. Motley, this time in the person
of Elizabeth Montgomery rather than Sophia Harris, was again in the fashion business, a development that led to further work designing fabrics for
the garment industry.

"I will never have another *South Pacific,*" said
Mary Martin. "Everyone in the world came to see

it. . . . Presidents, kings, emperors came to see
it."[7] The show ran for years in New York with
various changes of cast, closing on 15 May 1955
after 1,925 performances before Broadway audiences totaling more than three million. It won
eight Tony awards and the Pulitzer Prize for
drama. The sheet music sold two million copies.
A million copies of the soundtrack were sold on a
long-playing record.[8] The Broadway production
transferred in 1951 to London with Mary Martin,
but with a predominantly new cast. An Australian
company played it for over two years. In 1955, it
was re-staged twice by the City Center Light Opera Company—first, with different directors and

casts, but with Mielziner's set design and Motley's costumes.

Later that year the musical *Miss Liberty* made Elizabeth Montgomery herself feature-story material. Set in 1885, this pleasant musical tells the story of a French girl (supposedly the model for the statue in New York harbor) who comes to the United States to participate in a publicity stunt during the New York newspaper circulation wars. The show combined music, song, and dance in a dazzling production that ran for 308 performances. Its songs have passed into the popular repertory: "A Little Fish in a Big Pond," "Let's Take an Old-Fashioned Walk," "Homework," "Only for Americans," and "You Can Have Him." The production required ten sets. For its cast of actors, singers, and dancers, 265 costumes were needed. The production was backed in part by the fabric manufacturer Liberty's of London.

"'Liz' Guards Costumes for *Miss Liberty*" ran the lead in a Philadelphia paper. A feature article described her supervising the design, production, packing, and re-fitting of the *Liberty* costumes. Featuring the narrow shoulders, butterfly sleeves, bustles, and full skirts of the colorful 1880s, the women's costumes received notices in the popular press for being both enchanting and authentic. Authentic-looking they may have been, but the designs and newspaper photographs show that, just as she used a cotton fabric with "Everglaze" (a precursor of permanent press) instead of silks and satins, Elizabeth Montgomery modified the robust 1880s' lines to bring them close to the slender shape popular in 1949 women's clothes. To sum up her contribution: The *Times*' critic Brooks Atkinson deemed the play "disappointing," but was quick to say that with choreographer Jerome Robbins and set designer Oliver Smith, the Motleys "have found something fresh to contribute to an old show formula" (16 July 1949).

Occasionally musicals with Motley-designed costumes were less well received. Billed as a "musical fantasy," *Happy as Larry,* directed by and starring Burgess Meredith, closed early in 1950 after three performances. Later that year came another musical flop. While he was starring as Petruchio in the long-running *Kiss Me Kate,* Alfred Drake teamed up with the composer John Mundy and the lyricist Edward Eager to create a musical version of Goldoni's commedia dell'arte play, *The*

Liar. It closed after twelve performances. The tepid review in the *Times* (19 May 1950) nevertheless appreciated "nifty sets by Donald Oenslager" and "costumes by Motley that are, as we have come to expect, quite right."

For *Peter Pan,* the musical version of James M. Barrie's play, Elizabeth Montgomery designed costumes three times for three productions: one in 1950, a second, different version in 1954, and that production's transfer to London. The first, directed by John Burrell and choreographed by Wendy Toye, starred Jean Arthur as Peter, Boris Karloff as Mr. Darling and Captain Hook, and Marcia Henderson as Wendy. Celebrated composer and conductor Leonard Bernstein wrote the music. The "handsome settings" by Ralph Alswang pleased the critics, who reported a standing ovation when—thanks to Kirby's Flying Ballet from London—Wendy and the Darling children learned to fly (*Post,* 25 April 1950). "And Motley," concluded Brooks Atkinson (*Times,* 25 April 1950), "who never yet has designed a hackneyed costume, has dressed mermaids, Indians, buccaneers, and a boys' gang with equal simplicity and grace."

Despite the devastating experience of World War II, in this musical and others, one catches hints of post-war optimism. Atkinson commented: "In view of the ghastly things that have happened to our battered world since Barrie conceived *Peter Pan* out of tobacco smoke and childishness, your correspondent had a number of misgivings about this project for turning time back in the theatre. But the misgivings were superfluous. Time has not been turned back. No sense of time is involved in Barrie's invocation to a magic world." In New York the play ran for 320 performances. In 1952 the production toured the United States.

Paint Your Wagon in late 1951 added another to the string of Motley-designed hit musicals. Composed by Lerner and Loewe the show was set in 1853 at the end of the Gold Rush and featured rough and tough miners meeting dance-hall girls. Agnes de Mille choreographed the show. Its drama, music, and stage spectacle seem to have delighted everyone. Hit songs included "I Talk to the Trees" and "They Call the Wind Maria." "A caravan arrived at the camp, and all the ladies of the town stepped out of this wagon, looking absolutely gorgeous," remembered Elizabeth Mont-

gomery. "I had wonderful notices for that one.
The men's costumes were more or less authentic,
but decorative-authentic. The girls were very
colorful. When it transferred to London, Sophie
had my sketches. From them she supervised the
making of the costumes there." "The show,"
wrote William Hawkins (*Sun Times,* 13 November
1951), "is often startlingly lovely to look at, with
Motley's rich colors against the sun-washed shades
of Oliver Smith's sets." More than a hundred costumes were required for a cast of sixty-four. The
company subsequently toured the United States.
For the transfer to London in 1953, Sophia Harris
adapted Elizabeth Montgomery's costumes.

Critics may have faulted *Can-Can* for being thin
on plot and long on song and dance, but that
hardly mattered at the box office, where the
crowds kept coming throughout one season and
into the next. Set in Montmartre in the Gay Nine-
ties, it told the story of a judge (Peter Cookson)
who falls in love with the girl (Lilo) who stands
accused before him on a morals charge. For inspiration, Elizabeth Montgomery turned to the paintings of Toulouse-Lautrec. Cole Porter's songs
included "C'est Magnifique," "It's All Right with
Me," "I Love Paris," and, of course, "Can-Can."
Spiced up by Lilo, a French chanteuse and dancer
touted as "the French Ethel Merman," the real hit
of the show was Gwen Verdon, then making her
Broadway debut. "You couldn't go to dinner anywhere without having to talk about Gwen Verdon," recalled Charles Adams Baker.[9] *Look
Magazine* (8 September 1953) carried a color spread
on her as Eve. Motley received the by-now-usual
praise for the costumes: "The Motley costumes are
progressively eye-catching, from the working
clothes of the girls, through the Garden of Eden
costume ball, to the final Apache and can-can outfits," wrote William Hawkins. "Motley's costumes, especially those she has designed for the
Garden of Eden ballet, capture the wonderful absurdity of the period in a manner that must certainly disconcert the romantic ghosts of Du
Maurier and Toulouse-Lautrec," wrote Wolcott
Gibbs (*New Yorker,* 16 May 1953).

If the first *Peter Pan* in 1950 was a musical "fantasy," as the producers dubbed it for adding incidental music and a few songs to the English play,
the second *Peter Pan* in 1954, directed by Jerome
Robbins, was an unmistakably American musical

Can-Can, *Shubert Theatre, New York, 1953. Costume sketches for two "Apaches." Their dark red trousers and jackets are set off by a cranberry-red cravat and
a light striped shirt. Motley Collection.*

with spectacle on a Hollywood scale. It contained
dancing, flying effects, dazzling sets, and, of
course, costumes by Motley. Having already
played with the SRO sign on the sidewalk in Los
Angeles and San Francisco, the production tri-
umphed in New York as well. "Mr. Larkin's hu-
morously detailed scenery and Motley's fabulous
costumes are admirable. Especially the animals: the
lion, the kangaroo, and the ostrich have droll personalities in the designing as well as the acting,"
conceded Brooks Atkinson (*Times,* 31 October
1954), whose enthusiasm for Mary Martin was
tempered with quibbles about overproduction.
Other critics sprinkled their reviews with hyper-
boles for Mary Martin's Peter, for Cyril Ritchard's

Captain Hook, for Kathy Nolan's Wendy, for Sondra Lee's Indian Princess, and even for Joe. E. Marks's Smee. "Disney," pronounced Walter Kerr (*Herald Tribune,* 21 October 1954), "isn't in the running in this amiable, elastic nightmare."

After her many musical successes, it must have seemed natural that Elizabeth Montgomery design the costumes for the film of Rodgers and Hammerstein's *Oklahoma!* She did and the film credits proclaim "Costumes designed by Motley." Yet, as mentioned in the discussion of Motley's film work in chapter 13, she left the production before the costumes were made. "They had two costume designers, which wasn't a good idea," remembered Elizabeth Montgomery. "They couldn't get Karinska, whom I wanted, to make the costumes. So it didn't work out." After twenty-five years, the incident still rankled.

In 1956, Frank Loesser's *The Most Happy Fella* burst out, following a long dry spell after his *Guys and Dolls.* The new play had thirty musical numbers built around a solid plot. It was based on an old play about Tony, the Italian vintner from the Napa Valley who sends away to San Francisco for a mail-order bride, the waitress Rosabella. "For *The Most Happy Fella,* the costumes were for working people in California who were harvesting the grapes in the 1880s or 1890s," Elizabeth Montgomery remembered. "For my research I went to that wonderful picture library in the New York Public Library." As several critics noticed, it was a "music drama" (Brooks Atkinson's term, *Times,* 4 May 1956) that stood between musical comedy and light opera. Among the soon-to-be familiar tunes, the audience heard "Somebody, Somewhere," "Standing on the Corner," "Happy to Make Your Acquaintance," "Big D" (for Dallas), and "Song of a Summer Night." Beautiful sets by Jo Mielziner changed with the seasons, and Motley's rainbow of costumes colorfully evoked the time, place, and mood. After a very long run of 678 performances, it finally closed on 14 December 1957.

In *Shinbone Alley,* the last musical Elizabeth Montgomery designed, she found herself facing a whimsical variation on the problem of Andre Obey's *Noah*—how to make actors and singers appear as animals. Don Marquis, a columnist for the New York *Sun,* had invented the pleasant fiction that, during his absence from his typewriter at night, a certain cockroach named "archy" would write free-verse philosophy and reflections on the mores of his alley-cat pal "mehitabel." Everything was lower case because "archy" couldn't handle the shift key. From this unpromising material was fashioned *Shinbone Alley,* a musical comedy filled with dances, featuring Eartha Kitt as "mehitabel" and Eddie Bracken as "archy." Dressed as alley denizens, dozens of singers and dancers cavorted around Eldon Elder's spidery fire escapes and back streets. "Motley has been eminently successful in making the off-beat characters seem human. You'd recognize them immediately in side street bistros or dime-a-dance places," wrote Robert Coleman (*Daily Mirror,* 5 April 1957). A foreshadowing of *Cats,* it was a graceful near-hit, closing after forty-nine performances.

Beyond the splashy fame of musicals, Elizabeth Montgomery continued to design "straight plays," as the theatre world refers to what academics call "contemporary drama." These plays engaged her in both new historical drama set in earlier periods and contemporary drama using modern dress. The 1945–1946 season saw a "lend-lease" transfer of five productions from London: Chekhov's *Uncle Vanya,* both parts of *Henry IV,* Sophocles' *Oedipus Rex,* and Sheridan's *The Critic.* These "classic" plays made the Broadway critics and the New York audiences envious of the polish and versatility of the English cast, including Margaret Leighton, Laurence Olivier, Joyce Redmond, Ralph Richardson, and Harry Andrews. Although no one seems to have written on the subject, it is not hard to see a connection between American admiration of the English style and the popularity of Motley-designed costumes, especially for Shakespeare and other serious drama.[10]

Not every production designed by Elizabeth Montgomery succeeded. *He Who Gets Slapped* challenged her to improve on the Theatre Guild's original production of this Russian melodrama à la *I Pagliaci* about a disillusioned nobleman who joins a circus. The original production was a design success; the revival was not. "The set by Motley is spacious, cluttered, and realistic, whereas the original set was intimate and suggestive;" said the *World-Telegram* (21 March 1946), continuing, "the costumes are gaudy and circusy, whereas the originals were harmonious and drably moody." For *Second Best Bed,* a "trivial and tedious comedy" to

The Sun (4 June 1946), the best that the reviewer could say was that "Motley provided a cross-section of Anne Hathaway's seventeenth-century cottage which is charming enough to house something far better." It closed after five performances. "A dimly lighted, highly atmospheric Motley set featuring a very gray and Gothic spiral staircase that is constantly in use," reported Louis Kronenberger (*New York PM,* 7 June 1946) failed to redeem *The Dancer*—an unthrilling murder mystery that closed after five performances.

Towards the end of the 1946–1947 season, John Gielgud's celebrated production of *The Importance of Being Earnest,* which had enjoyed a series of revivals in London during the War, opened in New York at the Royale Theatre. The critics were ecstatic and Brooks Atkinson (*Times,* 4 March 1947) credited the designers' contribution: "Motley's settings are models of period decor; they can be played against without staring the acting out of countenance or overwhelming the performance with color. The costumes convey the character of the parts and the satire of the comedy without sacrificing beauty. What Motley has accomplished completes Mr. Gielgud's design for artificial comedy." Photographs make it clear that the designs were Elizabeth Montgomery's adaptation of the original designs by Sophia Harris for the 1942 London staging, which in turn was based on Motley's designs for the 1939 production.

More than a year elapsed between productions before Elizabeth Montgomery found an ideal vehicle in Maxwell Anderson's *Anne of a Thousand Days.* It was a costume drama about Henry VIII and Anne Boleyn starring Rex Harrison and Joyce Redman. Critics agreed unequivocally with Howard Barnes (*Journal-American,* 9 December 1948) that it was "the best play of the season," praising the script, the acting, and the costuming, with some reservations about Jo Mielziner's set. "Magnificent" was the word most often used to describe the costumes. Fashion designer Sally Victor liked the headdresses worn by Joyce Redman as Anne so much that she created hats she called "Tudor-tops."

Critics, however, particularly noticed Henry's costumes. John Lardner (*Star,* 10 December 1948) commented, "In the interest of verisimilitude, Rex Harrison manages somehow as the play goes on to convey an impression of bloat, and he splays his

legs in the genuine Holbein style in a very deft bit of incidental acrobatics." Having originally envisioned someone of Charles Laughton's burly build in the role (he had played the part on stage and in film), the designer found in the choice of slender Rex Harrison a special problem: "For *Anne of a Thousand Days* the author Maxwell Anderson said that it was good that I'd avoided the clichés of the period. We started off with a very elaborate set by Jo Mielziner. But that all got scrapped, and they had to start all over again in the middle of rehearsals. I remember we had to send to Hollywood for legs to be specially made for Rex Harrison—great, fat Henry VIII legs. Rex had rather skinny legs. The Hollywood legs cost a thousand dollars." It was more than just a simple theatrical trick with

Anne of a Thousand Days, *Shubert Theatre, New York 1948. Elizabeth Montgomery fitting Joyce Redman (Anne). The photograph comes from Motley's files.*

the legs, as explained in Motley's *Designing and Making Stage Costumes.* Rex Harrison wore padding to build out his chest and shoulders, thereby making his neck seem shorter. The sets had narrow doorways to make him appear bigger. Because the script demanded that Henry appear in many social settings—from casual undress to sporting dress to court dress—Elizabeth Montgomery looked to descriptions and paintings of Tudor costume for inspiration, so that "everything Henry wore had some basis in historical fact." To make possible the twenty-eight costume changes for Rex Harrison and his co-star Joyce Redmond, the designer had to invent "a device by which they could be 'snapped' on and off." The costume change for the coronation scene was made in thirty seconds![11]

In a cover story about *The Innocents,* a dramatization of Henry James's *Turn of the Screw, Life* (3 April 1950) called it "the most frightening Broadway play in years." William Archibald, a dancer turned writer known to Motley as the author of *Carib Song,* adapted the James novel. Praising the "stylish and sumptuous production," Howard Barnes (*Herald,* 2 February 1950) credited "the costumes by Motley for being in perfect keeping with the period and mood of the piece." Motley's taste and style in the costumes seems to have fit perfectly with Jo Mielziner's Victorian living room and Peter Glenville's deft direction. Brooks Atkinson (*Times,* 2 February 1950) called the overall effect "necromantic."

At the end of the same year, Elizabeth Montgomery again designed costumes for Guthrie McClintic and Katharine Cornell. Billed as "a traditional comedy," (meaning an English upper-class situation comedy), *Captain Carvallo* never made it past tryouts in upstate New York. It closed while still on the road. Nor was there much joy a year later at the next "straight play" she worked on, *The Grand Tour*—Elmer Rice's melodrama about a Midwestern embezzler who falls in love with a Bridgeport schoolteacher on the *Ile de France.* It was burdened with a script that the critics agreed no director, actors, or designers could rescue.

Bernard Shaw's *Candida,* with costumes designed by Motley, came to New York for a four-week stand after a national tour. Although she hoped it would display her talents in the theatre,

film star Olivia de Havilland fell flat. "I imagine that it must be difficult to mount a production of *Candida* from which all wit, all charm, all serenity have vanished," wrote Walter Kerr (*Herald-Tribune,* 23 April 1952). "This particular labor was triumphantly accomplished, however, on the stage of the National Theatre Tuesday night." Motley's costumes escaped mention. About the best thing that could be said about William Marchant's *To Be Continued,* which opened the night after *Candida,* was that it had a distinguished director in Guthrie McClintic, a fine cast, including Jean Dixon, Dorothy Stickney, and young Grace Kelly, attractive sets by Donald Oenslager, and "fastidious," graceful costumes by Motley. Nonetheless, the show flopped.

Elizabeth Montgomery began the year 1953 with *Mid-Summer,* a new comedy by Vina Delmar, staged in the refurbished Vanderbilt Theatre. While the critics thought the play rather weak, they were mightily impressed with Geraldine Page, who had been "discovered" the year before in an off-Broadway Greenwich Village production of Tennessee Williams's *Summer and Smoke.* (She had not come from nowhere, as the *Daily News* pointed out, but had played in Eastern and Chicago stock companies for some years.) Set in 1907 in a shabby 14th-Street hotel, the play tells the story of a schoolteacher trying to break into vaudeville while his illiterate wife patiently waits for a home and children—a wish she finally attains. Her rival, the kept woman with a heart of gold, "makes a dashing picture as an overdressed floozy of the period (overdressing artfully done by Motley)," said the *Daily News* (22 January 1953). The play had a good run of 109 performances, closing on 25 April 1953.

Mademoiselle Colombe, Jean Anouilh's play about the impossibility of true love in the lively, but all-corrupting theatre, drew together Julie Harris as the theatre-struck young wife, Eli Wallach as her husband, who sees through the glamour to the tawdry reality behind it, Edna Best as his prima-donna mother, and some fine character actors to round out the backstage crowd of roués and sycophants. Boris Aronson created "an amusing and flavorsome backstage production for the Paris of 1900," wrote Brooks Atkinson (*Times* 7 January 1954), going on to praise Motley for "beautiful costumes." "The audience really didn't like it, not because of any casting problems, but because it's cynical and bitter—'no nice people in this play' is the way they put it," recalled Harold Clurman,[12] who directed the play "because I liked working with Julie Harris." No doubt because of its anti-sentimental themes, it closed at the end of February after sixty-seven performances.

Fresh from their success in London at turning Henry James's *Washington Square* from a novel into a play—*The Heiress*—Ruth and Augustus Goetz approached Andre Gide with a request to do the same for his novel *The Immoralist*. He refused, saying that the subject of the book, homosexuality, was taboo in the theatre. They eventually won Gide over and the result was a play that Brooks Atkinson (*Times*, 9 February 1954) judged a "tragedy . . . austere, crushing, and genuine." The story closely paralleled Gide's own suffering. Geraldine Page played the wife whose husband (Louis Jourdan) finds that an earlier homosexual episode makes it impossible for him to accept her love. In the languid decadence of colonial North Africa, he is drawn to the flagrant overtures of his young colleague (David J. Stewart) and to "the insidious charm of James Dean as an idle native houseboy," Atkinson continued. Noting the power and delicacy with which both script and production treated a potentially sordid or melodramatic story, Atkinson gave ample credit to the design as well: "George Jenkins, scene designer; Abe Feder, lighting expert, and Motley, costume designer, have provided a physical production that expresses rueful beauty in harmony with the mood of the play." It closed after 101 performances—a good run for a serious play. "*The Immoralist* was the first thing James Dean was in, his first Broadway play," remembered Elizabeth Montgomery. "A strange little man, in blue jeans, and very, very shy. I had to take him to Bloomingdales once to buy a pair of blue jeans. He was that shy."

Through the pages of the *New Yorker* Roald Dahl had created a taste for his macabre short stories, in which death and destruction were never far beneath the bland surface of middle-class manners. He adapted his own stories to create *The Honeys*, depicting two suburban Boston sisters-in-law (played by Jessica Tandy and Dorothy Stickney) who successfully murder their husbands, the Honey brothers. Hume Cronyn played both men, contrasting the whining fussiness of one brother with the palsied martyrdom of the other. Wrote Robert Coleman (*Daily Mirror*, 29 April 1955): "The settings by Ben Edwards and costumes by Motley are so eloquently accurate as to almost speak. They heighten and suggest admirably the dizzy doings that take place." Lacking the broad humor of *Arsenic and Old Lace*, *The Honeys* closed after thirty-six performances.

The Young and Beautiful, by Sally Benson (who was otherwise known for her comedy *Junior Miss*), wove together incidents from F. Scott Fitzgerald's short stories. Set in Chicago circa 1915, it follows the spoiled adolescent Josephine as she lightheartedly and callously hurts the young men who court her. Walter Kerr caught each nuance: "Josephine descends a curving staircase, kicks off her chartreuse slippers, and flings herself expectantly into an Irene Castle pose. Josephine darts to a tasseled sofa, curls up like a kitten of prey, and pretends to enchanted astonishment as a neighborhood swain strolls in. Josephine lounges against living-room pillars, tilts her head hopefully for the newest visiting male, torments her escorts—and even the most casual visitors—until they are captives at her feet" (*Herald-Tribune*, 3 October 1955). As for the design, "Eldon Elder," wrote Brooks Atkinson (*Times*, 3 October 1955), "has provided a useful setting that expresses the ugly splendor of advanced interior decoration in 1915. Motley's costumes are superb—gorgeous as well as theatrical."

Ugo Betti's *Island of Goats*, for which he won the Italian National Drama Prize in 1950, did not translate well to Broadway. Despite praise for the acting of Laurence Harvey, Ruth Ford, Uta Hagen, and Tani Seitz, the critics were clearly puzzled and fed up by "the Italian bore," as Robert Coleman unflinchingly termed Betti (*Daily Mirror*, 5 October 1955). Although recognizing the power of Mielziner's symbolic set, they warned their readers away, and the play closed four nights later, after eight performances. Motley's costumes escaped critical notice, and Elizabeth Montgomery recalled nothing of the production.

Paddy Chayefsky's play, *Middle of the Night*, marked his Broadway debut after he had established himself with *Marty* as a scriptwriter for films and television. The "slice-of-life" love story about an older Jewish businessman and an already-married woman twenty years his junior marked Joshua Logan's debut as both producer and director. It brought Edward G. Robinson back to the stage after a twenty-five year absence. Set in the present with interiors by Jo Mielziner, the production won Motley praise for "atmospheric" costumes. The play opened in February and closed the following May after a long run of 479 performances.

On a visit to London with her young son John in the summer of 1956, Elizabeth Montgomery designed spectacular costumes for the "Esther Williams Water Show" at the Wembly swimming pool. The glamorous and svelte Esther Williams, an American film star renowned for her swimming prowess, put on a public display of her talents. "Everything had to come up out of the water looking absolutely dry, without a bit of water," Elizabeth Montgomery recalled. "We made taffeta feathers, which came up looking dry. My son John was six then, and he became a great friend of the fire-eater there at Wembly."

Eugene O'Neill's autobiographical *Long Day's Journey into Night,* a play he had written in 1940, explored the unhappy story of his family: the aging, hot-tempered actor father (Frederic March), the drug-addicted mother (Florence Eldridge), an elder brother whoring and drinking his life away (Jason Robards, Jr.), and young Tyrone immersed in romantic ennui (Bradford Dillman). Jose Quintero's direction, David Hays's dingy set, and, Brooks Atkinson (*Times,* 8 November 1956) adds, "the shabby, shapeless costumes by Motley and the sepulchral lighting by Tharon Musser perfectly capture the lugubrious mood of the play." In Elizabeth Montgomery's three costume designs for Mary Tyrone, one can see how the designer has traced her moral deterioration through the play: first the demure housewife, whose family hopes against hope that she has broken her morphine addiction; then the would-be femme fatale, high on drugs and trying pathetically to charm the men in her life; and, at the end, a pale wraith in her nightclothes, who has submitted to her addiction. "None of us can help the things that life has done to us," she says pitifully; "they're done before you realize it, and once they're done they make you do other things until at last everything comes between you and what you'd like to be, and you've lost your true self forever." The production enjoyed a long run interrupted by a summer transfer to the Paris Festival; O'Neill was awarded posthumously both the Pulitzer and the Critics Circle awards for the play. In 1957–1958 it toured the United States with a different cast.

In the film version of *Long Day's Journey into Night,* for which Elizabeth Montgomery also designed the costumes, Katharine Hepburn played Mary Tyrone. Film required detailed authenticity instead of the more impressionistic quality used in the theatre costumes, which affected her approach to designing them. "The curator of a New York museum," Elizabeth Montgomery recalled, "allowed Miss Hepburn to try on a priceless period dress. Pressed for time, we gratefully adapted the garment, in fabric and in style and, above all, in cut."[13]

"The First Gentleman," as George III's profligate son the Prince Regent was called, wishes to marry off his daughter Charlotte. She resists his choice. Around this conflict Norman Ginsbury built a costume drama set in 1814–1819. Directed by Tyrone Guthrie, it starred Walter Slezak—"a blond hippopotamus," John McClain called him (*Journal-American,* 26 April 1957)—the beautiful Inga Swenson, and Peter Donat. Even these first-rate professionals were unable to infuse Ginsbury's weak script with more than a moment or two of theatrical life, leaving the critics to delight in the costumes, if not in the drama. "Motley," wrote Brooks Atkinson (*Times,* 26 April 1957), "have piled one dazzling costume on the other, bankrupting the King's exchequer in the last scene when they dress the Prince Regent in robes of incomparable splendor." Wolcott Gibbs found them "wonderfully repulsive," (*New Yorker,* 4 May 1957). The costumes won Elizabeth Montgomery the Tony award in 1958, but the show closed after twenty-eight performances.

By the middle of the 1950s, the Motley enterprise in America mirrored that in England—both combined commercial productions with summer work at a Shakespeare festival. In 1951 Margaret Harris as Motley had joined forces with Glen Byam Shaw at the Shakespeare Memorial Theatre, Stratford-upon-Avon, sometimes joined by Sophia Harris, as discussed in chapter 10. In America, Elizabeth Montgomery joined the American Shakespeare Festival at Stratford, Connecticut. Built in 1955 by Lawrence Langner to Edwin Howard's designs, the American Shakespeare Festival was a brave attempt to match Stratford-upon-

Collage of costume sketches from Stratford, Connecticut. Clockwise from upper left: Lady Macbeth, rough costume sketches for the cauldron scene in Macbeth, *women's costumes for* As You Like It, *costume sketch for Francis in* Henry V. *Motley Collection.*

Avon and Stratford, Ontario. In its early years, it boasted a summer season of three productions, extended by tours and a short season in New York at the Phoenix Theatre. Performances for students and an acting academy directed by Helen Mencken extended its activities, none of which received government subsidy. With Motley in England designing Shakespeare sets and costumes for Stratford-upon-Avon, it was only natural that Elizabeth Montgomery as Motley in America should design for "Stratford-on-the-Housatonic," as the critics were fond of calling it. "The American Shakespeare Festival at Stratford, Connecticut, was delightful," recalled Elizabeth Montgomery. New York audiences rushed to see the shows in their pleasant seaside setting. A wardrobe at the theatre made the costumes under Elizabeth Montgomery's supervision. In all, she would design seven productions for the Festival, which was finally forced by lack of funding to close its doors in 1977.

The Merchant of Venice, her first production there, starred Katharine Hepburn as Portia playing opposite Morris Carnovsky as Shylock. Jack Landau directed performances that critic John Chapman found "remarkably contemporary," meaning possibly that they lacked the polish—and the affectation—of high-toned English productions. A unit set by Rouben Ter-Aruturian on the new theatre's thrust stage allowed for swift staging. "Motley has costumed *The Merchant of Venice* and in lavish and wonderful fashion," concluded Chapman in his rave review (*Daily News,* 11 July 1957).

The English branch of Motley returned to New York in 1957 with the American transfers of two London productions designed by the Harris sisters. John Osborne's *Look Back in Anger* transferred from the Royal Court Theatre in London to New York with the original cast and costumes designed by Sophia Harris, who did not come over with the show. With an American cast substituting for the original English actors, it continued in New York for a long run, playing for 408 performances and closing 20 September 1958, after which it went on an American tour until May 1959. George Devine's production of Wycherley's *Country Wife,* which also transferred to New York from London that year, was only a modest success. It ran for only forty-five performances, despite a cast that included Laurence Harvey as Mr. Horner and Julie

Harris as Mrs. Pinchwife. "*The Country Wife* wasn't successful in America. It played in Canada and in New York and in Philadelphia, but they didn't seem to like Restoration comedy. There's never been a Restoration comedy that's come from London that has been a success in New York, apparently," said Margaret Harris. "I think Americans find them coarse and vulgar and boring. They don't like them." After spending most of his review disapproving on grounds of taste, Wolcott Gibbs (*New Yorker,* 7 December 1957) ended his review saying, "Motley's sets and costumes are very handsome indeed." Margaret Harris designed the rather minimal sets, which evoked the eighteenth century by full-scale line drawings on transparent plastic, rather than built sets, thereby giving a feeling for the period without holding up the action for scene changes. Sophia Harris's costumes were witty indications of the period, making Julie Harris a smiling, wholesome innocent and Laurence Harvey a glamorous man-about-town. Elizabeth Montgomery helped with the costumes for both transfers.

Further indication of Motley's widespread popularity was an engagement as the designer for the untoppable spectacle of spectacles, the producer Mike Todd's "Birthday Party" in Madison Square Garden, 17 October 1957. It celebrated the success of his film *Around the World in Eighty Days.* Mike Todd, his wife Elizabeth Taylor, and their glamorous friends were costumed by Motley for the celebration. Tickets were sold to the general public, who were admitted to Madison Square Garden as spectators. Complete with elephants and other live entertainment, it turned into an extravagant public event. "We dressed Elizabeth Taylor as a Gypsy girl," Elizabeth Montgomery remembered. "They advertised it on carts going round the city. It was supposed to be a great supper party for the rich and famous. But then they only served hot dogs and coffee. There were lots of horses in it, and my poor step-daughter had to dress the horses. She's terrified of horses."

Motley's next show was *Look Homeward, Angel,* inspired by Thomas Wolfe's sprawling autobiographical novel. The adapter Ketti Frings created "a magnificent play," said John Chapman (*Daily News,* 29 November 1957), ranking it with *Death of a Salesman.* A wonderful cast starring Anthony Perkins, Jo Van Fleet, and Hugh Griffith garnered rave reviews. Director George Roy Hill and set designer Jo Mielziner used a revolving set to open out different facets of the dingy boardinghouse that the Gants call home. Walter Kerr, Brooks Atkinson, John McClain, Richard Watts, Jr.—all the New York critics—heaped praise on the production, not failing to include Motley's 1914-style costumes that, wrote Frank Aston (*World-Telegram*, 29 November 1957), "should bring a long sigh from the oldsters." The production won both the Pulitzer Prize and the Critics Circle Award. It closed 4 April 1959 after 564 performances.

Working in Theatre 74, in the spring of 1958 Elizabeth Montgomery designed the sets for an off-Broadway production of *Asmodee*, a new translation of Francois Mauriac's play. The production was notable principally for the scandal associated with Erroll Flynn, who had originally been in the cast. "He got very drunk in the middle of rehearsals," Elizabeth Montgomery remembered, "and so they put somebody else in. I know when they went to fit him, he was so drunk he could hardly stand, poor man." The play closed after three weeks.

Love Me Little, an arch comedy of manners set variously in a Connecticut girls' school and a New York City apartment, attempted without much success to build on the popularity of the novel by Amanda Vail. It seems to have irritated the critics by its superficial, contrived burlesque of the mating game as practiced by the older and the younger generations. The play opened at the Helen Hayes Theatre, New York, on 14 April 1958 and closed on 19 April after eight performances. Alfred Drake directed Joan Bennett and Donald Cook. The tricky sets on a revolve by Ralph Alswang were contemporary, as were the costumes by Elizabeth Montgomery.

Conflict between the realistic conventions of the modern theatre and the melodramatic plot and gothic horror of *Jane Eyre* led director Demetrios Vilan and set designer Ben Edwards to some extravagant special effects for the burning of Thornfield Hall. Elizabeth Montgomery's costumes established the period, but, according to Brooks Atkinson (*Times*, 2 May 1958), even strong acting by Eric Portman and Jan Brooks could not rescue the production, which closed in the middle of June.

In the 1958–1959 season that boasted such hits as Lorraine Hansberry's *Raisin in the Sun* and the long-running *My Fair Lady* and *The Music Man,* the plays for which Elizabeth Montgomery designed costumes were minor, not major triumphs. *The Cold Wind and the Warm,* S. N. Behrman's play about his boyhood in Worcester, Massachusetts, came close to being "his finest," said Brooks Atkinson (*Times,* 9 December 1958). Directed by Harold Clurman and starring Eli Wallach, Maureen Stapleton, Morris Carnovsky, and Suzanne Pleshette, it gathered warm reviews for its author, director, and cast. The sets by Boris Aronson and costumes by Elizabeth Montgomery were not mentioned, probably because they were quietly effective and naturalistic in evoking the American middle class in the early 1900s. It ran for 120 performances.

At the start of the new year, William Faulkner's *Requiem for a Nun* opened at the John Golden Theatre in New York. A serious challenge to American theatre, as discussed in chapter 9, this Royal Court production featured Sophia Harris's costumes, which Elizabeth Montgomery adapted, and Margaret Harris's set, which came over from London. As did *Look Back in Anger,* it advanced the banner of young, "angry," and serious drama against the unserious musicals and classics in the West End and Broadway. *Requiem* played for seven weeks before closing.

The Rivalry, Norman Corwin's play about the Lincoln-Douglas debates, dramatized the actual debates verbatim, with musical transitions. Starring Richard Boone as Lincoln and Martin Gabel as Stephen Douglas, it drew favorable reviews from all the critics and enjoyed a run of eighty-one performances. Elizabeth Montgomery's costumes, David Hays's raked plank stage, and David Amram's music "conjure authenticity of atmosphere and drama," wrote Lewis Funke (*Times,* 9 February 1959). One hundred years after the debates, the issues of racial segregation were again headline news, giving the piece a strong topical appeal.

In *A Majority of One* Leonard Spiegelgass paired a Jewish matron from Brooklyn (Gertrude Berg) with a Japanese industrialist (Cedric Hardwicke) against the wishes of the younger generation. Although principally a vehicle for Berg and Hardwicke in character parts, the production's colorful staging of the Tokyo scenes brought credit to Donald Oenslager, who designed the sets, and to Elizabeth Montgomery for "lovely Oriental costumes," to quote Robert Coleman (*Daily Mirror*, 17 February 1959). The production played well into the next season and then went on an American tour for the 1960–1961 season, with Berg and Hardwicke still in the cast. Gertrude Berg's costumes for the earlier scenes of the play deliberately over-emphasized the physical defects of the humdrum widow to allow for an almost complete transformation when she later changed into Japanese costume. "I bought clothes as well as designed them," said Elizabeth Montgomery, "and some of the buying was done at long range. The Japanese garments, both traditional and contemporary, had to be completely authentic. Since New York couldn't provide us with what we needed. all the oriental garb was imported from Tokyo, down to the underclothing worn by Sir Cedric Hardwicke, who was required in one scene to change costume onstage."[14]

During the summer of 1959, Elizabeth Montgomery was designing again for the American Shakespeare Festival in Stratford, Connecticut. *The Merry Wives of Windsor* brought together a talented team of American comic actors, with Larry Gates as Falstaff, Will Geer as Shallow, Edward Asner as Bardolph, Sada Thompson as Mistress Quickly, and Morris Carnovsky as Dr. Caius. Critics loved it. Elliot Norton in the Boston *Independent* (9 July 1959) praised it as "handsomely costumed by Motley, beautifully designed by Will Steven Armstrong." It featured dances choreographed by George Balanchine.

Il Trovatore, which opened the Metropolitan opera season, saw Elizabeth Montgomery designing both sets and costumes for a production that the *Daily News* (6 December 1959) trumpeted in a color spread as "decked out with spanking new costumes and scenery by Motley." The photograph of "the Gypsy encampment" shows a cast of sixty on a vast set with a hazy, mountainous backdrop. In keeping with the melodramatic and romantic Spanish story of thwarted love, mistaken identity, and a Gypsy's revenge, the sets were reminiscent of Utrillo's stylized late medieval landscapes. Not every critic approved. "The sets, which placed the action in a never-never land of Byzantine mountains and Gothic and Romanesque arches, did not in any way compare with the old *Il Trovatore* sets by Harry Horner, which reflected

the noble and simple tradition of Gordon Craig and Adolphe Appia, and were among the handsomest in the Metropolitan's repertory," wrote Winthrop Sargeant in *The New Yorker* (7 November 1959). The costumes were lavish: the Gypsies in muted russets and browns, the Spanish in shades of gray, and the principals in striking, vivid reds, blacks, and, for Leonora, white satin. Carlo Bergonzi appeared as the troubadour of the title, Manrico; Antoinette Stella sang the part of his beloved Leonora; Giuletta Simionato was the avenging Gypsy; and Leonard Warren, the ill-starred Count di Luna. In opera circles it is still remembered for the shock traditionalists felt when the diva turned away from the audience, revealing that her dress that was cerise from the front was magenta from behind. Quelle horreur! A major production, *Il Trovatore* absorbed Elizabeth Montgomery's energies, and she remembered it well: "We were living up in Connecticut by then, and I had to drive down. I was lucky in having the bass baritone Leonard Warren to work with; he was a most delightful man. He was the leading singer, and anything he said went. We got on fine, so it was easy. The nuns had fantastic headdresses, which were then beautifully made by Karinska."

Trovatore was the first of three operas Elizabeth Montgomery designed at the Met. For *Simon Boccanegra* in 1960 and *Martha* in 1961, however, she did the costumes only, and so was less involved with the productions.[15] Motley's graceful, evocative costumes represented a "theatricalization" of opera, moving away from the earlier stiff costumes and settings to a more fluid, dramatic style. Her ability to evoke the emotional atmosphere, the period, and the individual characters, a talent amply developed over decades of historical costume dramas, won her acclaim with the critics. Writing of *Simon Boccanegra*, Winthrop Sargeant stated simply, "the costumes, by Motley, fitted handsomely into the stage picture" (*New Yorker*, 12 March 1960). That Motley's costumes also flattered the singers, making them glamorous and beautiful, ensured Elizabeth Montgomery's good working relationships with them. Her experience ran counter to the common distresses that have made "Never dress a diva," the costume designer's watchword. She painted commissioned portraits of several of the opera singers, including Maria Callas, Victoria de Los Angeles, and Leontyne

Price, who made her debut on 27 January 1961 in a revival of the Motley-designed *Il Trovatore*.

Becket, Jean Anouilh's Tony award-winning "dramatic spectacle," as the credits had it, took top honors for the 1960–1961 season. Laurence Olivier played Becket; Anthony Quinn, Henry II. Translated from Anouilh's script (already a success in Paris) by Lucienne Hill and directed by Peter Glenville, this intellectual tour de force had a good run in New York—193 performances. It went on the road, then returned for a three-week engagement with Laurence Olivier playing Henry II, a change that Lewis Funke (*Times,* 9 May 1961) approved. Writing the opening-night review for the *Times* (6 October 1960), Howard Taubman found Motley's costumes and Oliver Smith's settings part of the "sparkle" of the production.

It was a major theatrical event. Critics in Boston, Washington, D. C., and New York heralded it as "superb," "brilliant," "powerful and distinguished." Yet it was not as good when it opened as it was after a six-month run and a tour, according to Judith Crist (*Herald Tribune,* 9 May 1961) who thought it went from good to great by the switch of Olivier from Becket to Henry (made necessary by Anthony Quinn's film commitments). Ever the experimenter, Elizabeth Montgomery used "Celastic," a new material similar to fiberglass, to fashion the crowns and helmets, an innovation she later revealed in *Designing and Making Stage Costumes.*[16] The costumes won her a Tony award, a recognition at the time almost overshadowed by her concerns as a wife, mother, and chatelaine of an old, historic house in Connecticut. "We were still moving to Connecticut while I worked on *Becket,*" she recalled. "I remember trying to cope with it in a hotel. We had to have men on horses, so we had a block for the man to stand on to give him height. Then we had a strap to support the horse's body, a hobby horse, really. The strap went round his waist, and his coat covered it. I don't remember seeing anything like it before; I think we invented it."

After beginning the new year with the extravagance of *Martha* at the Metropolitan Opera, Elizabeth Montgomery had several months to prepare her next shows: *As You Like It, Macbeth,* and *Troilus and Cressida* at the American Shakespeare Festival in Stratford, Connecticut. In *As You Like It,* well-known stage and film actress Kim Hunter

played Rosalind to Donald Harron's Orlando. Director Word Baker and set designer Robert O'Hearn moved the setting of the play to fashionable American suburbia, an innovation that shocked and mainly displeased the critics. Motley's designs—"uninhibitedly modern," said Howard Taubman (*Times,* 25 June 1961)—came in for their share of the criticism. Among the touches critics objected to were a courtier in a Madras jacket wearing a black eye patch (a tongue-in-cheek allusion to a shirtmaker's advertisements); Oliver in jodhpurs wearing a sports jacket with a cigarillo in the breast pocket; Orlando in overalls; Duke Frederick in an all-white suit; and the forest lovers in a pastiche of Elizabethan and Victorian fashions. Costumes for *Macbeth* were "the rough-hewn garments of ancient Scotland," as Howard Taubman noted with pleasure (*Times,* 25 June 1961) before going on to fault Pat Hingle's Macbeth and to praise Jessica Tandy's Lady Macbeth.

For *Troilus and Cressida,* director Landau with designers O'Hearn and Montgomery shifted the period from the Trojan War to the American Civil War, an allusion to the centenary of its outbreak, which had sparked a wave of Civil War nostalgia. Working on a low budget, they bought "a bale of almost obscenely new gray uniforms," which "had somehow to be made to resemble the tattered and faded rags worn by General Lee's starveling veterans in the last days of the great war."[17] To achieve that effect, the designers virtually destroyed the costumes, attacking them with scissors, dyes, bleach, and even wire brushes. Judith Crist (*Herald Tribune,* 24 July 1961), who approved of the change in historical period, noted parallels between Carrie Nye as Cressida and Scarlett O'Hara, Will Geer as Priam and Robert E. Lee, and Patrick Hines as Agamemnon and Ulysses S. Grant. Besides the blue (Greek) and gray (Trojan) uniforms and the crinolines, the critics noticed mainly the flattening effect of putting an American frame around the action. As Crist said, "Suddenly you find yourself watching the window-dressing rather than the play." Like the changes employed in *As You Like It,* this updating proved more distracting than effective.

Kwamina attempted to confront racial issues again coming to national attention in the United States through the civil rights movement. As Shakespeare set his more controversial plays in dis-

Kwamina, *Fifty-Fourth Street Theatre, New York, 1961. The costume sketch for an attendant shows how Elizabeth Montgomery used costumes to enhance an exotic atmosphere. Motley Collection.*

tant Italy, this musical took place in Africa, where an English-educated physician, Kwamina (Terry Carter), returns to his African homeland—now on the brink of independence. There, against a backdrop of "native" dances choreographed by Agnes de Mille, he falls in love with the missionary's daughter, Dr. Eve (Sally Ann Howes). Amidst "a glow of costume colors, many shades of pink and red, against the jungle green of the settings," wrote Cyrus Durgin (*Boston Globe,* 28 September 1961), playwright Robert Alan Arthur and composer

Richard Adler attempted a musical about changing African mores. Although praised for being "serious," "unusual," and "courageous," it closed within a month. Elizabeth Montgomery's colorful and lively costumes received scant attention.

Later in 1961 Margaret Harris came to New York with the West End hits *Ross* and *A Man For All Seasons.* With her came not only Glen Byam Shaw, who had directed *Ross* and who would help with the transfer, but also a crowd of theatre people who had worked together since the 1930s: Paul Scofield, Michael Redgrave, Googie Withers, Carol Goodner, Keith Baxter, among others. To complicate matters, besides managing the two transfers, Byam Shaw, Margaret Harris, and a cast of English and American actors were to stage Graham Greene's *The Complaisant Lover,* produced by Irene Selznick.

New York presented a demanding change after the ease of working in London, Margaret Harris recalled: "I hadn't been in New York often since the War, and that was the first time that Elizabeth and I had a chance to work together for a long time. *The Complaisant Lover* wasn't very pleasant to work on because of Irene Selznick, who was awful to both of us. She kept telling us what to do. We had silly, terrible arguments. It shouldn't have mattered to me at all, but I just dug my toes in because I resented being told. It was just a straightforward play about a dentist, but because it was in New York I found it very, very difficult to create what I wanted."

Directed by Glen Byam Shaw and starring Michael Redgrave, Googie Withers, and Richard Johnson, *The Complaisant Lover* garnered praise from all the critics for a well-turned, thought-provoking comedy enhanced by uniformly excellent acting. The play revolved around a love triangle in which the lover must be "complaisant," because husband and erring wife insist on continuing their sexless but comfortable marriage. Its contemporary setting, difficult for Margaret Harris because of the strictures of American stagehands' unions, offered further challenges to Elizabeth Montgomery as costume designer: "For one thing, the play was particularly and peculiarly British, depicting a stratum of society that, if something less than fascinating, must certainly be almost unique. The characters had to appear as though they purchased their clothes in the better London shops,

but on no account could they look chic. And need-
less to say, they were not permitted to appear
flashy. These were not Mayfair types; they were
stodgy middle-class characters betrayed out of
their formal molds by not very enduring passions.
At the point of the female lead's first entrance you
were supposed to be told, by the length of her skirt
and the height of her heels, by her jewelry and
her coiffure, that this was an upper-middle-class
English housewife who might be taken in sin, but
would never be taken completely out of character.
But the play's budget would not permit us to have
clothes made under contract with a recognized theatrical costumier, as they are in most Broadway
productions. It was staged in New York in winter,
and to procure one simple cotton frock for the
ingenue—the *right* sort of frock, we hoped—we
trudged through snow and bought four dresses.
They were eventually discarded by the producer
Irene Selznick and by the director Glen Byam
Shaw who became abundantly aware that, no matter what else New York might have, it didn't have
a Harrod's. The firm, penny-wise budget relaxed,
naturally, and finally went out the window. My
own chances of making a significant contribution to the play had, I believe, long since done
likewise."

Whatever its production difficulties, *The Complaisant Lover* enjoyed a good run of just over 100
performances, but was utterly overshadowed by
the London transfer of *A Man for All Seasons*. A
history play about Sir Thomas More, the heroic
statesman who defied Henry VIII's demand that
More sanction his divorce, it had opened with a
somewhat different cast in London six months earlier. Margaret Harris had designed the sets for the
London production; Sophia Harris, the costumes.
"Noel Willman's staging is immaculate," wrote
John Simon (*Theatre Arts*, 46 [1962], 10–11). "Like
the author Robert Bolt and Paul Scofield as
Thomas More, the director extracts maximum lu-
minosity from every spark of dialogue and action,
and no movement on the stage is anything but the
accurate graph of an idea. This atmosphere of all-
pervading intelligence and economy is fitted by
Motley's scenery and costumes like a glove—no,
better: like scenery and costumes by Motley. The
boldly curving ramp that leads from a Tudor balcony down to a few staunch pieces of furniture;
those elegant and evocative little flown units that

suspend themselves unassumingly above the action
and yet manage to envelop it in the sensuousness of
place, those gowns in shades that efface themselves
before the deeper coloring of ideas, provide the
fitting calligraphy for the playwright's noble dis-
course." It was "even a bigger hit in New York
than in London. . . . . Scofield, though long a star
in England, was making his first Broadway appearance."[18] A fabulous hit that ran literally for
years, it closed in June 1963 after 637
performances.

Ross, a play by Terence Rattigan about Lawrence
of Arabia, had opened in May 1960 in London.
John Mills took the title role that Alec Guinness
had made famous and Glen Byam Shaw directed.
The production met with the same unalloyed success as did the other London transfer. Using flashback to move from the point of a disturbed
Lawrence's incipient breakdown as the anonymous
RAF private "Ross," the play explores his adventures in fighting for the Arabs' freedom from
Turkish rule, his eventual capture by the Turks,
and, darkly hinted at, his rape by the minions of
a sadistic Turkish commandant. "Motley's sets and
costumes," said Howard Taubman (*Times*, 27 December 1961), "capture the atmosphere of the air
station, desert, general's quarters, and Turkish palace with impressive effect." The production ran
for 159 performances.

Dubbed a "musical adventure" and based on the
film *Viva Villa!* about Pancho Villa, *We Take the
Town* never made it into New York, closing after
playing in New Haven and Philadelphia early in
the spring of 1962. Not even Robert Preston in
the lead could save one of the few duds for which
Elizabeth Montgomery designed costumes. "Visually," she recalled, "it was a designer's holiday. In
the production, an actor playing a Mexican dicta-
tor was supposed to wear more medals than any
one man could ever carry. We made them of felt,
ribbon, wire, red, blue and white sequins, braids,
simulated pearls, rubber flex, old beads, and other
odds and ends. . . . [They] brought forth the de-
sired amount of laughter," but the fifty-plus original medals required "an incredible amount of
design work."[19]

Elizabeth Montgomery served as the house costume designer at the American Shakespeare Festival that summer for productions of *Richard II* and
1 Henry IV. *Richard II* was a design success but an

acting failure. Director Allen Fletcher was unable to help screen star Richard Basehart to get near the nobility of Richard, nor was he more successful with Hal Holbrook as John of Gaunt or Philip Bosco as Bolingbroke. The critics nevertheless appreciated the sets by Eldon Elder and Motley's costumes. The large auditorium and the thrust stage had made for difficulties until Eldon Elder solved the problem of linking the audience and the actors with a unit set, a single large arch across the stage with a grillwork, banners, and other impedimenta of the Middle Ages. Motley's costumes—"almost phosphorescent," said Judith Crist (*Herald Tribune,* 18 June 1962)—seemed to Arthur Gelb (*Times,* 18 June 1962) part of an overall strategy to make up for weak acting: "The stylized pageantry, richness of sets and costuming, and throbbing musical accompaniment are more of a piece than the acting. Indeed, they seem designed to cover up and gloss over the inherent weaknesses of the production rather than to underline a solid performance."

Henry IV, Part One fared much better. Directed by Old Vic veteran Douglas Seale, it starred as Falstaff Eric Berry, an experienced actor who had already won praise for his Falstaff at the Phoenix Theatre two years earlier. Hal Holbrook as Hotspur also took top honors. The sets and costumes received scant notice.

An ill-fated drama about war in the Renaissance, *Lorenzo* closed after four performances. Motley's next venture, the musical comedy *Tovarich,* settled into the Broadway Theatre for a run that carried it through to the end of the season. Well known in the United States as a drawing-room comedy by Jacques Deval and adapted by Robert Sherwood, the script had been made into a film starring Claudette Colbert and Charles Boyer (1937). The musical version had been in the making since 1959. Ironically entitled *Tovarich* ("comrade" in Russian), the play revolved around the plight of an exiled Russian grand duchess forced to work as a ladies' maid for an American family in Paris in the late 1920s. It featured Vivien Leigh as the sprightly maid Tatiana, the French film star Jean Pierre Aumont as her beau, Byron Mitchell as their American employer, and dozens of singers and dancers, giving ample scope for Elizabeth Montgomery's flair for glamorous costumes. From her point of view, it was not a happy production for the costume designer: "Vivien Leigh was wonderful look-

ing, but by this time she'd got very difficult to work with. It was after her separation from Larry. She was very haughty. Jean Pierre Aumont played the man. He was terrible to work with. There were stripes on his waistcoat, and he said, 'In our house, only a butler wears his stripes that way.' He was boasting that he knew all about butlers." The *Times* (20 March 1963) praised Vivien Leigh for giving "regality and lightness" to a musical that was otherwise "routine."

Far different from such elegant period costumes were Elizabeth Montgomery's costumes for Bertolt Brecht's *Mother Courage and Her Children,* a harsh drama about the Thirty Years' War in Europe, directed by Jerome Robbins and starring Anne Bancroft and Gene Wilder. Working with the young Chinese-American designer Ming Cho Lee, Elizabeth Montgomery created costumes that evoked the grim and timeless experience of war. "The great lumbering wagon," which Mother Courage pulls across battlefield after battlefield, "looms like another character," wrote the designers.[20] Although a success with the critics—"a work to welcome and cherish," wrote Howard Taubman (*Times,* 1 April 1963)—the somber themes and the disjointed plot did not greatly please audiences; it closed in May after fifty-two performances.

110 in the Shade, a musical based on *The Rainmaker,* brought together Harvey Schmidt (music) and Tom Jones (lyrics), whose runaway success *The Fantasticks* was playing off-Broadway. Joining them were the tried and true combination of Agnes de Mille (choreography), Oliver Smith (sets), and Motley (costumes). Inga Swenson starred opposite Robert Horton and Stephen Douglass. Yet the critics were severe. The book was "simpleminded," the acting so unconvincing that "Joseph Anthony's staging cannot irrigate the prevalent aridity, nor can the now familiar style of Agnes de Mille, who has done this sort of dance movement a good deal more eloquently in the past," Howard Taubman wrote (*Times,* 25 October 1963). Walter Kerr (*Herald Tribune,* 25 October 1963) liked Inga Swenson, but found fault with nearly everything else except "Oliver Smith's backdrop with small shadows creeping across the desert." When it opened in Boston, Elliot Norton (*Boston Record-American,* 10 September 1963) summed up his lukewarm reaction: "The costumes of Motley are designed to please the eye in this new musical comedy which remains to be lifted up from its present prosaic level to that giddy elevation where the hits are." Other critics in Boston and New York were more generous, but there was an implicit suggestion that the once-winning combination had now gone stale. True or not, the audiences kept coming. The show ran to the end of the season and then went on an American tour. (With the same designs and with Inga Swenson still in the lead, it was restaged in London under Charles Blackwell's direction in 1967.)

Later that season, Elizabeth Montgomery designed a dozen period costumes for Gilbert and Sullivan's *Patience,* performed at the New York City Center. It was a straightforward piece of work for which her name never appeared in the credits. She then had the summer to herself in Connecticut, or rather to herself, her husband, and a houseful of growing children. The American Shakespeare Festival was in the throes of financial and artistic distresses that would bring the whole enterprise to an unhappy end some years later and did not see fit to engage Motley as its costume designer again. This loss was easier for Elizabeth Montgomery to bear since the Festival's reputation had begun to decline.

Her big hit came the following season with *Ben Franklin in Paris,* a musical starring Robert Preston, whose acting and singing in *The Music Man* had given him super-star status. True, Walter Kerr (*Herald-Tribune,* 28 October 1964) complained that "the integrated musical has turned back into operetta again, and I do hope the town's costumers are happy," and Howard Taubman (*Times,* 28 October 1964) in the same vein wrote, "the trouble is that one takes pleasure in scattered bits, rather than in the work as a whole." Yet the other critics were unequivocal. "A very handsome enterprise designed by Oliver Smith and costumed by Motley," wrote John Chapman (*Daily News,* 28 October 1964); "a big, fat hit," trumpeted John McClain (*Journal-American,* 28 October 1964), who particularly praised it as "very stylish." Audiences, who loved to have their history served up as a musical, came in droves, keeping the doors open for 215 performances. It closed 1 May 1965.

As the director Hal Prince tells the story, the Sherlock Homes musical *Baker Street* could have been a "small, atmospheric show." Instead, although it turned out to be a box-office success, running for 313 performances, it became a direc-

tor's and producer's nightmare. Rather than focusing on Holmes (Fritz Weaver), the production revolved around Inga Swenson, fresh from *110 in the Shade,* as Irene Adler, the femme fatale who saves him from Moriarty. It received raves for the opening in Boston (*Variety* called it a combination of *Around the World in Eighty Days* and *My Fair Lady*), and expectations were high in New York. Yet, as it happened, the New York critics much preferred the season's "serious" musical *Fiddler on the Roof.* Calling it "three World's Fairs rolled into one gaslit playhouse," Walter Kerr (*Herald-Tribune,* 18 February 1965) panned it. Howard Taubman (*Times,* 28 February 1965) pronounced: "*Baker Street* falls short of consistency of style." Four years of work and huge expenses left the director proudest not of the production itself but of an effect he contrived to show Queen Victoria's coronation from the London rooftops by using a parade of miniature soldiers and a golden coach. Whatever its takings at the box office—enhanced by producer Alexander H. Cohen's advance-purchase ticket scheme—it did not rank as a great artistic achievement. Prince laconically reports that "after *Baker Street* I was not offered another directing job for three years."[21] Elizabeth Montgomery remembered it fondly. "*Baker Street* was one of the last things I did in New York. It was fun to make, and fun to do. It won several awards."

"A stunning play, one of the finest of our age, has come to town," proclaimed Howard Taubman (*Times,* 17 November 1965) in praise of John Whiting's *The Devils,* a play based upon Aldous Huxley's *The Devils of Loudun* and commissioned by the Royal Shakespeare Company, who had produced it in 1961. The play starred Jason Robards as a libertine priest and Anne Bancroft as a sadistic, deformed prioress. Because the priest rejects her sexual advances, she denounces him as a devil-worshiper to Richelieu and his torturers. A tight script that pleased Taubman left Walter Kerr cold, who called it "evil in one dimension" (*Herald Tribune,* 5 December 1965). With a glance or two at Motley's period costumes, Rouben Ter-Aruturian's Breughelesque sets, and Michael Cacoyannis's sometimes overelaborate direction, the critics largely ignored the production itself, preferring instead to analyze the merits of the script. The play ran for only thirty-one performances, closing on 6 January 1966.

Elizabeth Montgomery's last production while

she lived in New York, *Don't Drink the Water,* marked Woody Allen's debut as a Broadway playwright. The farce was set in the American embassy in Moscow and revolved around the antics of a Jewish businessman, who, pursued by evil Russians, seeks refuge in his embassy. Although Jo Mielziner's set was admired, Elizabeth Montgomery's contemporary costumes were not mentioned in the reviews. Production photographs show the businessman (Lou Jacobi) in a fedora and a loud "Hawaiian" shirt accosting the ambassador's son (Anthony Roberts), who wears a pinstriped suit. Looking on anxiously are Kay Medford as the businessman's wife in a modified "sack" dress clutching *Europe on 5 Dollars a Day* and Anita Gillette as their daughter, in a sleeveless minidress à la Jackie Kennedy, bubble hairdo and all. It had a long run and was still touring in 1968.

By 1966 Motley's "American period" was drawing to a close. Although the Woody Allen farce was the last New York production completed while Elizabeth Montgomery maintained residence in America, it was not the last New York Motley production. After having moved back to London, she returned for Peter Ustinov's *The Unknown Soldier and His Wife,* which opened on 6 July 1967 at the Vivian Beaumont Theatre, with "Scenery and costumes by Motley." Ustinov had first worked with Motley when he was a student in the London Theatre Studio before the War. That happy experience prompted him to commission Elizabeth Montgomery to design both sets and costumes. She came to New York from London with Ustinov and director John Dexter for the production. *The Unknown Soldier and His Wife* was

anti-war before that political stance was fashionable, moving by flashbacks through different historical periods, each demonstrating war's futility and human cost. "The actors wandered onto the stage and, with bits of costume and a few props, appeared to improvise the play. In keeping with this scheme, the setting was a nondescript area—perhaps an abandoned theatre or an old circus tent," wrote the lighting designer Jules Fisher (*Theatre Crafts,* November-December, 1967, 8–12). "Elizabeth Montgomery, the costume and scenic designer was well aware of the visual, as well as the dramatic, importance of the actors, and she approved of the darkened stage," he concluded. The production had a respectable run of 159 performances in New York. It was revived with a different cast at the Chichester Festival in England the following year. With Ustinov directing, it was restaged in Lyons, France, and eventually came into the New London Theatre. In these later productions, Elizabeth Montgomery was assisted by Margaret Harris in the set and costume design.

Sophia Harris's funeral in the spring of 1966 brought Elizabeth Montgomery temporarily back to London. Later that year, searching for better medical treatment for her husband, Elizabeth Montgomery returned with him to live in London permanently. She nursed him through his final illness until his death in 1968. Their son John became an artist living for a time in Denmark then moved to Australia. No longer active as a designer in her own right after 1967, Elizabeth continued as a close friend and collaborator with Margaret Harris. She died in 1993.

7
Motley in London
1940–1947

At the beginning of World War II Sophia Harris set out on a course distinct from her two partners in America. Although their paths would cross, in the years after the War the Motley women's three-fold collaboration became the exception, not the rule. During the War, Motley in the person of Sophia Harris remained an important part of the London theatre world. Her costumes continued to be seen in premiere London productions. Unfortunately, Sophia Harris was less inclined to save her drawings than either of the other Motleys. Only designs from productions she worked on with one or the other of them have been preserved. The public record partially documents what she did—although it is itself incomplete for the war years.

When she bade farewell to her sister and Elizabeth Montgomery in 1940, Sophia Harris remained behind in a city preparing for war. Newly married, she and George Devine awaited his call-up. She joined the Land Army to do her part for England. "When they learned that he would be sent to India," said Margaret Harris, "they decided to have a child, in case he didn't come back." George Devine departed for the Burma campaign. Pregnant and without the company of the other Motleys, Sophia Harris moved out of central London to Kingston-on-Thames. After she gave birth to a daughter, Harriet, she suffered a nervous breakdown. Mother and child were subsequently evacuated to the countryside as the bombs began to fall.[1]

The London theatre world was transformed by World War II. Either through call-up or emigration, theatre people departed. Most were engaged in some way in the war effort, either serving in the military or entertaining troops and civilians at home and abroad. Motley's close friends in the theatre community were almost without exception involved. "Larry Olivier was in the Fleet Air Arm for a bit. So was Ralph Richardson," recalled Margaret Harris. "Alec Guinness and Michael Redgrave were in the Navy. Harry Andrews, Tony Quayle, and Glen Byam Shaw were in the Army."

Some artists, such as Elizabeth Montgomery and Margaret Harris, left the country to work far from the battlefields. Christopher Isherwood and W. H. Auden, for example, had emigrated to America before war was declared, in protest against the appeasement of Hitler.[2] Despite the thinning out of available artists, the London theatre world for the most part tried to ignore the war, carrying on as if it were business as usual. In 1939, before the Blitz, theatre practices continued almost unaffected. Productions went into rehearsal, opened outside London, and then came into the city.

With the onset of the bombing and the blackout, the calling up of men into the armed forces, and the first shortages of goods and services, the theatre and the country at large shifted to wartime footing. Air raids moved up evening curtain times and changed the nature of theatre-going from a somewhat formal social occasion to something closer to popular entertainment. By 1943, Eric Johns reported in *Theatre World* (January 1943, 17–18), an earlier six-o'clock curtain time trimmed the period between matinee and evening performance to a single hour. "Only people of leisure have time to dress for the theatre these days when they have to be in their seats by six o'clock," he wrote," and there are so few of them that they would look sadly out of place in the stalls, sitting next to men in battle-dress and women in office jumpers. . . . In consequence, no one dresses at all. War workers have no time, and the others simply fall in with the majority. . . . Theatre-going is becoming more casual and consequently more popular than ever. It is a habit that is rapidly taking a firm hold on sections of the public who had never seen a play in their lives prior to the war. . . . The war is also taking stars out into the provinces more frequently than they went in the old days."[3] However cheery a picture Johns painted, there were the blackout and the bombs to contend with. At times it must have seemed to Londoners that the theatres were themselves targets. Stray bombs did destroy several.

Recognizing his unique contribution to the war effort, the authorities exempted John Gielgud from active duty, as they did for others deemed essential to the maintenance of theatre as part of the war effort. Throughout the War, theatre artists found work under the aegis of Hugh "Binkie" Beaumont of the theatre management firm H. M. Tennents.

Sophia Harris continued to specialize in costume design, as she did in her earlier position on the Motley team. Because she had been involved for years in a long-term relationship with George Devine and because she was in other ways the "domestic" Motley, she stood somewhat apart from her sister Margaret and Elizabeth Montgomery. Her designs in the 1930s had been done in collaboration with one or both of them. A sharp eye for fashion had made Sophia Harris the Motley who ran the firm's couturier house, "Elizabeth Curzon." Through this venue, she designed and supervised the making of fancy dresses for public events, theatrical productions, and films. The dresses were cut by Hilda Reader under the wing of Berman's, one of the big London costumiers. The premises in St. Martin's Lane housed a showroom and cutting room.

Couturier gown designed by Sophia Harris, from Motley's files.

Before the War, Elizabeth Montgomery and Sophia Harris had designed "collections" of clothes that were shown publicly, as top designers still do. Their exclusive clientele included the Duchess of Argyle, Deborah Kerr, Valerie Hobson, and other well-known actresses and society women, who bought clothes from the collections or had them specially designed for themselves. Their evening dresses were made of unusual materials—one very beautiful dress was fashioned from curtain lace. Sophia Harris was known especially for her combination of glamour and wit—placing a bouquet of silk roses in the décolletage of an elegant frock was typical of her mischievous sophistication. Motley also designed daytime clothes and street wear.[4] One can see in Sophia Harris's subsequent work in the London theatre and in film an extension of that initial focus on fashion. Whatever the setting, her designs expressed atmosphere and character, modifying the niceties of period fashion.

Although she was credited in her own name or in Motley's from time to time, much of Sophia Harris's work in the war years was done without attribution—a shortcoming that reflected the catch-as-catch-can business of mounting productions in wartime. Whether or not Sophia Harris was credited, the productions she designed were of consistently high quality. She is not mentioned in the credits for *The Cherry Orchard* (1941), for instance, although she and her partners had planned the production of the play before the War, as mentioned in chapter 4. It is listed, however, among Motley's credits as designers in *Who's Who in the Theatre*.[5]

George Bernard Shaw had written of the heroine of his play *The Doctor's Dilemma:* She was "beyond all dreams, an arrestingly good-looking young woman." For a revival of the play at the Haymarket in 1942, Vivien Leigh was costumed by Sophia Harris to reflect the height of fashion as it was circa 1906, when the play was first performed. She dressed Vivien Leigh as Mrs. Dubedat in showy hats and stunning tailored gowns—one of black velvet, another of white lace—that set off her fragile beauty. "Miss Vivien Leigh," reported the *Times* (5 March 1942), shows "how attractive the fashions at the turn of the century may yet appear." In keeping with the play's original period, Sophia Harris transformed what had once been a contemporary play into a classic. Attention paid by the newspapers to Vivien Leigh and her elegant costumes not only credited Sophia Harris's successful designs, but also reflected the pride in things English that infused the theatre and its audiences.

Based loosely upon the immorality of a doctor at St. Mary's Hospital, who callously asked "Is he worth it?" when a new patient was suggested for his tuberculosis cure, the play settled in for a long run that carried it well into 1943. An often repeated piece of theatre lore credits John Gielgud with the skill and delightful panache that enabled him to step into the part of Dubedat on twenty-four hours' notice, the principal actor and understudy both having become ill.[6]

In April 1942, following a smash year on Broadway, a new production of Lillian Hellman's *Watch on the Rhine* opened at the Aldwych Theatre, with sets by Michael Relph and, said the program, "with clothes by Sophia Harris." It was an instant hit. Set in Washington, D.C., it portrayed the plight of a good German engineer who finds himself and his family threatened by the pre-War Nazi government. Its topicality practically guaranteed box-office success, and Sophia Harris's costumes helped tell the story. The engineer's American wife, played by Diana Wynyard, put aside her glamorous frocks in favor of a practical blouse and wraparound skirt. As the American matriarch, Athene Seyler presided over a household full of children, European refugees, and, of course, intrigue and murder. Emlyn Williams directed.

"London's most finished and sparkling production," proclaimed *Theatre World* (January 1943) in assessing the revival of John Gielgud's production of *The Importance of Being Earnest,* which he directed and in which he starred with Gwen Ffrangcon-Davies, Cyril Ritchard, Jean Cadell, Peggy Ashcroft, and Edith Evans. In the glowing reviews one hears more than a hint of patriotic fervor for the best that is British; Sophia Harris's "Motley" costumes completed the picture of the glories of an earlier era.

What else had London theatre to offer? Not much of great pith or weight, if the listings for early 1943 are typical: Beverly Baxter's third extravaganza, *It Happened in September; Waltz Without End,* a musical romance based on Chaplin's life; *House of Jeffreys,* a horror play with Sybil Thorndike as a missionary who turns cannibal; and Cole Porter's *Let's Face It,* about three American servicemen and their girls. In the context of these shows, Sophia Harris's work associated her with solid quality.

Later that season she worked again with Emlyn Williams and set designer Michael Relph. The play was Turgenev's *A Month in the Country,* which Williams had adapted. Michael Redgrave starred as Rakitin and Valerie Taylor as Natalia Petrovna. Motley's costumes graced the period comedy with such elegance that, to one critic, Valerie Taylor looked like a Winterhalter portrait come to life. A few others complained of "over decoration" and "over costuming," likening it unfavorably to a "Hollywood stunner."[7]

The Last of Mrs. Cheyney allowed playgoers a chance to see what Tyrone Guthrie and a new cast would do with Frederick Lonsdale's popular "comedy of the day before yesterday," as the author coyly dubbed it. Another London drawing-room comedy full of lords and ladies, it starred Athene Seyler and Coral Browne. The play had been staged earlier at the Westminster theatre under a different director and with a different cast. For witty and elegant costumes, the director relied on Sophia Harris as Motley.

In 1945 Sophia Harris worked with Emlyn Williams once again. *The Wind of Heaven,* which he wrote, directed, and starred in, credited "costumes by Sophia Harris (Motley)." The play was set in a Welsh village during the Crimean War. A sentimental story of a young mystic whom the villagers hail as the Messiah, it was a distinctly British play and was never revived. British in a rather different way, Noel Coward's *Sigh No More* was a musical extravaganza choreographed by Wendy Toye, featuring Joyce Grenfell and Cyril Ritchard as the principals playing in front of a cast of "singing Sylphides." The play demanded plenty of work from the costume designer, but was not one of Coward's better efforts.

In the history of the theatre, wartime London is probably best remembered for its enthusiastic audiences and for the tens of thousands of servicemen who flocked to it—not for any major breakthroughs in play writing, direction, design, or acting. As Motley, Sophia Harris's contributions—sometimes fugitive and unrecorded—were as significant as those of any other artist who was able to function amidst the tension and uncertainties of the times. When the War ended and she was reunited with her husband George Devine, they faced a future that they hoped would bring together their former colleagues for a fresh start. What they could not know, however, was that they would soon be viewed as the old guard, not the promising newcomers, in the London theatre.

Margaret Harris returned to London on the *Queen Elizabeth* in the spring of 1946. Awaiting her were Sophia Harris and George Devine, recently returned from military service in Burma and the Far East. "I traveled over on the boat with Giles Playfair, and he came to London with us in their car. I remember thinking how small their car was, compared to American cars," recalled Margaret Harris. "They said, 'We've got a really big car, because we didn't know how much luggage you'd have.'"

"When I returned to England from America after the War," Margaret Harris said, "some of the theatres were damaged. There was not a lot of money to spend, but there was tremendous enthusiasm for the theatre—a boom in the theatre, really. Everybody needed something to cheer them up. London was a shambles, with great empty areas everywhere where they'd been blitzed."

The War's end saw the Motley ménage coming together again in a different configuration. Sophia Harris and George Devine were married and lived with their three-and-a-half-year-old daughter in Edwards Square, where they put up Margaret Harris briefly. As soon as they could, the couple went to France to restore professional ties with Michel Saint-Denis and his wife, Suria Magito, leaving Margaret Harris to look after their daughter Harriet. "She didn't like it at all," said Margaret Harris. "I had a rather worrying time because she wasn't well, and she got very upset, having never been separated from Sophie before. She was terribly jealous of George, because he took up a lot of Sophie's attention. She was very unhappy being left with me, and I was pretty scared, I must say." Shortly afterwards, Margaret Harris took over the flat in Earl's Terrace, Kensington High Street, which Michel Saint-Denis and Suria Magito had left when in France.

The Motley studio in St. Martin's Lane had been blitzed. "There's a story John Gielgud tells about it," said Margaret Harris. "He lived just up the road. One night when they were bombing, he sensed that they'd got the Motley studio. He went down the next morning to see, and the place was a shambles. It had been burnt. Skips of costumes had been blown open. He said his red costume out of *Richard II* was hanging on top of the iron staircase, flapping in the wind. The men who were clearing up the rubble had got hats out of *Hamlet* on, with feathers and things. All over the yard were the labels that we used to sew in the costumes, so it said, 'Motley, Motley, Motley, Motley, Motley, Motley, Motley,' everywhere. He said it was an extraordinary sight."[8] With the studio gone, the workrooms had to be closed down then and there. From that time on, Motley designed the costumes but had them made by commercial costumiers. Instead of using a studio, the two Motley women designed costumes and sets at home.

In 1946 and 1947, as the theatre artists who had been scattered by the War returned to London, theatre began to develop again in the British capital. The Motley women were at the center. Even though they continued to receive credit as "Motley," their partnership after the War saw their paths diverging. Life began to settle down with demobilization over and the theatre returning to something near normal. Margaret Harris and Sophia Harris as Motley became part of a new "company" of directors, designers, actors, and student-apprentices similar to the London Theatre Studio but centered around the Old Vic, as described in the next chapter. Sophia Harris became caught up in the formation of the company and with family concerns as the theatre moved on to peacetime footing.

In the meantime, foreshadowing Motley's work in Stratford-upon-Avon, in 1946 Margaret Harris designed *Antony and Cleopatra* at the Piccadilly Theatre in collaboration with Glen Byam Shaw as director—thereby forming an artistic alliance that would carry on until his retirement in 1978. "*Antony* in 1946 was the first time I'd done a big show entirely on my own, without either of the others," recalled Margaret Harris. "Glen Byam Shaw began working on *Antony and Cleopatra* when he was wounded in Burma. Glen had been getting awfully bored, and his brother Jim, who was in the next bed in the hospital, said, 'Why don't you work out a production that you can do when you get back.' And so he worked on *Antony and Cleopatra,* and kept at it for years. When he came back, Binkie Beaumont asked, 'What do you want to do?' '*Antony and Cleopatra,*' said Glen." Having kept London-based theatre people going during the War, after it ended Binkie Beaumont re-established the ones who returned—Glen Byam Shaw, George Devine, Tony Quayle, and many others.

In the 1946 *Antony*, Godfrey Tearle played Antony, with Edith Evans as Cleopatra and Anthony Quayle as Enobarbus. The design was based on Tiepolo's paintings of Antony and Cleopatra. "We thought that, with Edith Evans not in the first flush of youth," said Margaret Harris, "it would be better not to give her Egyptian costumes. So we did it seventeenth-century baroque. I did a lot of research, making sketches from art books and drawings of their sandals and other details. The set was no good at all. It had a big central column,

fluted, with a platform all round it with sliding doors in the platform, like a lift. I made some very bad sketches of it, as I'd never done any set sketches. Elizabeth had always done the sketches, and I'd done the model and the practical work.

"Glen made me take all the actors one by one out into the corridor and ask them to roll up their sleeves and roll up their trousers so that I could see what their legs and arms were like. I had to give a report on it all. They weren't bare-legged, any of them, except some of the Egyptians. They had Roman costumes—seventeenth-century baroque Roman costumes with breeches. I tried not to show too much, because actors are never, or hardly ever, muscular. They're getting better now, but then they were rather skinny characters."

Antony and Cleopatra at the Piccadilly Theatre was hardly a box office success, despite generous reviews. The *Times* (21 December 1946) especially praised the permanent set and fluidity of the staging. *Theatre World* (March 1947) proclaimed it "one of the most memorable revivals of Shakespeare's play London has seen." Anthony Quayle made a first-rate Enobarbus. Nevertheless, all was not well: The Piccadilly Theatre was in disrepair and Edith Evans as Cleopatra was well past her salad days. Postwar shortages plagued the practical side of production. "A Mr. Trimmingham, playing one of the eunuchs, was heard to say," recalled Margaret Harris laughing, "'Mr. Tearle and that old lady are sure going to lose a lot of money.' I suppose they did." The run was short and Tennents may have absorbed a loss. Yet the production was a success artistically because it reunited theatre people dispersed by the War. In the end, it served as a prototype for the successful staging of the play in 1953 at Stratford-upon-Avon.

Now re-established with her family and with her sister nearby, Sophia Harris as Motley continued in the mainstream of London theatre as it branched out after the War. Margaret Harris's American experience and prestige added to the firm's already stellar reputation, and Motley continued their pre-War success as designers. In combination with director Glen Byam Shaw, Margaret Harris as Motley was taking the firm into a fresh dimension in which she and the director would conceive the direction and design of the production. For both women, exciting plans were taking shape to establish new companies centered on the

Old Vic Theatre. These developments were already in process as 1946 drew to a close, and the country began to rebuild after the War.

Behind this excitement, however, lay changes that would make it impossible to recreate the atmosphere and achievements of the talented crowd who had imbibed of Gielgud's dreams and Motley's tea in St. Martin's Lane in the years before the War. Gielgud himself had felt somewhat excluded—or he was going off on a separate path—when Michel Saint-Denis and the others had founded the London Theatre Studio. The War had changed everyone, dividing them by their separate and individual experiences. Glen Byam Shaw had been wounded in Burma. His plans for *Antony and Cleopatra* unofficially committed him to directing rather than acting. George Devine's service had thrown him out of the cloistered worlds of academe and the theatre. He returned changed, as his wife had also been changed, by the experience of the War and the birth of their daughter Harriet. That George Devine and Sophia Harris were about to set up a proper domestic arrangement meant that the Motley establishment that had been would be no more. With extensive experience in the West End, on Broadway, and in Hollywood, Margaret Harris saw stretching before her design work at the highest reaches of the British theatre, a goal for which she had returned home. Old friendships realigned themselves. What could be called "the Motley decade" in British and American theatre design was about to ensue.

8

The Old Vic, The Young Vic, and the Old Vic School 1947–1953

George Devine and Sophia Harris had first discussed "The Plan" with Michel Saint-Denis and his wife Suria Magito on a visit to France in 1946. It evolved rapidly into a concrete proposal to renew the Old Vic and extend its mission to include the training of younger theatre artists. Devine and Saint-Denis, with their colleague from before the War, Glen Byam Shaw, put the idea into practice beginning late in 1946. It went through a number of transformations, both in the planning and the implementation. Although the three men were officially in charge of the operation, in practice they consulted widely with their colleagues in the theatre and worked in very close cooperation with Sophia and Margaret Harris, who were responsible for the design component. In more recent times the two women probably would have shared more visibly in the management of the enterprise. As it was, their substantial contributions went beyond the design credits listed in the programs. Imbued with the wish to restore and improve English theatre, this group of idealists worked at low salaries, often against their best financial interests. For additional income, they could occasionally command higher pay from commercial theatres in the West End.

The "Plan," or more formally, the "Vic Expansion Scheme," envisioned four conjoined undertakings: (1) the already-established Old Vic

Company in London; (2) the Young Vic Company, which would tour the provinces; (3) the Young Vic Players, a student group that could travel to and perform in venues lacking theatres; and (4) the Old Vic School, a reincarnation of the London Theatre Studio. Profits from the Old Vic Company would help underwrite expenses for the "Old Vic Centre," as the last three activities were named to distinguish them from the professional Old Vic.[1]

The common aim of the Old Vic Centre's three divisions was to train actors, directors, and designers who would create productions for nontraditional audiences and whose work could feed into the mainstage work of the Old Vic Company. Fully professional, the Old Vic Company was first formed from experienced actors, some of them stars. Directors, designers, and actors maintained a loose affiliation with the company, rather than a permanent relationship. Their productions played in London at the Old Vic Theatre, occasionally transferring to the West End, with graduates from the Old Vic School playing minor parts and walk-ons.

The Young Vic, conceived as a professional touring company, was made up of less experienced actors, most of them graduates or students from the school, except the actors playing leading roles. The Young Vic toured the provinces, playing important theatres there, and completed a short season at the Old Vic Theatre in London.

The Young Vic Players, in which all parts were played by actors from the school, were a separate small-scale, low-budget company launched in 1949 to tour in places where there were no theatres—church halls, secondary schools, and other small-scale venues. These arrangements would shift over the course of time as the Old Vic Centre evolved.

Although everyone worked together, George Devine took responsibility for the Young Vic Company, Glen Byam Shaw for the School, and Michel Saint-Denis for the overall direction of the enterprise. Motley in the persons of Margaret and Sophia Harris were the resident designers and teachers of design for all three divisions. As such, they designed sets and costumes for several of the Centre's productions.

Shows produced by the Old Vic Companies were important both in themselves as theatre and as training for the students—the next generation of actors, directors, and designers. Each production had its own director, designer, and cast. Guest directors—Tyrone Guthrie and Hugh Hunt, among others—came in from time to time, as did guest designers. Not all guest directors shared the selfless vision of the founding triumvirate, resulting in conflicts of interest that ultimately brought the Old Vic Centre down.

Glen Byam Shaw's Old Vic School, which began just after the War in 1947 and closed in 1951, maintained an acting course, a design course, and a technical production course for the training of stage managers and directors; an advanced design course trained about four of the best directing and design students each year. These advanced students worked in director-designer pairs under Michel Saint-Denis with some help from Margaret Harris. Several of the Old Vic School's actors and designers came to be well known: the actors Lee Montague and Keith Michell, for instance, and the designers Malcolm Pride, Carl Toms, Richard Negri, Stephen Doncaster, and Alan Tagg. Margaret Harris supervised designers-in-training and brought back the concept of a basic costume for the students, a refinement of the idea launched in the L.T.S. Sophia Harris occasionally consulted on designs and lectured, as did Elizabeth Montgomery when she visited London.

Everyone in the School—actors, designers, technicians—collaborated to produce an annual show, two programs performed in the course of a week on the Old Vic stage. They worked within three broad categories of style: "Shakespearean," "Restoration," and "modern." For actors and designers of the time, these terms meant something quite specific. "Shakespeare" meant a "big style," suitable for classics from the Greeks to Shakespeare. "Restoration" embraced a more improvisational style suitable not only for Restoration comedy but also for the *commedia dell' arte,* in which actors playfully acknowledged the audience. In the "modern" style (Devine called it "aquarium theatre") the audience was treated as if it were not present. For designers, as Wardle reports, this meant that "Shakespeare moves in curves; Restoration comedy, being set in front of cloths, presents a flat picture; and modern plays reflect the random complexity of the real world." Such unifying theories aside, however, what mattered was that the design students "consider space architecturally, always starting with a ground-plan." "The criterion of a successful design," Wardle continues, "was whether it faithfully translated a dramatic style into spatial form and assisted actors in articulating the play's rhythm."[2]

Late in 1946, George Devine directed and Motley designed the first play the Young Vic produced. *The King Stag* by Carlo Gozzi, a contemporary of Goldoni, is a fantasy play about a prince who turns into a stag. Sophia Harris created the costumes, Margaret Harris, the set. The set design was based on Douanier Rousseau's primitive paintings of jungles. "We used outsized leaves," remembered Margaret Harris. "A pretty setting by Motley," wrote the *Times* (27 December 1946), "made the whole thing great fun." The company chose the play, Wardle states, because it was popular in East European children's theatres. It opened at the Lyric, Hammersmith and then toured.

The Young Vic's production of *The King Stag*—stylized, imaginative, and enjoyable—also inaugurated an interesting aspect of actor-training at the Vic School: Actors were told in rehearsals to imagine themselves to be animals. As they had for the actors in *Noah* and for the student actors at the L.T.S., Motley created masks for the students to wear as part of exercises that continued throughout the training period. The practice became part of

The King Stag, *Lyric Theatre, Hammersmith, 1946.*
The set and costumes were inspired by the paintings of
Henri Rousseau. The actors have not been identified.
Production photograph from Motley's files.

the regular Vic School training program. To some it was a notoriously irrelevant distraction. Wardle reports that a representative of the Vic Governors who visited one of these sessions later used it against the School, because it seemed childish to him. Yet for many of the actors it represented a freeing up of inhibitions. At the same time, it provided a difficult and challenging experience shared by everyone. In the parlance of the School, such training was part of the "tunnel" through which one must go before emerging as a professional.

In 1947, a year during which Sophia Harris was mainly concerned with designing for films and Margaret Harris with the Old Vic School, Motley designed a production at the Young Vic—*The Shoemaker's Holiday* by Thomas Dekker. For this episodic play with its swift scene changes Margaret Harris created a small set that could be changed

almost instantaneously. Three metal uprights were set in a triangular pattern onstage. Each had three small flats attached to it, like a revolving door. For a scene change, the flats could revolve. "They weren't solid prisms like Greek periaktoi," explained Margaret Harris, "but open, so that the flats swung round on a central pin. With them we could make different shapes and different areas."

The costumes, which she also designed, had to be done very inexpensively. The stylish men's costumes were made of "huckaback," a linen used to make face towels. "It's very firm, and you can only get it in white, so we dyed it and painted it," said Margaret Harris. The women's clothes were made of linen and painted in patterns that emulated embroidered Elizabethan clothes.

In 1947, too, Elizabeth Montgomery came with her husband to London from New York. She executed drawings for the costumes for the second Young Vic play that year, *The Snow Queen*. A fantastication written and directed by Suria Magito based on Hans Christian Anderson's fairy tale, the

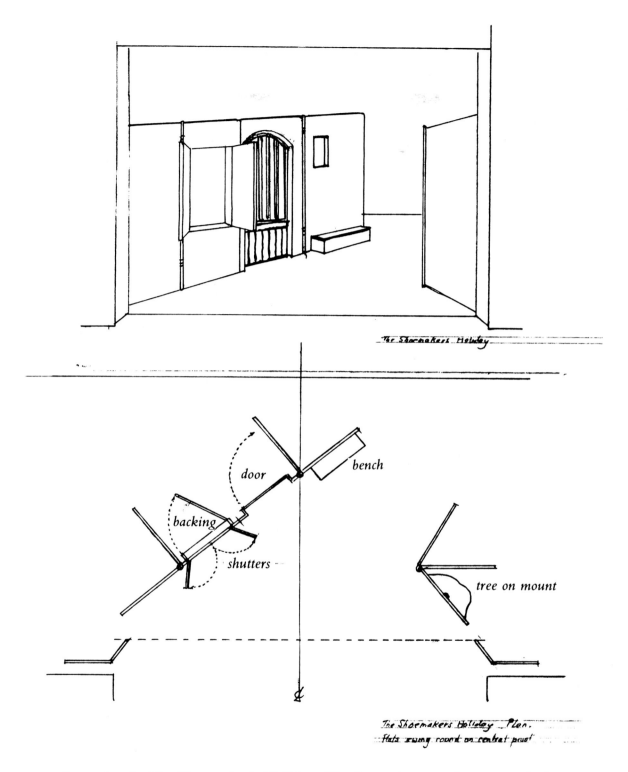

Stage plan for The Shoemaker's Holiday. *The flats swing around on a central pivot.*

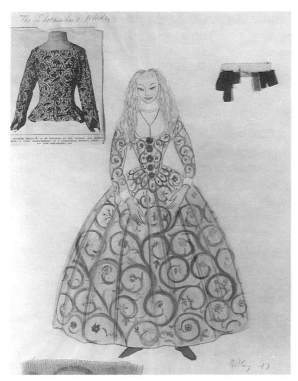

The Shoemaker's Holiday, *Young Vic, 1947; trans-ferred to the Toynbee Hall Theatre, 1948. Costume designs for Rose and Sibyl. Pinned to the design for Rose (left) is the illustration of an Elizabethan dress that inspired the designer. Motley Collection.*

production began as a Young Vic project aimed at younger audiences and toured for a year. It then came into the Old Vic around Christmas time, when the West End theatres were featuring traditional pantomimes. The play's magical effects required ingenuity. "When the Snow Queen had to come in through the window, a rose tree had to fade and die suddenly," said Margaret Harris. "We made the stems of rubber tubing with stiff wire running down them. To make it fade, we pulled the wire out; when it had to grow again, we pushed the wires up—they were padded at the top to prevent them from cutting into the rubber tubing. The rose, in a pot, was on top of a chest, which was hollow, open at the back, and set up against a flat. A hole was also cut in the flat and a stage manager crawled through and sat inside the chest to operate it." The *Times* (21 December 1948) admired the adaptation. Animal costumes and masks for this production once again hearkened back to Motley's designs for *Noah*, which, along

with *The Shoemaker's Holiday*, had been revived as part of the Young Vic repertory for 1947.

Important as they were for training actors and passing along Motley's principles to young designers, the Young Vic productions drew minimal attention from the reviewers. Chekhov's *The Wedding*, directed by George Devine at the Old Vic School in 1948, received little notice—even when it was revived in 1951 by the Old Vic Company at the Old Vic Theatre. In its cast were Devine, Sheila Ballantyne, and Powys Thomas. "It is one of those plays that's full of entertaining and amusing characters, which George understood perfectly," remembered Margaret Harris. "It was delightful, and terribly funny."

Early in January 1949, London audiences saw *As You Like It*, directed by Glen Byam Shaw. It was a Young Vic production for the Old Vic. Margaret Harris, who designed both sets and costumes, explained that "we based it on the medieval *milles fleurs* tapestries—very different from the *Richard of Bordeaux* tapestries. The costumes were seventeenth century, roughly Charles I. We had Jeanne Wilson, a big girl, playing Rosalind. We wanted to put her in breeches rather than tights, because I think girls look so awful trying to look like boys in tights. So we had to decide what her clothes should be like, and from that we decided on the period we would do it in. We decided to make her clothes look as if she'd borrowed them. They were too big for her, so she looked gauche, and rather delightful." Amidst general, if somewhat condescending praise for the efforts of the young actors, the *Times* (4 January 1949) complained that the director "lets his designers do one or two queer things, such as making part of the Forest of Arden resemble the submarine forest in which Captain Nemo went hunting and where all the branches grew vertically." Obviously, simplification and stylization put off this literal-minded critic. Just as obviously, the heady days of post-War euphoria had yielded to a sharper-eyed, less tolerant critical scrutiny as a new decade approached.

By 1950 the entire Old Vic organization was under strain. Expressing concern over costs, the Old Vic's Board of Governors questioned the value of the Old Vic Centre. Competition for funding and public support had emerged with the push for a "National Theatre" distinct from the Old Vic. Guest artists at the Old Vic Theatre—star actors such as Lawrence Olivier and directors such as Hugh Hunt and Tyrone Guthrie—quietly espoused emphasis on the Old Vic Theatre at the expense of the Young Vic activities, much to the consternation of the "Three Boys," as Saint-Denis, Devine, and Byam Shaw had been nicknamed.

Even as these shifts were underway behind closed doors, Margaret Harris designed the set for *Hamlet* at Kronborg Castle, Elsinore, where it had become an annual event. This *Hamlet* had originated at the New Theatre—the play's director Hugh Hunt was suspected of being antipathetic to the Young Vic and the School. When called upon by Hunt to design the set, Margaret Harris acquiesced and went to Denmark with him to plan it. "It was not a very happy experience," she recalled, saying that "Hugh was not very generous about 'The Boys.'" J. C. Trewin remembered it as "Michael Redgrave's Hamlet, unfussed, highly intelligent, and suitably acclaimed at Elsinore—where the company appeared early in June in the Kronborg courtyard."[3]

Almost as if to demonstrate how mistaken were Hugh Hunt and others who wished to eliminate the Vic School and the Young Vic, the next two productions designed for them by Motley reflected the strength of the original plan. *Bartholomew Fair* showed that the Young Vic and the School had matured into an operation that could mount a production using talent from the School, play it successfully outside London, and then bring it into the Old Vic for performances in December. *Henry V* demonstrated the integration of established talent with the newcomers in a wholly professional, innovative production.

Ben Jonson's *Bartholomew Fair* required a sizable cast with a large and intricate set that evoked the hurly-burly of the Renaissance fair. The revival was staged first at the Assembly Hall for the Edinburgh Festival in August 1950. For that venue, Margaret Harris ranged the stalls for the fair along the gallery at one end of the hall, with the main stall in the middle of the gallery. The action began on a built-out platform on the lower level, then moved through the stalls of the fair. At the Old Vic in December 1950 the designers put the stalls in short "streets" running downstage from the back rather than in a straight line across the back of the stage as they had done at the Edinburgh Festival. Because the play lampoons Puritans, Margaret Harris slightly caricatured the costumes. She padded people to make exaggerated shapes, adding excessive make-up and slightly comic wigs. "It was a massive prop show—hundreds and hundreds of props for the vendors in the play to sell," she remembered. "The students from the Design Course helped to make and set them up onstage."

"On the stage of the Old Vic," *Bartholomew Fair* "is twice as effective as it was in the vastness of the Edinburgh hall," reported the *Times* (19 December 1950). The concept behind the staging, as Frances Teague says in her account of the production, was to evoke the feeling of the fair itself, an ideal difficult to realize in the large Edinburgh space, less so at the Old Vic's smaller space.[4] Clouding the production, however, was the dissolution of the Vic Centre and the threatened resignations of the "Three Boys." J. B. Priestly said in *The Listener* that *Bartholomew Fair* deserved praise for "some astonishingly good character acting from the younger members of the Old Vic Company. . . . It will be a great pity if he [George Devine] together with his two brilliant colleagues, is allowed to resign from the Old Vic."[5] Yet of course, early in 1951 they did.

Bartholomew Fair, *Edinburgh Festival (transferred to the Old Vic Theatre), 1950. Clockwise from upper left: costume designs for Ursula, Troubleall, Cokes, and Busy. Motley Collection.*

That season the Old Vic itself had been refurbished. Bombed during the War, it was in need of extensive repair. There was an immediate short-term restoration, followed by substantial re-design of the stage for the 1950–1951 season. In an effort to break out of the proscenium arch, the designer Pierre Sonrel extended the forestage over the orchestra pit. "The Old Vic stage was rather special," recalled Margaret Harris. "It was a convex curve, projecting towards the audience. At the front there was a shallow, lower forestage, about two steps down, also convex, curving out from one proscenium door to the other. In the middle of the curved mainstage was an oval lift. If it was up it made the mainstage bigger, and if it was down, it made the forestage bigger." To bring the action nearer the audience, forestage entrances were also added in an arrangement "reminiscent of the Elizabethan stage," reported Alice Venezky with approval.[6]

Despite shaky funding and conflicts over the continued activity of the Old Vic Centre, the Old Vic Company's reputation for excellence in Shakespeare and classic drama continued. The Company presented the work of Britain's most experienced actors, directors, and designers. It was a showcase for excellence and theatrical innovation.

Henry V, directed by Glen Byam Shaw and designed by Margaret Harris, involved minimal settings. Evocative rather than representational, these settings, as the Chorus suggests, called upon the audience to complete the stage picture with their imaginations. The staging reflected powerfully the experience of combat in World War II, still fresh in everyone's minds. Without obvious updating, the play took on a contemporary edge. Alec Clunes as Henry, Dorothy Tutin as the Princess, and Paul Rogers as the Dauphin, joined by Mark Dignam and Richard Pasco, made a strong cast. The play opened 30 January 1951 to critical approval. Speaking for the consensus, Alice Venezky appreciated the "fluidity of staging, purity of text, and ensemble presentation with careful attention to each detail as well as to the over-all production. . . . The decor by Motley is as effective as the direction, with three carts of war creating the setting for the battle scenes, which take place in the several acting areas."[7]

"*Henry V* at the Vic with Glen Byam Shaw was one of the shows I always think of as a step forward," said Margaret Harris. "It was the first time I thought of using the stage with practically nothing on it. It's a natural play for minimal scenery, because the Chorus keeps apologizing for the lack of scenery. We had a bare stage, a low rostrum about three feet high round the back, and a cyclorama. Before the play began, the audience saw nothing on the stage but six apparently empty poles topped with crossbars, in two lines of three set from downstage to upstage. Then Roger Livesey as the Chorus appeared in Elizabethan costume for the speech 'O, for a muse of fire' and the 'Wooden O' and all that."

A basic problem in design for *Henry V* is the differentiation of the English and French without time-consuming costume or scene changes. Motley could draw upon their earlier experience with the play in 1937. "It was very different from the earlier *Henry V* we had done with Tony Guthrie, which was much more formal," Margaret Harris explained. To provide clear distinctions between the English and the French, she used a basic costume for all the extras, who could be transformed from English to French by a change of coat and hat. They had very close-fitting trousers, similar to tights, with one red and one blue leg. On opposite sides on the top were one red sleeve and one blue sleeve. When the extras were English soldiers or English attendants, they wore red coats and yellow hats, so that the legs and the sleeves of the basic costume were exposed. When they played the French, they wore long white tabards. When they played soldiers at war, they had rough coats and boots. The Duke of Burgundy was set apart from the other characters by his pale gray costume. "The actors didn't like the costumes much, because they were made of such thick stuff," said Margaret Harris, "but it allowed us to make very clear shapes, like fifteenth-century paintings."

When six extras came on for the first scene, they each stood next to an apparently bare pole with the crossbars at the top. On a certain cue, each pulled a halyard, and dark green velvet banners painted with a coat of arms came fluttering down the pole. The stage was dressed, and the King entered.[8] For the tennis-ball scene the English were dressed in reds and grays and browns, and the French were dressed in blues and whites. The French wore silver accessories, and the English wore gold. To represent Southampton, Motley arranged for masts with yardarms and rigging to be stored out of sight behind the back rostrum. By pulling on a single rope the masts could all be raised, providing a background that looked like ships in a harbor, instantly changing the scene. White banners were flown in to form a V shape with the point downstage over the heads of the actors when a scene took place in the French court. For the Princess scene, Motley used a painted cloth which dropped down from the flies. As it descended, a "canopy" painted on it swagged open to form an entrance, and the Princess and her maid entered through it, as if entering a pavilion. While that scene played, the cloth closed off the stage to allow for a set change behind it.

During the war scenes the stage was bare except for carts and a few guns. Because the carts were moveable, the acting areas became completely flexible. "It was the first time we'd used that idea" explained Margaret Harris. "If you wanted somebody in an elevated position in a certain part of the stage, you just took a cart there. The soldiers moved the carts about, brought them on, took them off, always for a reason of transporting something or fetching something." In the night scene, tiny campfires glowed onstage, evoking an army deployment. "We showed the model to Michel, going through it very carefully with him," said Margaret Harris. "He was rather mystified to start with. Suddenly, he said, 'Ah, I see what you are at.' He was very excited by the way we were doing it. It really did work."

Another Motley innovation for this show was a special lighting arrangement that eliminated the need for scene changes during the battle. The forestage ceiling contained openings so that lights could shine straight down. "When we had a very quick crossing scene of French soldiers, for instance," Margaret Harris explained, "we could black out the stage, then bring up the ceiling lights and make a light curtain. You could see the stage if you really tried, but not very clearly. The French soldiers were in pale costumes, which took the light well so that they could play scenes running across. We didn't have to change sets for them."

"The whole wartime experience of being on a campaign was very clear in Glen's mind," said Margaret Harris. Laurence Olivier, who had directed and starred in the wartime movie of the play, came to see the Old Vic Henry V. It pleased director and designer that their old friend appreci-

ated the military truth of the production. "What is marvelous is that you've made Henry's two big speeches so different," Margaret Harris recalled Olivier saying. "In the first one [IV, i, 1–34] Henry is clearly talking to the officers. He's planning things and his whole attitude is that of a general talking to his staff. In the 'Crispin, Crispian' speech to the army [IV, iii, 19–67], he is talking to the men. He's in charge of the situation in both directions, with the officers *and* with the men— but his attitude is different. I would never have thought of that, but it absolutely makes the play clear." As for Olivier's film, designed by Roger Furse, Margaret Harris thought it was "a bit of a hotchpotch between the pictorial scenery and the very real characters—the battle scenes, with the horses charging, were wonderful."

In the end, the visionary Old Vic plan as conceived by Saint-Denis, Devine, and Byam Shaw foundered for several reasons having to do more with the conflicting aims of the Old Vic Theatre, the Old Vic Centre, and plans for the National Theatre than with any inherent flaw in the plan itself. It left many who had been involved quite bitter. As Wardle recounts the ins and outs of the collapse, the "Three Boys" found themselves blocked by lack of funds and, in their view, betrayed by the Governors and by the directors Hugh Hunt and Tyrone Guthrie, who accepted the Governors' invitation to take over the running of the Old Vic Theatre and to close the Old Vic Centre. The Old Vic School simply stopped when the entire staff resigned in protest at these actions. No students applied, and the School closed at the end of the 1951 classes.

King John in 1953 was the last Shakespeare that Motley would design at the Old Vic. Despite a strong cast that included Michael Hordern, Richard Burton, and John Neville, the production did not succeed. Nor was it a happy experience for the two old friends who worked together on its staging. It was uncomfortable, even painful, for George Devine as director and Margaret Harris as designer to return to the premises, which everyone concerned with the School had vowed to shun after its breakup. Michel Saint-Denis had departed for France, the victim, it was whispered, of Francophobia among the supporters of the Vic and the National Theatre, one of whom was said to have vowed that "Britain's national theatre will not be run by a Frenchman!"[9]

The Old Vic Theatre itself was at this time being run by Michael Benthall, who had commissioned the designer James Bailey to build a permanent set for all the productions that season. With this arrangement in place, Motley were asked to do the sets and costumes for *King John,* with results that were hardly satisfactory to the designers or the critics. The play itself is difficult, best known as a vehicle for pageantry in the spectacular theatre of the nineteenth century and little produced in this century. Added to intrinsic problems with staging was the tension Motley encountered between the dark—almost black—neoclassical Renaissance permanent set and the medieval period of the play.

James Bailey's permanent set resembled the Renaissance Teatro Olimpico in Vincenza, with a heavy triple arch upstage and with two arched assembly entrances downstage. "Faced with this Renaissance permanent set for *King John,*" said Margaret Harris, "we decided that we would do the costumes basically Elizabethan, with medieval additions to suggest the period of the play. We didn't know quite what to do about the permanent set, so we put medieval cannons and various other medieval pieces behind Bailey's arches. The effect was not really very successful." For the costumes, Margaret Harris used a basic "Elizabethan" ensemble—trunks, tights, tunics; and distinguished the English in dark green suits from the French in black. She brightened the stage picture with brilliant colored canvas pieces, such as canvas cloaks, armor, shields, helmets, and twelfth-century weapons. Amidst praise for the actors and complaints about the episodic plot of the play, the critic for the *Times* (28 October 1953) faulted the directing, the sets, and the costumes: "The permanent set which has already done duty for *Hamlet* and for *All's Well That Ends Well* is much less friendly to this medieval play. It seems to be particularly unfriendly to the fighting scenes. Mr. Devine seems

to not have made up his mind whether to stylize them or to play them realistically, and to furnish the knights with casques that suggest visitors from Mars is to make the best of neither style." With this production Motley's second period at the Old Vic ended on a rather sad note.

During the post-War years between 1947 and 1951 Motley had once again found themselves part of a company. Working at different levels of professional skill, playing for different audiences, however battered by administrative and political distresses from outside, the Old Vic company fulfilled an ideal that would carry over in Glen Byam Shaw's company of experienced stars and young apprentice actors at the Shakespeare Memorial Theatre, Stratford-upon-Avon, and George Devine's English Stage Company at the Royal Court Theatre, London. At a time when other designers concentrated on remunerative commercial work, the two Motley women put first their dedication to their art and to their teaching. The breakup of the Vic School, disheartening as it was to all, did not destroy the company ideal, which flourishes today: That collaboration among director, actors, and designers marks the central ethos of theatre in Great Britain.

Decades later, one can see in the Vic efforts an attempt to rekindle the easy collaboration and the involvement of younger people that characterized Motley's studio and the London Theatre Studio in the 1930s. It is also true that the entire nature of theatre and theatre education were changing then and have changed since. Now, ad hoc theatre companies spring up overnight. Theatre training has become part of the mission of universities and community colleges in the United States and of universities and polytechnics in Great Britain. The great plan of the "Three Boys" plus Margaret and Sophia Harris lives on in the celebrated national companies of the Royal Shakespeare Theatre and the Royal National Theatre.

9

The English Stage Company and The Royal Court Theatre 1954–1966

During the early 1950s, the marriage of George Devine and Sophia Harris suffered in the turmoil surrounding the demise of the Old Vic. Devine was stretched thin by the tribulations of the Vic and by his insufficiencies (as he perceived them) as father and husband. She strained to combine the raising of her daughter Harriet with her husband's concerns and with her own design work. While Devine was consumed with the Vic, Sophia Harris became surrounded by a number of younger theatre artists, designers especially, who looked to her as an inspiration. She acted as the emotional and spiritual mother to many of these up-and-coming artists, among them students and graduates from the London Theatre Studio and the Vic School.[1] As her sister's partner in Motley, she continued designing costumes for West End plays, Shakespeare productions, and opera—work described in other chapters.

"The image I have of her as a designer, seats her at her scrubbed kitchen table in Lower Mall, with an up-turned dinner plate and poster paints for a palette, licking her paintbrush, painting design after design with casual elegance. She knew the human figure, and she handled the actors and fittings very well," remembered director Peter Gill. Her assistant, Reg Hanson, who later specialized in stage millinery, remembered her design process, which he watched unfold again and again: "First she read over the script and made notes, often talking to us about it. Then she discussed it with the director and the actors. *Then* she did the drawings, found the fabric, and ordered the costumes made. Next came the first fitting—there were usually three. 'Here,' she used to say, 'is where the design begins.' She had a wonderful eye for form and line and would take the line of the period and adjust it to suit the actor or actress and to express the character. She came to the dress rehearsal, of course, to make further adjustments. It was usually about five weeks from 'Will you please?' to "Thank you very much.' I don't know what she was paid, not more than £500 for a show, I wouldn't have thought."[2]

"So far as Motley were concerned, we were well established by the 1950s. We had all the work we wanted—*more* work than we wanted," said Margaret Harris. Whatever their burden of personal distresses Sophia Harris and George Devine continued to collaborate artistically. Despite the termination of the Vic School, Sophia Harris was in effect continuing to train young designers by keeping her home and studio open to them, discussing her work with them, and occasionally taking them on as assistants, most often for West End shows or films.

After a period of freelance work as a director, George Devine began to seek out new playwrights, young actors, and directors—among them William Gaskill, John Dexter, and Lindsay Anderson—to found the English Stage Company at the Royal Court Theatre in Sloane Square. In this enterprise Devine nurtured younger writers, later called the "Angry Young Men"—John Osborne, John Arden, Arnold Wesker, and other playwrights who turned against the idealizing bent of the theatre to confront social problems. These in turn inspired the next generation of English playwrights—Edward Bond, Howard Brenton, David Hare, and others. The wave of young playwrights and their concern for social issues would spread throughout the English theatre to the Royal Shakespeare Company, the Royal National Theatre, and the West End. What Devine got underway would affect the course of English drama in the latter twentieth century.

The nucleus of the English Stage Company, dedicated to new English plays and revivals of classics, began to form around the production of *Hedda Gabler* in 1954.[3] Led by George Devine, who took over from Peter Ashmore as director, the company were determined to bring the best in English talent to such plays as Ibsen's often-produced modern classic. The play presented Margaret and

Hedda Gabler, Lyric Theatre, Hammersmith *(transferred to the Westminster Theatre), 1954. Rough costume sketches for Peggy Ashcroft as Hedda. Motley Collection.*

Sophia Harris with a challenge: how to lighten the play's atmosphere of "sexless, penitential gloom, where, as Guthrie once pointed out, high thinking takes place in a world of dark crimson serge table-cloths and huge intellectual women in raincoats and boots."[4] The set was bright, sunlit, and elegantly pleasant. The production starred George Devine as Tesman, Michael MacLiammoir as Brach, Alan Badel as Lovborg, and Rachel Kempson as Mrs. Elvsted. It opened in Dublin, where, Peggy Ashcroft recalled, "They thought it was the greatest, wittiest, funniest play ever." When the production transferred from Dublin to the Westminster Theatre, the company toned down the comic business. *Theatre World* (October 1954, 24) called it "brilliantly successful," especially Peggy Ashcroft's "great triumph" as Hedda. It later transferred from the Westminster Theatre to the Lyric, Hammersmith. In early 1955, it toured Holland, Denmark, and Germany.[5]

By 1956 the English Stage Company had found a home in the Royal Court Theatre—once Granville-Barker's theatre. Again Devine used principles derived from those of Michel Saint-Denis's Compagnie des Quinze: ensemble acting, a "company" esprit de corps, and the primacy of the author's text governing production decisions. "To me it was an attitude to life, as well as to the theatre. It was a rejection of fame and wealth. What was important was one's work," remembered Jocelyn Herbert, who designed many productions for the Royal Court.[6] At that time, she recalled, Motley's work had become somewhat more "classical," suitable to history plays and established classics. It contrasted her own work, into which she tried to incorporate ideas from contemporary painting.

Following George Devine's idea that the theatre ought to open out into the reality of the world outside, Margaret Harris designed a permanent surround for the stage in this venerable theatre: "George and I had been trying for a long time to make a permanent surround for the Royal Court, a cloth with wing pieces. What we evolved was used for the first few productions, but it really wasn't very valid. I always think when a designer works out a permanent surround in the theatre, *that* designer can use it on any production, but when other designers come in, they can't accept it. When *I* used it, it worked; others found it difficult, if not impossible." As shown in the illustration, two white S-shaped vertical "surrounds," or curved legs, stood on either side of the stage with a back-panel that could be dropped in upstage to connect them. In front of the S-shaped side pieces hung a layer of netting—transparent most of the time—that with different lighting could create the illusion of hazy, indefinite distance. "We wanted something which will seem as impermanent and of the moment as the life that takes place on the stage," Devine told Wardle.[7] As things worked out, the beautiful effect of the gauze and the curved backdrop—inspired, some thought, by Brecht's stage in Berlin—proved impracticable because on that small stage the gauze kept getting snagged on movable sets or props.

The English Stage Company was dedicated to both classics and new plays—with particular interest in English authors. Whether new or old, the plays were selected for their engagement with contemporary social issues. Of the first season's five offerings, all were English except Arthur Miller's very American play *The Crucible*. The inaugural production of the season was by the novelist Angus Wilson. Since its premiere at the Bristol Old Vic, Wilson had extensively rewritten *The Mulberry Bush,* an "Oxford play" that exploited that familiar setting to probe social issues. The production received gentle treatment from W. A. Darlington in the *Daily Telegraph* (3 April 1956) and John Barber in the *Daily Express* (3 April 1956), yet it did not please the *Times's* critic (3 April 1956), who faulted the play, but praised some of the acting. Gwen Ffrangcon-Davies played Rose Padley, "who is so used to doing harm with the best of motives that she has become incapable of recognizing the harm she does." By June it had been "withdrawn from the repertory," reported *Theatre World* (June 1956). Motley's contemporary costumes and setting went unnoticed.

The House Un-American Activities Committee hearings chaired by Senator Joseph McCarthy had sparked Arthur Miller to write *The Crucible* in 1953. Though the Committee no longer posed a severe threat, the play still had great power. Staged at the Old Vic in 1954, it was re-staged under the direction of George Devine and Tony Richardson at the Royal Court in 1956. The excellent cast included Mary Ure as the accusing Abigail, Joan Plowright as her accomplice, George Devine as the judge, and Michael Gwynn and Rosalie Crutchley as John and Elizabeth Proctor, the accused husband

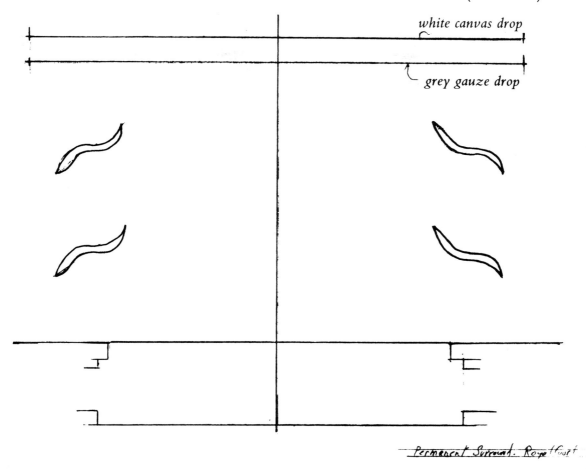

Stage plan for the Royal Court Theatre. Top: Permanent surround. Bottom: Detail of side masking. 20′0″ high.

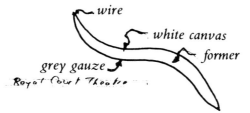

Timber former top and bottom, white flax canvas up stage, grey gauze down stage. Top former suspended, bottom former screwed to stage. To prevent bowing of onstage edge a wire dropped through small pocket and through a hole in the stage, and weighted down.

and wife. The *Times* (10 April 1956) cited Stephen Doncaster's setting and Motley's costumes as "simple to the point of severity and completely effective." *Theatre World* (June 1956) said flatly: "This is the production that should have inaugurated the English Stage Company's regime at the Royal Court Theatre."

By the beginning of the 1956–1957 theatre season, the English Stage Company were seen as saviors of British drama in the face of foreign challenges. "The need for such a bold venture was imperative," proclaimed *Plays and Players* (August 1956): "What these rebels have in common is a determination to bring our drama back to grips with the harsh realities of life and to give expression to whatever angry sentiments they might feel. All have something of value to say and, equally admirable, the guts to say it." Such sentiments, then rare, would take more than a decade to mature into the protest drama of the later 1960s.

George Devine was concerned with developing new directing talent as well as new playwrights. Like his mentor, Tony Richardson was an alumnus of Wadham College at Oxford and past president of the O.U.D.S. (1949–1951). After a stint at BBC Television, he joined Devine's English Stage Company as Associate Director in 1955. That year, he directed his first play for the English Stage Company—a new work by a young man his own age named John Osborne. *Look Back in Anger* was to mark a new direction in British theatre, rejecting in its content and staging the values of the comfortable middle class. Along with Brecht's *Mother Courage* and Beckett's *Waiting for Godot,* both staged in London in 1955, *Look Back in Anger,* said the authoritative theatre critic Harold Hobson, "set the course of the British theatre for the next quarter of a century, begat a host of inferior imitators, almost destroyed the commercial theatre, stimulated the move towards the establishment of a National Theatre, encouraged the proliferation of fringe theatres, and, though they were all extremely entertaining themselves, enabled their less talented followers to propagate the theory that entertainment in a play is a mark of mindless frivolity."[8]

The play tells the story of the idealistic Alison (Mary Ure), who meets and falls in love with her university classmate, the working-class Jimmy Porter (Kenneth Haigh), a scholarship student. They complete their studies and marry. As the play opens, they are living together in a squalid flat. Neither is happy, despite honest efforts on both their parts and well-intended pressures from friends and parents. As the play unfolds, the couple's differing social backgrounds, exacerbated by interfering parents and friends, ignite one conflict after another.

Sophia Harris's costumes evoked the pathos and conflict of Alison and Jimmy's ill-fated love. In Alan Tagg's setting—the dingy flat inspired critics to coin the term "kitchen-sink drama" for plays of this genre—Alison in her silk slip stands beautiful and vulnerable as she struggles to understand and

Look Back in Anger, *Royal Court Theatre, 1956 (later transferred to the Lyric, Hammersmith, and the Lyceum, New York). The working-class Jimmy Porter (Kenneth Haigh) confronts his distraught upper-class wife Alison (Mary Ure). Photograph courtesy of the Raymond Manders and Joe Mitchenson Theatre Collection, London.*

comfort her angry, embittered, and dangerous husband. Jimmy finds himself caught between the dreams of his education and shabby reality. These costumes marked a new dimension to Sophia Harris's designing. For the new plays—and films—of social realism the designer had to have an extraordinarily accurate eye for the way "real" people, especially working-class people, dressed. Anything slightly wrong would be picked up by the contemporary audience. Her costumes were unobtrusive, but exactly right.

Reviewers at first panned the show. "In the opening night reviews," recalled Margaret Harris,

Hamlet, *New Theatre, 1934.*

Hamlet, *New Theatre, 1934.*

The Happy Hypocrite, *His Majesty's Theatre, 1936.*

Three Sisters, *Queen's Theatre, 1938.*

Miss Liberty, *Imperial Theatre, New York, 1949.*

Henry V, *Old Vic Theatre, 1951.*

Colombe, *New Theatre, 1951.*

Paint Your Wagon, *Shubert Theatre, New York, 1951.*

Antony and Cleopatra, *Shakespeare Memorial Theatre, Stratford-upon-Avon, 1953.*

Antony and Cleopatra, *Shakespeare Memorial Theatre, Stratford-upon-Avon, 1953.*

Antony and Cleopatra, *Shakespeare Memorial Theatre, Stratford-upon-Avon, 1953.*

Antony and Cleopatra, *Shakespeare Memorial Theatre, Stratford-upon-Avon, 1953.*

Othello, *Shakespeare Memorial Theatre, Stratford-upon-Avon, 1956.*

The Merry Wives of Windsor, *Shakespeare Memorial Theatre, Stratford-upon-Avon, 1955.*

The First Gentleman, *Belasco Theatre, New York, 1957.*

King Lear, *Shakespeare Memorial Theatre, Stratford-upon-Avon, 1959 (five costume sketches).*

The Tulip Tree, *Haymarket Theatre, 1967.*

Il Trovatore, *Metropolitan Opera House, New York, 1959.*

The Merchant of Venice, *Haymarket Theatre, 1967.*

Margaret Harris in her office at the Motley Design Course.

"it was absolutely slated." *The Times* (26 May 1956) ran a follow-up article, two weeks after the first review, arguing that the play did not speak for today's youth: it misrepresented them. By the end of the summer, however, critical opinion had shifted. *Plays and Players* (August 1956) saw the production as the restoration of serious drama to the English theatre. With the exception of *Separate Tables,* said the reviewer, "every stimulating play in London was an importation from either Paris or Broadway, and it seemed as though our own writers were going to spend the rest of their lives turning out pot-boiling thrillers or insipid tea-table comedies. . . . John Osborne has launched a bitter attack on smugness and hypocrisy wherever he sees it in the world around him. . . . And the result is exciting theatre, bold, full-blooded and provocative." Audiences agreed, and the production went into an extended run before it toured England and then transferred to New York, perhaps even ensuring the existence of the English Stage Company. Margaret Harris, who went to Moscow with the touring production in 1958, recalled that from a design standpoint "there was nothing particularly remarkable about the production." In London it won an award for best new play. Summing up the positive responses to the play, Kenneth Tynan (*Observer*) said it presented "post-war youth as it really is." The *Financial Times* called it "a play of extraordinary importance."[9]

Nigel Dennis's *Cards of Identity,* based on his own zany novel, followed in the Royal Court repertory. It enjoyed nothing like the success of Osborne's play. An interesting sidelight on an otherwise dismissable satire on psychoanalysis: playwright John Osborne played the small part of Dr. Scavenger. "Baffling but stimulating," *Plays and Players* (August 1956) said sympathetically. "The satire," said the *Times* (27 June 1956), "comes out as a spray of cold and clever ideas which have been imperfectly dramatized." "It was quite a funny play," said Margaret Harris. "Sophie had great wit and designed wonderful comedy costumes."

Following *Cards of Identity,* in a gambit to bail themselves out of a deficit of £13,000, the English Stage Company performed William Wycherley's *The Country Wife* as a special Christmas show. The bawdy Restoration comedy revolving around the rake Jack Horner's escapades with other men's wives—escapades made easier by his giving out that he is no longer a danger to women—must have seemed a rather radical departure from the ESC's dedication to putting on new plays with contemporary relevance. With Joan Plowright as the wife and Laurence Harvey as Horner, however, it was a great success. The production transferred to the West End and then to New York, where Elizabeth Montgomery helped with the costumes originally designed by Sophia Harris. Its stylized costumes and sets gave it a distinctly contemporary twist.

The sets were made of transparent plastic, with only line-drawings of architectural details. Motley built a gently raked stage over the real stage. Narrow and deep, the false stage led from upstage right downstage with a slight false perspective getting wider as it came downstage. "As I made the model," said Margaret Harris, "I was thinking of making all the sets and furniture with metal work. Because it was very difficult to make in model form, I drew it all on perspex [transparent plastic] with black or white ink—the furniture, all sorts of inn signs, doorways, and arches. George [Devine] came to see the model and he said 'Why don't we do it like that? Why don't we draw it on cobex [another strong and fireproof transparent plastic]?' So that is what we did." They applied the cobex to a light wooden framework and then drew the architectural designs in outline with black or white paint. The scenery was simply dropped in—a doorway, or an archway, or some inn signs, a window, or the like—to permit continuous acting through changes of scene. There was a problem with the blinding reflection of light off the cobex into the audience, but if the lines that held it vertical were eased slightly, the cobex leaned forward a few inches at the top, and the light was reflected entirely onto the stage. The floor was shining black, painted with a linoleum paint and white lines to appear tessellated. Onto the front of the stage Motley built a false stage, a box with a trap containing rolled up carpets: one yellow and one blue. When it came time to change from one scene to another, these carpets could be pulled upstage with various mechanical devices so that they changed the floor from one interior to another—or to exteriors. "It was fun to see the carpets slowly running upstage," remembered Margaret Harris. "It meant we had to have wires on the stage to

The Country Wife, *Royal Court Theatre, 1956 (transferred to the Adelphi Theatre, New York). In the costume sketch, the only touch of color was the bright Chinese red trim on the lady's fan. This style carried throughout the costumes and set, stylizing and lightening the mood of this Restoration comedy. Motley Collection.*

serve as guides when the carpets were rolled up. The wires were always there. They were flat on the stage and didn't seem to worry the actors."

The costumes were caricatures of seventeenth-century fashions. Horner's brass earrings, yellow sash, and cherry-red high heels came in for some commentary. Their simplified lines made it clear that this was a contemporary re-staging, rather than a period piece. "Both costumes and sets were entirely in black and white with tiny touches of color in the accessories or in the carpets," recalled Harriet Jump, Sophia Harris's daughter. "Each character had just one spot of primary color—a red fan, a blue handkerchief, or a yellow head-dress. The 'town ladies' were mostly in black, with a little white. The virtuous Althea was in pale gray. Margery Pinchwife, the country wife, was mostly in white, with touches of black. So, though there was no color to speak of, the costumes were able to give very good indications of the characters' traits. Although the play's setting was contemporary when it was first performed in the 1670s, she moved the period to the early 1700s, when they had those very, very straight Persian coats and the women had fontanges [tall headdresses]," she said. Margaret Harris especially remembered the hats: "We didn't have much money to spend, and Sophie made these wonderful hats. All the feathers were made out of cut and curled muslin. If you draw a knife down a strip of muslin, it curls. She made all the feathers that way. It was quite enjoyable."

Apparently nostalgic for three-dimensional sets and broad farce, the *Times* (13 December 1956) wrote that "Motley's cellophane settings make an intrinsically pleasing effect of light and cool elegance, but it is an effect which somewhat emphasizes the tendency of the playing to thin out the full-blooded jokes." Kenneth Tynan (*Observer*, 13 December 1957) saw it another way: "Motley's costumes, clever as they are, do not quite come off. . . . But the décor, teased out of what seems to be wrought iron and perspex, is of a delicacy almost Gallic." Even with the popular Julie Harris taking over Joan Plowright's part, the New York critics were less than kind: "Decrepit Romp But Julie Tries," ran the headline on John McClain's review in the *Journal American* (29 November 1957). The show inaugurated the ESC's conception of "pylon" productions—productions of classic plays that would anchor the company by providing a traditional standard against which to measure new plays. It was hoped that they would underwrite those new plays with solid box office. For Margaret and Sophia Harris as Motley, the policy meant opportunities to bring their gift for period costumes into play.

In June 1957 George Devine announced the formation of the English Stage Society—as distinct

The Country Wife, *Royal Court Theatre, 1956.*
Lady Fidget (Diana Church), Horner (Laurence Har-
vey), and Mrs. Pinchwife (Joan Plowright). Photo-
graph courtesy of the Raymond Manders and Joe
Mitchenson Theatre Collection, London.

from the English Stage Company—as another vehicle for developing new plays: staging them
"without decor" on Sunday nights when the theatres would be otherwise dark. His assistant John
Dexter took charge of the initiative and Sophia
Harris was from time to time involved, even
though costumes and scenery were ostensibly to
be absent. "'The aim of the English Stage Society,'
explained Mr. Dexter, 'is to get a play performed
as cheaply as possible so that its genuine value can
be assessed. . . . When a play is chosen for production by the English Stage Society, it is rehearsed
almost to dress rehearsal level and played before a
Sunday night audience without any embellishment
in the way of staging. Only absolute necessities

in the way of scenery and properties are used,'"
reported *Theatre World* (July 1957, 37).

The premiere of Faulkner's *Requiem for a Nun,*
directed by Tony Richardson at the Royal Court,
starred Zachary Scott and Ruth Ford, who had
come to London from America to do it. The play
and the production won accolades for the playwright, the director, the designers, and the actors.
"There is nothing on the London Stage today one-
tenth as powerful as this tense drama," began the
notice for *Requiem for a Nun* in the *Times* (27 November 1957). Indeed, Faulkner's play, which had
sought an American staging in vain, found a home
at the Royal Court in London, where its controversial subject matter raised no objections. For its
first run, the actress Ruth Ford, a friend of Faulkner's for whom the part of Temple Blake was said
to have been written, urged George Devine to
stage the play. He did, with such success that the
production then transferred to New York. Ford

did play Temple Blake—a lawyer's wife whose sojourn in a cathouse during her college days put her in such a moral quagmire that her baby's black nanny murders the child, lest it be raised by such a harridan. Margaret Harris designed the sets; Sophia Harris, the costumes. It had a very simple set. Two big louvered doors upstage center backed somewhat stylized representations of a courtroom, a living room, the governor's office and the jail. Above them all hung an American eagle clutching the scales of justice. Sophia Harris designed the costumes in period and in character.

However successful the production, it was an unpleasant experience for Margaret Harris: "I simply *hated* the play. I can't *bear* it! Then again I don't like any of those plays about the American South. I find Faulkner and Tennessee Williams very unpleasant. There is something so terribly sordid about them to me. The Southern attitude to me is very frightening." She remembered Richardson as a rather brash young director: "Tony Richardson was away while I was working on it. When he came back, I presented him with whatever idea I'd had. He said, 'Oh yes, that's all right. But I want you to do ten different ideas, and let me choose.' I said, 'I can't!' [*Laughing*]. The set we eventually used, we evolved together."

Bernard Shaw's *Major Barbara*, which had had its premiere at the Royal Court in 1905, returned to the same theatre in George Devine's 1958 production. It benefited from an "operatic style . . . advocated by Shaw," as the *Daily Telegraph* (29 August 1958) put it, meaning that Devine minimized stage business and let the ebb and flow of the dialogue-debates stand on their own. Alan Webb played Undershaft as "unusually dangerous"; Frances Rowe, Lady Britomart "in the grand manner of high comedy"; and Joan Plowright, Barbara, as, "merely adequate." Margaret Harris's sets and men's clothes and Sophia Harris's costumes for the women were done realistically in period. There was a touch here and there of gently burlesque exaggerations of the period. "We wanted the effect of a sepia photograph," Margaret Harris said. "We tried to do it very, very simply because as always at the Royal Court there wasn't very much money. I tried to make the set look a bit like those Victorian drawings of slums. The first scene is in a Salvation Army yard with Salvation Army hut, then there is the drawing room, and then a scene on the

Rosmersholm, *Royal Court Theatre, 1959. Costume sketch for Rosmer's companion Rebecca West (Peggy Ashcroft). Motley Collection.*

lookout up at the top. We used hessian instead of scene canvas, which was painted to give the feeling of a drawing."

A modern classic, *Rosmersholm* by Henrik Ibsen was Motley's next show at the Royal Court, by now a thriving theatrical institution in Sloane Square. It starred Peggy Ashcroft as Rebecca West, Eric Porter as Rosmer, and Mark Dignam as Kroll. "Sophie and I did it quite simply," said Margaret Harris. "The back wall had four wooden columns with a door in the middle and portraits hung between them. It was the normal Royal Court approach, played very straightforwardly but understood in depth." Garbed in costumes that emphasized an atmosphere of oppressive conformity, in which "every character has the bright, alert hostility of a duelist," as Harold Hobson put it in the *Times* (19 November 1959), *Rosmersholm* presented "Peggy Ashcroft at her best." When the show transferred to the Comedy Theatre in the West End, W. A. Darlington proclaimed it "the highlight of 1959." *Theatre World* (January 1960, 19) called it simply, "one of the finest productions now to be seen in London." The talented cast could have been betrayed by sets and costumes that were historically true to the play's period, yet unable to express it afresh. Rather, as Carol Brahms wrote in *Plays and Players* (January 1960, 11), Motley avoided "the usual cluttered scene with the usual green plush chairs waiting, as usual to be sat upon heavily in moments of stress. . . ." By choosing drab colors and dull furnishings, the designers helped the actors create a world of middle-class conformity in which a housekeeper could drive her mistress to suicide and a staunch conservative could discover too late the validity of his rivals' causes.

Motley designed a courtroom trial play, *The Naming of Murderer's Rock,* at the Royal Court the next season. It was a docudrama written by Frederick Bland and directed by John Bird about a famous New Zealand murder trial. As "powerful, somber, and extremely effective," as critic Bernard Levin found it (23 November 1960), the show failed to please the *Times*'s critic (31 November 1960), who seemed puzzled that such a well-acted play could be so inconclusive. For Margaret Harris and Sophia Harris, it was a straightforward task made problematical by having to present a courtroom in the theatre and the hanging of the men at the play's end. "There was a court scene with the usual problems of a court scene—where to put the Judge," said Margaret Harris. "If you put him upstage facing downstage, everybody else has to play up to him. If you don't, he has to play up to everybody else. We did, in fact, put him upstage center. Then came a scene with the gallows where they were hanging the men. Those being hanged each had a harness on, so when they went through the trap they were caught around the waist and not the neck."

With the exception of costumes for *Song in the Theatre,* a Christmastime revue by Dudley Moore, for three years Motley's name appeared in the Royal Court credits for only one production, *You*

in Your Small Corner, which opened in October, 1960 and was revived the following March. Critics found flaws in this second play by Barry Reckord. Set in Brixton, it is the unhappy tale of interracial romance—Jamaican boy and English girl—complicated by class strife. His mother is a successful club owner, her family are down on their luck. As a photo of the set model shows, this revival of an earlier staged reading "without decor," extended the line of "kitchen sink" plays.

By 1964, when she designed costumes for her last production at the Royal Court, the Ben Travers farce *A Cuckoo in the Nest,* Sophia Harris and George Devine had come some distance from the earnest encouragement of young playwrights and the presentation of socially relevant drama at the ESC's beginnings. George Devine, still artistic director, had by now separated from Sophia Harris and had been living with Jocelyn Herbert for several years. When their household dissolved, as Margaret Harris remembered, "Sophie and George went through all her things and chucked out a lot of designs and records, which was a great pity." Sophia Harris, in turn, had become more and more involved with designing costumes for films, as described in chapter 11. Her period costume designs for Frank Wedekind's *Spring Awakening* in 1965 were the last she did for the Royal Court. The revival of the once-controversial 1890 play about awakening adolescent sexuality, "palpably a one-night affair," according to the *Times*'s disgruntled critic (22 April 1965), was redeemed by "a brilliant performance by Nicol Williamson." For her part, Margaret Harris had since 1960 been working principally in the West End and at the English National Opera.

After she and George Devine separated, Sophia Harris remained in close contact with the community of artists that had grown up around the English Stage Company and the Royal Court. Not only did she often design costumes for their productions, but she continued to serve as an informal teacher to the young designers with whom she worked, extending an earlier pattern from the London Theatre Studio and the Old Vic School and anticipating Margaret Harris's instruction at the Design Course at the English National Opera, then in embryo. As recalled by her protégés Peter Gill and Reg Hanson, as well as by her daughter Harriet, who was then a teenager, the house on

Sophia Harris in her studio, Lower Mall, Hammersmith, 1956. Standing behind her on the balcony is her daughter Harriet. The photograph comes from Motley's files.

Lower Mall, Hammersmith, became a kind of informal clubhouse to which young designers and actors came to meet with "Sophie," who presided there as the unassuming chatelaine. "The last thing she said to me, when I stopped in and she was dying," said Peter Gill, " was, 'Darling, there's something in the fridge.' She was witty, elegant, and full of affection for us all."[10] In their recollec-

tions, one catches echoes of Motley's early years in the Chippendale studio on St. Martin's Lane and of Margaret Harris's later "open house" and exhibitions at the Motley Design School. Surrounded by friends and in the midst of her work, Sophia Harris nonetheless did not meet an easy death, succumbing to cancer in 1966.

10
The Shakespeare
Memorial Theatre
1948–1959

The work for which Motley came to be known most widely were their designs for Shakespeare plays in Stratford-upon-Avon. Collaborating closely with directors Glen Byam Shaw, George Devine, and Anthony Quayle, the Motleys, and particularly Margaret Harris, crafted a coherent, thoughtful approach to Shakespeare's plays. Their productions were flawlessly executed, using the resources of a great theatre and a great acting company. As Motley in New York had come to mean the very best in theatre design, Motley at Stratford marked another pinnacle in their career. At Stratford, their shows were seen by hundreds of thousands, who came from all over the world, and by more hundreds of thousands in foreign capitals as the productions toured. For many, these productions represent the best Shakespeare of the 1950s.

The first Stratford production designed by Motley had been the updated *Twelfth Night* directed by Irene Hentschel in 1939. After the War, when Elizabeth Montgomery came from New York for a visit in 1948, she joined Margaret Harris at the invitation of Anthony Quayle. He was directing two plays for the Shakespeare Memorial Theatre, Stratford-upon-Avon: *The Winter's Tale*, starring Esmond Knight, and *Troilus and Cressida*, starring Paul Scofield and Heather Stannard. In preparation for the productions, Margaret Harris and Elizabeth Montgomery, accompanied by Elizabeth's hus-

band Patrick Wilmot, journeyed to Stratford-upon-Avon to design the sets and costumes. As the plays went into production, the two women travelled back and forth from London. "I don't remember much about those two productions," said Margaret Harris. "Probably because I was also working at the Old Vic School at the same time. Elizabeth did most of the coping with them."

For *The Winter's Tale*, Motley chose a Russian milieu: "There is nothing soft, or even Sicilian, about the Sicilian king's court, as Motley presents it," said the *Times* (7 June 1948): "The curtain rises on a Bacchanalia, a scenic overture preparing our minds, by Motley's memories of Bakst, for the notion that Hermione, daughter of a Russian emperor, has caught a Tartar for a husband. . . . The Asiatic setting is not only strange and beautiful in itself but the strangeness suits a tale which asserts at every turn the right of romance to laugh at psychology." While other critics admired the innovation, the *Manchester Guardian* (7 June 1948) complained that the "plangent spectacle . . . of Scythian Sicily" made Bohemia "by contrast flat and tepid."

In a rare staging, *Troilus* was transported to a time and place remote from Troy. "In spite of Motley's odd determination to persuade us that the Greek camp outside Troy resembled a Polar explorer's advanced bivouac," quipped *Punch* (14

July 1948), the production "is a fair success." To the *Manchester Guardian* (5 July 1948), "the Greeks looked Partisan-like, with their rough jerkins and enormous medal-ribbons," and the Trojan's city recalled a "war-time Cairo." The shifting of period, which had been a controversial design concept for decades, snapped the reviewers to attention. They focused on the designer's concept, an approach Motley generally decried.

In 1949–1950, as the Old Vic enterprise was collapsing, Stratford was also in the midst of change. Before the War, it had gained a reputation for good, sometimes experimental Shakespeare. During the War, shortages of goods and people pulled down its artistic standards. In an effort to improve Stratford's reputation, immediately after the War the governors of the theatre had appointed Barry Jackson as artistic director. The founder of the Birmingham Rep, Jackson was a director known especially for staging Shakespeare in modern dress. When he ran up a huge deficit at Stratford, so the story goes, the governors turned to Anthony Quayle, expecting him to bring in stars from the West End. By employing London stars and top-flight production standards, the governors hoped to draw the crowds that would rescue the box office. Thus, in 1949, Quayle was appointed artistic director.

After directing shows at Stratford during the 1951 and 1952 seasons, Glen Byam Shaw was named Quayle's co-director in 1953. It was a natural alliance, because the two had worked together since the 1930s. Quayle, in turn, took the 1953 company on tour to Australia and New Zealand. Byam Shaw took over as sole director in 1957, holding the position until 1959, after which Peter Hall succeeded him. The royal charter granted in 1961 changed the name from the Shakespeare Memorial to the Royal Shakespeare Theatre.

In the decade under Quayle and then Shaw, the theatre attained international preeminence, due in no small part to the high standard of directing, acting, and production brought to it by the two men, their colleagues from before the War, and the new actors and directors they were fostering in the nascent Stratford company. Quayle and Byam Shaw brought in Gielgud, Ashcroft, Olivier, Richardson, and Devine, as well as such younger actors as Roy Dotrice, Ian Holm, and Dorothy Tutin and young directors Peter Brook and Peter Hall. Al-

though they by no means monopolized design at Stratford, Motley in the person of Margaret Harris, sometimes with Sophia Harris creating costumes, designed more productions than anyone else during this period.

As these collaborators put together one season after another, the Stratford theatre evolved from a sometimes interesting provincial theatre to an international showcase for the best British talent.[1] It drew hundreds of thousands of visitors from home and abroad. In 1955, reported *Plays and Players* (April 1955, 22), "The bookings for the first eight weeks of the season has been sensational." For 81,900 seats at sixty-three performances, the hard-to-reach Shakespeare Memorial Theatre had received 500,000 booking requests.

The remarkable success of the Shakespeare Memorial Theatre in the 1950s was not only a matter of big names and a busy box office. It also fostered the company spirit that gave rise to the present-day Royal Shakespeare Company, in which actors, directors, and designers all collaborate closely. With this growth in stature, the company gained international renown. The first tour outside Britain and Europe to Australia in 1953 featured the Motley-designed production of *As You Like It*. Motley's contributions belong to the decade during which the Stratford company's rise to international fame gathered force.

"I loved Stratford," Margaret Harris recalled. "The staff and the whole atmosphere were marvelous, and it got better and better with Glen. He took so much trouble with the people in the town and with the staff. Fred Jenkins, the construction carpenter, was a wonderful craftsman, carpenter, and engineer—a real man of the theatre. It was a small staff, perhaps twenty men on the stage, whereas at the London Coliseum now they have about seventy—three shifts round the clock. These men worked all the shifts, and they really enjoyed doing it. The audiences, too, were marvelous. The majority were foreign, but they really enjoyed it very much; the theatre was always completely packed. Glen made a great deal of money for the theatre with the productions and the tours. They had a big bank balance when he left in 1959. I think one of the reasons Tony Quayle got Glen in was because he was going to go to Australia with a tour, and he wanted to have somebody he could really trust there. I suppose Tony was also thinking of leaving Stratford himself. Glen enjoyed it tremendously, even though it was such an enormous responsibility.

"It was, I think, the happiest time I ever had, those eight years in Stratford. I used to stay very often in Glen's cottage. He had a little room there where I could work. But I always had a workroom in the theatre. The nicest one was a room up on the balcony in the Conference Hall, the big rehearsal room. [The space was remodeled and named the Swan Theatre in 1986.] I had a little room up there, and I used to be able to pop out and look at rehearsals. It was very, very nice; I liked working up there.

"The Shakespeare Memorial Theatre was also marvelous, because you were part of a company. It wasn't like London, when you just go in, do a show, and that's that. There it was really a 'company' feeling; it was marvelously enjoyable. When Peg [Peggy Ashcroft] was there it was especially wonderful. There was something about Peg. She was a great leader for the company. Everybody loved her, and everybody enjoyed doing things with her. She enjoyed everything so much, and she really worked at it. She was there for two years at least when I was there. Some of the time I stayed with Glen and Angela [Baddeley, his wife], and some of the time I stayed with Peg out at Avoncliff, a lovely house that was always given to the leading actors or directors for the season."

The 1952 Stratford season marked the beginnings of the company's rise to international fame with the announcement that Stratford was committed to a second season in London. There would now be two companies. One company would prepare and perform plays in Stratford, some of which would transfer to London, and a second company would be formed for the following season in Stratford. By bringing in Glen Byam Shaw as his co-director, Anthony Quayle was able to take on responsibility for activities outside Stratford. And, for his part, Byam Shaw could count on the help of Margaret Harris, his preferred designer.

Coriolanus, the first play produced by the new regime, saw Anthony Quayle as Coriolanus, Mary Ellis playing Volumnia, Michael Hordern as the patrician, Menenius Agrippa, and Laurence Harvey as Tullus Aufidius, with Byam Shaw directing. Margaret Harris used Roman costume for the Romans and Cretan costumes for the Volscis. "Laurence Harvey was marvelous to dress," she remembered. "He had the most amazing figure, and he wore clothes very glamorously." The sets were another matter. Her original idea for a raised platform running around the back of the stage became overly complicated, she later thought, with a large ramp coming down from a center door for Rome, pikes that stuck up from below for Corioli. "It was clumsy and heavy, from my point of view," she said. The production must have had special appeal to audiences who so recently had seen military service. "Anthony Quayle," wrote *The Times* (14 March 1952), for example, "presents the hero as a tough soldier with a parade ground rasp in his voice." It was a domestic interpretation, rather than a political one; more about a soldier than a patrician. For a play generally thought to be unpopular, the production won the critics' approval. "Motley's decor is dignified and soberly beautiful," wrote the *Stratford-on-Avon Herald* (21 March 1952), "and the producer probably has his good reasons for neglecting the spectacular possibilities of fights, crowds, and processions."

To avoid the expected pastoral greensward, Margaret Harris set the 1952 *As You Like It* in winter, put the women in Louis XIII gowns, and dressed the men as Van Dyck cavaliers. Margaret Leighton and Laurence Harvey as Rosalind and Orlando received warm praise from the critics. "They were very much in love then," remembered Margaret Harris. "It always seems to happen when people play Rosalind and Orlando—they fall in love with each other." Michael Hordern played an excellent Jaques, she added.

Traditionally the play had been set in high summer. Byam Shaw and Margaret Harris's idea was to begin the play in winter, then move into spring and end in summer. The first scene with Orlando on the farm was snowy. A white felt floorcloth gave the impression of snow on the ground. The wintry forest contained a cave built of branches and plants that were painted as if they were snow-covered. After the interval, a different set evoked springtime. As the tenor of the play became happier, the set became more and more summery. "Sometimes, to change the location of the action, a front gauze appliquéd with great sweeps of leaves came down. It wasn't quite as good as I wanted it to be," recalled Margaret Harris. "It drove me mad doing the model, and then they never could quite make enough leaves to do it. It could have worked rather well, but the images behind didn't quite push through properly."

The *Manchester Guardian* (30 April 1952) found the staging "rich and picturesque in a rather cramped way, with much use of the arras curtain," and *The Times* (30 April 1932) pointed out that "the elegant fashion of the French court, all silk and lace," couldn't do much to keep the actors warm. Nor did the press approve of Rosalind's disguise. As the *Stratford-upon-Avon Herald* (2 May 1952) complained, Margaret Leighton was "hampered by the clothes assigned to Ganymede, for, in an effort to get away from the hackneyed (but becoming) doublet and hose, Motley provided her with an adaptation of the costume affected by transatlantic girl cyclists on long, dusty tours." Others objected to "tropical vegetation" in the Forest of Arden. When the production was being readied for touring Australia and New Zealand, notices such as that in the Birmingham *Gazette* (4 December 1952), called it "the one unqualified success of the recent Festival season." It was well received overseas.

The Shakespeare Memorial Theatre attracted the attention of the newly crowned Queen Elizabeth and her consort Prince Philip. What was to have been a solemn event—a royal visitation—turned out to be somewhat informal. "They came to a big lunch laid on in the theatre restaurant, with everybody else kept out," Margaret Harris recalled. "The Queen was at one end of the table, and Philip was at the other end. It was a long, long table. She came in with Glen and Fordham Flower, chairman of the theatre's Board of Governors. Queen Elizabeth sat down, because she has to sit down before anyone else could. Prince Philip shouted from the other end of the table, 'You'll have to stand up again. There's a chap here wants to say Grace.' And so she stood up, the Canon said Grace, and we all sat down again. After the performance they came onto the stage and met the cast. Prince Philip was very interested in what the leaves were made of, because they were plastic, and he was promoting plastic at that time."

The following year, the 1953 "Coronation Season," featured five plays alternately directed by Byam Shaw and Anthony Quayle. Now co-directors, the pair assembled a star-studded company that included Harry Andrews, Peggy Ash-croft, Tony Britton, Marius Goring, Yvonne Mitchell, and Michael Redgrave. Motley designed both *Richard III*, starring Marius Goring, and *Antony and Cleopatra*, starring Michael Redgrave and Peggy Ashcroft. The eight-month season broke box-office records, drawing 360,000 people and taking in nearly £180,000 sterling. Quayle then took *As You Like It* on tour to Australia.

For Motley, the Coronation Season brought a small triumph in the crisply designed *Richard III* and a far greater one in the world-renowned *Antony and Cleopatra*. As good designs, both stand up to examination. Margaret Harris's sets and costumes for *Richard III* nicely distinguished the competing factions, elegantly suggested the period, and, with some allowance for better production resources and a growing taste for minimalism in the theatre, recapitulated the style of such earlier historical dramas as *Richard of Bordeaux*. It was quality Motley, yet not sufficiently exciting for the critics to notice especially, particularly when they had the shortcomings of the established star Marius Goring to analyze.

Although the scholar Clifford Leech aptly pointed out that the Stratford *Richard III* took on special interest as the sequel to the Birmingham Rep's *Henry VI* trilogy, others focused on Marius Goring's Richard.[2] Newspaper critics faulted Goring for his overly naturalistic acting. The *Times* (25 March 1953) wrote, "Such villainy can be represented on the stage only in the grand style, and for this style Mr. Goring has little natural taste." Even the lank, long, red hair, the beetle-like carapace of the black armor for his deformity and the club-foot shoe given him by Motley were not enough to help the actor convince the audience of his malignity. Motley's stylized spiderweb-like setting evoked a kind of distorted medievalism consistent with the play's heightened, almost melodramatic reality, but at odds with Goring's acting style. In an interview with the author years later, he confessed that he had been "terribly awestruck by Olivier's film, but ever grateful for his advice: 'Remember it is the longest uninterrupted role in Shakespeare. For God's sake, hold back so you've something left at the end.' But I didn't. I couldn't, even though I tried, and I did make less of it than I'd hoped for." Critical praise for Motley's sets and costumes, for Byam Shaw's direction, and for the supporting cast of Harry Andrews and Yvonne Mitchell did not save the production from being an also-ran.

A resounding success that season, *Antony and Cleopatra,* immediately followed *Richard III.* Starring Michael Redgrave and Peggy Ashcroft, it opened to acclaim in Stratford, went to London for a run, and then on tour to the Continent. The production is notable because the full production records and nearly complete Motley designs allow one to examine it in some detail.

Of course no Shakespeare play can ever appear as if entirely new. When Byam Shaw and Motley staged *Antony* at Stratford in 1953, some in their audience would recall their 1946 production at the Piccadilly Theatre with Edith Evans and Godfrey Tearle. Others would remember Olivier's 1951 London production with Vivien Leigh as Cleopatra in Shakespeare's play and in Bernard Shaw's *Caesar and Cleopatra,* both productions that benefited from the glamour and notoriety of the Oliviers. The challenge for Glen Byam Shaw and Motley with *Antony* was to present Shakespeare's play as Shakespeare, not as a star vehicle or a box-office oddity—for the Oliviers's work together had by now been tainted by gossip that their marriage was faltering badly. At Stratford the play took on a much different coloration.

Michael Redgrave made a handsome, credible Antony, and Peggy Ashcroft a passionate, beautiful Cleopatra. Although a few critics thought Peggy Ashcroft slightly miscast (perhaps her warm personality suffered in comparison with Vivien Leigh's cool beauty), they were extravagant in their praise of the production. In no small way, Margaret Harris's sets and costumes were responsible. Michael Billington, who saw the production as a schoolboy, remembered that they made the "transition from Rome to Alexandria with cinematic speed and simple lighting-changes. A rope looped with canvas indicated Pompey's galley. Two purple poles suggested Octavia's court. Stratford's hydraulic lift enabled the central area of the stage to rise and become Cleopatra's monument."[3] Echoing Billington, T. C. Kemp reassured his scholarly readers that "Miss Ashcroft . . . justified the assertion that 'her voice and words were marvelous pleasant.'" Writing for the academic record, he found no fault, judging that "Glen Byam Shaw achieved a fine production."[4]

The Scotsman (30 April 1953) described Motley's achievement. "The play is not hampered by unnecessary decor. Both scenery and costumes have been designed by Motley, and yet in the strict sense there is no set scenery. The stage, save for a couple of slender pillars, is as bare as possible. Almost all the rest is 'props.' A simple sail let down from above, with the addition of some sparse ship's furniture, suffices for Pompey's galley. One set for Cleopatra's monument is a simple piece of arched masonry with gigantic Egyptian figures. . . . But during most of these tense three hours the stage is bare except for a flight of shallow steps, and sometimes a simple figure or two figures at parley are sharply etched against the sky." Richard Findlater wrote in the London *Tribune* (20 November 1953) at the end of the London run, "A theatrical Everest, . . . the supreme virtue of this production, indeed, is that Shakespeare is its hero."

After the close of the Stratford season, the production had a London run at the Prince's Theatre before leaving early in January 1954 for a European tour to The Hague, Amsterdam, Antwerp, Brussels, and Paris. "The only place it was a dead flop was Paris," recalled Margaret Harris. "The Paris critics hated it. I don't know why, exactly. Perhaps it was because they had to wait for somebody, an actor or a dignitary in the audience, and the curtain went up twenty minutes late. The actors had got themselves into a fine frenzy by then. The Parisians hated the look of it, too. They said that the colors were '*fondant,*' like those pastel sweets. They weren't at all, but anyway they despised the English color sense. Any attempt at being an artist, they think is hopeless in England. I went into Peggy's room the next morning to read the notices. Everywhere else there'd been absolute raves, and when we got the Paris papers we couldn't believe our eyes—the notices were all absolutely terrible!" "French audiences could accept neither the play's blend of comedy and tragedy nor the carryings on and banter of the hero and heroine," Billington reported.[5] With that exception, this notoriously difficult play was an unusual success among the critics and at the box office.

Margaret Harris took as her inspiration the classical Roman stage—spare, with as little scenery as possible. She built up the stage—easy to do at Stratford by raising the stage lifts and building around them. There were four steps down to the forestage, which was semicircular. Two large columns rose on either side, leaving two-thirds of the stage as the center. A rostrum stood across the back of the stage.

At the play's beginning, Antony and Cleopatra entered together under a yellow canopy and walked down the steps for the first scene. That arrangement remained for most of the act. The scenes in Egypt were localized without additional scenery by bringing on slaves carrying objects— often Cleopatra herself sitting or lying down on a litter. At other times, she stormed on. To shift the scene to Rome, the designer changed the color scheme completely—the costumes, the props and set pieces, and the sky (the cyclorama backstage on which colored light was projected). In Egypt, the sky was either blue or yellow—usually yellow—for a hot effect. In Rome, everything was gray. "For the first scene in Rome, they flew in a big Roman eagle carrying a bar, which held a curtain—not soft, but treated with plaster, so that it looked sculptured," Margaret Harris said. "Three thrones for the triumvirs were set center, far downstage. The scene changed to Egypt when the Roman eagle went up again into the flies, the color of the sky changed, and Cleopatra entered on a litter. The Egyptians were all dressed in white and very brilliant pieces of color. Cleopatra was always dressed in a very strong color. The Romans' costumes were all gray and silver. For the second Roman scene, a big screen made of metal with a map etched on it allowed the Romans to plan their campaign."

After the first interval, the physical layout of the stage space changed from the horizontal symmetry of part one. The center steps in front of the back rostrum were removed. Off to stage right, a set of concave curved steps formed a corner entrance for the actors. Above them hung a large blue drape, like a tent, for all the interior scenes. "The drapes were up in the flies, and were lowered down," explained Margaret Harris. "We had attached a line that held up the center of the drape, so that as it lowered, an entrance was opened in the middle by the swag the line made. For the 'Great Fairy' scene, Cleopatra dressed herself up in very light things, with a great feather headdress. It was dark, and she came down the steps, with all the slaves carrying little lights, quite small, so that the entire scene was speckled with lights. Antony was waiting for her on the stage."

After the last interval, the stage had nothing but a low rostrum around the back. The scene changes were all made with light, except the scene at Antony's tent. For that, a swagged curtain dropped in; Antony played the scene with Eros in front of the curtain. After Antony had stabbed himself, soldiers came on to carry him off stage right, and the tent went up into the flies. "As the tent went up, the center section of the rostrum rose slowly on the lift, following the tent. It was all in rhythm," said Margaret Harris. When the lift reached the top, a trap in it opened. Cleopatra and her women stepped out of the trap. The scene had changed, and they were now on top of Cleopatra's monument. Under the center of the lift, the large opening created an entrance high enough for an actor to walk through. As the women stepped from the trap above, the men came through the center opening carrying Antony. They set him down on the forestage, and the women hauled him up onto the top. "It is a difficult moment to stage," Margaret Harris continued. "We had a rig, like a wooden davit, and a rope through it so that the stagehands backstage could help them. But it looked as though the women were hauling him up by themselves. Cleopatra helped him on when he got to the top. She had to swing him back, because he had to come up in front of the lift. He was no lightweight, Michael Redgrave."

After the tour, the production came to the Shaftsbury Theatre, London, which lacked a lift. Margaret Harris improvised with a scene truck, but, as she said, "The effect was spoiled. Indeed, for the whole tour, those effects didn't work, because we couldn't have the lift."

For the 1954 season, Margaret Harris again designed sets and costumes for two of the five plays: *A Midsummer Night's Dream,* directed by George Devine, and *Romeo and Juliet,* directed by Glen Byam Shaw. Both, of course, were plays Motley had designed before, and audiences expected innovation. In neither case were the innovations wholly successful.

Adapting an earlier idea for the Young Vic production of *A Midsummer Night's Dream,* Margaret Harris put a painted gauze a few feet in front of a back cloth, which was painted with stylized temples to represent Athens. Inspired by Paul Klee, the gauze represented the forest. Varied lighting made the gauze appear or disappear. "The trees were made of a wire frame covered with gauze and mesh, with leaves applied to it quite formally," Margaret Harris explained. "It looked like a painting." More than the stylized settings, the music and the costumes for the fairies ran the risk of disappointing devotees of the romantic-ballet-opera school, who expected Mendelssohn's music, dainty fairies, glamorous Greeks, and clownish rustics. Instead of Mendelssohn, George Devine used music composed by Henry Boyes. "George Devine felt that Oberon and Titania are very unpleasant, cruel, nasty people," said Margaret Harris. "Why should they be surrounded by pretty little dainty fairies?" Oberon wore a net cloak covered in leaves. When he was supposed to disappear, he could turn his back, put his arms up over his head, and the cloak would spread out in the shape of one of the trees, so that he looked like another tree. "I made Titania's four little fairies very grotesque," said Margaret Harris. "Cobweb was really like a little spider, and Mustard-seed was very spiky and nasty. We made them grotesque because of the names and because of the things that they do and say." Puck, "who wobbled bowlegged like a Simian, was dressed like a bird and equipped with claws" said the *Birmingham Mail* (24 March 1954). "Oberon too, wore a make-up which was irreconcilable with my sort of Fairyland. . . . Titania was not so much a fairy queen as a rather defiant little suburban wife." "Queer, aquatic insects," the *News Chronicle* (24 March 1954) called them. Bottom and the other mechanicals wore tunics and trousers of no particular period, but with Greek patterns painted on them. Margaret Harris dressed the upper-class mortals "as if they had just stepped off a Grecian urn," said the *Stratford-on-Avon Herald* in admiration (26 March 1954). Anthony Quayle played Bottom; Vanessa Redgrave was Helena; Keith Michell, Theseus; and Jean Wilson, Hippolyta. "The production impresses with the good taste of the stage spectacle; it amuses with the richness of the drollery; still, it does not enchant," deemed *The Times* (24 March 1954).

For the second play in 1954 Motley returned to *Romeo and Juliet,* this time seeking fresh inspiration from Giotto. For their productions in 1932 and 1935 they had turned to Carpaccio and Botticelli. In their attempt to give the set both a Renaissance and a modern feeling, they used a setting of unstained wood that incorporated Renaissance archi-

tectural forms. "We always had trouble with both *Romeo* and *Hamlet,*" Margaret Harris admitted. "Because both Glen and I had been tied up with the original Gielgud productions, we found it very difficult to see either of them fresh. With any *Romeo,* we thought that you either have to have a permanent balcony, or you have to bring the balcony on. In either case, it's a bit of a difficulty. So we decided to have a permanent set, with an upper level which went right round, part of which could be used as the balcony. The set was semi-circular, concave with columns round, a balcony above, and little buildings on each end, so that the actors could come out of those buildings, leaving the central area to play in. It was all made of oak veneer. We didn't paint or stain it, it was just the pure wood." For the Capulets' mausoleum, Margaret Harris added grilles and "tombs" under the balcony, so that the actors entered above and then descended to stage level, as if entering the mausoleum. "It was not altogether successful," she admitted.

Some critics panned the set. "Like a Swedish bank," complained one critic unkindly of the unvarnished wood. "I realized afterwards that if I had put touches of gold on it," Margaret Harris said, "I could have avoided that response." The set was by no means a failure. *Shakespeare Quarterly* praised the artistic allusion and dramatic utility of the setting: "As befits a play that is cast in a somewhat antiquated (for Shakespeare) and formal mode, the staging followed a convention older than Shakespeare. The set consisted of little more than a wide balcony almost spanning the stage and flanked on either side by squat, square towers, the color being of that palest pink or 'natural wood' color that characterizes the views, in miniature, of Florence or Bergamo or Verona, in the background of so many quattrocento pictures. The balcony, besides its obvious use in the love scenes, served as the street-block from whose upper windows the citizens of Verona looked fearfully out upon the brawling factions, and, embellished with a chandelier and streamers, as the minstrels' gallery at the Capulet ball. . . . It was the actors who really dressed this stage, which bristled with human detail in the crowd scenes but became withdrawn and statuesque (as things are in moonlight) when only the lovers were on it."[6] "Too calculating, too cold a person, Laurence Harvey wasn't

The Merry Wives of Windsor, *Shakespeare Memorial Theatre, Stratford-on-Avon, 1955. Rough set sketches show the changes from the Garter Inn (left) to Ford's House (right), from which Falstaff is being carried in the bum-basket. Motley Collection.*

good as Romeo" said Margaret Harris. "He didn't get on with Zena Walker, and it didn't work." The production was pleasing to academics, perhaps, but Margaret Harris concurred with the critics who found the production lacking. She would re-design the play once again in 1958.[7]

Margaret Harris's year had found a new rhythm. From late summer into autumn she designed in London, almost invariably in collaboration with her sister Sophie, productions of classic drama, "straight plays," and opera. As the new year approached, she and Glen Byam Shaw would discuss the plays for the next Stratford season. Sometimes Byam Shaw, his wife Angela Baddeley, and Margaret Harris would go for a working winter holiday to lay the groundwork. By February Margaret Harris would have done the preliminary sketches—"storyboards"—of individual scenes

and rough sketches for sets and costumes. In turn, Byam Shaw would be putting his thoughts down on paper, making a notebook full of remarks to the actors and a carefully choreographed personal promptbook detailing entrances, exits, and stage business. Using Margaret Harris's ground plans and set model, he moved toy soldiers and pipe-cleaner figures around to visualize the play moment by moment. Rehearsals began five or six weeks before opening night. At the same time, Margaret Harris had produced the scale plans for the settings and, sometimes with Sophia Harris's help, the detailed sketches of the costumes for the wardrobe staff and costume shop. As the celebrations for Shakespeare's birthday on 23 April drew near, the productions came together through the installation of mock-up sets, costume fittings, technical rehearsals for lighting and set changes,

the dress rehearsal, and, finally, opening night. New productions opened every two weeks or so from late March onward to run in repertory throughout the summer and into the early autumn, after which some of them might transfer to a theatre in the West End.

Motley's *Merry Wives of Windsor* revealed Margaret Harris at the peak of her form as a set designer. The play is a difficult one to stage because of its logistical complications. It moves among scenes in the Garter Inn, the outside and inside of Ford's House, the street, a field, and the vicinity of Herne's Oak. To keep the action continuous and to minimize the time for set changes, she came up with a novel solution: an intricately devised— almost a Rube Goldberg—contraption of sliding panels, folding screens, two-sided Venetian blinds, roll-up interiors, flying pieces, and a tree (Herne's Oak) that emerged in sections from the stage floor. An example of the designers' legerdemain, the set itself could win rounds of applause. As an expression of the play's witty change-and-change-about sitcom, it was entirely appropriate.

At first, street scenes were interwoven with changes from one interior to the other. Eventually,

however, the scenes changed directly from one interior to the other without a street scene between. To keep the stage alive rather than closing it off completely at any time, Margaret Harris made the set part of the entertainment. A central structure, roughly V-shaped, pointed upstage. By means of sliding panels within the structure, two small three-dimensional pieces that slid forward, and a venetian blind over the fireplace that could flip over to show different locales on each side, the designer transformed the setting from the Garter Inn to Ford's House and back again. During the transformation from one interior to the other, the interiors could be hidden from view by five small flats, built up in low relief, that represented the facades of houses, with windows, doors, and snowy roofs. The flats could fly in and out and were so arranged that they masked the interiors during the change, but allowed the sides and front of the stage to be used as a street. "All these changes required a lot of delicate adjustment to make the masking and the scene changes work," she explained. "When the street was set, it was possible to come up a trap, upstage, and enter the interior set without being seen, so that furniture

The Merry Wives of Windsor, *Shakespeare Memorial Theatre, Stratford-on-Avon, 1955. Set sketches for the street scenes (left) and for Herne's Oak (right) in the last scene. Motley Collection.*

could be changed and actors could be 'discovered' at the start of an interior scene."

There came a point in the play when the set changed from one interior to the other, in sight, with the audience watching. Panels slid across, revealing some parts of the set and concealing others. The three-dimensional pieces that rolled forward contained panels and sliders that changed the scene from the Garter Inn to Ford's house and back. When the scene changed, the panels and sliders moved and—instantly-the interior of the Garter Inn became the rooms in Ford's house. *But* the venetian blind showing a painted panel remained unchanged from the Garter Inn to Ford's house. There was a pause. The audience began to accept that the blind would stay as it was, but suddenly the blind flipped over, revealing the other side—another panel painted a different color. "When it was well timed it got a laugh and a round of applause," said Margaret Harris. "When it did, the stagehand who operated it used to run over the road to his wife, who worked in the wardrobe, saying 'I got my laugh.'" For the scene at Herne's Oak, the whole structure, which was built on the permanent sliding stage, slid off to stage left, out of sight, and the tree came up slowly on the stage lift. Because the lift could accommodate only eight feet below the stage, the tree was built in two sections; the top section slid up behind the lower section, then the lift came up, bringing the base of the tree to stage level.

In combination with the witty costumes by Sophia Harris and robust comic acting by William Devlin (Sir Hugh Evans), Angela Baddeley (Mistress Page), Anthony Quayle (Falstaff), Keith Michell (Master Ford), and Rosalind Atkinson (Mistress Quickly) and "cracking speed," as *Punch* (20 July 1955) said, it was one of the season's hits. To many, the wintry sets and scenery in low relief suggested a Christmas card—a welcome thought

in the middle of an English heat wave, but not an original one. The *Birmingham Post* (14 July 1955) credited Oscar Asche with having come up with the idea forty years earlier.

By 1956, a little more than halfway through their tenure at Stratford, Glen Byam Shaw's directing and Motley's designs had placed their well-tuned Shakespeare productions at the center of the Stratford magic. Byam Shaw and Margaret Harris by no means monopolized production there. As artistic director, Byam Shaw brought in upcoming directors Peter Brook and Peter Hall, as well as designers Tanya Moiseiwitsch and Lila de Nobili. That year five plays were directed by five directors, collaborating with five designers. The constant was the season's acting company, headed by Emlyn Williams and Harry Andrews, two actors from Motley's 1930s circle. Of the five plays on offer—*Hamlet, Love's Labour's Lost, Measure for Measure, The Merchant of Venice,* and *Othello*—-the only one Glen Byam Shaw directed and Margaret Harris designed was *Othello*.

"I took a completely different attitude from when I had designed *Othello* with Orson Welles, which was a one-off, unique," remarked Margaret Harris. "It was one of the more successful productions at Stratford from my point of view, and Glen was quite pleased with it." The set marked an innovation for the flexible Stratford stage. The stage lift was dropped down to its lowest position, so that the center of the stage became a deep hole. A cyclorama was dropped into the lift opening, so that the cyclorama went all the way down to the bottom of the opening. A rostrum was then placed in the lift, to form a convex semi-circular area downstage. On the stage floor was painted a circular design. With this arrangement, the entire play took place downstage, mostly on the forestage. It created a space that seemed open at the back and focused on the forestage. In the downstage "assembly" entrances on stage right and stage left were built structures of mahogany-veneered timber—to get the color and the feeling of the wood. Both side structures had balconies, each of a different design. Staircases descended from the balconies to stage level.

The Venetian scenes, which took place downstage of the lift, were indicated only by Venetian lions or a lantern. For the court scene, the doge was carried in on a throne, and servants brought on elaborate branched candelabra. "Then, for the harbor in Cyprus, one could imagine that the whole stage was overlooking the harbor," explained Margaret Harris. "We had guns pointing outwards as though they were defending it. All the people who were coming from the ship came up from below, via the upstage lift, as if coming up from the sea front." For the scenes in Cyprus after the Venetians once settle in, the action took place beneath a large silk canopy that was pale orange on the outside and white on the inside. The canopy was of two layers of Japanese silk, held up

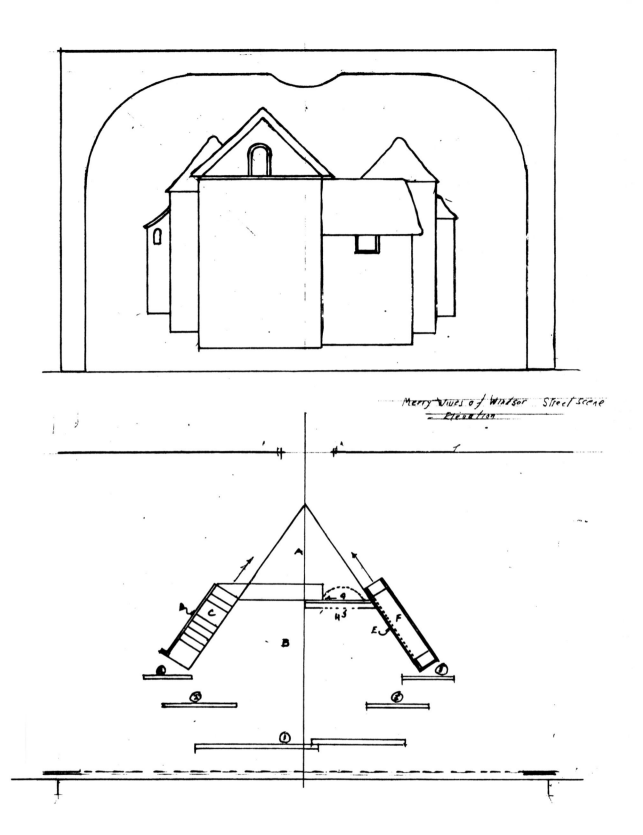

The Merry Wives of Windsor. *Street scene elevation (top) and stage plan (bottom). House pieces 1, 2, 3, 4, and 5 fly in for the street. Access to A is through the center of the back cloth, and to B from A during street scenes. C, D, and F slide into place for the Garter Inn, and D, E, and F for Ford's House. G slides across and the shutter at H rises to disclose a fireplace for Ford's House. The venetian blind is above the fireplace at H.*

Othello, *Shakespeare Memorial Theatre, Stratford-on-Avon, 1955. Storyboard for Othello and Desdemona's confrontation with her father before the Duke and the Signory of Venice. Motley Collection.*

by poles and swagged up over the stage, with huge tassels hanging down from its lowest points. "One imagined the whole thing was played on a terrace where they had a canopy to keep the sun off," said Margaret Harris. "We kept the lifts upstage down all through that time to create a sense of a drop-off behind the acting area and thereby to give the feeling that the actors were high up." The stage remained canopied until the last scenes when the canopy flew out, the lift came up, and the entire stage became level.

For the willow scene a drape was dropped in; the bed was upstage behind it. "When the drape flew out, the bed with Desdemona in it rolled slowly downstage towards the audience until it was very, very near," Margaret Harris said. "They played the whole of that scene there. At the end, they all died on the bed, a huge four-poster, or on its platform. Because the bed had come too far downstage to bring the curtain in, it very, very, very, slowly went back upstage with all of them on it. The lights gradually faded until the bed was far enough upstage for the curtain to come down, and the stage was dark except for a single spot on Desdemona and Othello. Then the curtain fell slowly. It was very dramatic. It worked rather well."

The costumes were Elizabethan-Jacobean, the period in which the play was written, because neither director nor designer saw any reason to put it in another period. "Glen wanted Othello to be very military," said Margaret Harris. "He was dressed in red throughout, until the very end—almost a military uniform. Harry Andrews, a fine figure of a man, played Othello absolutely as a black African. The part has often been played as if Othello were a lighter-skinned Arab. Yet he says himself, 'Because that I am black.' When you have a white actor you can't really be very convincing about it, but Harry looked pretty good from that point of view."

The critics were extremely appreciative. "We owe Motley gratitude for a Venice night glittering with stars, a sea-coast Cyprus ominous with cannon, and a silken tent whose roof ensnares the warmth and glory of the southern sun," rhapsodized Harold Hobson in the *Sunday Times* (3 July 1956). The *Birmingham Post* (31 May 1956) reported that "the center of the stage can become Venetian lagoon, Doge's council chamber, Cypriot citadel, or Desdemona's bedchamber; all suggested with imaginative economy. Nothing is done to blur the play." For the same critic, Motley's costumes transformed the otherwise non-villainous Emlyn Williams into "the stocky, leather-jerkined, black-beard, with the face of a Judas in a Renaissance painting." John Russell Brown wrote that director and designer were "unobtrusively resourceful; apart from a penchant for the splendid—the scene in the council chamber resembled a portrait group for Van Dyck or Rembrandt rather than an emergency meeting under threat of war—they were chiefly intent on showing off the chief characters."[8] "The forestage is hard, symmetrical and prosaic, with wooden stairways on either side, like a lecture hall," wrote Harold Matthews (*Theatre World*, July 1956, 14), continuing: "Motley have let themselves go on port-wine colored robes for the magnificoes, which give richness to the scene in the Sagittary." The drop of a great swagged drape above the stage, a shift to harsh Cypriot sunlight, and a blue sky projected on the cyclorama changed the scene to Cyprus, where the action continued with changes in lighting and props to indicate changes in time and place.

In 1957 an explosion of Shakespearean production from the Shakespeare Memorial Theatre and the Old Vic was filling theatres across Europe, as well as in London and Stratford. It looked to be "a great vintage year," speculated Muriel St. Clare Byrne in the pages of *Shakespeare Quarterly*.[9] Motley's productions that season were two of the classics—*As You Like It* and *Julius Caesar*. As had *Othello*, the perennially popular *As You Like It* presented Margaret Harris with a Shakespeare play Motley had already designed. The challenge was to come at the play fresh, without losing what had succeeded in the 1952 production.

The 1957 *As You Like It* benefited from fresh casting and costumes, but retained the idea that the play moved from winter into spring and summer.

To set this production off from the earlier design, Margaret Harris kept the sets almost the same, but chose a different, later Renaissance period for the costumes. The greater innovation, however, was to cast a young Orlando, played by Richard Johnson, opposite a more mature Rosalind, played by Peggy Ashcroft. "Richard Johnson had a certain name when he played Orlando," said Margaret Harris, "but nothing yet glamorous." Robert Harris, who played Jaques, came from Gielgud's generation. His beautiful speaking voice and maturity gave him a magisterial melancholy. "As Rosalind, Peggy was cunningly accoutered by Margaret Harris in dark red jacket, breeches, and boots to disguise that slim boyishness was not perhaps her first attribute," wryly observed Michael Billington, calling attention to the inevitable fact that Motley and their contemporaries had moved from youthful innovation to the solid accomplishments of artistic maturity.[10]

As in the 1952 production, a winter setting for the first scenes in the Forest of Arden seemed obvious to the designer and director. The Duke speaks of "the churlish chiding of the winter wind (II, i, 7) and his followers sing of "winter and rough weather" (II, v, 40). Yet the winter setting could still provoke the critics' displeasure. The *News Chronicle* (3 April 1957), among others, complained peevishly that although "it is not all a play of spring and summer, it surely should not begin with hoarfrost and continue to look quite chilly almost throughout the evening." In the end Byam Shaw's deft direction and Peggy Ashcroft's charm won audiences over, even as the setting avoided sentimentality. "The chill wind of man's ingratitude blows nor-east by the weather-vane on the stables" where Orlando lives neglected, wrote Muriel St. Clare Byrne. "Old Adam's mittened hands and his warm crimson comforter [add] the one touch of color against the pale wintry sky and the delicate landscape-with-chateau, reminiscent of the miniaturists, which sets the scene firmly in France," she continued. "It is Winter in the Forest, too, where Amiens is glad of his shaggy cloak and Corin of his sheepskin and muffler. And then Spring comes to Arden. The water of the brook is still icy as a barefooted Touchstone dips up a bucket-full, shudders 'Br-r-r!' as he sluices face and hands, and then tosses the sparkling drops up into the air . . . And from that moment the gaiety begins to bubble over like a fountain. The slender, larch-like trees with their light foliage stand out against clear skies: we are ready to fleet the time carelessly as they did in the golden world: Rosalind will appear to lead the chorus of lovers through the contrapuntal melodies of the lyric theme of love, into which, with most giddy cunning, they are now lured by parody and a false gallop of verses. It is the turn of the play, the enchanted moment. *Vera incessu partuit dea?"* These raptures from an academic critic were echoed in the praise of her brethren of the press. A year later, her colleague Roy Walker confirmed her judgment stating simply: "The production abounded in touches of poetry."[11]

Julius Caesar, the second Motley-designed production of the 1957 season, presents director, designer, and actors with three major problems. First, it is often used as a school text based upon a story so well-known that many in the audience may find it familiar, boring, and tedious. Second, it is set firmly in classical Rome, so that the range of choices in sets and costumes runs to fluted columns and white togas—updating having produced some notoriously unsatisfactory results. Third, its casting is difficult: The main character, Caesar, dies halfway through; Brutus' wordy philosophizing slows the pace; and Mark Antony's well-known request for Roman ears easily can steal the latter part of the show. To overcome these problems, Byam Shaw and Margaret Harris re-thought the play in terms of military attitudes, deportment, and etiquette familiar to actors and audiences, for whom the memory of the War was hardly a dozen years distant.

Margaret Harris concentrated on fluidity in the scene changes to avoid the stodgy, "forumesque" stasis associated with classical Rome. Exploding the scenes with light and movement, she used bright colors for the togas. "We were bored with white togas," said Margaret Harris. "I found some early Roman paintings with togas in very strong colors. We made them a thick rayon jersey, which took dye very well, and put the different armies in different colored togas and tunics."

The scenes changed with magical ease. "The curtain rose on a stage dominated by a larger-than-life statue of Caesar, raised on a tall plinth in the center of the stage. After the disrobing of this image by the envious tribunes, the statue pivoted

backwards out of sight, and the two walls of gray stone parted. Against the blue sky at the back of the stage the living Caesar was acclaimed. The statue might easily have dwarfed the human figure, but the magnificence of the gold-embroidered crimson toga and the majesty of Cyril Luckham's bearing made him the incarnation of an immutable and pivotal principle of order. This ordered Rome was visible in the massive fluted monoliths of light gray stone, which ranged outwards from Caesar as their personal center in two symmetrical lines, continued in the tall stone portals flanking the forestage. Here was the wide perspective of Caesar's Rome with Caesar himself the keystone," observed Roy Walker. He discerned in the staging a willingness to see Caesar more as the hero vilified than as the dictator-in-the-making that the experience of World War II had made popular.[12]

To achieve both the atmosphere of marmoreal Rome and the swiftness of Shakespearean staging, Margaret Harris created six pale gray stone structures that could be moved in and out, and rearranged from scene to scene. The structures were set at an angle, with a fluted "return,"—a short vertical piece joined to the longer vertical flat, which enhanced the illusion of three-dimensionality, but remained clearly representative, not realistic. These two-sided flats on six big scene trucks were arranged in a shallow V shape that pointed upstage. In this unlocalized "Roman" acting space, scenes changed by shifting and rearranging the sliding pieces. For the first scene, they were pushed in close to center stage for a sharp V shape with a statue of Caesar at the apex. (Please see the drawing, below.) After rearrangements for the subsequent Roman scenes, they were pulled back to form wings, with a rock-like structure at center stage. "I think that rock arrangement was wrong," said Margaret Harris. "It seemed as if it had come from a different production."

For these changes to work, they had to be swift and seemingly effortless, or the flow of the action would be disrupted. "Glen told Fred Jenkins, the wonderful construction carpenter, 'I want them to move like butter. I want them to be *absolutely* silent and to slide *absolutely* evenly and smoothly,'" remembered Margaret Harris. "Fred said, 'Oh yes, I can do that.' He then had them made and set up on the stage. In the first rehearsal, Glen and I said, 'This is splendid! They really are what we were

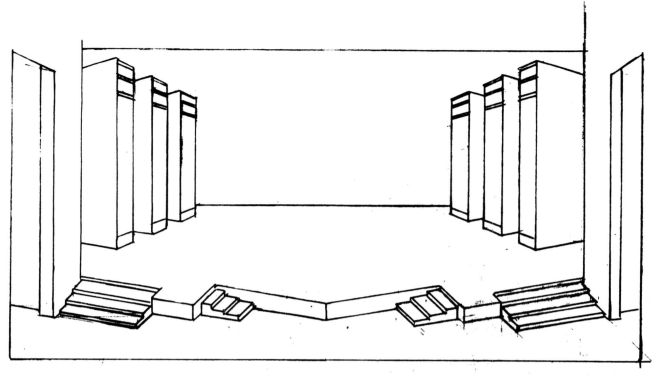

Julius Caesar Elevation

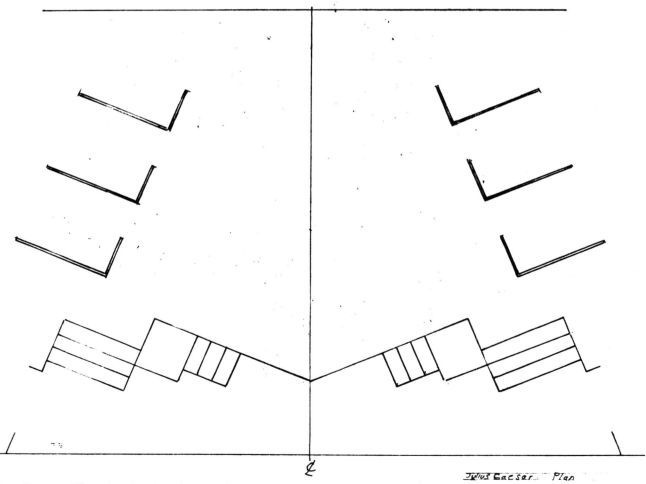

¢

Julius Caesar Plan

Julius Caesar. *Elevation (top) and stage plan (bottom).*

hoping for. Fred said, 'Thank you very much.' Next morning we came in, and they were all lying on the stage, flat on their sides. Fred was working away on them. 'What happened Fred?' we asked. And he said, 'Well, they weren't good enough, were they?' Which is so marvelous! The director accepts the work, but the carpenter thinks that it could be better. Fred was like that. He was a perfectionist. He was a wonderful man."

The transformation of the stolid school-text classic to exciting theatre worked. "A sharp, swift revival," stated J. C. Trewin (*Illustrated London News*, 8 June 1957), "set with ingenuity by Motley." "Mr. Shaw infuses his production with remarkable freshness," said the *Stage* (30 May 1930); "with its massive square pillars, which are skillfully moved about for change of scene, and Motley's rich red, blue, and gold costumes, which are contrasted with gray and black, the conception asserts its dramatic flourish from the outset."

Certainly it is one of the ironies of the theatre that young designers create exciting productions wishing that they had the ideal stage, director, and cast to realize their slim-budget ideas more fully—only to find that, when they have achieved success and ample resources, theatrical taste has changed. And so it was, to some degree, with Motley. *Romeo* and *Hamlet,* two of their biggest hits in the 1930s, they found difficult to re-imagine in the idiom of the 1950s. Taste was shifting away from the painterly, glamorous style Motley had cultivated. Even as their ingenuity as set designers and improvisers had become standard practice, the "finished" beauty of Motley's Shakespeare was being challenged by designers who sought to put their own idiosyncratic stamp on a production. This approach was anathema to Motley and, one might add, to disgruntled academics who had begun to complain of newfangled "gimmicks."

In the 1958 Stratford season, *Romeo and Juliet* did not win many accolades. With some faint praise for the actors Dorothy Tutin and Richard Johnson, several critics took Motley to task for the sets. "The pillared open balconies . . . are much too high for the lovers' midnight duet," carped the *Times* (3 April 1958), "but fitted with shifting screens and hung with chandeliers or crucifixes they serve most of the play's pictorial needs, giving interesting depth to the exterior scenes and elegance to the interiors." Sophia Harris's costumes

were fifteenth-century Italian. Her period wig for Richard Johnson was styled of very long dark hair, inadvertently anticipating male fashion a decade later. In the late 1950s, however, men never had long hair, so Romeo's wig was not accepted by the critics. "They said he looked like a spaniel!" remembered Margaret Harris. "Of course if it was done now nobody would notice or object. Eventually, he abandoned the wig and did it with his own hair, which wasn't nearly as good." The set had two tall structures made of dark green columns decorated with gold and with gold Renaissance arches. It was based on a painting in the National Gallery that was brought out of storage for Motley to study. The approach had merit, but lacked audience appeal.

"Why," asked W. A. Darlington (*Daily Telegraph,* 9 April 1958), "was poor Romeo condemned to an unromantic turn-out and hairdo which makes him look only one degree less sinister than the furious Tybalt himself? And why was the balcony scene played in semi-darkness so that the faces of the lovers could hardly be made out?" *Theatre World* (July 1958, 16) too, disliked the setting: "Motley's scenery was undeniably Italianate. A balcony there must be; Juliet's balcony. The stage was filled with two large square balconies mounted on pillars. Such symmetry on the stage not only restricts action; it has a rather similar effect on the imagination." Remembering the earlier *Romeo* of Peter Brook, Alan Dent (*News Chronicle,* 9 April 1958) thought this *Romeo* "more conventional. It harks back . . . to the famous Gielgud-Olivier version of 1935. . . . Motley this time has gone to a different Italian painter, one of the school of Perugia, for the delightful staging and brilliant clothes." Changes in theatrical taste from 1935 had made an approach that struck everyone then as sharply innovative now merely conventional.

Any doubts that Motley had lost their touch were put to rest by *Hamlet*. Feeling that they were influenced by their designs for Gielgud's 1934 *Hamlet*, Margaret Harris sought to simplify the color scheme and the set design, which consisted mainly of two large, gray, metallic-looking columns set either side of the stage. "I disliked it so much I can hardly remember it," said Margaret Harris, citing her displeasure with Michael Redgrave's performance as a factor. Critics also faulted Michael Redgrave's and Dorothy Tutin's restrained acting as Hamlet and Ophelia. In the *Observer* (8 June 1958), Kenneth Tynan waspishly called her "a mouse on the rack." Yet they were ecstatic about the sets and costumes. "Motley's settings are incomparable," wrote Rosemary Anne Sisson (Stratford-upon-Avon *Herald,* 6 June 1958); "the tall, silvered columns give an ennobling majesty. The Court scene blazes with richness and color. This is not a *Hamlet* acted out upon some indefinite platform. Instead, we move intimately about the rooms and battlements of the Castle, never aware of ingenuity, but constantly warmed and satisfied by beauty and propriety." "Dignified and simple black and gold pillars and the magnificent glowing scarlets, rich and gleaming, almost took the breath away as the curtain rose on the second scene," echoed Ellen Foxon in the *Birmingham Weekly Post* (6 June 1958); and the *Financial Times* (4 June 1958) wrote of "an agreeable, picture-book background." Less kind, Tynan said that "the setting, an arrangement of shiny hexagonal pillars, appears to have been inspired by the foyer of the old Paramount Cinema in Birmingham"; and J.W. Lambert (*Sunday Times,* 8 June 1958) described Dorothy Tutin as laboring under "the handicap of being dressed not as a girl of the Court but as Little Orphan Annie."

Sophia Harris's work at Stratford that season ended with *Much Ado About Nothing,* which Tanya Moiseiwitsch had designed but could not complete because of illness.[13] At the request of the director Douglas Seale, she completed the set design and supervised its construction. She designed the costumes as Italian in the Garibaldi period. Apparently the director thought a change of period necessary to distance this production of *Much Ado About Nothing* from John Gielgud's in Stratford in 1950, which Harold Matthews (*Theatre World,* October 1958, 27) recalled, was "so excellent . . . it was generally conceded that *Much Ado* could not be done better." "Many details are most pleasurably apt" in the 1958 production, he continued. "Motley made a varied and tasteful display of military uniforms, crinoline dresses and 'national' costumes. More sartorial advantages accrued to the men than to the women. Crinolines have little variety. The men had different costumes for different occasions. Once, in smoking caps, they recalled an old advertisement for honeydew." The *Times* (27 August 1958) found the shift in period "a stumbling block." "Purists," said *Punch* (10 September 1958) "have some reason to be shocked; myself, I was greatly entertained and driven to think again about the play."

The *Romeo* and the *Hamlet* subsequently toured in Russia. Margaret Harris remembered a designer's nightmare. The *Romeo* set had been damaged in transit. On the stage of the People's Palace in St. Petersburg (then Leningrad), she worked alone. "I was left there to touch it all up overnight," she remembered. "I had a huge 'A' ladder that I couldn't move except by pulling and pushing it because I couldn't pick it up. They didn't have any scene color, so I had to get big pots of poster color. I had a frightful night. Nobody was in the theatre except a very old lady who kept puttering through giving herself tea which she didn't offer me, but she did indicate that I could smoke if I liked which I didn't do. The production was a tremendous success with the audience."

In *King Lear* during the 1959 Stratford season Margaret Harris wished to evoke primitive Britain. Her original idea had been to place the court scenes in Byzantium. Charles Laughton, who was to play Lear, persuaded her to shift it to Britain, a change with which Glen Byam Shaw as director concurred. At Laughton's insistence, for the opening scene Margaret Harris dressed him in a white robe, which he wanted made too long for him, so that it would create the illusion of height when he stood on the top steps of his throne. "But of course, he had to come in and walk up the steps," she remembered. "He got in a great tangle, so it had to be cut off to a reasonable length." As with other Motley productions, the color scheme differentiated the groups. Lear was in white, Cordelia and the French were in pale blue. Edgar was all in gray and white. Regan was in purple and black, and her soldiers wore purple tabards. Goneril's people wore clothes of a dull ochre. "It wasn't quite as bald as it sounds, because of course they had other colors and textures as well," she explained. "The color was interesting and worked quite well, as did the costumes, which were absolutely *simple*."

A wonderfully realized production, it received an uneven critical reception due chiefly to Charles Laughton's Lear. Not well physically and very aware that this performance, paired with Bottom in *A Midsummer Night's Dream,* marked the high-water mark of his career, Laughton desperately wanted to succeed, and sometimes he did. "There were moments when Charles was amazing," remembered Margaret Harris. "He was good in some of the quieter scenes, and he was rather marvelous in the mad scene. But when he had to use a lot of power, he hadn't the strength. It didn't mount up to being very complete." At times overwrought and in bad voice, Charles Laughton's performance varied greatly from night to night. On some nights, in some scenes, he was inaudible even at the front of the stalls. On other nights, as people who were there still remember, it was the *Lear* of a lifetime. Others in the cast gave memorable performances. Ian Holm, who was then just making a name for himself in theatre, played the Fool. Robert Hardy, known to television viewers as the veterinarian in *All Creatures Great and Small,* played Edmund. Albert Finney was very successful as Edgar. "When he had to do 'poor Tom's a cold' he crouched in a corner of the orchestra pit," said Margaret Harris. "He had just a loin cloth on, and he insisted on having things that he could stick on himself as though he was stuck with thorns. So one had to make little balsa wood thorns. He was very, very good, a marvelous actor."

Amidst glowing praise for Byam Shaw's direction, Motley's sets also reaped critical accolades. "Highly original without being in any way unconventional," said the *Financial Times* (19 August 1959); "we are presented with a green flat plain and a low horizon of the sky behind it, broken up by a few bare properties—masts of ships, engines of war, a wattled hedge—that adequately suggest the appropriate place and also preserve throughout the sense of some prehistoric simplicity." Muriel St. Clare Byrne devoted her entire piece to the production: "It was one of the most widely-discussed productions of recent years . . . [which] may come to be regarded as the most revolutionary treatment of one of the great tragedies we have seen since the modern-dress *Hamlet* of thirty-five years ago." Recognizing that Laughton's performance could unduly polarize audiences, she called attention to the "fundamental brain-work of the director and designer," concluding "I have never seen a clearer production than Mr. Byam Shaw's nor grasped more fully the logic of its dramatic structure, the bones of the play."[14] This production brought to a close the collaborations of Glen Byam Shaw and

Margaret Harris at Stratford.

Having accomplished what he set out to do—creating a "company," producing plays that raised Stratford productions to the best international standard, and building up a huge cash surplus—Byam Shaw turned the artistic direction over to Peter Hall, who in turn would leave his distinctive stamp on the operation that came to be known during his tenure as the Royal Shakespeare Company, or simply "the RSC." One of Peter Hall's distinctive achievements is thought to be his formation of a "company," a group of artists on long-term contracts whose commitment was to the RSC, not just to a production here and there. Although it is not generally acknowledged, what Peter Hall did in this respect was to formalize the practices of Glen Byam Shaw and Anthony Quayle in the 1950s. In their case, the long-term contracts were unnecessary, as they were essentially asking friends and colleagues to collaborate in a common undertaking. Within that framework of experienced, older actors, directors, and designers accustomed to working with each other, the directors consciously brought in younger actors, moving them up through the ranks. The Stratford enterprise in the 1950s was in essence the nascent Royal Shakespeare Company and Royal National Theatre rolled into one, a fact that becomes evident by comparing the cast lists and credits from the 1950s, 1960s, and 1970s. The big names were all there: Peggy Ashcroft, Laurence Olivier, Vivien Leigh, Charles Laughton, Michael Redgrave, Anthony Quayle, and John Gielgud. Further down the cast lists appear the names of actors who have since become stars, their talent nurtured in the company. Albert Finney and Ian Holm were only two of many who first appeared as walk-ons in the 1950s and then moved into the title roles in the decades following. Young directors grew up in the Stratford company: notably Peter Brook and Peter Hall. New designers also came to work in Stratford: Tanya Moiseiwitsch, Lila de Nobili, and Roger Furse. Rather than a disjunctive break with the past, the renaming of the Shakespeare Memorial Theatre as the Royal Shakespeare Theatre and the new directorship under Peter Hall were an evolution whose roots went back to the London Theatre Studio and Motley's workshops before World War II. It is hardly surprising that Margaret Harris saw those years at Stratford as the culmination of her work.

Free to experiment with the considerable resources of the Stratford wardrobe and scene shops, she subordinated her designs to the needs of the director and actors, always bearing in mind the characterizations and dramatic effects they were striving for, effects that everyone assumed were to be discovered in the words of the script. However obvious such an approach may seem to people trained first as readers of Shakespeare, and there were droves of them in the Stratford audiences, it would be seriously challenged in the decades to come by directors and designers for whom the text was a jumping-off point for sometimes drastic interpretations, interpretations that many "purists" felt imposed new meanings on the plays. Peter Brook's experimental *Titus Andronicus* in 1955 anticipated in spirit his white-box circus *Midsummer Night's Dream* in 1970, a production whose departure from the traditional Victorian fairies must

have owed at least indirect inspiration to Motley's earlier break with tradition in 1954. Now that several decades have passed and the theatrical styles of the 1950s can be seen for themselves—rather than as objectionable recent traditions to be shucked off, as in the 1960s and 1970s, there has come a new appreciation for what Byam Shaw and Margaret Harris accomplished at Stratford. When one looks at productions at the Royal Shakespeare Theatre or the Royal National Theatre today that are not dominated by a forthright symbolic statement, but rather gently moved to an unexpected period and allowed to flow swiftly and gracefully, with attention to clarity and dramatic structure, the design and directing one sees go back to the intentions and inspirations that Motley taught. These principles were not only evident in their productions, but also in their "Motley Design Course" for young theatre designers, as discussed below in chapter 14.

11

The Sadler's Wells Opera and The English National Opera 1952–1978

Motley's set and costume designs for opera in London were part of a general movement to re-invigorate British opera. As mentioned in chapter 6, Elizabeth Montgomery also designed several operas during her years in the United States. Although those were significant productions, especially *Il Trovatore,* for which she designed both sets and costumes, opera design was not central to her work. It was different for the Motley women in London, especially for Margaret Harris, for whom opera came to be a major focus during the last two decades of her career. As they did for theatre, for opera Motley designed productions in which sets and costumes expressed atmosphere, character, and drama.

As far back as its origins in Covent Garden, opera in London traditionally meant spectacular stylized productions. International stars stood and sang in languages other than English in front of massed choruses. Sets were made of heavy, painted scenery. The music soared, but, as the performers moved from one beautiful tableau vivant to the next, the sense of drama and theatrical power in the action was minimized. After the War, Covent Garden productions were usually sung in English, even by international stars such as Elizabeth Schwartzkopf.[1] The Sadler's Wells Opera, so named for the theatre in north London in which the company performed, offered a homegrown al-ternative: operas sung in English by British, Australian, and Canadian singers. In 1970 the Sadler's Wells Opera moved to the London Coliseum in St. Martin's Lane, changing its name to the English National Opera at the beginning of the 1974–1975 season. Throughout the 1960s, Motley were the principal designers for this company.[2]

Opera poses special challenges to a designer crossing over from theatre work. Casts are large and the singers are purported to be temperamental. Emotions are larger than life. The story line is melodramatic. Settings are often exotic and fantastical. Opera audiences are renowned for their passionate engagement with the performance. They often know the opera inside and out, and they can be fiercely critical of what displeases them—whether it be in the singing or in the staging. A designer must expect that innovation will meet with distrust. Because the cost of producing an opera is high, once a production is mounted it will often be "revived" in subsequent seasons. In turning to the Motley women, opera producers were seeking designers experienced with the large casts and the varying demands of musical theatre.

Although they had designed *The Beggar's Opera* in 1939 for the Glyndebourne Festival, Motley's involvement with London opera came during the 1950s and 1960s. Between 1952 and 1962, Sophia and Margaret Harris only occasionally designed

155

operas for the Sadler's Wells Opera company.

In 1961, Glen Byam Shaw became director of productions, Colin Davis became musical director, and Margaret Harris became the head of design of the Sadler's Wells Opera. For nearly a decade afterwards, she remained in that role. She usually designed one new production each season and supervised revivals of productions that she had designed previously. Sometimes she collaborated with her sister or with Elizabeth Montgomery.

After Sophia Harris's death in 1966, Margaret Harris continued at the company on her own. When they moved into the London Coliseum her pace slackened somewhat, although she designed several major operas and re-designed revivals of operas she had originally done for the smaller Sadler's Wells stage. She closed the decade with the opera company in 1972 by designing a mammoth production by Colin Graham—Prokofiev's *War and Peace*. Her operatic design work ended in 1978 with Gian Carlo Menotti's *The Consul*.

"When we began to design operas in the 1950s," said Margaret Harris, "the worlds of opera and theatre had just begun to move closer together, bringing theatre directors and designers into opera houses." With the breakup of the Old Vic enterprise in 1951, the Old Vic's theatre manager, Stephen Arlen, moved to the Sadler's Wells Opera as general manager, working under the director, Norman Tucker. The company's legal charter specified that only British singers could appear; thus Sadler's Wells Opera could not use international stars, except the few who were British. Faced with a potential box-office shortfall, Tucker decided as a matter of artistic policy that unified production with ensemble singing and action would be the company's strength. His aim was a "dramatic" production style—as opposed to a spectacular "operatic" style. The emphasis on drama came to be regarded as an "English" approach to opera, distinct from the prevailing European mode. To improve the acting and establish a company feeling, he brought in theatre people dedicated to those ideals—Stephen Arlen's former colleagues from the Old Vic. For directors, he called upon Glen Byam Shaw, George Devine, and Michel Saint-Denis. For designers, he turned to Margaret and Sophia Harris.

As a theatre director, Arlen wanted to make opera appeal to a wider audience—people who were

Eugene Onegin, *Sadler's Wells Opera, Sadler's Wells Theatre, 1952. Costume sketch for a dancer at the ball. The off-white gown is accented by a deep red stole. Motley Collection.*

interested in the drama as well as the music. Having seen them work with students at the Old Vic School, Arlen hoped that his newly recruited colleagues would benignly educate the musical directors, conductors, and singers. At first working on an opera-by-opera basis, by 1961, as part of the company's artistic staff, Byam Shaw and Margaret Harris were given responsibility for the company's productions. In the years that they worked with the Sadler's Wells company, this team created a company spirit and a production ideal widely aspired to in the smaller British opera houses in years to come.

Their first production was Tchaikovsky's *Eugene Onegin,* which follows the poignant, star-crossed love of Onegin for Tatiana, whom at first he spurns when she declares her love for him in the famous "letter scene." After killing his best friend in an unfortunate duel, he leaves Russia, hoping to ease his conscience by travel. During his absence, Tatiana marries an elderly prince. Onegin returns and begs her to accept his love. When she refuses out of loyalty to her kind husband, Onegin sinks down into his romantic grief and the opera concludes. Arlen, who was also production manager, asked George Devine to direct and Motley to design—Margaret Harris the set, Sophia Harris the costumes.

"We approached it as if it were a play, with the added emotional inspiration of the music," Margaret Harris recalled. The musical director and conductor encouraged this approach—which paid off. "Motley's sets suggest sumptuousness without ostentation," said the music critic for *The Times* (23 May 1952). The same critic especially appreciated the "ingenious house in cross-section for Tatiana's letter writing and the pillared hall for the dances." Later revivals met with compaints about "shoddy" sets (Andrew Porter, *Financial Times,* 19 October 1955) and "wilting" sets and costumes (Mark Taylor, *Music and Musicians,* February 1962). These faults aside, Taylor appreciated the St. Petersburg scenes in Act 3 that "still glow in black, gold, and burnished crimson splendor." John Amis in *The Scotsman* (12 January 1962) praised the production's passionate acting. "An Onegin without inhibition," he proclaimed in a rave review.

For dramatic continuity, Margaret Harris reduced the number of sets to four, from the six the libretto requires.[3] She linked the two dance scenes by variations on pillars—rustic for the birthday party, ornate for the St. Petersburg ball—economically indicating two different social settings. She placed the house on a revolving stage that could turn to show the interior of Tatiana's bedroom upstairs, about four feet above stage level. It provoked consternation among some opera aficionados, who complained first about the color—they wanted it pink, not blue—and then about the height to which it raised the singer. "We wanted to get the feeling that she was lifted up," said Margaret Harris. "The opera people said that musically she shouldn't sing it in that position. It was all a lot of nonsense. All those 'operatic' ideas!" For the first season, the designer prevailed, but for the revivals the bedroom became pink.

In 1954, *Nelson* by Lennox Berkeley and Alan Pryce-Jones made its world premiere at Sadler's Wells. George Devine directed, and Villem Tausky conducted. In the annals of opera, *Nelson* is a specialist piece—a heroic opera best suited to British audiences, familiar with the life and adventures of a national hero. The confrontations and embarrassments of Nelson, his mistress Lady Hamilton, and his wife Lady Nelson took place in elegant drawing rooms, giving Sophia Harris ample scope for glamorous costumes. Her bright naval uniforms reflected a sharp eye for historical detail. Neoclassical settings by the painter Felix Kelly were crowned by the tableau of Nelson's death scene on the *Victory,* possibly inspired by the painting by A. W. Devis.[4]

The new opera faced stiff competition in a London season that saw world premieres of four other new English operas: William Walton's *Troilus and Cressida* and Michael Tippett's *Midsummer Marriage,* by Covent Garden; *Benjamin Britten's The Turn of the Screw* and Lennox Berkeley's *A Dinner Engagement,* by the English Opera Group. In *Opera News* (October 1954) Penelope Turing faulted *Nelson* for its cumbersome plot and uneven singing. The score and libretto were revised for the revival the next year, but not enough to please the critics for the London *Times* (23 March 1955), *The Stage* (24 March 1955)), or Noël Goodman in *Truth* (7 April 1955). With their attention focused on deficiencies in plot, score, and singing, none of the critics mentioned the direction or design.

In 1955, Margaret Harris and George Devine took on Mozart's elaborate fantasy *The Magic Flute.* Rudolf Schwartz conducted. The director and designer approached the opera as if it were a Shakespearean play—an episodic drama unified by a single, permanent set. "We felt the opera has a crystal quality and wanted to make a shining, translucent set," explained Margaret Harris. Because they had to use plywood, canvas, and painted silver foil, rather than lighter, transparent materials (at that time unavailable), she found the set ineffective—"much too heavy, solid, and coarse." As an experiment, it did not succeed.

Nor, in the designer's opinion did the scene where the singers pass through fire and water, a test based on Masonic rituals. Motley represented the two elements by gauze banners with fire or water painted on them. The banners were held so as to allow the singers to walk behind them. "It didn't work," she concluded, "but I don't think it was really a disaster."

The costumes were also an experiment that did not quite work. Sketches suggest that Margaret Harris's inspiration from Egyptian paintings of Osiris and Isis created an elegant, exotic look appropriate for Masonic ritual. To save time and money she made the costumes of stiff netting with strips of plastic tape glued on them to look like pleats. The alternatives—actual pleating or sewing strips onto the costumes—would have been impossible. The principals' costumes were fine. But time ran out in making the costumes for the chorus because at first she chose tapes that were too wide, unflattering to the singers' figures. "I didn't know how very difficult it was to dress singers!" she shuddered. "I had been used to actors, who are a very different matter. At that time singers were fat and unshapely and hadn't got very much know-how about wearing costumes."

The critics were not at all pleased. "The sets mistake vulgar cheapness for fantasy" and are a "downright travesty of the music," the *Times* (4 March 1955) sneered, adding "but do designers *ever* listen to music?" *Punch* (9 March 1955) took them to task for a "distractingly ingenious" set in which "shutters drop to hide one scene from the next; trick temple doors are folded up in full view of the audience to give the priests elbow room"; and "jetty-like ramps for ceremonial entries are masked at other times by a jungle of standard lamps." "Costumes," complained the same critic "have a geography quite their own," indicating that Pamina was made to look like "Montezuma's daughter," Tamino like "a pure-blooded Aztec" who "found himself in the Nile Valley" where he met Sarastro wearing a "black miter and bleached cheetah skin."

These disappointments in sets and costumes notwithstanding, director and designers did achieve their overall goal—a unified production that ran without breaks or curtains for scene changes, except at the interval. "As with Shakespeare, we made scene changes by having the singers carry on props," remembered Margaret Harris, "perhaps for the first time in opera."[5]

In 1959 Margaret Harris and Sophia Harris designed sets and costumes for Wagner's *Tannhäuser*. The opera is difficult because it stands between Wagner's earlier recitative-and-aria style and his later, more unified dramatic style. Director Anthony Besch and the conductor Colin Davis had not worked with the Motley women before. For the designer, the transformation from the Venusberg to the Valley of the Wartburg requires particular ingenuity. Preparations got off to a bad start, Margaret Harris said, when Anthony Besch called from the Bath opera where he was based, to summon her for a meeting to discuss the opera. The results were not happy, from the designers' point of view. "We tried to base the sets on Turner paintings in the National Gallery," recalled Margaret Harris. "The whole production was really terribly bad; it simply didn't work at all. None of us really liked the piece—neither the music nor the story. I think it showed in what we did."

The critics were divided, in part because anything Sadler's Wells Opera could do with *Tannhäuser* would be better than "the unforgettable horror of the 1955 Covent Garden performances," as David Cairns wrote in *The Spectator* (18 December 1959). In *Music and Musicians* (January 1960) Evan Senior praised the production and conducting for giving the opera new life, but complained that the "very fine costuming was somewhat marred by the odd, angular sets." "Grand opera in miniature," proclaimed Peter Heyworth in *The Observer* (13 December 1959). The *Financial Times* (4 February 1960) particularly disliked "Venus's ugly costume," and expressed general dissatisfaction with the sets and costumes. Harsher yet, David Cairns in *The Spectator* (18 December 1959) deplored the design unequivocally: "Motley's plastic and plywood, antiseptic, hundred-per-cent-washable decor totally fails to conjure up the richness and romantic color of the medieval German storybook past; the May morning setting suggested, to my indignant gaze, the country-life section of a big department store." Despite poor reviews, the opera "has proved a popular addition to Sadler's Wells's repertory," reported the *Times* (4 February 1960) later in the season.

In the midst of the 1961–1962 season, *The Rake's Progress* by Igor Stravinsky brought director Glen

Byam Shaw, conductor Colin Davis, and the two Harris sisters a fully satisfying success in combining theatre and opera.[6] Before the production opened on 2 February 1962 at Sadler's Wells, preparations for it began in New York, where Margaret Harris and Glen Byam Shaw were staging *Ross, A Man For All Seasons,* and *The Complaisant Lover,* as described in an earlier chapter. Although it was Byam Shaw's first opera, he and Margaret Harris could draw upon years of collaboration as they re-imagined Stravinsky's work for the Sadler's Wells stage, where it had appeared only once before in a production by the visiting New Opera Company.

Aware that Stravinsky's score included sophisticated imitations of Mozart and other eighteenth-century composers, the director and designer stylized the production. When the curtain rose, it revealed another small "curtain" that proclaimed "Sadler's Wells Opera" in eighteenth-century letters. This curtain then rose to reveal a stage-upon-the stage decorated with modern renderings of eighteenth-century wrought iron and architectural bric-a-brac, thereby underscoring the opera's artificiality. The spare, minimalist sets were balanced by lavish costumes that evoked Georgian London. No theatrical period piece, the design only glanced at the famous Hogarth paintings that had inspired the composer and his librettists, W. H. Auden and Chester Kallman. The production unfolded in a series of tableaux vivants connected by full-bodied acting and swift scene changes.

The critics were nearly unanimous in their appreciation. "The stylishly ingenious Motley sets' spare elegance matches that of Stravinsky's neoclassical masterpiece," proclaimed Frank Granville Barker in *Plays and Players* (March 1962). "One of the best things the company has done for a long time," said David Drew in the *New Statesman* (9 February 1962), drawing attention to the transformation of the brothel scene—"the chorus suddenly frozen in their posture of lustful teasing," so that "Tom can sing his wonderful Cavatina." Only Andrew Porter of the *Financial Times* (3 February 1962) complained that the artifice and lack of curtains between scenes went against the opera's structure of scenic finales.

"We did *The Rake's Progress* very lightly and simply," said Margaret Harris, who designed the sets. Sophia Harris designed the costumes. "Being

Stravinsky, it's very, very light music. We didn't want the production to get weighted down by Hogarth, who took a sharper point of view." She created a unit set with a raised center-stage rostrum, to suggest the eighteenth-century stage within the Sadler's Wells stage. The scene could be altered by "drops"—pieces flown in from above. These scene changes were exacting for the designers and the stage crew because the drops had to fit in precisely with the perspective of the stage. The set was built of very thin wood, with wire sculpture for details, creating effects that were representational, rather than realistic. Successful and popular, *The Rake's Progress* played at Sadler's Wells, had several revivals there, and was finally revived at the Coliseum when the company moved there. "Because it had only a half chorus, it was very small for the larger Coliseum stage, and it had already been small for Sadlers Wells," said Margaret Harris. "Sophie was happy with the costumes. They were some of her best. I was quite happy with it." So were the management of Sadler's Wells Opera, who had appointed Glen Byam Shaw, Colin Davis, and Margaret Harris to the company's permanent artistic staff at the start of the season.[7] A revival of the production toured Europe in 1965.

The 1962–1963 season saw Glen Byam Shaw as director, Colin Davis as conductor, and Margaret Harris as designer again working together at Sadler's Wells in *Idomeneo,* the only full-chorus opera Mozart wrote. Among opera lovers it was often dismissed as a museum-piece *opera seria.* Set in ancient Crete, it tells the story of Idomeneo, the king of Crete, who was shipwrecked in a terrible storm. In the midst of the chaos, he had taken an oath to Neptune that, if he were brought safely ashore, he would confront and kill the first person he met. Washed up on his homeland, he meets his own son, and at first attempts to avoid carrying out his vow. When, tragically, he does prepare to kill the young man, Neptune appears and commands him to abdicate so that the son and his bride can become king and queen. Everyone is saved. From such unpromising, stiff material Mozart fashioned a beautiful opera. By emphasizing its dramatic power, the director, conductor, and designers created a production that changed critics' minds about the opera's reputed inadequacies. It played to packed houses.

Margaret Harris's design for *Idomeneo* went

Idomeneo, *Sadler's Wells Opera, Sadler's Wells The-atre, 1962. Sketch showing Ilea on the shore. Motley Collection.*

against the opera's traditional baroque setting, last seen at Glyndebourne in 1951, in the only other professional production of *Idomeneo* in England.[8] Instead of putting the opera in Mozart's period, she and Byam Shaw turned to the ancient Crete of the story. In a spirit of classical simplicity they created four giant steps onstage with four large platforms. These ran straight across the stage, each one higher than the one in front. For the storm at sea, ropes and tackle rigged behind the platforms suggested a ship. Sliding sets—or shutters—could be moved in from the wings between each of the rostrums to form settings suggesting temples or entrances. The colors resembled those on Greek vases—rust and black, with some red and mauve-pink.

The critics were enormously impressed by the music and the staging, less so with the decor, which many thought too sparse. "The scenery, though admirably spare, like the nondescript, shaggy costumes, has a curiously negative effect,"

wrote Philip Hope-Wallace in the *Guardian* (12 October 1962). The *Times* (12 October 1962) credited Motley for "the stern, Minoan, utterly un-Baroque sets. . . . The Bull from the Sea properly makes its appearance in one set, and there is a swirling, impressionistic front-drop of the oft-invoked ocean." Edmund Tracey in the *Observer* (14 October 1962) enjoyed the "colorful fantasti-cal" costumes and the "bizarrely handsome wigs." The *Sunday Times* (14 October 1962) complained that Motley "floundered in a mixture of styles." The critic praised the design for being "simply stylized," in some scenes and damned it as "penny-plain to tuppence-colored" in others. Antony Mer-ryn (*Stage and Television Today,* 18 October 1962) saw "uncluttered decor, with scenes subtly sug-gested by nets or ropes, at once picturesque, practi-cal, and economical." "That first performance brought a ton of bricks on our heads," recalled Margaret Harris with a wry smile. "Then when it was revived, they liked it, saying 'Of course, the classic setting is the only way to do it.' We were quite pleased with it." It was often revived, the last time in 1976.

In 1963, *Così fan Tutte* opened at Sadler's Wells.

The production was created by a team now familiar to critics and opera lovers. Glen Byam Shaw staged the opera. Colin Davis conducted. Margaret Harris created the sets. Sophia Harris designed the costumes. "Così is a very delicate little opera," Glen Byam Shaw told the cast at rehearsals. By that, Margaret Harris said, he meant that the score is wonderful, but that the plot is ridiculous—"and it is," she added. Colin Davis, the orchestra, and the singers won the critics' acclaim for the music.

For both the director and the designer, particularly the designer, the opera poses problems. The plot is implausible, however delightful. It requires a deft hand to set the tone that hovers between elegance and operatic self-parody—Mozart was gently spoofing his contemporaries' operatic clichés. Two young soldiers in love with two girls are challenged by an older man who asserts that no woman can be faithful. Taking up the challenge, the young soldiers pretend to go off to war. "They go off in a boat—you have to see the boat going," said Margaret Harris, recalling a difficult stage effect. "The soldiers wave. The girls look through their telescopes and wave good-bye." Shortly thereafter, two mustachioed "Albanians" arrive. They are, of course, the two men disguised. Each makes a play for the other one's girl, and both win—without going too far. The girls are very excited by their new beaux and prepare for a wedding. At the wedding supper, they hear the army band in the distance. In a panic that they might be discovered by their soldier-lovers, the girls tear off their bridal veils as they shoo the two foreign men away. The men dash out—"and have an appallingly quick costume change," said the designer—so that they can re-enter in their own uniforms. One of the "returning" men finds the wedding contracts, implicating the girls with two foreign strangers. The men go off, determined to find and kill their rivals; they come back wearing the foreigners' hats over their uniforms. Chastened at their folly, the girls sing with their swains a delightful finale, and the opera ends.

To capture the spirit of the opera, Motley designed a small and delicate permanent set—the ladies' villa—with a view of Naples in the background. Tiny ships rode at anchor on the painted sea with Vesuvius behind them. Downstage two rows of white arches on light, fluted pillars formed an arcade. A false proscenium

Così fan Tutte, *Sadler's Wells Opera, Sadler's Wells Theatre, 1963. Costume sketches for the lovers. Motley Collection.*

framed the set, so that the actors could enter from upstage or downstage. Drapes were flown in occasionally to change the scenes. Sophia Harris's costumes were light and amusing. After their lovers left for war, there was a costume change for the women. Instead of changing their costumes completely, recalled Sophia's assistant Reg Hanson, "she had them wear dresses of the same design—only in black. The trick was typical of Sophie's wit."

"Motley's sets are light, airy, elegant, and beautifully composed," Philip Hope Wallace pronounced in the *Guardian* (23 March 1963). His colleagues concurred. "Motley's settings made the strongest contribution to the evening," said the *Observer* (24 March 1963). "Their slender columns, transparent blue ornamental hangings . . . and cool aqueous coloring perceptively reflected the character of the opera," he concluded. Desmond Shawe-Taylor in the *Sunday Times* (24 March 1963) pointed out the designers' compromise between "puritanical severity" and "daintiness." John Warrack (*Sunday Telegraph*, 24 March 1963) enjoyed the "touch of whimsy and fantasy in Motley's delightful settings." "An elegant affair," Anthony Merryn reported, "its silver-gray decor is very pleasant to the eye, particularly in the garden scenes, with the blue Bay of Naples stretching realistically in the background" (*The State and Television Today*, 28 March 1963). Even the persnickety *Financial Times*' critic Andrew Porter admitted that "Motley's flimsy decor is all right in a Peter Jonesey sort of way" (23 March 1963). Ever severe, *Punch* (3 April 1963) called the design "delicious," but, on reflection, "over-chic." In subsequent revivals, the same critics came to see the design as wanting zest—afflicted by "visual pallor," said *Music and Musicians* (November 1972). It remained in the repertory when the opera company moved to the Coliseum, where the critics commented that it was not only too small for the Coliseum's larger stage but also old-fashioned.

The next season at Sadler's Wells opened on 12 September 1963 with *Der Freischütz* by Carl Maria von Weber. Colin Davis conducted, Glen Byam Shaw directed, and Margaret Harris designed both sets and costumes. *Der Freischütz*, or "The Gamekeeper," as it might be translated, tells the story of a huntsman in Bohemia who makes a pact with the Devil. Together the huntsman and the Devil go into the magical "Wolf's Glen" where they forge seven magic bullets. With these bullets the huntsman will be able to hit whatever target he chooses. All is well in this gothic tale—from Germany's early nineteenth-century romanticism—until, alas, the Devil tries to trick the huntsman into shooting his beloved Agathe with the last magic bullet. Good triumphs, Agathe is spared, and the Devil is thwarted. Inspired by this strange plot, von Weber created magic in the music, and the director and designers responded with a powerfully suggestive staging.

For the designer, the depiction of the folkloric scenes of medieval Germany and particularly of the magical denizens of the Wolf's Glen presented an invitation to flights of fancy. "There were some wonderful beasts in the Wolf's Glen—extraordinary apparitions of birds and animals," recalled Margaret Harris. The Movement Group (a ballet troupe) performed the parts of the apparitions against a dark background. To appear invisible against the background, the dancers wore black body stockings and black hoods. On top of their body stockings, the women wore lighter-colored bird heads and bird wings. When they perched on the men's shoulders and the men raced across the stage, the audience could see only the birds' heads and wings, so that it appeared the birds were flying. For apparitions of other animals, the same principle applied—light for the apparitions, black for the dancers who carried them. "It was like the Trocadero show we'd done with the Samoiloff lighting in the 1930s," explained Margaret Harris.[9] "It was really quite exciting. The entire production was quite a happy experience."

In one scene, she remembered, the production utterly lost the audience's sympathy. The huntsman is supposed to shoot an eagle. In the theatre it is an old vaudeville schtick for someone to fire a gun up into the flies over the stage and to have a bird fall down, astounding the shooter and convulsing the audience with laughter. Margaret Harris defied the wise advice of others, who foresaw a similar result if the fatal bullet brought down an eagle onstage. "I had a wonderful eagle made so that it was the right weight, with its wings flexible and with real feathers. At the dress rehearsal, the huntsman shot up into the flies. BANG! This bloody great thing came down and there were roars of laughter. So then we said, "That won't work! We'll have him shoot into the wings, and he can go out and drag it onstage by its wings." BANG! He comes back on with the eagle. Roars of laughter. So finally he had to bring in only a few feathers. It was rather a waste of that beautiful eagle."

The critic for the *Times* (13 September 1963) summed up the consensus: a curious, romantic opera with wonderful music but a story full of "naive folk matter." "The horrors of the Wolf's Glen," the reviewer continues, "are portrayed with pantomime vividness, and for the rest, we inhabit a true-to-life romantic Bohemia of forest, mountain and moonlight. Though Motley's sets have the naive simplicity of illustrations in a child's storybook, the costumes themselves are very much the real thing: the bride and bridesmaids in the last act are enchantingly authentic." Such praise notwithstanding, *Der Freischütz* did not find a place in the company's repertory. Although it received good notices when it opened at the New Theatre, Oxford, and then came to Sadler's Wells, it never transferred to the Coliseum with the other operas in the repertory, not because of any difficulty with the staging, but simply because it is not a very popular opera.

In 1964 Sophia Harris joined her sister at Sadler's Wells to design the costumes for *The Makropulos Case*.[10] John Blatchley directed and Charles Mackerras conducted. Leos Janacek's opera tells the story of Emilia Marty, an opera singer whose father's magic potion has kept her youthful for more than 300 years. The "Makropulos Case" refers to her lawsuit to regain the formula from the heirs of her long-ago lover. In the course of three strange acts—she reminisces with a former lover, now a dotard, for example—she wins the case, and regains the formula, only to welcome death in her final aria as the formula is burned.

In keeping with the opera's period, the early twentieth century, the Harris sisters aimed for an art nouveau feeling. "Not Beardsley, more French and very colorful," said Margaret Harris. In the first scene, set in a lawyer's office, they distorted the perspective slightly to create a strange, surreal effect. Her favorite set for this opera was based on a sketch by Leon Bakst of a bare stage: "It had huge, swagged curtains, a great throne, surrounded by ladders and lights and props. Flats and bits of scenery were faced to the wall."

The Makropulos Case, *Sadler's Wells Opera, Sadler's Wells Theatre, 1964. Costume sketch for Emilia Marty. Her gown is a rich purple hue. Motley Collection.*

Written in 1924–1925, the opera had its premiere in Brno, Moravia, in 1926. Until its premiere at Sadler's Wells, it was unknown in England. The critics' responses ranged from appreciation to ecstasy over the music, the staging, and the performances, especially Marie Collier's in the title role as Emilia Marty (known as Elina Makropulos in her past life). Ernest Bradbury called her "larger than life in her brilliant red costume and the enormous feathered hat of a Gainsborough painting" (*Yorkshire Post*, 13 February 1964). Among others, Peter Heyworth in the *Observer* (16 February 1964) found fault with "John Blatchley's clumsy and nerveless production" in making her an aged crone in the final scene. "A stunning achievement," said Desmond Shawe-Taylor in the *Sunday Times* (16 February 1964). "Motley's designs catch the seedy-sumptuous provincial atmosphere well," said Wilfrid Mellers (*New Statesman,* 21 February 1964). In 1965 Sadler's Wells Opera won a Theatre of Nations Prize for *The Makropulos Case.* The opera was revived in that year and in years following, and later re-staged in the Coliseum. It was last revived there in 1976, drawing praise from *Musical Opinion* (January 1976) for "Motley's evocative designs."

"Gounod's *Faust* was an utter disaster," said Margaret Harris of the production that opened the 1964–1965 season at Sadler's Wells. "I think it's a horrid opera. We didn't do it well, because none of us liked it." Glen Byam Shaw directed and Colin Davis conducted. The production team had plenty of company in their dislike for the piece. In the past, Wagner is said to have stalked out, calling it "that sugary, vulgar, nauseating, bungling piece of work!" When comparing the work to Goethe's drama, he and others objected to this hero's pathetic sentimentality, to say nothing of music that was pale and popular beside the mighty strains of the *Ring* cycle. For opera lovers, however, it was a long-standing favorite whose popularity dated back to Victoria's time. Sadler's Wells brought it back by popular demand. Woe to any who dared tamper! On the first night, when the director, designers, and conductor walked onstage, the audience booed. "Colin walked off the stage," Margaret Harris said, "but Glen dragged him back and said, 'You can't do that just because somebody's booing. You've got to stay till the curtain comes down.' We brought him back on with us."

Many critics roundly faulted the production. After praising the new translation by Leonard Hancock for excising some spurious additions, and the conducting of Colin Davis, the *Times* (17 September 1964) took the rest of the production team to task for lacking "heart"—they had dared to unsentimentalize a favorite. Others complained about the loss of favorite melodies and scenes—the Walpurgisnacht in particular. "To say that Glen Byam Shaw's is a new production laughably understates the case," wrote Charles Reid (*The Spectator,* 25 September 1964), continuing "he has jettisoned and innovated right and left, giving what amounts

to a basic reconception." "Motley's sets lash out wildly in every direction," warned John Warrack (*Sunday Telegraph,* 20 September 1964). He held up for special ridicule Marguerite's "vile little thatched tea-cosy of a cottage set in a garden still awaiting the delivery of the plastic gnomes, that is not only hideous in itself but flatly contradicts the nocturnal rapture, subtly tinged with menace, that Gounod hangs over the closing pages." Even the sympathetic Edmund Tracey in the *Observer* (20 September 1964) who enjoyed "Motley's very careful and accurate costumes" and "successful blend of genuine sixteenth-century Germany (the costumes in the Kermesse) and of nineteenth-century sentimental-medieval (the angels at the end)" nevertheless pounced on "Marguerite's twee thatched cottage" as "a disaster."

From a designer's point of view, however, the production was not entirely without merit. "At the beginning of the opera Mephistopheles has to appear in Faust's study—SNAP!—just like that," recalled Margaret Harris. "So we used an old trick. The scene was very dark and part of the background was black. Mephistopheles walked on holding a stick with a black cloth in front of him. He stood there until the moment he had to appear, then he dropped the stick, there was a flash, and he appeared. A string offstage pulled the stick and cloth off. To the audience, it seemed miraculous. It was one of those very simple old theatrical tricks that works every time if you do it right." She was also pleased with the effect at the end of the opera of Marguerite's apotheosis in prison, for which they brought on ballet dancers as baroque angels—an innovation, however, that some critics singled out with displeasure.

Late in January 1965, Verdi's *A Masked Ball* opened at Sadler's Wells with Glen Byam Shaw directing, Colin Davis conducting, and Motley (Margaret and Sophia Harris) designing sets and costumes. The opera has a curious history. In 1792 King Gustavus III of Sweden was assassinated at a masked ball in Stockholm, supposedly by the husband of his mistress. Assisted by the composer Maurice Auber, the playwright Eugène Scribe wrote a runaway opera blockbuster, *Gustavus III,* that opened in Paris in 1833, playing in London later the same year. In Italy, Verdi hired the poet Antonio Somma to rework the libretto. The Italian censors objected to showing the death of a king onstage, an objection overcome by shifting the action to Boston and altering the social status of the characters. Its melodramatic plot brings the King (in disguise) and his best friend's wife Amelia to visit the same sorceress. Her advice leads them to meet at midnight under a gibbet. In the last act, during a melee at the masked ball the King is assassinated, but he clears Amelia's name before he dies. With sound common sense, Margaret and Sophia Harris put the setting back in Sweden, a shift anticipated in an earlier Covent Garden production.

"I didn't like what I did, and I didn't particularly care for what Sophie did," she stated. "The material for the costumes was too flimsy. For the masked ball in the last scene, I thought it should be very mysterious and dark, but Sophie didn't agree. She wanted the costumes to be very light. So she made very light things, and I made the set light. To me it didn't make any impact." Nor, in her opinion, did the other scenes—the fortune-teller's cellar, the gibbet on top of a hill, and the courtier's study. To change scenes, the designer used four or five "book" flats (two flats joined together so as to make a free-standing screen) with different covers on them. In the ball scene the covers were white with gilt candlesticks, for instance, and for the gibbet scene they were black, rough and dark. "Really, I don't like the opera," explained Margaret Harris. "Maybe I didn't do it very well because I didn't like it, or vice versa. I can't tell which."

The opening night was a disaster. The lead tenor's cold so impaired his singing that the management came onstage to beg the audience's indulgence. At the final curtain the gallery booed the conductor, director, and the two Motley women, reported Eric Mason in the *Daily Mail* (28 January 1965). Amidst general complaints of dullness in the staging and the design, the *Sunday Telegraph* (31 January 1965) summed up the critics' consensus: "The visual side of the evening . . . failed to evoke the Versailles-like atmosphere of Gustavus III's Stockholm court. Motley's last scene of the masked ball itself was magnificent. The colors and costumes combined to make the stage picture look like an old print. For the rest the settings were very ordinary." Nevertheless, the production was quite popular. Byam Shaw's staging was modified by Tom Hawkes in a subsequent revival. The opera remained in the company's repertory and was later restaged for the London Coliseum where "Motley's settings still look well (especially the spacious palace scenes, with their decorative eighteenth-century classical designs)," said the *Times* (28 October 1974).

La Bohème is a favorite among opera lovers, but the 1966 production of Puccini's opera initially met with mixed reviews. The Harris sisters found themselves designing a production with director John Blatchley and conductor Mario Bernardi, instead of the familiar team of Glen Byam Shaw and Colin Davis. Traditionally, the artist's garret in which the young gentlemen art students live is a huge studio, into which the frail, consumptive Mimi comes on her way up to her garret. The scenes that follow drew on the same sentimental, romantic view—the bustling Paris street scene outside Café Momus, the pathos of the winter scene outside the gates of Paris, Mimi's collapse and death of consumption in the final act. John Blatchley wanted to make the characters and the setting more contemporary. Basing his interpretation on the joking in the text, he envisioned the four young artists as "real young men like the Beatles, who are always kidding each other," recalled Margaret Harris.

She approved of this realistic approach. Accordingly, she scaled down the studio to make it a little room with a window in which hung a piece of sacking where a pane of glass was missing. The staircase could be seen coming up from below and going on upwards beyond the garret. For their first meeting, Mimi stops for breath outside the garret door, her candle goes out, she knocks to ask for a light, Rudolfo opens the door—and they fall in love. In earlier productions, she was not seen until Rudolfo opened the door. In this one, because the stairs were visible, her approach and hesitation before knocking could be seen. The critics complained that this ruined "the surprise." The director and designers "ruin the exits and entrances by showing us the passage outside" the garret, complained John Warrack (*Sunday Telegraph*, 6 March 1966). Their reaction vexed Margaret Harris. "What surprise?" she asked. "She's supposed to be living on the floor above them, so they must know her—and besides, before he opens the door Rudolfo says that it's a woman." To placate the critics, the director changed the blocking to have her come *down* the stairs from above, thus keeping her partially concealed in the dim light. "To me that made nonsense of the whole thing," continued Margaret Harris. "Why should she get out of breath coming *down* the stairs?"

Other implausibilities also bothered the designer. For the scene in the market square, the young men are having supper at the café. Margaret Harris reversed the usual orientation of the scene, so that the café awning rose up into the flies, facing the audience, as if they were sitting inside while the lovers were eating outside. "To me their eating outdoors is madness," she said, "because it's in the snow. However, it's in the text. Oh, that opera is dreary! You see them at the gates of Paris, then in the last scene you go back to the attic, and Mimi comes in and dies. Really horrid."

The critics and the audiences did not entirely agree with her bleak assessment. While some critics thought the "naturalistic" approach too "cold and calculating" (*Music and Musicians,* April 1966), others felt, with the critic for the *Times* (3 March 1966), that it was "opera for the young." "Motley . . . have miraculously caught the atmosphere of the production: their attic, crammed and cornered with a panorama of rooftops and chimneys, and with a visible staircase to the room that allows many good dramatic effects (particularly the exit at the end of the first act), is exceptionally skillful, and in style quite unlike their recent work." Going further, *The Stage* (10 March 1966) declared that "Motley's settings establish the contrast between the squalor of the tiny garret—for once really small—the bleakness of the toll-gate scene and the busy Paris street outside the café." The review concluded that the staging was a "splendid piece of collaboration between producer, conductor, designer, and lighting man, with the artists responding sympathetically."

La Bohème remained in the repertory at Sadler's Wells, transferred to the London Coliseum when the company moved there, and then went to Opera North in Leeds. "In 1981 the Coliseum gave it to Opera North, and I went up there to resuscitate it. As before, irrationally, Mimi still came *down* the stairs."

"A triumph," crowed one reviewer after another, praising Sadler's Wells production of *The Mastersingers of Nuremberg,* Wagner's only comic opera, which opened on 31 January 1968. They fell over each other with praise for the conducting of

Reginald Goodall, the playing of the orchestra, and, with a few nitpickings, for the singing in a fresh English translation. The direction of Glen Byam Shaw and John Blatchley received similar appreciation. The sets designed by Margaret Harris and Elizabeth Montgomery divided critical opinion, garnering faint praise on the one hand as "suitable," and eliciting harsh criticism on the other for being wrong for the opera. At best the notices were a dull reward for their efforts. They fulfilled the fears of theatre people working on opera, that by concentrating on the music, opera critics are apt to underestimate the contributions of the designers.

In part, one can guess at some diminution of effort or inspiration in Motley's personal circumstances. Sophia Harris had died in April 1966. Elizabeth Montgomery, her husband ailing, had been involved in making arrangements to move him, their young son, and the household from Connecticut to London. In 1967 no new Motley-designed operas appeared. Between them, the two surviving Motley partners, Margaret Harris and Elizabeth Montgomery, designed only three theatre productions for London, although there were two shows at the new Chichester Festival theatre, as described in the next chapter. Whether consciously or not, Margaret Harris was turning her attention more and more to the new Design Course at Sadler's Wells and curtailing her other work, a reasonable adjustment for someone approaching seventy years of age.

By the time the two women began work on *The Mastersingers,* Sadler's Wells Opera Company was completing plans to move from the medium-sized theatre in Sadler's Wells, Islington, into the larger and grander London Coliseum in the heart of the West End. It was the designers' last major undertaking in their customary theatre in North London. Wagner's opera calls for two choruses, thereby requiring Sadler's Wells to combine their at-home and their touring companies. The production took shape under Reginald Goodall's conducting and the supervision of two directors—Glen Byam Shaw and John Blatchley. Responsibility for design was also divided: Motley designed the sets and David Walker created the many, many costumes.

The opera posed two areas of difficulty for designers: how to arrange for the comings and goings of the two choruses on Sadler's Wells's small stage, and how to evoke the piece's folksy comic atmosphere without becoming kitsch. On Motley's side, Margaret Harris enlisted Elizabeth Montgomery's help. Neither of them had ever worked with David Walker, and they seem not to have collaborated well. Margaret Harris did not think Walker's realistic costumes fitted with Motley's fanciful sets. Because the opera is set in sixteenth-century Germany and because Wagner wished to express the folk origins of his music, Motley turned to the period's colorful Majolica pottery as inspiration for the sets. They imitated its yellowish greens and blues, and its colorful depiction of houses and people. "It's a comedy, and we thought that the 'Majolica' look would suit it," said Margaret Harris. Yet David Walker apparently did not agree. "We designed the sets before he did his costumes. He could have cooperated, but I suppose he didn't like our idea. If he had done both sets and costumes, it would have worked well, because his costumes were very good. Unfortunately, they made the critics say our sets looked like toy town."[11]

Critics who went into raptures about the music and the staging faulted Motley's sets and Walker's costumes. David Cairns (*Spectator,* 15 February 1968) admired the "lifelikeness" of the production's physical environment—the cobbler's workshop "makes its effect despite some not very distinguished Motley sets." After stating plainly that the production "is the most intelligent and perspicacious I have seen anywhere since the days of Beecham," *Musical Opinion* (March 1968) complained that "Motley's sets are not of the same artistic standard. . . . From a purely utilitarian point of view, however, the outdoor sets all make room on the small stage for the necessary action." Noël Goodwin (*Truth,* March 1968) felt that "Motley's sets were more successful in the first and last scenes than in the poky site of the street brawl or the spartan comforts of Sachs' dwelling," thereby shifting from "evocative impression and naturalistic illustration." "Motley's sets gave an impression of artiness," said the *Musical Times* (April 1968). The transfer to the London Coliseum allowed the set designers to make adjustments, with apparently happy results for some critics. "The Motley sets come into their own on this larger stage," wrote William Mann (*Times,* 26 August 1968). "The hor-

rid sketch of distant Nuremberg has gone, leaving a plain yellow cyclorama, some rudimentary hillocks, and a collection of carnival floats, not perfectly satisfying but undeniably festive." On the whole, the reviews continued to be sprinkled with complaints about the design, even as the production itself became opera legend.

A fire in the costume stores at the Coliseum later damaged the costumes for *The Mastersingers.* After David Walker declined to re-do them, Margaret Harris had a chance to integrate the costume and set design. "The new costumes brought the production into better proportion and unified its palette, but they still didn't quite work," she recalled, "because they looked contemporary." At that time stylish young men—"Mods"—were wearing short jackets, very tight jeans, and long hair, in the style of the Beatles. Except for codpieces, Motley's sixteenth-century costumes for the men resembled the trendy fashion of Carnaby Street. This attempt to make them understandable to contemporary young people misfired.

The same revival gave Margaret Harris a chance to re-design the last act, in which the chorus comes on singing. To represent different guilds to which the singers belong, she hung huge banners on either side of the stage, borrowing an idea from her 1937 production of *Henry V,* which had used banners to distinguish the English and the French. Each guild's cohort of mastersingers entered singing—in carts. Practical reasons lay behind this innovation. The chorus needed elevation so that they could see the conductor. And they needed to enter singing. The carts functioned as movable platforms that made sense within the medieval setting of the opera. "It made a wonderful picture to assemble them all," said Margaret Harris with pride. "I thought that worked very well." Unfortunately, the conductor Reginald Goodall complained that the chorus could not sing properly in carts because some of them had to pull the carts as they sang, recalled Margaret Harris. "He is *the* Wagner conductor. He's wonderful, and he's tiny. When he's conducting, you don't see him at all because he doesn't come over the rail. You only see these little hands up in the air." Nevertheless, the carts remained. However beautiful visually, the dramatic side of the production clashed with the demands of the music, in the conductor's opinion.

By the late 1960s, as she became more involved

with the design course and less with designing new productions herself, Margaret Harris remained active as Head of Design for Sadler's Wells Opera and later for the English National Opera—as the company was re-named. As Motley productions were revived, she helped to stage them.

When the company moved into the Coliseum in 1968, its large stage required modification of the Sadler's Wells sets, which were too small for the space. She also altered the stage opening, which measured a huge fifty-six feet across the bottom of the proscenium arch. To make the stage seem smaller, she added a neutral filler around the inside of the proscenium arch. Within that she put a false proscenium painted darker than the original proscenium's pink faux marble. Assembly entrances on either side of the stage permitted large groups to enter and exit swiftly. Her changes decreased the stage opening to forty feet, still ten feet wider than Sadler's Wells, but small enough so the sets were not completely lost when they were transferred to the Coliseum stage. Eventually, set designers for new productions wanted to use the full stage opening, so the management took out the false proscenium, against Margaret Harris's advice. "I warned them, but they didn't take me seriously," she said. "It led to spending a great deal of money. A designer is not going to have that huge space and not fill it with large—and expensive—sets. So it has cost the English National Opera a lot of money, and it still does."

For her first production designed for the company's newly refurbished West End theatre, in 1972 Margaret Harris designed the sets and costumes for the English premiere of Sergei Prokofiev's *War and Peace*. David Lloyd Jones conducted. Colin Graham directed and collaborated on the design. As Motley, Margaret Harris took principal responsibility for set and costume design, working closely with the director, who also received credit for design in the program. No British opera company had ever staged the opera. Its cast includes, by one critic's count, seventy-two principal roles.[12] Add to these a full chorus and a corps de ballet.

A period study of aristocratic Russia, the first part of the opera moves in seven scenes through the garden, drawing rooms, and ballrooms in which Natasha meets Andrei and her elopement with Kuragin is foiled. The six scenes of the second part begin on the battlefield, moving from the Russian side to the French side and back again before culminating in the conquest, the sack, and then the burning of Moscow. It concludes with the French in retreat and the Russian people triumphant. "The opera is complex and has a set of costumes to match its complexity," stated an internal memo. Other working papers document a staggering number of details to attend to: costumes for the principals plus a chorus of seventy-five with six extras. The running plot calls for change after change of costume as the cast switch from drawing room to battlefield, from the Russians to the French. With costumes came innumerable props— for the conquest of Moscow, for instance, there were "French soldiers in stolen furs," " soldiers stealing Muscovites' boots," "luggage, clothes, icons, pillows, pictures"—the lists are endless.

Even with a large stage to work on, the director and designer still had to overcome problems of scale—how to move large choruses on and off stage and how to arrange them so that they could see the conductor and be seen and heard themselves. The director asked Margaret Harris to design a set with six large trucks—moving platforms—three on each side. The upstage truck was high, the next was lower, and the downstage one lower still, to form a giant set of steps for the chorus. Vertical wooden slats made the steps resemble the board-and-batten siding of Russian country architecture. Whether the platforms were pushed onstage empty, as rostrums for the chorus to climb onto, or pushed onstage with the chorus already standing or seated upon them, they served the purpose of getting the chorus up and out of the action on the stage.

Across the back of the stage Margaret Harris hung a huge projection screen, forty feet by twenty-six feet. On it were projected slides of paintings and drawings. "We couldn't represent the battles or Moscow being burnt or those kinds of things, so we showed a picture on the back that stated—'This is what's happening'—without trying to represent the event." The screen was so big that it required two projectors whose images overlapped. "The difficulty of having the two slides match up invites human error—the electricians *could* and very occasionally *did* put in one half of one slide and one half of a different slide," she recalled. "That did happen once or twice, and it was pretty agonizing."

For the drawings themselves, Margaret Harris expended substantial effort. She went to Paris with the director to collect reproductions of the events in the opera as seen by French artists. When they asked Russian museums for similar material, the Russians refused. Margaret Harris enlisted the artistic help of John Wilmot, Elizabeth Montgomery's son. She sent him reproductions of French paintings from the period of the opera to guide him in creating drawings to be projected on the screen—a parade, for instance, with regiments passing. Since the text of the opera names the regiments that have to march across the stage, both John Wilmot in his drawings and Margaret Harris in the costume designs had to take care to reproduce the uniforms accurately. According to Margaret Harris, "He did huge drawings, twenty by thirteen inches, to fit the forty-by-twenty-six foot screen, in scale so we could show them on the model of the set. At the time he wasn't interested in color. So he sent me his wonderful drawings in ink on paper. On the first one, I started coloring his original—rather than a copy. It didn't go very well. I was panic-stricken, because to ask him to do them all over again would be impossible. I got it right in the end. After that I always had the drawings reproduced, so I could try things out. John had never had a drawing lesson in his life. Only twenty years old, and he did these marvelous sketches!"

The combination of slide projection and realistic costumes and sets seems to have worked well. "Huge success," read the headline in the *Evening Standard* (12 October 1972). Philip Hope-Wallace in the *Guardian* (12 October 1972) was only half-joking when he said, "If I were a millionaire, I would put the thing on for a three-year run and make a killing." Critic after critic praised the effects, which had been attained with no little effort. For the war council of Fili, in which Russian generals appear, Margaret Harris brought in an expert on Russian military decorations. When the scene was staged, a painting of the meeting appeared, projected on the backcloth behind the generals who held their council at a table in the same position with the same decorations. On opening night, Ronald Crichton (*Financial Times*, 13 October 1972) thought the "uniforms in War are so decorative that there is some danger of prettification."

War and Peace, *Sadler's Wells Opera, London Coliseum, 1972. Costume sketch for Helene (Anne Hood). Her empire-waisted gown is trimmed with green. Motley Collection.*

For the earlier ballroom scene, Margaret Harris used a similar arrangement. She found a painting of a ballroom lit by chandeliers, copied it, and then modified the chandeliers to match those in the stage set. When it was projected on the backcloth, it did not blend in with the actual set, but instead showed a picture related to what was happening onstage. For the burning of Moscow, she had about forty paintings from France reproduced in black and white. For the Russian winter, a single huge white groundcloth gave the effect of endless snow. "I nearly went mad painting the projections," she remembered. Between scenes, brief synopses of the scene that followed were projected on a small front-drop screen à la Brecht.

War and Peace enjoyed a great success with the critics and at the box office. Some critics argued that the quality of Prokofiev's own work had been tainted by the Soviet Ministry of Culture, whose "suggestions" for greater patriotism he had heeded when composing the opera. None had anything but praise for the production. Rodney Milnes (*Spectator,* 21 October 1972), for instance, especially praised the scene changes and "a stunning tableau of Napoleon in the ruins of Moscow."

The opera was revived several times during the 1970s and toured the United States in 1984. Reviewing the production just before the American tour, the *Telegraph* (2 April 1984) stated unequivocally: "The complex problems posed by the almost cinematographic switches of time and place within the work's two massive panels have been solved by the producer, in close collaboration with his designers, with an absorbingly fluid and inventive skill, to create with a gripping immediacy the rapidly changing panoply of history as it affects both the personal relationships of the characters and the national Russian consciousness." A dozen years and several revivals after its opening in 1972, the production had lost none of its power.

After the enormous *War and Peace,* Margaret Harris devoted herself almost exclusively to her design course at the English National Opera. Her last full-scale opera at the London Coliseum was Puccini's *Tosca,* an opera vastly popular with the public, last staged by the Sadlers' Wells company in 1963. Much in the minds of critics and opera lovers was the landmark production—Franco Zeffirelli's much-acclaimed, glamorous, naturalistic staging at Covent Garden ten years before. Featured in that production were the international opera stars Maria Callas as Tosca and Tito Gobbi as Scarpia. The production team flouted opera conventions to distance the English National Opera's production from its Covent Garden predecessor. Besides Zeffirelli's hard-to-beat precedent, the production faced another difficulty: When translated into English the melodramatic plot can provoke giggles as easily as thrills at Scarpia's nefarious doings. Former opera critic Edmund Tracey, by now a director of the company, was

commissioned to prepare a new translation in hopes that the problem could be avoided. To these difficulties add Margaret Harris's intense dislike for the opera. "It's so schmaltzy and awful," she protested. She objected in particular to its melodramatic plot—"not a very nice story."

The reviewers chronicled a long list of faults with the production, taking the designer and director to task for "deglamorizing" *Tosca,* as Ronald Crichton put it in the *Financial Times* (6 February 1976). "Margaret Harris, obsessed with dingy browns, made a clutter of the church scene, presented Scarpia in an apartment of the Palazzo Farnese looking as though it had been occupied by squatters," wrote Frank Granville-Barker in *Music and Musicians* (March 1976). Mostly the critics noticed what they disliked. There was occasional praise—Robert Henderson in the *Telegraph* liked "the carefully observed Empire drawing room of the second act." Opera lovers, Margaret Harris recalled, even created an uproar over which of two "San Andrea" churches in Rome was meant by the text. She decided to use the smaller church as the model for her setting because she found it more interesting artistically. "The critics and audiences were furious because the *other* San Andrea was traditional. Opera's full of conventions, and if you go against the traditional convention, bricks come down on your head!" she laughed. "Then for each revival there's a different Tosca, who has to have different costumes. It drives you crazy! That's part of opera, they always have a new principal singer and you always have to change the costume." Subsequent revivals fared no better with the critics. The production was dismissed as "an unedifying shell," by David Murray (*Financial Times,* 21 April 1980), and passed off—"*Tosca* survives anything"—by Rodney Milnes (*Spectator,* 19 January 1985).

Margaret Harris's penultimate "opera" was the British premiere of Benjamin Britten's *Paul Bunyan,* a little-known work from the composer's youth. More a musical entertainment or operetta than an opera, its staging nicely coincided with the celebration of the American bicentennial. It was presented in Snape, a village in East Anglia near the place Britten and his friend Peter Pears lived. There they had converted an old malt house into a theatre called "The Maltings." Britten had composed the opera in America with W. H. Auden before World War II, but it was performed only once in New York. Britten and Auden quarreled and the composer claimed to have lost the score. After Auden died, Britten agreed to permit Colin Graham to direct the opera for the Aldeburgh Music Festival and then to transfer it to Sadler's Wells. Graham was co-artistic director with conductor Steuart Bedford of the English Music Theatre company, which they had helped to found in 1976.[13]

Centered around the legendary lumberjack Paul Bunyan, the piece featured loggers of every nationality and their girlfriends. Its musical numbers gently parodied Americans and American musical forms—the blues, a hoe-down, Christmas music, even a mock funeral march and an advertising jingle, leading Stephen Walsh to liken it to a "May Week 'entertainment,'" put on by University students (*Observer*, 8 February 1976). Margaret Harris decided to do the lumberjacks' checked shirts in their respective national colors, with yellow and blue for the Swedes, red, white, and blue for the French, and a striped yoke and then stars for the Americans.

Because the production was meant for touring, sets were simple, consisting "of two pairs of decorator's steps," wrote William Mann (*Times*, 7 June 1976), "the taller metamorphosed into a lovely Christmas tree topped by a corn fairy doll; a Stars and Stripes flag [gained] extra stars as the evening proceeded; some logs and stockades, little else." "The set was very light, little fences," she recalled. "It was fun. It's a comedy. They were a delightful young company," recalled Margaret Harris. "They could dance, they could sing, and they could act. It was a very enjoyable time. Britten sometimes looked in at rehearsals, although he was partially disabled by a stroke."

The Consul by Gian Carlo Menotti was the last opera Margaret Harris designed. Although she had stepped down as resident designer some years earlier, her continued association with the English National Opera through the Design Course made it natural for them to turn to her in an emergency. In the summer of 1978 the chorus went on strike. This "industrial action" over pay led management to select Menotti's opera, which needs no chorus. It was directed by David Ritch, one of the com-

Paul Bunyan, *English Musical Theatre, Snape Maltings, Aldeburgh Festival (transferred to Sadler's Wells Theatre, London, 1976). Costume sketches for four lumberjacks. Motley Collection.*

pany's staff directors. Howard Williams conducted. The opera was the first production of the two artists at the Coliseum. Set in the context of the Cold War, the story revolved around the escape efforts of a woman trapped in an unnamed totalitarian state. Her activist husband flees, but she is unable to obtain a visa to find political asylum in an unnamed Western country. Her mother and baby die. The Scarpia-like chief of secret police threatens her. Her husband returns, only to find that she has killed herself to release him from the last hold the secret police might have over him. When it was first staged in 1950, the opera took America and Europe by storm. By 1978 it seemed "a farrago of melodrama and sentimentality" to Paul Griffiths of the *Times* (14 August 1978). Nevertheless, the majority of the critics approved. They were especially pleased with Margaret Harris's designs. She "has taken the only possible course in giving the piece an authentic Fifties feel,"

Paul Griffiths said in his review. Philip Hope-Wallace (*Guardian,* 14 August 1978) praised her "good simple pictures."

Looking back on Motley's work as designers for opera, Margaret Harris discerned a tension between their simple, straightforward approach to design and the elevated expectations of opera audiences: "I think our belief that we should be truthful to the text, even though we did, of course, consider the music, meant that our designs didn't always meet the grander and more opulent needs of opera—especially the 'big' operas we designed—*Tannhäuser, The Magic Flute, Faust,* and *A Masked Ball.*" Taking the long view, it is evident that their designs, as much as the direction of Glen Byam Shaw and others who came to opera from the theatre, formed a new and distinctly British approach to opera that emphasized a balance between the drama of the story with beauty of the music and spectacle.

12

In the West End
1949–1975

Involved as they were with the Old Vic, the Royal Court, and the Stratford-upon-Avon theatres in the 1950s and with the English National Opera in the 1960s and 1970s, Motley nevertheless worked without letup as designers for the popular and powerful commercial theatre in the West End. That Motley continued to be sought after there attested to their great influence and prestige. Among some forty-two productions over nearly thirty years, they scored remarkable successes with *Colombe,* directed by Peter Brook; *Ross,* directed by Glen Byam Shaw; *A Man for All Seasons,* directed by Noel Willman; and *Hay Fever,* directed by Noël Coward. Only occasionally did they meet with outright failure, and that often due to difficulties with the director or cast—as with Orson Welles's notorious *Othello*—rather than to shortcomings in the design.

After the War Motley did not design a West End production until 1949, when their modern-dress *Antigone* was at the New Theatre and *The Heiress* played at the Haymarket. They designed the Greek classic as if it were contemporary. Dressed in formal evening wear, Laurence Olivier was the one-man Chorus. Before the action started, he moved among the silent actors to begin the play in which his wife Vivien Leigh played the title role. She won praise for "pathos" and "the appeal of an exquisitely carved statuette," but drew censure for lacking "the power that splendid defiance requires" (*Times,* 11 February 1949). Creon in a helmet and

great coat completed the updating, which did not greatly please the critics, according to Kenneth Hurren (*What's on in London,* 18 February 1949).

The Heiress, an adaptation by the Americans Ruth and Augustus Goetz of Henry James's novel *Washington Square,* had been staged earlier in New York. With John Gielgud directing the London production, Peggy Ashcroft starred as the plain-Jane American heiress; Ralph Richardson, as her wealthy father; and James Donald, as her gold-digging suitor. J. C. Trewin judged it "good, solid, leisurely drama."[1] His colleague Harold Hobson saw it as a watershed in which Peggy Ashcroft "marked the fact that Britain now had an actress worthy of comparison with the great feminine figures of the Continental stage."[2] The designs by Sophia Harris and Margaret Harris drew an accolade from *Theatre World* (May 1949, 13): "The staging of the play calls for the highest praise, a further tribute to the genius of the stage designers, Motley." However, as Margaret Harris remembered, the triumphs of her old friends Peggy, John, and Ralph were achieved in the midst of arguments between the American author-producers and herself as the English designer, to say nothing of squabbles among the cast that drove John Burrell, the original director, to quit.

"We had an idea that we wanted to make it look like the Rothenstein painting: dark figures against light backgrounds. The sets would be very light and the figures very dark against them, even though the New York production had had very dark sets. Binkie Beaumont and the Goetzes came to my flat, which was by then in Earl's Court Gardens. They didn't like my set design. I tried to explain what we were trying to do, and I remember Ruth Goetz saying, 'Well, I don't care about that.' I was very angry, and I flew into a rage, and said, 'There's a shelf of books up there. Pick out the colors you want the set painted, and I'll paint it that color.' So they did. I painted the set dark green and dark red, and all those conventional Victorian colors. They came back and said, 'Oh, that's absolutely marvelous! It's absolutely right! Don't you like it?' I said, 'I think it's appallingly vulgar.' Binkie was very, very angry. He said I'd been insolent. I probably was, but I was terribly annoyed at being told that what I was trying to do was nonsense. It ran for a long time and was quite successful."

Jacques Deval's *Marriage Story* at the end of the 1948–1949 season ("a tortoise," said the *Times,* 5 May 1949, dismissively) and Jordan Lawrence's *For Love or Money* at the beginning of the 1950–1951 season ("sadly unreliable," said the same paper, 25 August 1950), both employed costumes designed by Sophia Harris. Aside from these productions, Motley's name did not appear in the West End credits for two years due to their involvement with the various phases of the Old Vic, as described in chapter 8.

Towards the end of the 1950–1951 season, perhaps in anticipation of the throngs of American tourists that now made the summer almost a season to itself, director Basil Dean attempted to repeat at the Cambridge Theatre the runaway success of his 1923 production of *Hassan.* It required exotic "Arabian Nights" costumes, a "Dance of the Beggars," and other bits of extravagant stage spectacle. He turned to Motley to provide the sets and costumes. Sophia Harris's costumes were based on Indian miniatures. They were made in bright, clear colors—pinks, reds, and darker colors—of delicate fabrics in patterns suggesting the Orient. Unfortunately, the critics found the whole thing hopelessly dated. Margaret Harris dismissed the production as "a complete and utter disaster!"

In 1951, Margaret Harris seized the chance to work with Orson Welles, who had achieved great stature as a film director and would-be Shakespearean. His earlier efforts, a controversial "voodoo"

Macbeth and other projects in New York for the Federal Theatre Project, had been popular successes. By coming to London to direct and star in his own production of *Othello,* in collaboration with Laurence Olivier Productions ("LOP"), he set himself a challenge that he found difficult to meet. "He was a very undisciplined stage actor," said Margaret Harris. "It occurred to him to do something, and he just did it, without considering what it was going to do to the other actors. He was terribly nervous about doing Shakespeare in London. He was in Larry's theatre, you know, so he was a bit scared about it. It was a terrible ordeal for him."

The production was only moderately successful. *Theatre World* (December 1951, 24) credited him with a "personal triumph." *The Times* (19 October 1951) termed him "an impressive but an unexciting Othello." Archie Nathan rather charitably recalled that Welles was "a wonderful Othello, very much looking the part," paying more homage to Motley's costuming than to Welles's acting.[3] Looking the part could not overcome his bad case of nerves and lack of preparation. Among theatre people, the production became a minor legend as an example of everything going wrong that could. In an interview with the author, Maxine Audley, who played Emilia in that production, remembered Welles getting carried away and flinging a handful of coins at her face, not the floor, when he told her to leave him alone with Desdemona. For the designer too, it was an experience fraught with difficulties.

Welles asked Margaret Harris to create a scene-changing effect that was like a film "wipe" in which a new scene sweeps across from one side of the screen to the other. The set was divided into two halves. A curtain could run back and forth across the front of the stage. On one side the action could continue while the set was changed on the other. The full stage, without the curtain, could also be used. "We had a big brown curtain made, but the effect never worked, because the track was made badly," said Margaret Harris. "We were trying to get a filmic feeling to it." The critics zeroed in on the clumsy arrangement, condemning the whole idea. "The Motley set produced some pretty effects," wrote T. C. Worsley (*Daily Telegraph,* 19 October 1951), "but the device of drop scenes with a curtain half-drawn was not effective, while the noise of preparations going forward behind the shrouded half of the stage was thoroughly distracting." *The Times* (19 October 1951) repeated that judgment, saying "the half-curtained scenes fail of their effect because they are not one thing or another."

Working with Welles himself proved to be a trial to the designer. "Orson used to come and work in my studio in Earl's Court Square," Margaret Harris recalled. "He used to arrive in the morning and say he must have some coffee; before he could do anything he had to have coffee. And he had to have coffee all day long, without cease. My flat was on the ground floor. There was a basement below where the landlord lived, and there was a yard out at the back, where the landlord's little lame boy used to play. He had a little wagon made of tin. He would go clippity-clop, clippity-clop, running round dragging this thing. Orson said to me, 'You must stop that, I can't stand it.' So I said, 'I can't stop it, it's his yard. He must do what he likes in it.' So Orson said, 'I'll stop it.' The kitchen windows opened out onto the yard. He went into the kitchen, and he opened the window. He stood there, for two or three minutes. What he was doing I don't know, but the sound stopped, and the boy had a slight heart attack—not a serious one, but he collapsed—and the toy wagon never reappeared. I suppose Orson just made faces at him, I don't know. That huge creature must have absolutely terrified the boy."

When *Othello* went onstage, problems multiplied, recounted Margaret Harris: "That production was a very difficult situation, because everyone who had anything to do with it was completely drunk. *Nobody,* including Orson, I have to say, could do anything. We got to Newcastle, where it was going to open, and Orson said, 'Do you know anybody who can get this on for us?' The stage director was drunk, the management was drunk. Everyone was drunk. So I said, 'Well, George Devine could, but I don't suppose for a minute that he will.' And Orson said, 'Ring him up, ask him to come.' So I rang him up, and reluctantly he decided to come. Orson was furious when I had to go back to London to deal with the School after we opened in Newcastle. Christopher Morahan was then my assistant. A graduate of the Old Vic School, he has since gone on to be director of drama at the BBC, then a director at the Na-

tional Theatre, and now an important film director—he directed *The Jewel in the Crown.* Anyway, Orson said to him, 'Well, if Percy goes, you must stay.' And Chris said, 'But I'm working at the School too, I can't.' There was a terrible scene at a party. The whole party was brought to a standstill by this awful row going on between Orson, Chris, and myself. So I left and so did Chris.

"Orson had a dresser, a tiny little lady called Betty Martin. She had a cold and Orson wouldn't have her in the dressing room. So he said to me, '*You* must dress me.' So I had to dress him. I don't know how she managed, because he had to have earrings, and she'd have had to stand on a chair to get them onto him. It was a very horrid experience. The difficulty was, he absolutely poured with sweat, and the black makeup wouldn't stay on. It would just run off. Poor Gudrun Ure, who played Desdemona, was always black from head to foot, because wherever he touched her, it came off on her."

Opening night brought its own disasters. "On the first night in London, when he came down a long flight of steps into the bedroom on his way to kill Desdemona, he was carrying a candle, which went out on the way down the stairs," remembered Margaret Harris. "That wasn't too good, because he says 'Put out the light' just before he goes to kill her, and it was already out! Then, when he was throttling her, or suffocating her, he slipped, and he fell on top of her, CRASH!!! Her head went plonk against the end of the bed, which was a plywood box, covered with bedding. It didn't seem really to damage her, though. When they came to take their curtain call, she was completely black, her white nightgown, her face, everything was black. When he was supposed to fling the coins down, as if paying for Desdemona, he flung them in Emilia's face. Maxine Audley was naturally very angry. As soon as the curtain went down, she dashed across the stage and caught him a great clip in the face. She could just reach. When the curtain went up, they bowed, and he tried to be conciliatory."

After the *Othello,* the 1951–1952 season held more excitement for the Motley women. As noted in other chapters, Sophia Harris designed costumes for *The Card*—a film starring Alec Guinness—and for *Eugene Onegin,* the first Motley-designed opera, for which Margaret Harris did the sets. In the

West End Sophia Harris designed costumes for period plays: *The Happy Time*, a comedy based on Robert Fontaine's novel about a French Canadian household's preoccupation with love, and *Colombe*, set in late nineteenth-century Paris. "I saw *The Happy Time*," said Margaret Harris. "Sophie's costumes were full of character, delightful, and amusing." Directed by Sophia Harris's husband George Devine, the play starred Devine, Rachel Kempson, and Peter Finch. It opened in January, in the midst of the ongoing struggles at the Old Vic and was not especially memorable, despite the praise of the *Times* (31 January 1951) for "gaiety sauced with Gallicism."

Motley's next West End production created considerably more excitement. Jean Anouilh's *Colombe* at the New Theatre brought together several currents in the evolution of the theatre. Anticipating the unsentimental theatre of the absurd, the French playwright used the backstage drama of Parisian theatre to question contemporary values. In brief, the play follows young Mademoiselle Colombe from her introduction to the theatre by her lover's mother, an aging prima donna, and her subsequent delight in its corruption and decadence. Viewed one way, the play traces a fall from innocence; from another, the absurdity of romantic love in an unsentimental world. The young director Peter Brook, who later became one of the century's most famous directors, himself designed the sets. Sophia Harris's costumes combined with the sets to create a realistic, period ambiance. Her daughter Harriet, who remembered her mother's reaction at the time, said, "collaborating with Peter Brook was one of the most creatively exciting experiences of her working life. 'He strikes sparks off you,' she told me. She found him sometimes infuriating, but she felt she did some of her best work for him. Using Toulouse-Lautrec as inspiration for *Colombe*, the figures in her sketches had a shadow painted down one side, like his posters." *Theatre World* (February, 1952, 9) credited Peter Brook with a "masterly production . . . of colorful theatre." Two years later in New York, Elizabeth Montgomery would design a production of the same play, directed by Harold Clurman. From photographs of the two productions, one can see how much Sophia Harris's sympathetic, bittersweet costumes for Joyce Redmond as the flower girl-become-ingenue differed from Elizabeth Montgomery's sexy, flirtatious costumes for Julie Harris, who seemed to epitomize the insouciant Broadway girl who leaves her poor, simple-and-sincere lover for the adventures of the theatre. The critics identified Toulouse-Lautrec as the inspiration, praising Peter Brook's direction and the Motley designs as "decorative, ingenious, and slightly fantasticated."

As Motley's seasons in London went, the 1952–1953 season was relatively slow. Two Motley-designed productions came to London from New York. For *The Innocents*, the adaptation of Henry James's gothic novella *The Turn of the Screw*, Sophia Harris created original costume designs. For *Paint Your Wagon*, she adapted Elizabeth Montgomery's. As usual, the critics loved the "beautiful period costumes" in the Victorian thriller and the splashy, sexy outfits for the showgirls in the Wild West musical—"ravishingly dressed by Motley" (*Times*, 12 February 1953). On an entirely different note, in *The River Line*, a new play by Charles Morgan, Paul Scofield portrayed a man slipping into insanity. Sophia Harris's realistic costumes reinforced the split between the hallucinations he imagined and the sane world the audience perceived.

Charley's Aunt, Motley's first show in 1954, did not please the critic for the *Times* (11 February), for "the picture is delicately composed and exquisitely tinted, but it is only moderately funny." To that critic, Gielgud and Motley seemed to have treated a broad farce as if it were a variation on *The Importance of Being Earnest*. Photos of the set model show drawing room sets that suggest rather than represent the play's upper-class interiors. Although billed as "entirely new," this thirty-sixth revival of the play with John Mills as the cross-dressed "aunt" simply failed. Sophia Harris designed the costumes. Margaret Harris designed the sets so that they "looked as if they were drawn in pen, and just washed with color," she said, adding that from the designers' point of view, "it was quite satisfactory." Motley's next show, Dodie Smith's *I Capture the Castle*, also failed to set the box office afire. It was dismissed by the critics as a romantic comedy, "predictable in the 1930s style."

Testy reviews highlighted the Anglo-American rivalry sparked by the juxtaposition in the West End of *Wedding in Paris*, a home-grown English musical, and *Can-Can*, an American musical imported from New York. The two shows were set in Paris, and Motley designed the costumes for both. *Wedding in Paris* by Vera Caspary opened at the Hippodrome late in the 1953–1954 season. It revolved around the efforts of an English divorcée (played by the 1930s English leading lady Evelyn Laye) to complicate the lives of the young and innocent Canadian, Angy (Susan Swinford), her intended (Jeff Warren), and a wily European roué (Anton Walbrook). "Nothing could be more English," complained the *Times* (15 October 1954), adding "altogether, a disappointing evening, in which the scenery deservedly comes in for more spontaneous applause than anything else." Thea Neu, not Motley, designed the sets.

If the English musical was too English, the same critics thought the American musical lacking in dramatic interest. Coming on the heels of *Paint Your Wagon* the previous season, *Can-Can* garnered more criticism than praise for anything but Mielziner's sets and Motley's splashy costumes, which Sophia Harris had recreated using Elizabeth Montgomery's sketches.

In *A Likely Tale* by Gerald Savory, Motley's only West End show in the 1955–1956 season, Robert Morley, Margaret Rutherford, and Judy Parfitt joined forces in an odd mixture of sentiment and comedy revolving around an expected inheritance. Peter Ashmore directed. The comic highlight was Robert Morley's departure as a middle-aged man and his entry almost immediately afterwards as that man's scapegrace son, decked out in a motorcycling outfit. Sophia Harris designed the costumes, which slightly caricatured their wearers' personalities.

Theatrical tastes were changing as the 1950s progressed. Some of the critics wanted drama with more bite. Leading them was Kenneth Tynan. *The Chalk Garden,* he thought, would stand as the last of an old West End tradition—the drawing-room play centered around the mores of the upper class—that "went out with a flourish, its banners resplendent in the last rays of the sun."[4] Playing the mysterious governess in the household of Mrs. St. Maugham, Peggy Ashcroft "created a real character out of the dumpy shape of Miss Madrigal," wrote Michael Billington.[5] And Motley contributed to her characterization of a shy, stubborn, incalculable spinster. "The hands," Billington continues, "clutch the little black handbag for security,

a trim, belted governessy sort of hat perches on her head, the white blouse is secured by a chaste brooch at the neck. Every physical detail is right." Possessing the "spirited eloquence of a Mozart quartet," according to one critic, the play was subsequently staged in New York (Cecil Beaton did the sets and costumes) and made into a film. It was revived in London in 1971. Tynan's elegy proved premature.

In the two seasons that followed, Margaret Harris worked mainly at the Shakespeare Memorial Theatre; Sophia Harris, at the Royal Court. In the West End, they collaborated on a revival of Chekhov's *Seagull* at the Saville in 1956. When Motley were just beginning, they collaborated with John Gielgud in the Queen's Season production of Chekhov's *Three Sisters* (1937), as described in chapter 4. Their designs helped to validate the Russian playwright's worth. Now his works had become classics, so that the production of *The Seagull* at the Saville Theatre was billed as part of the "Classic Season." Using a new translation by David Magarshack and starring Diana Wynyard as Arkadina and Hugh Williams as Trigorin, the production drew high praise from the critic for *Theatre World* (September 1956, 9), who said: "We must acclaim the production by Michael MacOwan and the setting and costumes by Motley, all of which blend into a perfect artistic whole still rare on our stage."

In the 1957–1958 season, Sophia Harris's dashing costumes were seen in *Lady at the Wheel* at the Lyric, Hammersmith (subsequently at the Westminster Theatre). Another mildly successful British musical comedy, it featured Vivienne Bennett, Henry Longhurst, and Frederick Schiller in a play about a woman who dared to drive in the Monte Carlo rally.

Although not strictly speaking in the West End, the Old Vic was no longer the poor relation of the commercial theatre. It was on the brink of becoming the "National Theatre"—a flagship of the Arts Council, enjoying government subsidy. Motley's returning there after a long absence hardly represented a restoration of their earlier dream of a "company." Rather, as famous designers, they were part of the theatre's mission to feature the best of British theatre.

One of the Old Vic's productions of non-Shakespearean classics, Pinero's nineteenth-century farce *The Magistrate* opened late in the 1958–1959 season. Margaret Harris was called in to design the sets, Sophia Harris to design the costumes. This witty period piece almost inevitably raised the question for the director Douglas Seale: "Can we get Motley?" For the designers themselves, it was odd to return to the Old Vic, where they had worked first with Gielgud before the War, then as a part of the grand Old Vic scheme with Michel Saint-Denis, Glen Byam Shaw, and George Devine in the late 1940s, only to have that enterprise fold. "It was very straightforward. I based the sets on late nineteenth-century interiors," said Margaret Harris. "An overmantel had little niches and shelves for ornaments, and an elaborate painted frieze went around the room." In any event, the critics acknowledged the Motley touch: "the costumes and setting help establish the stiff social respectability upon which the farce turns," wrote Philip Hope-Wallace (*Manchester Guardian,* 20 March 1959). He did not, however, appreciate their wit in undercutting that stiffness, writing that "the Motley sets are charming, but the ladies' clothes (of electric blue and orange) make nonsense of a basic element in the joke of respectable matrons trapped in the police station after a police raid." Said the *Times* (19 March 1959) headline simply: "Old Vic Revival Fails to Reap the Laughs."

With the close of the 1959 Stratford-upon-Avon season, Margaret Harris's work there came to an end, leaving her free to focus on projects in London. She occasionally helped out with a design or production problem at Stratford, but did not design any more productions there. Until Sophia's untimely death in 1966, the two sisters often collaborated on Motley productions in London.

Motley's designs in the early 1960s were seen across the dramatic spectrum. As the decade progressed, they gradually came to concentrate on English-language opera at Sadler's Wells. Margaret Harris's association with the English National Opera led her to found the Theatre Design Course, where students could study set and costume design. Having worked together on Shakespeare productions and occasionally on opera during the 1950s, in the next decade the designer-director team of Margaret Harris and Glen Byam Shaw continued together on straight plays in the West End and on Broadway, as well as staging operas

at the English National Opera. Sophia Harris now had separated permanently from George Devine and was raising their daughter Harriet by herself. The sisters continued to design for the West End plays, the Royal Court, the English National Opera, and for films. For Motley the main change as they entered the new decade was that they were centered in London, with the work in Stratford-upon-Avon at an end.

In the 1959–1960 season in the West End, *The Aspern Papers* and the smash hit *Ross* kept Motley's work before the public. Based on Henry James's novel, Michael Redgrave's adaptation was a thriller about the recovery of controversial papers by a literary sleuth of dubious reputation. Starring Redgrave as the sleuth and Pauline Jameson as the young woman guarding the papers, its turn-of-the-century ambiance required realism heightened for melodrama. Sophia Harris designed the costumes. "An artistic success beyond expectation," crowed Philip Hope-Wallace (*Manchester Guardian,* 16 August 1959), echoed by Harold Hobson (*Times,* 16 August 1959) and Alan Pryce-Jones (*Observer,* 16 August 1959).

Ross, Terence Rattigan's play about Lawrence of Arabia's life, presented particular challenges to Margaret Harris. The action moves by flashback from the moment that Lawrence of Arabia returned to England to serve anonymously under the pseudonym "Ross," to his earlier experiences in the Middle East. Besides the difficulty of moving from the English present back in time to the Middle East, the designer had to face the fact that many in the audience were familiar with the region, having served there in the War or with British commercial firms. A recent biography by Anthony Nutting had polished Lawrence's image, making him paradoxically both a romantic cult figure and a mysterious, pathetic victim of public misunderstanding.

To prepare for the production, the director and designer went to Jordan, "where we picked up valuable feelings about that area," said Margaret Harris. The play had many different scenes. Rather than trying to create separate sets for each, Margaret Harris designed a desert set. A cyclorama created the sense of the desert sky, and the stage was covered with a sand-colored felt. A saucer-shaped ground row ran around the bottom of the cyclorama and the felt went up over it, creating the

Ross, *Haymarket Theatre, 1960 (transferred to the Eugene O'Neill Theatre, New York, later that year). Sketch for the opening scene. The army building was flown out to reveal the desert for the scenes following. Motley Collection.*

effect of continuous desert. "It got quite a feeling of sand and of nothingness," she said. Built flats, dropped in or trucked on, established different locales for varying scenes.

The play begins in an R.A.F. office in a hut in Uxbridge where Lawrence was stationed. A flat representing the hut dropped in for the scene and flew out at the end of it. "All we used," she said, "was the flat, a table, and a chair." All those scene changes, however, made more work for the stage crews. In production, the sets worked best in Liverpool, where the play opened. "When it came to the Haymarket in London," recalled Margaret Harris with some exasperation, "it wasn't as well managed by the staff. They were used to drawing-room comedies, and they resented having a play

for which they had to work all evening."

The *Times* (13 May 1960) found the "desert scenes convincing." Lawrence, played by Alec Guinness, was famed for his glamorous Arab dress, which he wore in the field and at ceremonies. The role required costumes that were both elegant and virile, a combination Margaret Harris strove for by making slight modifications to R.A.F. uniforms, the Arab robes, and Turkish military dress. "It was all based on our research," she recalled. The sets and costumes pleased the director Glen Byam Shaw, the designer, and the audience, who flocked to the performance in London. *Plays and Players* (July 1960, 18–19) featured the production as the "play of the month." A new production starring John Mills was mounted in New York the following season, 1960–1961. "The New York production used the London scenery," recalled Margaret Harris, "and they made new scenery for London, where it continued to run. In New York, it didn't go at all. I don't think anybody in New

A Man for All Seasons, *Globe Theatre, 1960 (transferred to the ANTA Theatre, New York, later that year). Sketches for Act I, scenes 1 and 2, and for Act I, scene 7, two set sketches. Motley Collection.*

A Man for All Seasons, *Globe Theatre, 1960 (transferred to the ANTA Theatre, New York, later that year). Sketches for Act II, scene 1 and 4, and for Act II, scene 9. Motley Collection.*

York knew or cared anything about Lawrence of Arabia. It's a very British play, and they weren't interested, so it didn't do well." The film *Lawrence of Arabia,* starring Peter O'Toole, followed the New York production; it was not designed by Motley.

A Man for All Seasons, directed by Noel Willman and starring Paul Scofield, was a runaway success on both sides of the Atlantic. Robert Bolt's play was about the heroic Sir Thomas More, the Lord Chancellor who defied Henry VIII's wish to divorce Katherine of Aragon and marry Anne Boleyn. As Motley, Margaret Harris's sets and Sophia Harris's costumes added another triumph to their long list of successful historical plays. The production pleased the London critics and, surprisingly, in view of its immersion in a distant period of English history, it also pleased American audiences, reaping rave reviews in New York. Along with designing *Ross* and a new play, Graham Greene's *Complaisant Lover,* Margaret Harris oversaw the remounting of *A Man for All Seasons* in New York that autumn. The play was made into a film starring Paul Scofield and Leo McKern as Sir Thomas More and Thomas Cromwell, both from the original cast, and Orson Welles as Cardinal Wolsey.

Motley's ingenious set drew particular praise for the way it created individual scenes within a unit setting—a long, spiral slope turned into stairs curving around from midstage left to downstage right center. A metal handrail and a slightly "sixteenth-century" screen at the top completed a setting that was essentially timeless. Into this neutral setting, small scenic indications changed the location. To represent Wolsey's palace, a huge miter flew in and hung suspended above the stage. A front gauze with a water design represented the River Thames. For the trial scene, royal coats of arms built in bas relief were hung over the stage. Except in More's house, there was no furniture. The pieces of scenery and notice boards coming down to announce scene changes created an effect the *Times* (2 July 1960) thought "Brechtian." Margaret Harris found it a straightforward task: "While we were doing *Ross* in Liverpool, they rang me up from Tennents to ask if we would we do *A Man For All Seasons.* So we started working on it up there. The author Robert Bolt, the producer Binkie Beaumont, and the director Noel Willman

Toys in the Attic, *Piccadilly Theatre, 1960. Costume sketch for the plain-Jane character Anna Berniers (Diana Wynyard). It is one of the few Motley-designed shows that flopped. Motley Collection.*

all came up to work on it. I really thought that I was just doing what Robert Bolt said he wanted in the stage directions—a staircase. I had two weeks to do it in. I didn't really see why he wanted that, but I didn't have time to argue, so I just did it. Sophie did the costumes. They were traditional, but had a good sense of individual character. It was an amazing success, a tremendous success, that play." It opened in July.

Later that summer came *Waiting in the Wings,* by Noel Coward. "A light whimsy," the *Times* (9

August 1960) called it. The play about a group of aged actresses made for a nostalgic, sentimental evening in the theatre. It focused on their conflicts and reminiscences as boarders in "The Wings," a home for retired actresses. Margaret Webster directed Sybil Thorndike, Mary Clare, Edith Day, Mary Lohr, and Norah Blaney. "I think that he had written it to help out the elderly retired actresses who were in it," said Margaret Harris. For her and her sister, it was another drawing-room job with contemporary fashions, somewhat exaggerated to suit the actresses' styles. It opened in Dublin and played at the Duke of York's Theatre in London.[6]

Of the English production of Lillian Hellman's *Toys in the Attic* (1960) perhaps the less said, the better. Hoping to capitalize on its success in New York by bringing in Diana Wynyard and Wendy Hiller under the direction of John Dexter, the producers retained the New York designer Howard Bay's sets and featured new costumes designed by Sophia Harris. The production flopped, closing at the end of January, with a loss of £10,000 to London ticket agents. Critic Robert Muller (*Evening Standard*, 11 November 1960) simply said it was "a pathetically bad English production of a good American play."

Whenever possible, Glen Byam Shaw and Margaret Harris, sometimes accompanied by Byam Shaw's wife, the actress Angela Baddeley, would travel to the location where a play was set. For Ibsen's *Lady from the* Sea, Tennent's sent the director and designer to the fjord Andalsness and to the seacoast of northern Norway. "It was invaluable experience," said Margaret Harris, "because the play is about the feeling of someone who returns to the sea after being shut in by a fjord." As in all their work, Motley's aim was to capture the feeling of the place and to express the emotional environment of the play—in this case about a wife obsessed with her drowned lover. The production brought together a stellar cast—Margaret Leighton as the wife, Ellida, John Neville as her ghostly lover, Andrew Cruickshank as her husband, Vanessa Redgrave and Joanna Dunham as her daughters, Bolette and Hilda. Esmond Knight played the painter Ballested, and Richard Pasco, the young sculptor Lyngstrand. "Vanessa Redgrave was absolutely marvelous as Bolette," said Margaret Harris. Sophia Harris's costumes expressed the period

and the play's strongly defined characters.

Calling it "one of the finest pieces of theatre to be seen in the West End," *Theatre World* (May 1961, 31) credited Motley with "outstanding decor," and Robert Muller called the settings "marvels of naturalistic detail." Joining the chorus, hard-to-please Kenneth Tynan (*Observer,* 19 March 1961) judged that "the settings by Motley would not disgrace the Moscow Art Theatre." Ingeniously, the setting was capable of suggesting movement up and down the mountains. The first scene was in the garden just outside the house. In order to get the feeling of the fjord, a stretch of water appeared upstage. To represent the mountains in the distance that hemmed in the fjord, two large cloth pieces hung from metal rods. To suggest the silhouette of a mountain range, each rod was bent to form the mountain-top shape. From the rods hung cloth backdrops painted to resemble a forest. A layer of cloth gauze, hung over the backcloths, broke the sharp outline of the mountain ranges making them appear distant. The two cloths crossed over each other, one hanging in front of the other, as if there were two separate mountain ranges separated by a deep fjord. When, in the next scene the action shifted up the mountain to a look-out place, the perspective of the mountains shifted. To accomplish this, Motley lowered the hanging backcloths, which were soft, so they piled up on the stage. More sky could now be seen, and the action seemed to be much higher up in the mountains. To enhance the feeling of being higher up, the actors climbed up from backstage onto a slightly raised platform. For the next scene, the "mountains" rose up and the action returned to the garden.

In the seasons following, the London Motley women were concerned mainly with work outside the West End—opera at Sadler's Wells for Margaret Harris, film for Sophia Harris. Nevertheless, "Design by Motley" appeared in the credits for M. J. Farrell and John Perry's *Dazzling Prospect* at the Globe Theatre. Directed by John Gielgud, it was a fairly conventional drawing-room play about life in a decaying Irish mansion. It starred Margaret Rutherford, Joyce Carey, and Hazel Hughes. The play drew little critical attention, being appreciated mainly, as the *Times* (2 June 1961) said, by "those who collect Margaret Rutherford performances." Margaret Harris designed the sets, and Sophia

Lady from the Sea, *Queen's Theatre, 1961. Rough set sketches. Note the changes in the mountains in the distance for scenes at different altitudes. Motley Collection.*

Lady from the Sea, *Queen's Theatre, 1961. Rough set sketches. Motley Collection.*

Harris, the costumes.

At the end of the next season, 1961–1962, although busy with her work on major films, Sophia Harris found time to design costumes for *Playing with Fire,* a one-act comedy by Strindberg directed by John Blatchley. It opened at the Aldwych Theatre, then the London home of The Royal Shakespeare Company. The production was part of the initiative by the new artistic director Peter Hall to expand the company's repertory to include non-Shakespearean classics and new plays. "Beautifully dressed by Motley and imaginatively set by John Bury," wrote Philip Hope-Wallace (*Manchester Guardian,* 19 June 1962) of *Playing with Fire.* The review in the *Times* (19 June 1962) more or less dismissed it as a slight play, worthy of little notice.

Of more interest to the Motley women were their four West End plays of the following season, 1962–1963: a musical adaptation of Thackeray's *Vanity Fair,* a contemporary comedy *The Tulip Tree,* another revival of Bernard Shaw's *Doctor's Dilemma,* and an adaptation of E. M. Forster's novel *Where Angels Fear to Tread.* Sketches and renderings that document these productions, as well as the reviews, suggest the continuation of Motley's straightforward blend of beautiful period costumes and sets with a light touch of glamour.

N. C. Hunter's middle-class comedy *The Tulip Tree* starred George Benson, Lynn Redgrave, and Celia Johnson and was directed by Glen Byam Shaw, with sets by Margaret Harris and costumes by Sophia Harris. As the title suggests, the play took place around a tulip tree in a garden, with a village in the distance. The critic for the *Times* (30 November 1962) pointed out how the production drew "extensively on the garden setting for images of natural decay." For the designers, there was a practical problem: how to depict the change of seasons. "Glen and I went to Kew Gardens to look at a tulip tree," said Margaret Harris. "We took a lot of photographs of details. For the set, we had a great big tulip tree built with removable branches so that it could be adjusted to show spring and summer. Just before the play opened, all the leaves had got buckled up from having been packed. We had to get the whole company to straighten them out, including Lynn Redgrave, who said, 'How many leaves are there? There must be at least a million!'" Sophia Harris's costumes caught the mood of the slightly fussy middle-class household.

Compared to the *Doctor's Dilemma* in 1942, for which Sophia Harris had also designed the costumes, the 1963 production directed by Douglas McWhinney, made a rather slight impact. The *Times* (23 May 1963) warned, "Shavian revival leaves play's weakness undisguised," and *Theatre World* (July 1963) commented on "a hesitant and colorless Act I." Motley nevertheless received credit from the first critic for "sets that are elegantly apt." Margaret Harris disagreed. "I don't think that what I did with the sets was very good."

Where Angels Fear to Tread, written by E. M. Forster and adapted by the American Elizabeth Hart, starred Michael Denison, Dulcie Gray, and Keith Baxter. The play is about a woman who goes to Italy and has an adventure with a young Italian. Because it required several three-dimensional settings on the small stages of the Arts and then St Martin's Theatres, Margaret Harris used a revolving stage. "There was a difficult scene in which Dulcie Gray has to bathe a baby," she recalled. "Of course we used a flexible dummy. Glen managed it marvelously. The baby and the bath were upstage, Dulcie was facing away from the audience. It was a nice play, but it was quite difficult to design and stage." However effective Byam Shaw's direction, the *Times* (7 June 1963) spent most of its review talking about the "drastic effect of adaptation."

Motley's West End plays in the 1964 season fared better: *Hobson's Choice* by the "Manchester realist" Harold Brighouse and *The Right Honourable Gentleman* by the more conventional M. Bradley-Dyne. Although greatly different in subject matter, for the designers the two plays fell within a common, nineteenth-century frame of reference. The difference came in social milieu and ambiance.

Hobson's Choice was a successful play dating back to the early years of the century. It revolved around Henry Horatio Hobson, the hard-boiled owner of a shoe-and-boot shop. By putting on an English play written before World War I as a production of the National Theatre at the Old Vic, Laurence Olivier was making a statement about the quality of homegrown drama. John Dexter, who had been a young director at the Royal Court, directed the production. Joan Plowright as young Maggie Hobson played the "new woman" who struggled against her traditionalist father, played by Michael Redgrave. Assisted by Piers Haggard, son of the actor Stephen Haggard, Margaret Harris

Hobson's Choice, *Old Vic Theatre, 1964. Costume sketch for Tubby (Reginald Green), who wears a leather apron. Motley Collection.*

went to Manchester to take photographs for details of the set. The sets were on a revolve on the Vic's raked stage, sloping upwards away from the audience. To make them appear perpendicular, the sets had to be wide at the base and narrow at the top. "It was tricky," she recalled, "but it worked." "An atmospheric piece, it was helped by Motley's interior sets . . . particularly Maggie's cellar with its long grimy window at street level," reported the *Times* (8 January 1964).

For *The Right Honorable Gentleman* the Harris sisters found themselves on the familiar ground of upper-class London society. The play followed the politician Dilke as he was brought low by a past love affair, the scandal keeping him from a potential term as prime minister. Anthony Quayle played Dilke, Anna Massey, the girl, and Coral Browne, her mother. Motley used a revolve for the set, with an innovative design. The setting switched back and forth between two interiors. The spaces from the edge of the revolve to the tormentors (narrow flats set up and down stage just inside the proscenium arch to help with the masking) had to be filled. The director Glen Byam Shaw wanted the changes to take less than half a minute—just long enough for the revolve to get around. There was no time to change the flats, and since the rooms were different in character, the filler pieces couldn't remain the same. To solve the problem, Margaret Harris designed a frame of pillars with a cornice above and developed a system whereby one piece of scenery was hinged to the upstage side of the arch and another piece hinged to the downstage side. They scissored—when one swung out, the other swung in, assisted by a stagehand in the wings. "People were always very astonished," Margaret Harris recalled. "They didn't know how the change took place. The arch pieces were neutral, and they simply didn't notice that it was the same for both interiors." It was quite successful with the critics and at the box office.

Emile Littler produced the show. He and Motley had had a serious falling out years before over *Book of the Month.* Director Glen Byam Shaw told Littler that he wanted Motley to design the play. "Emile said 'No.'" Margaret Harris reported. "Glen said, 'Well who do you want, then?' Emile brought up designer after designer, and Glen said, 'No, no, I don't want to work with him. I don't want to work with her. Won't do.' So finally Emile gave in. But he got back at us. He offered us a miserable fee, and Glen having fought so hard for us, we couldn't turn it down. He paid us something like £150 for designing both scenery and costumes. He also snaffled the costume designs and kept them. For years they were on display in a fast-food restaurant in the West End."

As the 1960s ripened, Motley in London—Margaret and Sophia Harris—found their energies divided among the ongoing work at the Royal Court (new plays and new stagings of classics), Sadler's Wells (English-language operas), and the West

End. Sophia Harris continued to work in film as well. Their work in the West End ebbed and flowed. The 1964–1965 season saw Motley's name on only Noel Coward's *Hay Fever* at the Duke of York's Theatre, a transfer from the Old Vic where it had followed *Hobson's Choice* as a modern English classic of another sort. It had only one set, but it presented a problem: The iron safety curtain had to come down straight through a staircase. Margaret Harris had the handrail and one of the steps hinged so that they swung out of the way when the curtain came down. For Sophia Harris, the light comedy set in the 1920s had become a witty period piece, ripe for her deft talent in creating amusing costumes. "The use of costumes is one of the many delights of the production. . . . Lynn Redgrave, a hilariously discomforted Jackie, flops nervously into a chair and manhandles her beads on to her lap like a chain and anchor. Maggie Smith, equipped with a truncated bustle embellished with pearl buttons, scoops her train into position with a cigarette holder like a fairy's wand," reported the *Times* (28 October 1964). "The Motley decor, like the author's direction," said *Theatre World* (December 1964, 17), "avoided burlesque of this vintage but indestructible comedy.

For Margaret Harris, the memorable part of the production was Edith Evans's return to the Old Vic. "We opened in Brighton," she remembered. "Edith was quite old by then, and she was worried. She said, 'I can't play. I can't go on. I can't go on.' Noel was absolutely stumped. He didn't know what to do, so he sent for John Dexter. John said, 'I'll get her on.' He went to see her and he said how terribly sorry he was she wasn't well, and all that sort of thing. Then he said, but don't worry at all, because the understudy's very good and she'll give a very good performance. Edith went on! That's the sort of man John was; he could do that sort of thing."

In Chichester, the cathedral city sixty miles from London, Laurence Olivier had helped to inaugurate and direct a festival centered around a new, state-of-the-art, open-stage theatre, almost a rough draft for the National Theatre on the South Bank in London. In 1965 Arthur Wing Pinero's *Trelawny of the "Wells,"* with sets by Alan Tagg and costumes by Sophia Harris, opened its fourth season. The Chichester Festival was a going concern by then, its productions transferring from

time to time to London. The production very nearly did not come off. It was directed by Desmond O'Donovan, who, said Margaret Harris, "could carry the rehearsals through till they got nearly to the end, but he couldn't give the actors the final push. The actors got nervous because he didn't give them the confidence they needed. So John Dexter came in to help him with *Trelawny* at the end."

The play presented a considerable problem for director and designers. Pinero had been nostalgic himself about the theatre of the early 1800s when he wrote the play a century later—the "Wells" was an old, affectionate nickname for Sadler's Wells Theatre. For this production, a double displacement in time compounded the play's difficulty. How, in a brand-new, late twentieth-century theatre, to evoke Pinero's late nineteenth-century evocation of the earlier nineteenth-century theatre? On Chichester's open stage, all set changes have to be done in sight. "Desmond was not able really to cope with the set changes, so John Dexter did them," said Margaret Harris. "He is miraculous at that sort of change. They had to change everything, including the carpet, because it had to go from a touring actors' place to a very grand drawing room. John had six people dressed as footmen who worked the change, which was drilled to the last instant. It always got a round of applause—it was marvelously done. Then, when it came to London, for some reason Alan couldn't or wouldn't do the set. I was busy, so Sophie was asked if she would do it, though she'd never done a set in her life. She got her daughter Harriet's husband Peter Key to work with her, and they did a set which balanced with the costumes. It was the first and only set Sophie ever did."

The critics' praised not only the acting, but also the set and costume designers' success in evoking the feeling of a box-set theatre on the open stage at Chichester. Billed as the "National Theatre," Olivier's company found favor both in Chichester and London. Indeed, the *Times* (18 November 1965) favored the open stage over the "tall, wobbling flats" at the Old Vic in London, where it subsequently was transferred. Alan Tagg's minimal sets put more attention on Sophia Harris's costumes—Dickensian, Pickwickian, and lightly Victorian as they were. Her costumes for George Colman and David Garrick's *Clandestine Marriage* and Anouilh's *Fighting Cock* at Chichester the next season were the last she designed for Chichester.

By the 1960s, Bernard Shaw's plays had joined the ranks of the "classics." His 1900 play, *You Never Can Tell,* directed by Glen Byam Shaw and starring Keith Baxter, Cyril Luckham, Ralph Richardson, Harry Andrews, and Angela Thorne, came to the Haymarket Theatre in 1966. Margaret and Sophia Harris as Motley designed the sets and costumes. The production by these people who had worked together for decades—Byam Shaw, Harry Andrews, and Ralph Richardson since the 1930s, Cyril Luckham since the Shakespeare Memorial Theatre—looked dated to some critics. For the *Times* (13 January 1966) the production was "everything that the phrase 'The Haymarket play' suggests," implying that it was deft, but conventional. As the theatre world changed, what had once been directing, design, and acting that seemed exactly true to the spirit of the play now seemed somehow dated, despite a dateless script. It was the last London production Sophia Harris designed before her death.

Margaret Harris remembered Ralph Richardson's performance as "absolutely superb. In one scene he had a long speech to the character played by Harry Andrews, on a terrace where they've had a lunch party. Ralph said to Glen, 'I can't think what to do with this, it's such a long speech. I need something to do.' Glen said, 'Well, why don't you clear the table?' It had been a lunch party for eight or ten people, and so he thought that was a very good idea. So Ralph went to a hotel and got a waiter to show him exactly how to do it. He performed it absolutely miraculously. It looked the most natural thing in the world. He put everything onto a great tray, he whisked the cloth over it, and carried it out. I thought, 'He's never going to get done in time.' But I saw it many times, and it was absolutely precise. On such and such a word, he picked that up and put it on the tray, and on another word, he picked up something else. It was always exactly the same and it was brilliant, absolutely marvelous—it always got a round of applause."

Although Sophia Harris's death in 1966 by no means meant the end of Motley's work in the West End, it marked a significant change. Through the work of the Royal Court Theatre, Sophia Harris's costume designs had continued to associate Mot-

ley's name with the avant-garde, both new plays and new approaches to classic plays. Otherwise, Margaret Harris and Elizabeth Montgomery, who returned to London in 1966, as Motley remained a bulwark of the theatre establishment—the West End, the Shakespeare Memorial Theatre, the English National Opera. With the English National Opera and the Design Course now giving a new focus to Motley's work and with changes in the London theatre and the culture of the times, Motley were no longer in the mainstream. Carnaby Street and the Beatles signaled larger changes at work, changes that made the Motley's style more appropriate to the conservative opera or to the big-budget West End shows.

In the mid-1960s The Theatre Royal in the Haymarket had become the haven for traditional, "first-rate British" theatre. Productions "directed by Glen Byam Shaw and designed by Motley" became a fairly regular feature. To Londoners and tourists such plays meant good solid entertainment, not the controversial and often sordid new plays at the Royal Court, the classics at the National, or the hit-or-miss shows in the rest of the West End. Staging Sheridan's *The Rivals* with Glen Byam Shaw directing, Ralph Richardson and Margaret Rutherford starring, and Motley designing must have seemed sure-fire. But the *Times* (7 October 1966) was tepid: "Played in front of Motley's pleasant evocation of eighteenth-century Bath—a handful of sets which owe nothing to recent fashion but which might have come from the same artists at any point in their career—Mr. Glen Byam Shaw settles for simplicity of interpretation conveyed with style."

In the end, Margaret Harris was not entirely satisfied with her contribution to the production, as she explained: "I think I overdid it for *The Rivals* at the Haymarket. The play was difficult. Glen and I went to Bath to see what it looked like, and we got quite a lot of information out of the North and South Parades. Obviously it couldn't work to have them as they are, parallel to each other. So we decided to do something like what we'd done in *The Merry Wives.* We would have the *central* house, and then have flats going out from the center forming a V, slightly in false perspective. We made them look like houses in the North and South Parades. We also found interesting the way the names of the streets are all put up very beautifully with this incised Roman lettering; so we did all that with *trompe l'oeil* painting. We were able to set the furniture for the other scenes behind the street scene. However, we were not able to do the sets as we had wanted. We had thought of having the sets very, very lightly built, either dropping in or coming on, but we allowed ourselves to be talked into having each piece on a truck. They'd built them on trucks. We shouldn't have given in because it made it all much too heavy and noisy. After it had opened, I met at a party the lady who owned the Haymarket Theatre. She said, 'Do you realize we have more stagehands than actors in this production?' I said I hadn't realized it. And she said, 'We shall have to get another designer, shan't we?' I didn't bother to explain. What's the point? She was an old lady and she didn't really know technically about anything. But she was quite right; it was wrong that it should be so heavily built."

"An experience not to be missed," wrote Martin Esslin (*Plays and Players,* April 1967), of Strindberg's *Dance of Death* at the Old Vic. Laurence Oliver played Edgar, the small-time army captain who is dying; Geraldine McEwan was his wife; and, completing the triangle, Robert Stephens was Kurt, the friend who comes to visit. A grim, sadomasochistic piece that spans two generations, Strindberg's long drama won high accolades from the press as a triumph for the National Theatre. It represented the mature talent of Motley and friends in a season in which *Fiddler on the Roof, The Prime of Miss Jean Brodie, The Royal Hunt of the Sun,* and Joe Orton's *Loot* were all vying for box office. *Dance of Death* was to be the last play at the Old Vic Motley designed.

Following their customary approach, for background Glen Byam Shaw and Margaret Harris went to Sweden to visit the army museum in Stockholm and the museum at Vaxholm, which provided a wealth of material. The production found the old friends working comfortably together. "Larry had a wonderful story about himself in that play," said Margaret Harris. "He said to Joan Plowright, his wife, 'It says in the text that he's a very ugly man. What shall I do about my makeup?' and Joan said, 'Don't make up at all!' He laughed at himself about that. He was extraordinary in that production. The dance he did was absolutely amazing. He spent *hours* rehearsing it. He

used to rehearse it, and rehearse it, and rehearse it, and rehearse it. At the end of the play, he's terribly lonely, upset, and miserable. He picks up the cat and he strokes it, and he goes offstage. On the first night, he had a real cat. Well, he picked up the cat, and he came down to the footlights, and he stroked it, and the cat looked at the audience, and said, 'Meowr?' The audience laughed, but Larry didn't. After that it was always a dummy cat. It was never the same with a dummy cat, and it had been simply marvelous when it was a real cat. However, of *course,* he didn't like it."

Motley's last Shakespeare in London was a lavish *Merchant of Venice* at the Haymarket Theatre, starring Angela Thorne as Portia. "For some maniacal reason, Ralph wanted to play Shylock," said Margaret Harris. "Anybody *less* Jewish in the world you couldn't find! He was determined to do it, and so Glen Byam Shaw reluctantly agreed to direct it." Elizabeth Montgomery and Margaret Harris worked together on the *Merchant;* as in earlier times, Elizabeth did the costumes and Margaret, the sets. "Because it's all so Venetian, we decided to do it in eighteenth-century period costumes à la the painters Longhi, Canaletto, and Guardi," Margaret Harris explained. "Elizabeth did some very glamorous costume designs. They were made very well at Nathan's the costumier's. I did some poor sets: I was *trying* to do people in gondolas, and it didn't really work. I don't think any of the scenery was very successful. The whole production was a bit of a failure, except the costumes. They were very handsome." Looking forward to that production, John McLeod in *London Look* (10 June 1967, 20–21) reported a retrospective exhibition of Motley designs at the Wright Hepburn Gallery in Belgravia. The Haymarket Theatre Royal Company, who put on the play more as entertainment than as serious drama, said Irving Wardle (*Times,* 8 September 1967), made it "resemble a musical comedy libretto." However excellent the acting by Ralph Richardson, the same critic felt that the sets and costumes set the wrong tone: "In spite of the opening parade of Venetian props, there is no continuous sense of place: and the choice of Regency costume—although it affords fetching displays of silks and velvet—gets between the actors and the text. They get little support from Motley's bare stage, equipped only with Shylock's house in one corner and a translu-

The Dance of Death, *production photograph, with Margaret Harris and Lawrence Olivier in his dressing room at the Old Vic Theatre, 1967. The photograph comes from Motley's files.*

cent green back wall." Period sets, glamorous dresses—ever Motley's forte—had gone out of fashion for Shakespeare.

"It was Glen's last Shakespeare, and ours, too," recalled Margaret Harris. "He had said a long time before that he never wanted to do another. 'I *can't* do any more,' he said. He left Stratford in 1959 because he felt that he had come to the end of what he could contribute that was fresh and interesting. He thought it was time to find somebody young to take over, and of course Peter Hall did. 'It's awful to hang on after you've finished,' he said. He really did the same thing at the English National Opera. He was very definite and tough about all that."

Wise Child at Wyndham's Theatre, Simon Gray's

first play, challenged contemporary mores. John Dexter directed Alec Guinness as a whiskey-tippling, transvestite gangster and his "son," an apprentice hoodlum (Simon Ward) who is coveted by a hotelier. Praising Guinness for "his masterly best," Michael Billington (*Times,* 11 October 1967) thought the playwright was trying to do too many things at once. For Margaret Harris and Elizabeth Montgomery, "it was a perfectly straightforward play."

The Bells by Leopold Lewis may have made Henry Irving famous overnight as Mathias the Jew, but the classic melodrama failed to fulfill Marius Goring's hopes for similar success. The *Times* (25 January 1968) castigated the cardboard play—the sets and costumes by Motley escaped censure—and spared no scorn for Goring's "fanatically artificial" acting. Margaret Harris recounts a story of the leading man's peculiar vanity: "Marius called me in his dressing room during rehearsals and said,

'I've got something rather interesting to show you. I've got Irving's costume that he wore in the part. They lent it to me from the London Museum. They say that I may wear it on the first night, if you don't disapprove. I'll put it on and show you.' And so he did. 'It fits me perfectly,' he said, 'even the shoes. Absolutely perfect.' I think he felt like a reincarnation of Irving. It was a very nice costume. He put it on, and it looked fine. I never saw the production. I was in the hospital, because the night before the opening I fell off the rostrum and broke my hip."

In a strange detour, Margaret Harris and Elizabeth Montgomery designed two sets of three one-act plays, centered around the husband-wife team of Michael Denison and Dulcie Gray. The first, billed as *Trio*, featured *The Will* by Barrie, *Village Wooing* by Bernard Shaw, and *Ways and Means* by Noel Coward; Michael Denison directed. It played at the Yvonne Arnaud Theatre, Guildford. The second, billed as *Three*, contained three Shaw plays: *How He Lied to Her Husband*, *Village Wooing*, and *Press Cuttings*; Nigel Patrick directed. It played at the Fortune Theatre, London. In common was Bernard Shaw's *Village Wooing*. Reviewing the latter group, Irving Wardle (*Times*, 27 January 1970) especially enjoyed Motley's touch in *Village Wooing*—" lovingly naturalistic shop, crammed with forgotten brand names." "There wasn't very much money to spend, and we tried to simplify it very much, with one set of flats which turned round," Margaret Harris commented.

Morris West's *The Heretic*, a play about the martyrdom of Giordano Bruno, failed to repeat the earlier success of *A Man for All Seasons*, another historical play about a martyr. Because it was historical and concerned with matters religious, it might have been a natural follow-up, but turned out to be a flop. Irving Wardle (*Times*, 17 July 1970), usually a generous critic, dismissed it as "period hokum . . . undisciplined and vulgar," in script and acting. Elizabeth Montgomery's costumes were not mentioned, though the designs are appealing.

Not much better were the reviews for Ibsen's *Wild Duck*, which Margaret Harris and Elizabeth Montgomery designed and Glen Byam Shaw directed. Hayley Mills starred. Eddie Kulukundis produced it for Knightsbridge Productions. The production had a few difficulties. In Leeds, where

it opened, Elizabeth Montgomery fell and injured herself. In the Criterion Theatre in London, there were no flies, which made set changes difficult. "The first scene is in a rather grand house at a party," said Margaret Harris. "We based the whole set for that scene on velvet curtains, draped, and hung on a semicircular rod, so that it was quite rich looking. The whole thing dropped in, inside the attic set. There had to be a very, very quick change from the house party to the attic, where they lived. It was worked out very carefully so the curtains flew out, most of the furniture for the attic was already set, and there was just one big piece to swing in. When the show came to London, we had to reconceive the whole thing. There are no flies at the Criterion and no space. It's a *tiny* stage. So we had to split this set up onto tiny trucks— about six tiny trucks, and we tried to fit the furniture onto the trucks. The change was supposed to be practically instantaneous, and we did get it down to two and a half minutes. They had to wheel all the trucks off and pack them exactly right.

"It was an interesting set because the attic was made all of wood—actual wood stained so that the grain showed. We used a wonderful scene painter called David Lawes. He's absolutely the tops. There was a little ceiling piece that had to lift up to let another piece come in. I said that it should all be wood. The management said, 'We can't have wood for this piece, it's too heavy. It can't be wood, it's got to be canvas.' And I said, 'I can't accept it.' They said, 'I'm sorry, canvas is the only way we can do it.' So, that was that. The set was set up, I came in and I looked up. I said, 'You've made it of wood after all!' But they said, 'David painted it.' It was simply amazing. He's really extraordinary. I was standing underneath it and I still thought it was made of wood. It just shows you that you can be obstinate for no reason. I was terribly annoyed and upset that they weren't going to do it of wood because I thought canvas would look awful. You can forget how very well things can be done." After spending his review faulting the acting and Byam Shaw's balanced directorial compromise between comic mania and tragic gloom, Irving Wardle perversely advised his readers to see *The Wild Duck* because "there is no better play in London."

The Unknown Soldier and His Wife came to the

London stage in 1973, six years after its premiere in New York. "A comic strip history of mankind at war," wrote Irving Wardle (*Times,* 23 May 1968) when he saw the play at Chichester in 1968. After its New York opening, the play by Peter Ustinov had been staged and re-staged first at the Chichester Festival in England, then in Lyons, France, and finally at the New London Theatre. Having designed the original New York set and costumes, as mentioned in chapter 6, Elizabeth Montgomery worked on the other productions with Ustinov, who had begun his theatre career with Michel Saint-Denis and Motley in the 1930s. Margaret Harris designed the sets for the London production—"very badly," she thought. Despite the fact that anti-war fervor ignited by the Vietnam War had been burning for some time, the *Times* praised Ustinov's prowess as playwright, director, and actor, yet found him and the play wanting: "A classic demonstration of Ustinov's strengths and his inability to project hatred even on the most hateful theme in the world."

For *A Family and a Fortune* in 1975, the Motley women found themselves designing sets and costumes that evoked nostalgically the manners and mores of England before World War I, the England of their childhood. The play was an adaptation by Julian Mitchell of a novel by Ivy Compton-Burnett. Alec Guinness and Margaret Leighton starred. In it Margaret Harris tried to make an effect on the set with sound. The play has one set, comprised of a room, a terrace, and a garden path. She designed the floor of the room in wood, the terrace of artificial stone, and the garden of gravel, so that the actors' steps would sound different, depending on where they were walking. "The wood and gravel worked, but the stone didn't," she said, "I think because it had to be mounted on wood and was hollow." It was Motley's last West End production.

★ ★ ★

Looking back over Motley's work in the West End over three decades, one can see a record of steady accomplishment. In the early years, they were part of the movement to re-establish excellence in the British theatre. That excellence was attained, signaled most visibly by the foundation of the National Theatre at the Old Vic and the rise of Arts Council subsidies for that enterprise, the Royal Shakespeare Company, and other, smaller companies in London and the provinces. Motley became one strand among many in British theatre design, standing for excellent period set design with evocative and often ingenious set changes, and a representational (as opposed to a realistic) approach. In costumes, Sophia Harris and Elizabeth Montgomery especially excelled in creating variations on period dress that brought out a play's atmosphere and helped to establish character. Their high level of achievement continued unabated. On a practical level, however, the mix of plays in the West End changed as time went on. Proportionately, the sorts of plays that Motley designed—all the rage in the 1950s—had come to be seen in the later 1960s as old-fashioned, belonging to another generation.

In terms of artistic style, the 1960s proved to be a watershed in British theatre design. New courses in the art schools and polytechnics had produced a different way of thinking about design—glitzy, technically inventive, self-proclaiming to the point that directors and actors spoke with scorn of "designers' theatre" that overshadowed the acting. So prominent was the shift in artistic approach that three of Motley's better known contemporaries either quit designing entirely, as did Cecil Beaton, who turned to photography, or drastically cut back their work in London, as did Tanya Moiseiwitsch and Leslie Hurry, both of whom found Stratford, Canada, more hospitable. Yet, as the theatre historian Roy Strong notes, despite the departure of these three designers and major changes in taste, in the 1960s "the painterly tradition did not die. It took a new direction, responding to the *verismo* style of Franco Zeffirelli and Lila de Nobili. This took on board the change in perception generated in the public by both film and, by 1960, television."[7] Hearkening back to nineteenth-century realism, all the more possible with new lightweight materials, this approach remained bound by single-point perspective. "Painterly" design was most comfortable in the opera house or the ballet, sharing with Motley's approach a delight in period accuracy and beautiful effects. But it was not in the mainstream.

More than anything, however, the changes in theatre design wrought in the 1960s and thereafter came from the emergence of new directors, new designers, and new theatres. Glen Byam Shaw and

Margaret Harris epitomized the directing and design of Gielgud's generation, perfected in its maturity during the 1950s and extending well into the 1970s, for certain sorts of plays or operas. Their successors in Stratford, director Peter Hall and designer John Bury, were twenty years younger and university-educated. Following a course not unlike Byam Shaw's and Motley's, Hall and Bury also gravitated towards opera as their careers ripened into maturity, even as the next generation of directors—Trevor Nunn and Terry Hands—and designers—Hayden Griffin, Farrah, Tim O'Brien and Tazeena Firth, John Napier—came to the fore in the 1970s.

The open stages of the Chichester Festival and the National Theatre responded to—some would say required—a non-representational approach favoring swift set changes and sometimes elaborate use of stage machinery—platforms rising and revolving, spectacular lighting effects, and symbolic, surreal, or abstract images that commented forcefully on the tenor and meaning of the drama. Inspired by these innovative spaces, designers began to see the stage and the auditorium as a part of the set design, rather than as neutral frame for settings. For the *Henry* plays in 1975, for example, the stage at the Royal Shakespeare Theatre was extended forward into the auditorium and backwards to the bare brick of the whitewashed back wall to make a huge, black wooden platform. Its remote resemblance to Shakespeare's Globe was enhanced by wooden facades that clad the galleries on either side of the proscenium arch. The designer Abdul Farrah and the director Terry Hands made it deliberately non-representational, beginning *Henry V* with the actors in rehearsal clothes, putting on their costumes only when the French ambassador is announced. In the battle scenes in the *Henry IV* plays, Northumberland, mounted on stilts, stepped powerfully down the stage like a great predatory bird in a feathered black cloak. For the tavern scenes, an enormous aubergine drape hung in midair suggesting an interior, but hardly representing any imaginable medieval tavern. Only some props: a table, stools, and tankards indicated the nature of the setting. For Motley, such "distortions" of Shakespeare would have been unthinkable.

Speaking years later of productions like this one—productions she rarely saw, but heard of through her students and the newspapers—Margaret Harris commented on the changes evolving in the theatre during the 1990s: "Theatre design is utterly different now—different sense of color, if there is any, different ideas about how the design should relate to the play and the actors. I decided not to go on designing because I hadn't the energy to be tough enough with myself. I don't go to the theatre anymore because I don't expect I'd like what I see very much." From the perspective of the 1990s, however, one can see that Motley's innovative and pioneering work laid the foundations for just such developments. They became possible when the younger designers and audiences could look beyond Motley's standard approach to design through the paintings of the past, to approaches through the discontinuities and symbolism of twentieth-century art. Although Motley had by the later 1960s largely confined themselves to designing for the English National Opera and only occasionally for the West End, their influence on the upcoming generations of designers continued through Margaret Harris's teaching. By no means dedicated to the sterile perpetuation of outmoded traditions, the Motley Theatre Design Course has been an innovative meeting ground for the best young designers to work with leading directors and designers, a story that is told in chapter 14.

13
Film
1933–1966

Motley's work as film designers formed a small but important part of their output. Although they were not always credited, the three women designed several films in England before World War II. During the war, Elizabeth Montgomery and Margaret Harris designed costumes in Hollywood for the Nelson Eddy-Jeanette MacDonald extravaganza, *I Married an Angel*. In America after the War Elizabeth Montgomery designed costumes for *Long Day's Journey into Night,* which adapted her designs from the stage production. She also designed costumes for *Oklahoma!,* but the Motley designs were used without her supervision. In England after the War, Sophia Harris designed costumes for more than a dozen films, credited sometimes in her own name, sometimes in her married name: Sophie Devine. The list of titles is impressive: *Great Expectations, Blanche Fury, Captain Boycott, The Courtneys of Curzon Street, So Evil My Love, The Card (The Promoter* in the United States), *The Innocents, The Loneliness of the Long Distance Runner, A Taste of Honey, Night of the Eagle, This Sporting Life, Night Must Fall, The Pumpkin Eater, The Spy Who Came in from the Cold, Fog (A Study in Terror* in the United States), and *Dance of the Vampires.*[1] Of the three Motley women, Sophia Harris made the greatest contribution to costume design for film, ranging from romantic costume dramas of the 1930s and 1940s to the gritty realism of the 1950s and 1960s.

Although Cecil Beaton and Oliver Messel are the "big names" who usually are mentioned as film designers, they themselves didn't design many films. More important, for instance, was work by Elizabeth Haffenden, who began designing for the theatre with Laurence Irving, came into costume design for films in the 1930s, and made a career designing the "Gainsborough melodramas" in the 1940s for Stewart Granger, James Mason, and Margaret Lockwood. In this context, Motley's work stands as representative, reflecting the mainstream development of British cinema.

Designing costumes for films differs from designing costumes for the stage. In film, Motley found, one designed more for the personality of the actor than for the character, more for the silhouettes in long shots and for the detail—the head, the hair, and the hat—in close-ups. The production process put costume design under the responsibility of the production designer (PD) and the art director (AD). In theory, the production designer was responsible for the overall "look" of the film; the art director, for carrying out that concept in detail. Costume designers worked with both; the production designer having final say. In practice, of course, their efforts were collaborative. Motley often worked as a team with production designer John Bryan and art director Wilfrid Shingleton. Occasionally, they worked with a single "art director" who was also production designer.

A serious difference between film design and design in the theatre rests in the sharing of artistic responsibility with a wider group of artists. Motley as film designers—principally Sophia Harris—had considerably less control over their work than they enjoyed when designing sets and costumes in the theatre. Where they had once done it all themselves in the theatre in London, in films they were constrained by union work-rules and by the expectations of the crafts people, who had set ideas about the quality and look of fabrics and props. Motley preferred the cheap material that would look right onstage; Hollywood preferred authenticity adapted to the film camera.

Costumes look different on film. Under stage lighting in the theatre, they may be made of fabrics and in colors that would appear too rough or too strong under natural lighting. They are meant to register with an audience seated at some distance from the performers and must hold up under the stress and strain of nightly performances. For films, especially color films, costumes must be finished in more detail in colors and fabrics that subtly suggest period and character. The bright colors of stage musicals must be muted for film, a point that one can see plainly when comparing the sketch for the film *Oklahoma!* with sketches for, say, the stage production of the musical *Paint Your Wagon.* "You must learn how colors will look," warn Motley in *Designing and Making Stage Costumes,* "and the rules here *are* quite arbitrary. Certain colors, notable among them a particular shade of blue, 'bleed': that is to say, the tone is dissipated by the light and the outlines appear frayed" (20). The authors caution designers against the use of white and urge them to consult with the cameraman and sometimes with a color expert from the studio for help in selecting costume colors.

Among the Motley films, their designs for *Great Expectations* perhaps came closest to theatrical costuming. This is not surprising, as Dickens relies on exaggerations of characterization and plot that in the hands of a less skilled writer would degenerate into caricature and melodrama. For films set in the past, such as nineteenth-century America for O'Neill's *Long Day's Journey* or Victorian England for *The Innocents* (the adaptation of Henry James's *The Turn of the Screw*), Motley needed to adapt clothing so that it would seem neither too exotic nor too uncomfortable to modern audiences. Films set in the present raise another problem. For *The Loneliness of the Long Distance Runner* and for *A*

Taste of Honey, both made and set in England in the early 1960s, Sophia Harris had to design costumes that audiences would scrutinize and interpret with the same acuity they would exercise in the world around them. Granted, not all audiences would be familiar with the two films' actual settings—a boy's school and working-class living quarters—but those who were would notice any false note. She had to have a keen eye for the way "real" people dress and to use those observations to help establish character.

Happily, film has a permanence denied the theatre. Even with careful research, one may only reconstruct and re-imagine Motley's accomplishments in the theatre. On film one can see their costumes as they actually appeared. Although some of the earlier films may be viewed only in archives, many of them remain current through videotape rental companies and art cinemas, thereby keeping Motley's name and work before audiences long after their theatre productions have vanished.

When Motley were first getting started in the 1930s, the British film industry was struggling to compete with the American. After World War I, during which the European film industry had gone into suspended animation for four or five years, the United States dominated the market and stayed there. Douglas Fairbanks, Mary Pickford, Charlie Chaplin—American stars and their film companies—took over the industry. As soon as new European talent emerged in the 1920s, Hollywood bought them up, offering more money and glamour than the European producers could. Britain's response was the protectionist Quota Act of 1927 for which the British film industry campaigned fiercely. This legislation required movie houses to show a certain proportion of British-made films. The British film industry responded with "quota quickies"—feature films that met the act's minimal requirements and fulfilled its aim of keeping the British studios open. Though they employed British artists, their artistic value came to little.

At the other end of a broad spectrum that included some solid, mid-range feature films, were the prestige productions of Alexander Korda and Michael Balcon, intended to compete in the world market with big-budget features from America. Korda's *The Private Life of Henry VIII*, starring Charles Laughton, was the first British film to succeed in the United States. It won an Academy Award. In a class by themselves, Hitchcock's *The 39 Steps, The Man Who Knew Too Much,* and *The Lady Vanishes* also found audiences in America. Despite such exceptions, the rule for British films in the 1930s were the low-budget quota quickies and mid-range films for the home market, which usually played as second features with the American blockbusters. For film history, these films are important. They record fresh talent on the rise and older talent on the way down, as well as big names from the silent days or American actors in starring roles, who would be hired to play only supporting parts in the United States. The films of the 1930s for which Motley designed costumes stand in the middle ground—serious artistically, well-financed, but not international features.

The American actor Charles Bickford—apparently on loan from an American studio—came over to Britain early in his career to star in Motley's first film, *Red Wagon* in 1933. With a cast rounded out by Raquel Torres and Greta Nissen, the film attempted to blend the appeal of British aristocratic tone with the adventure of the circus. It was not a hit. "What is designed as the big kick in the film is the circus atmosphere, on which a lot of time and money has been spent," said *Variety* (26 December 1936) when it was released in America. The article concluded that "it was all very well done. But this has ceased to be a novelty." Motley's name does not appear in the credits. Their contribution seems to have been more as costume consultants on the set. "We went out on location and helped with circus costumes," Margaret Harris remembered. "We did one for Charles Bickford that had a long red cloak."[2]

Motley's next film, *Brewster's Millions,* was more ambitious, even though their contribution was not remarkable. The film boasted the Hollywood director, Thornton Freeland, the British producer Herbert Wilcox, the stage and screen star Jack Buchanan, the top designers Schiaparelli and Norman Hartnell—and Motley. Not to be confused with subsequent remakes, the 1934 *Brewster's Millions* had already proved itself a star vehicle for Gerald DuMaurier onstage. The story is about a young man who will inherit a fortune only if he finds someone who will marry him by a certain date. Jack Buchanan, the film's actor-producer, had seen Motley's work and asked them to do *his*

clothes, with Schiaparelli and Norman Hartnell doing the rest of the costumes. The success of that venture led to other film work, principally for Sophia Harris, who began to specialize in it.

Sophia Harris designed the costumes for *Marigold* on her own. This 1938 film was directed by the silent-film director Thomas Bentley. The mid-range Korda actress Sophie Stewart played Marigold, a proper Edinburgh lass who strikes out for London where she meets dashing young officers. Others in the cast included Phyllis Dare, a stage star from early in the century, and the character actor Edward Chapman. Their presence marked it a solid film with well-known British talent. The theme of women's emancipation anticipated issues that only later would appeal to a large audience.

A "little film" packed with artistic talent, *I Met a Murderer* was almost a family production. James Mason, his wife Pamela Kellino, and her father Roy Kellino produced it; Roy Kellino directed; James Mason and Pamela Kellino starred. Its plot followed the accused murderer on the run (Mason) who is cleared by the help of a good woman (Pamela Kellino). Sophia Harris designed the costumes on her own, after Margaret Harris and Elizabeth Montgomery had left for America.

Despite a downturn at the end of the 1930s, the British film industry appeared to be finally coming into its own. When World War II broke out, the government wanted to close down the film studios, but the industry resisted, claiming that films were "propaganda" essential to the war effort. Moreover, the argument ran, keeping theatres and movie houses open would sustain public morale and defy the German onslaught, despite the danger of bombs falling on such concentrations of unprotected people. During the War the British studios turned to documentaries and big features—*The Life and Death of Colonel Blimp,* for example, or *A Matter of Life and Death* with David Niven. By the mid-1940s, the British film industry had begun to revive. David Lean made *Blithe Spirit* and *Brief Encounter,* for instance, and, perhaps better known to American audiences, Laurence Olivier produced, directed, and starred in *Henry V.* Independent from the American studios, they were able to be uniquely British, rather than imitative.[3]

In the meantime, Margaret Harris and Elizabeth Montgomery in America experienced filmmaking in Hollywood. *I Married an Angel* was the only

Great Expectations, *film, 1946. Production photograph, Miss Havisham (Martita Hunt). Still from the film by courtesy of the Rank Organisation Plc and the British Film Institute.*

film Motley designed in America, and they worked on it more as a means of qualifying for their union cards than for any other reason, as mentioned in chapter 5. George Cukor, whom they had met through the Olivier *Romeo and Juliet,* invited them to come to Hollywood, where he promised them a job at MGM. *I Married an Angel,* the last Jeanette MacDonald-Nelson Eddy musical, was a leaden dream-fantasy. It was optioned from the stage play of 1938, then shelved until 1942 because of the War. "As the 'angel' Jeanette MacDonald had to wear large, clunky angel's wings," Margaret Harris recalled. Contrary to film folklore—that Jeanette MacDonald was an "iron butterfly"—Margaret Harris found her "perfectly amiable, though a bit *old.*" Nelson Eddy, generally thought to be easygoing, allowed his pretensions to artistic taste to cause him to reject Motley's designs for his costumes in favor of his own designs. In the film he plays the son of a banking family in Budapest. Around the bank and estate house are portraits and busts of ancestors. Nelson Eddy made them himself, using his dressing room as a painting and sculpture studio. They were all self-portraits, with additional whiskers or mustaches to indicate antiquity. For Motley the experience was not particularly happy, although it did establish their union credentials as designers. "A rather disappointing experience," recalled Margaret Harris. "All we could do was make a thumbnail sketch, show it to Cedric Gibbons, the art director, and listen to him tell us how he had done something quite like it in the 1920s. He marked each design 'OK. Gibbons,' which meant that he approved it. We were glad to leave."

Great Expectations (1946), which Sophia Harris designed in England, followed in the wartime tradition of British films that celebrated Britishness. The War had ended and British film people were eager to make prestige films that would do well in America. Shakespeare's and Dickens's works were natural choices. The cast featured the best British film stars: John Mills, Jean Simmons, Valerie Hobson, Bernard Miles, Francis L. Sullivan, Martita Hunt, Alec Guinness, and Finlay Currie. Based on a stage adaptation written by Alec Guinness for George Devine and the Actors' Company, the play had been staged in Rudolph Steiner Hall at the beginning of World War II, as mentioned in chapter 4. When David Lean decided to produce and direct the film, he asked Alec Guinness to star as Pip's friend Herbert Pocket. Motley were commissioned to do the costumes. Besides Guinness, there were other members of the stage cast who appeared in the film—Martita Hunt as Miss Havisham, in particular. In an arrangement typical of the closely collaborative British film and theatre community, Sophia Harris designed the costumes with her former colleague Margaret Watts, whom she had met when Watts was working at Motley's studio as the manager. Since those days, Watts had married the designer Roger Furse and worked with him on the design for the famous Olivier *Henry V* film. She now worked as a designer in her own right under the name "Margaret Furse." The production designer John Bryan and the art director Wilfrid Shingleton strove to create a distinctive treatment of light and darkness, an effort that was recognized with an Oscar for production design and art direction. It was an early triumph for David Lean as "a brilliant technician, sensitive and serious about cinema, probably the most skillful of all the young British directors," wrote Paul Rotha in *The Film Till Now.*[4]

Filmed in black-and-white, the costumes bring Cruickshank's illustrations to life, creating delicate caricatures of the fashions of the times. The Christmas dinner at Gargery's looks like an old-fashioned Christmas card; Mrs. Haversham's treasured bridal gown—"a sick fancy," as she herself admits—is a threadbare relic of her youth; it proves fatal when it catches fire at the end. In London, the young men sport enormous bow ties; Jaggers (Francis L. Sullivan) proclaims his wealth with lush neckcloths, a lavish vest, and frilled shirtcuffs, and Joe Gargery, a caricature of a caricature, appears so outlandish that Pip tells him he is "dressed grotesquely in that new suit." In these instances and throughout the film, the costumes serve as markers of social status, symbols of London corruption or, in the case of Miss Havisham's gown, of the distorted values of the Havisham establishment. *Variety* (11 December 1946) said cautiously that the film "may take its place alongside the best British pictures now being made." It did. The film is regarded as a classic of the cinema.

Revivifying the British past through Dickens represented part of a wider trend to "escape into romanticism and historical set-pieces," as Paul Rotha observed.[5] In 1947, the same design team—

Great Expectations, *film, 1946. Production photo-graph, Pip (John Mills) and Herbert Pocket (Alec Guinness). Still from the film by courtesy of the Rank Organisation Plc and the British Film Institute.*

with some of the same actors—created *Blanche Fury,* Sophia Harris's next film. The head of the team, John Bryan, was the first film art director in England to be called a "production designer," a designation he campaigned for. He worked with David Lean, Cineguild, and Two Cities Films. Having come from the theatre, where he had worked with Laurence Irving, he later became a producer. In film circles he was known for "de-signed perspective," as he called it, meaning forced perspective—shots from unusual, often low, cam-era angles. Moreover, the settings he chose were unusual, infusing Bryan's films with a distinct sense of the camera's presence and the director's control. Wilfrid Shingleton, who had been work-ing in British film since the 1930s, served as art director for *Blanche Fury.* He and Bryan went on to create together such films as *The African Queen* and *Hobson's Choice.*

Blanche Fury was one of the first British films in Technicolor after World War II. It was directed by the Continental art film director, Marc Allegret. The plot is melodramatic simplicity. The beautiful Valerie Hobson, of noble birth but penniless, comes to the great house as a governess. Forced to marry the despicable young heir apparent, she falls for the dispossessed Stewart Granger, an em-bittered scoundrel who betrays her in the end. The

film illustrates Bryan's approach as production de-signer: the "look" of the sets and costumes is heightened, glamorous, romantic realism. The scenes of the English countryside look like post-cards come to life—bright sun, bright colors, "au-thentic" country great house. The costumes follow suit. Each phase of the heroine's development from impecunious governess to impassioned se-ductress to grieving widow is marked out dis-tinctly by Sophia Harris's elegant, picturesque, and glamorous costumes for Valerie Hobson. Cos-tumes for the rest follow the same pattern—ro-mantic, Byronesque clothes for the dastardly Granger; formal, prissy propriety for Valerie Hob-son's ill-fated husband; a "huntin'-and-shootin'-squire" look for his father; and so on. In keeping with Bryan's "forced perspective," in typical En-glish scenes (the manor house, the steeplechase, and so forth), the film could almost be seen as propaganda for the glory and travails of the Britain that was. It seemed both magical and as remote from post-War England as was Scarlett O'Hara's ante-bellum South in America.

In the same year, Frank Launder and Sidney Gil-liat, a producing and writing team, brought out *Captain Boycott,* based on the life of the Irish rack-rent lord. Known for thrillers—they wrote Hitch-cock's *The Lady Vanishes*—they misfired with this

Blanche Fury, *film, 1947. Production photograph, Blanche Fury (Valerie Hobson) and Philip Thorn (Stewart Granger). Still from the film by courtesy of the Rank Organisation Plc and the British Film Institute.*

big costume film, despite Sophia Harris's contribution. A socially conscious plot; proven writers and director; a cast filled with stars and vintage character actors; the art director Edward Carrick, Gordon Craig's son and Ellen Terry's grandson; and wonderful costumes by Motley all signaled a prestige film. But it was not a great commercial success. Its message may have been too heavy, without enough "entertainment value," as the industry moguls would say, and it has since faded into film history.

The Courtneys of Curzon Street (*The Courtney Affair in the* U.S.A.) came out in 1947 as another in the "Mayfair" series of films directed by Herbert Wilcox and starring his wife Anna Neagle. These romantic comedies were "top box office." Audiences paid to see handsome Michael Wilding paired with ladylike Anna Neagle, gowned in elegant costumes, lovingly photographed and directed by her husband Herbert Wilcox. According to Margaret Harris, Neagle was a good friend of Sophia Harris, whose name appears in the credits for this film. That is not the case for other "Mayfair" films, though she may have advised Valerie Hobson informally. People would go to Anna Neagle's films simply to see how gorgeous she looked in her elegant gowns—yet the costume designer's contribution was not always recognized in the credits. Ironically, wardrobe mistresses were more likely to appear in the credits than were the costume designers.

As wartime shortages eased and a new economic order began to emerge, British and American film efforts re-joined—or rather the Americans opened up subsidiary studios in England, as they had in the 1930s. MGM became MGM British; Twentieth-Century Fox, Twentieth-Century Fox British; and so on. Paramount British produced *So Evil My Love,* a prestige feature film with producer Hal B. Wallis and Lewis Allen, then a rising American director. A *"Gaslight"* film, in which the wife was being manipulated by others, it brought together a first-rate cast: Ray Milland—who was then seen as an American star, although he was in fact British—Ann Todd, Geraldine Fitzgerald, Leo G. Carroll (known to American television audiences as the star of *Topper*), Martita Hunt, and several British character actors. Edith Head, who did the women's costumes, gave the picture Hollywood prestige. Sophia Harris brought to it the luster of

London. The art director Tom Morahan, who worked with Hitchcock several times, was the father of Christopher Morahan, who later worked with Margaret Harris in the theatre and then went on to become a film and television director in his own right.

When the American distributors promoted *The Card,* Sophia Harris's next film, they insisted that it be renamed *The Promoter,* guessing correctly that the American slang meaning of "joker" would miss the point of the British "card," meaning "a self-promoter." Its plot, based on the novel by Arnold Bennet, follows the adventures of an ingratiating social climber, played by Alec Guinness, who cons his way up the social ladder. The rest of the cast also featured established British theatre stars: Glynis Johns, Valerie Hobson, Frank Pettingell. Sophia Harris's husband George Devine played a small part, as did Petula Clark, who would later become famous as a pop singer ("Downtown"), and the character actor Wilfrid Hyde-White (he later played Professor Higgins's friend Colonel Pickering in the film version of *My Fair Lady*). Set in the 1890s, it provided ample opportunity to show off British glamour with beautiful costumes by Motley. Its director, Ronald Neame, who later became famous for *The Poseidon Adventure,* had begun working in films as one of Britain's top cameramen. Although John Bryan had moved up from earlier work as art director, as producer he nevertheless supervised the film's design by his assistant Tim Hopewell Ash.

Caught up with the demands of George Devine's Royal Court venture, raising her daughter Harriet, and a disintegrating marriage, Sophia Harris did not work with film again until *The Innocents* in 1961.

Meanwhile, Elizabeth Montgomery as Motley was asked to design the costumes for the film *Oklahoma!* in America. An obvious choice in view of her Broadway musical experience, she began the design of the costumes, but came down with the flu before she could finish them. The producers brought in Hollywood designer Orry-Kelly to carry on. In the end, because the producers would not allow her to employ her own cutter and assistants, Elizabeth Montgomery left the film without supervising the making of the costumes. Unaware of this and other production problems—the film took a year to produce—*Variety* (12 October 1955)

Oklahoma! *film, 1955. Costume design for the women. Attached to the design are swatches of fabric. The pastel shades reflect the designer's response to filming in Technicolor. Motley Collection.*

said it "rates with the industry's best." Bosley Crowther in the *New York Times* (11 October 1955) said the film "magnifies and strengthens all the charm that the play had upon the stage." The new Todd-AO filming and projection system, however, left John McCarten complaining in *The New Yorker* (22 October 1955) of "an air of magniloquence hardly suited to the simple rusticity of its theme." "It was a hotchpotch," Margaret Harris said, "because Elizabeth wanted to do costumes that were true to the American Western style, and the other designer from Hollywood didn't." Nevertheless, the credits proclaim "Costume design by Motley." A single surviving sketch shows the farm girls' pastel frocks, colors toned down for Technicolor. The film was released in 1955. It was the last film Elizabeth Montgomery would design.

Sophia Harris returned to designing costumes for films in 1961 with *The Innocents*, a black-and-white film based on the stage adaptation of Henry James's novel *The Turn of the Screw*. Motley had also designed costumes for the stage productions, as noted elsewhere. The turn-of-the-century aristocratic setting and glamorous costumes gave an elegant face to the atmosphere of gothic terror. Deborah Kerr and Michael Redgrave starred, with the character actors Peter Wyngarde and Megs Jenkins in supporting roles. The film was directed by Jack Clayton. An "in" director at the time, he had gained fame through the film *Room at the Top*. Art director Wilfrid Shingleton was also considered topnotch. Produced by Achilles, an independent studio, the film received some support from Twentieth Century-Fox. Deborah Kerr's contract assured that the filmmakers would have a big budget to work with.

Despite the appreciation of literary audiences, *The Innocents* failed to impress the critics. Bosley Crowther (*New York Times,* 26 December 1961) spent most of his review explaining why it was unscary, "bland but inadequately motivated along psychological lines." More sympathetic, *Variety* (6 December 1961) found it "powerful and gripping, though somber and disturbing."

By the later 1950s and early 1960s, big-budget studios were being challenged by independent producers. Such respected directors as David Lean struck out on their own. Following that trend came *A Taste of Honey* from Woodfall Films, a production company founded by the Royal Court Theatre's Tony Richardson, Lindsay Anderson, and others. Naturally, they turned to Sophia Harris, their colleague from the Royal Court, for costume design. With the exception of *Tom Jones*, designed by Jocelyn Herbert, Woodfall's films were socially conscious—usually concerned with working-class issues. Their first film of this genre was John Osborne's *Look Back in Anger*, with costumes designed by Jocelyn Rickards, then living with Osborne. Many, however, were designed by Sophia Harris, who remained in close contact with Richardson and his circle. Despite her separation from George Devine in the later 1950s, her flat and studio in Lower Mall remained a magnet for these artists and others from the Royal Court.

As a play, *A Taste of Honey* had premiered in Stratford-upon-Avon in 1958, after which it enjoyed long runs in London and New York. Director Tony Richardson worked closely with the author Shelagh Delaney to keep the film as close as possible to the play. The bittersweet romance of a working-class girl (Rita Tushingham) with a black sailor (Paul Danquah) is the "taste of honey" that brightens a life made dreary by her poverty, her lower-class social status, and her slatternly mother (Dora Bryan). Rita Tushingham and Murray Melvin (playing a homosexual who befriends her) won the Cannes Film Festival acting awards. The film took the British Film Academy awards for Best Picture, Best Actress (Dora Bryan), Best Screenplay, and Most Promising Actress (Tushingham). *Variety* (20 September 1961) found it "vital and absorbing." A. H. Weiler in the New York *Times* (1 May 1962) said the work was "more memorable on film" than the popular play. *Saturday Review* (quoted in *Film Facts*, 25 May 1962) proclaimed it "the best English film to come along this year." Set in a working-class port city, it represented a radical departure from Sophia Harris's earlier, glamorous films. Her sharp eye for dress as an expression of character enabled her to capture the coarse floozy in the mother, the young girl's innocence, and the exotic appeal of her lover. The pop song "A Taste of Honey" came later; it had nothing to do with the film, except that it benefited from the film's popularity.

In 1962, for *Long Day's Journey Into Night* by Embassy Pictures—an American studio—Sophia Harris adapted Elizabeth Montgomery's costume designs for the play's premiere in 1956 in New York. Ely Landau directed. The film starred Jason Robards, Katharine Hepburn, Ralph Richardson, Dean Stockwell, and Jeanne Barr. Costumes for Hepburn as the morphine-addicted mother effectively traced her progress from an attempt at dowdy respectability in the first act to her pathetic "femme fatale" in the second, to her utter, disheveled decline in the last act. The costume designs provide a perceptive visual interpretation of the character. The credits recognize "Motley." Although Bosley Crowther said it was "generally stunning," in the New York *Times* (10 October 1962), *Variety* (30 May 1962) praised it unequivocally as "a lesson in filmed theatre . . . [that] allows the playwright's work to speak for itself." It remains a classic American film.

The Loneliness of the Long Distance Runner, another Woodfall film, portrayed the suffering and triumph of a "Borstal boy," or, in American parlance, "juvenile delinquent," placed into a reform school. Tom Courtenay's first big film, it won him the British Film Academy's award for Most Promising Newcomer. Believing that sports can make a gentleman out of anyone, the uppercrust headmaster (Michael Redgrave) encourages the young man (Tom Courtenay) to train for a race against a nearby posh public school. The training allows him freedom to leave the Borstal grounds. Although tempted to flee, he continues to return day after day. In the end, he slows down as he approaches the finish line, throwing the race to defy the aggressive pride of the headmaster. In the United States the film was sometimes billed as *Rebel with a Cause*, echoing the title of the James Dean film. As with *Taste of Honey*, Ralph Brinton was the art director; Sophia Harris, the costume designer. "She got some help from Peter Gill for that, I think," recalled Margaret Harris, "because he lived in her house." The costumes were not designed in the sense of "made-up." In cases like this, the clothes were chosen carefully from those in department stores so that they would be both "authentic" and interpretive. These thereby reinforced the strong social conflicts in a film in which as much was conveyed by what was not said as by what was said. Tom Courtenay's clothes, for example, are deliberately ill-fitting and large to make him appear poor and weak in comparison with the natty headmaster. The New York *Herald-Tribune* (9 October 1962) hailed the film as "a brilliant piece of work . . . the latest of Tony Richardson's sharp film expressions of the attitude of the 'angry young men' of England." It has become a classic.

Night of the Eagle, a horror film also released in 1962, was reminiscent of a cinematic genre known in the trade as "Hammer horror films."[6] These remakes of horror classics, or new color horror films on traditional plots and themes—the "son of" and "return of" variety—emphasized literal, gory, photographic reality. The stake that goes through the vampire's heart off-screen in the first version now is seen entering stroke by stroke as the blood spurts. In this film, set in a posh Oxford college, a candidate for an eagerly sought professorship gains help from his wife's powers of white witchcraft. His rival for the post receives assistance from *his* wife, a black witch. After several harrowing twists in the plot, the evil witch dies, a victim of the forces she has unleashed. The eagle of the title is an ominous statue on top of the college entrance that falls at the end of the film and crushes the evil witch who had fought the professor and his well-intentioned wife. Janet Blair plays the good wife; Peter Wyngarde, the good professor; Margaret Johnston, the bad witch; and Anthony Nicholls, her husband, the rival professor. Its producers, Albert Fennell and the team of Julian Wintle and Leslie Parkyn were known as medium-budget commercial producers. Jack Shampan was art director. Sophia Harris's costumes portrayed contemporary college dress—cocktail party frocks, house dresses, professorial garb. All were bought "off the rack." Why she worked on the film—other than for fun or for money—is unclear, as its subject matter, director, and cast were not especially familiar to her.

Based on a novel by David Storey, *This Sporting Life* continued the Royal Court group's series of stage and film productions set in the north of England among working class people. It was directed by Lindsay Anderson, formerly of the Royal Court. The link-up with producers Albert Fennell, Karel Reisz, Julian Wintle, and Leslie Parkyn suggests a tie to the commercial resources of that association. In his first big film, Richard Harris plays

a muscular, working-class thug who cannot understand why the sensitive Rachel Roberts finds him unappealing. William Hartnell, also in the cast, later became known as the television character Doctor Who. Colin Blakely, Arthur Lowe, and Leonard Rossiter rounded out a cast of good, mid-level British talent. The story follows the ill-fated romance of Frank Machin, a miner-turned-rugby-player and Mrs. Hammond, a factory worker's widow. As with the other "angry young men" films, Sophia Harris's costume designs reflected contemporary working-class fashions. The film was released in 1963.

Night Must Fall was based on a play by Motley's long-time associate, the director and playwright Emlyn Williams. The original play had been written, directed, and starred in by Williams in the 1930s, with a 1937 film adaptation as well.[7] With this film, released in 1963, the Woodfall people, along with Karel Reisz and Albert Finney, were turning to an older, established British "property." In doing so they were in keeping with the Royal Court's mandate to foster British plays and British talent—somewhat incongruously in this case, as the play hearkened back to an earlier era when social concerns were less an issue. MGM had produced the film in 1937; thus, MGM retained the rights and their subsidiary MGM British produced the remake. Albert Finney was then a big name because of the films *Tom Jones* and *Saturday Night and Sunday Morning.* In *Night Must Fall* he starred as the young opportunist who tricks a wheelchair-bound old woman (Mona Washbourne) into leaving him her money. The production designer Timothy O'Brien usually worked in the theatre, rather than in film. Sophia Harris's costumes were suitable. It was not in any way a remarkable film.

In Harold Pinter's adaptation of the popular novel *The Pumpkin Eater* by Penelope Mortimer, Anne Bancroft played the conventional upper-class housewife, always pregnant, (hence the "pumpkin eater") married to Peter Finch. In the course of a stormy marriage, she contemplates abortion to break out of her entrapment—sounding a theme that was then quite controversial. The film's plot and themes fit with the interests of the director Jack Clayton, whose *Room at the Top* had examined upper-class malaise. "In this slow, strong, incisive film, the ironing out of a well-kept wife's unkempt psyche is portrayed with harrowing perception by

Anne Bancroft," said *Time* (quoted in *Film Facts,* 4 December 1964) when the film was released in 1964. She was nominated for an Oscar for the part. A prestige British film in black-and-white, its cast also featured prominent stage actors: James Mason, Cedric Hardwicke, Richard Johnson, Anthony Nicholls, Maggie Smith, Eric Porter, and Cyril Luckham. Its production studio Romulus Films was known for high-quality films such as John Huston's *The African Queen* and *Moby Dick.* Sophia Harris designed (or selected) elegant contemporary clothes. At this point in her career, she was designing costumes for two or three films each year.

John Le Carré's *The Spy Who Came in From the Cold* followed in 1965. It ran directly opposite to the excitement and glory of Ian Flemming's James Bond. Instead, the film looks closely at the gritty, grim world of agents and double-agents, heavy drinking, blighted romance, and sudden death in London and Berlin. A big-budget thriller about a British spy disillusioned with the spies' games of cat-and-mouse in Berlin, the star-studded cast included Richard Burton as the spy and Claire Bloom as the innocent librarian who falls for him. The strong cast is completed by Sam Wanamaker, Oskar Werner, Peter Van Eyck, George Voskovec, Rupert Davies, Cyril Cusak, Michael Hordern, Beatrix Lehmann, and Esmond Knight. Ironically, Martin Ritt, the director of this anti-Cold War film, had been blacklisted for alleged communist sympathies during the 1950s in America. Bosley Crowther (*New York Times, 23 December 1965*) judged the film "realistic and believable," a welcome relief from "romantic and implausible" spy movies. Burton was nominated for an Oscar for Best Actor. The British Film Academy awarded it Best British Film, Best Actor (Burton), and Best Black-and-White Art Direction (Edward Marshall). As with her other costume designs for the Royal Court group, Sophia Harris's costumes had to indicate class and character subtly but precisely.

Fog exploited audiences' seemingly endless appetite for Conan Doyle.[8] In this minor film, Sherlock Holmes stalks Jack the Ripper through the streets of London. Its British director James Hill, whose career went back to the 1940s, is best known for his later film *Born Free.* The cast brought together some of the best British actors of the time: Robert Morley, John Neville, Anthony Quayle, Frank Finlay, Judi Dench, Cecil Parker, Donald Houston. Funding for the production came from several independent producers, with Columbia joining in. An offshoot of the Hammer-horror tradition, and the second Sherlock Holmes film in color, it shifted Holmes to real-life crimes, made him younger and more physically active than the cerebral original, and deprecated his virtuosity on the fiddle. "A pleasant diversion," said A. H. Weiler in the New York *Times* (3 November 1966). *Time* found it "sly and stylish" (quoted in *Film Facts,* 5 November 1966). Sophia Harris's Edwardian costumes established the period amidst the rather hygienic and well-lit East End sets.

Dance of the Vampires was the last film for which Sophia Harris designed costumes, working with the new director Roman Polanski. As suggested by the American title, *The Fearless Vampire Killers; or Pardon Me, But Your Teeth Are in my Neck,* it was a tongue-in-cheek takeoff on horror movies that has since become a cult film. It starred Polanski and his wife, the ill-fated Sharon Tate. Sophia Harris worked again with the production designer Wilfrid Shingleton. Although she was unable to finish the film before she died, the credits still read "Sophie Devine." Anthony Mendleson, who completed her designs, had been Ealing Studios' resident costume designer from 1947 until the studio closed in 1955. He then had a successful freelance career, winning Oscar nominations for *Young Winston* and *The Incredible Sarah.* Mendelson preferred to credit Sophia Harris and to leave his contribution to this film unmentioned.

Motley is a name well-known among British and American film designers. "Sophia Harris" or "Sophie Devine" are less readily recognized, except among the colleagues who worked directly with her. Out of more than 100 people who designed costumes for films, her costume designs for twenty films represents a significant output. More often than not, although many of the films Sophia Harris worked on were important, fame and credit went to the art director or the production designer. Motley's costumes were remarkable for their characterization, their glamour, and their aptness to the overall look of the production. As a costume designer for films, theirs was the art that conceals art, seldom recognized or credited outside the special world of the theatre and film designers.

14
The Motley Legacy
The Design Course (1966–   )

The more Motley's reputation thrived on both sides of the Atlantic, the more their influence among other designers grew. Although much of that influence was indirect, spread by example that was imitated unconsciously by others, much was direct, for Motley were also teachers. As described in chapter 4, they began teaching as part of the London Theatre Studio (1936–1939). After World War II, Saint-Denis, Devine, and Byam Shaw, with Motley, set out to implement "the Plan" for the Old Vic Centre, which included the Old Vic School, as described in chapter 8. Margaret Harris took charge of the courses in set and costume design, occasionally helped by her sister and by other established designers, until the Old Vic Centre and the School came to an end in 1951.

Having been drawn into the orbit of the Sadler's Wells (later the English National) Opera, in 1966 Margaret Harris began teaching young designers through that venue. She called the undertaking simply "The Sadler's Wells Design Course." One of the young designers, Hayden Griffin, later became her assistant and co-director of the course. His contribution to the school's administration and his teaching have been central to the course for nearly three decades.

In 1968, when the opera company moved from Sadler's Wells to the London Coliseum, the Design Course moved into rooms at the top of Sadler's Wells Theatre. In 1971, they moved into the company's rehearsal and wardrobe space at Camperdown House in Aldgate. These arrangements were ideal, in that the students worked on their own projects in close association with Margaret Harris, Glen Byam Shaw, and John Blatchley, who were close at hand. Each year a new group of students assembled in September. For ten months they worked with various theatre artists, attended dress rehearsals, and created their own individual design projects. At the end of the third "term" in July, their projects—set models and costume designs—went on display in the annual exhibition. To this showcase of new talent year after year came theatre artists—directors, designers, actors—for an opportunity to evaluate and often to employ the new designers, as well as to visit with friends and catch up on each other's doings. Thus a tradition formed that continues to this day, albeit with younger people taking on more responsibility, because of Margaret Harris's advanced age.[1]

Every few years, changes in the theatre company's management or funding made it necessary for the Design Course to find new quarters. When the ENO moved their workshops to West Hampstead in the late 1970s space and funds for the Design Course could not be provided; the course moved to the Riverside Studios in Hammersmith. Then an outpost of experimental theatre housed in the former BBC studios, the Riverside Studios made a name for itself as a venue for new work—or avant-garde treatment of the classics. It also served as a showcase for new work from abroad, under the directorships of Peter Gill and David Gothard. In 1987 a change in management forced the Motley designers to find an alternative studio at the Almeida Theatre in Upper Street, Islington—ironically only a few doors from the building where they had worked decades before with the London Theatre Studio. The Design Course maintained an informal partnership with the avant-garde, low-budget Almeida company for several years, but was forced to move again in 1991. As a temporary rescue measure, the Royal National Theatre on the South Bank generously agreed to house the course for one year. They adapted their paint frame, the large space where scenery flats were painted, for use by the Design Course. In 1992 the School moved into quarters in Shelton Street, near Covent Garden. In 1994 it moved into the Drury Lane Theatre workshops. The loyalty and devotion the Course inspired in its graduates account for its ability, like John Barleycorn, to rise again and again without any formal institutional status or affiliation.

Through all these changes, the course remained consistent in its aesthetic and organization. "It's all based on the work of Michel Saint-Denis . . . [who] believed that the most important person in the theatre was the dramatist, then the actors, and then the director and designer," Margaret Harris told critic Michael Billington (*The Guardian*, 31 January 1991). "He argued that the designer's job was to show the play and the actors to the best possible advantage. Also that they should not decorate: they should design. I suppose that is why our designers are very popular with dramatists. Edward Bond has said he couldn't have written for the theatre if it hadn't been for the Course, especially Hayden Griffin."

Over the years the number of students has increased only slightly from the original eight to ten. Each year more than 100 submit portfolios of their work and are interviewed. From these, about twenty-five applicants are selected for second interviews by Margaret Harris, Hayden Griffin, and, since 1992, Alison Chitty. In that crucial evaluative interview, emphasis falls not only on abilities but on personality: "We look, of course, for talent, imagination, and energy, but we also take great account of suitability of temperament, attitude, and approach," warns Margaret Harris in the school's prospectus. Her aims hearken back to the L.T.S. ideal of a "company" who work in happy collaboration, rather than a group of individuals in creative competition with each other. Over the nine months' work a bond forms among the students that carries over into later collaborations among the graduates of the Design Course and the many theatre artists who have worked with them.

By no means exclusively British or Anglo-American, the Design Course's graduates work in theatres all over the world. Most of them, it is true, work in Britain, Canada, Australia, and the United States. The roster of the graduates' homelands, however, reads like a miniature United Nations: Australia, Austria, Canada, Chile, Colombia, France, Germany, Gibraltar, Great Britain, Greece, Holland, Hong Kong, Ireland, Israel, Italy, Japan, Jordan, Libya, New Zealand, Nigeria, Norway, South Africa, Switzerland, the United States, Uruguay, and Yugoslavia. Referrals from graduates have kept up its international scope. It is no exaggeration to say that through these graduates Motley's influence continues in theatres throughout the world. (See the appendix for a complete listing.)

What distinguishes the Motley Design Course from courses in design at the Central School, the Slade, or the Royal Academy of Dramatic Art, for example, is its close connection with the working theatre from the highest levels—the Royal Shakespeare Company, the Royal National Theatre, the West End, and the BBC—to the more modest experimental and regional theatres. Other theatre training programs grew out of art schools. Motley's came from the theatre world and remains immersed in it. "Students are encouraged to approach design for theatre as an organic process involving the script, the actors, and the space, so that the final product is a cohesive theatrical event," states a description of the course from the 1970s. Its instructors are active theatre professionals who come in as part-time lecturers or tutors. In an average year, two dozen directors, three choreographers, four designers, four lighting designers, and four theatre technicians come into the School, sometimes giving lectures and often working closely with individual students. These theatre artists, in turn, invite the students to dress parades, technical rehearsals, and performances of plays, ballets, or operas in production. The opportunity to receive instruction from such a wide spectrum of theatre artists has prevented the development of any recognizable Motley "house style," other than the unremitting respect for the text's meaning, the actors' needs, the director's concept, and the audience's understanding.

Neither Margaret Harris nor the Design Course has espoused anything like a flashy, high-tech environment. Its quarters have always been workmanlike to the point of shabbiness, caused in part by scarce funds, but also by the minimalist—"use only what you must"—Motley approach. On a typical winter's day in the early 1990s, for instance, one could pass through the Almeida Theatre and climb stone stairs to an upper floor. After negotiating a room filled with the detritus of the theatre—some broken props, a hat-rack, a very dilapidated sofa, empty coffee cups—one could climb more stairs, at last stepping into a large studio well-lit by a skylight. On paint-spattered worktables sit

half-constructed set models; costume renderings are pinned to a drawing table; paintbrushes and paints, pencils, sketches, bits of model-making material, old newspapers, more coffee cups abound. In silent concentration, several students are hard at work; two are constructing set models, another frowns over a costume rendering, another is cutting balsa wood into what will become timbers for a set model. In one corner, three others visit about the dress rehearsal at Covent Garden the previous evening. Later that day a director renowned for his biting intolerance of below-standard work will be coming to assess the projects and to talk about his own work. A few jokes are being made about what he'll say about whose work. The atmosphere is secure, almost familial.

The telephone rings in an office down a narrow hallway. Ranged on shelves along the hall are scripts and art books; in filing cabinets are folders sorted by year and subject, fashion photographs, and items of interest clipped from *Vogue* and the Sunday supplements. Everything seems a jumble, albeit an interesting jumble, for it is here in the "library" that students will look first for ideas; later they will look in London's art galleries, museums,

Photograph of the "Design by Motley" exhibition.

or research libraries. At a battered desk in her office, Margaret Harris is on the phone talking with people looking for design work or looking for a designer. She will later join the students for the assessment of their work by the director, whom she has known for many years. Sitting at another desk, administrative director Chris Rodgers is speaking with a public relations firm that is launching a fund drive in aid of the school's ailing finances. The school, she is explaining, is entirely supported by donations or by fees paid by the students, not by government grants or subsidies. The occasion for the fund drive is an exhibition, "Design by Motley," opening at the Royal National Theatre later that week—a transfer from America. One o'clock, and time for Margaret Harris to meet a publisher and his assistant about the revision and reissue of Motley's *Designing and Making Costumes for the Stage*.[2] Then comes the director's visit, followed by a general summing up with the students after he has gone. About seven o'clock or so, Margaret Harris leaves for her flat in Barnes in her blue Renault.

In a typical year, students design several productions, making sketches for costumes and sets. When these are satisfactory, they make scale models that depict the appearance of different moments onstage under theatrical lighting. These "projects"—designs for sets and costumes for actual scripts in extant theatres—are often initiated by directors considering productions in particular theatres. For them, the Design Course offers an experimental laboratory in which they can test production ideas with a willing design student. Such collaborations often bear fruit in the form of later employment. During the Course students receive instruction in lighting, technical drawing, costume design, period costume, cutting, scene painting, propmaking, and makeup. Throughout, the emphasis is upon making designs and set models that would work in actual productions. No pat, how-to training, the Motley Design Course encourages its students "not to accept the easy and conventional solution but to dig deeper into the possibilities." It is that quest for the "imaginative, inventive, and adventurous" that has characterized Motley's own work and the work of their students.

The Course culminates in an opportunity for each student to design an actual production for a drama school, an opera school, or another low-budget but real-world theatre organization. The results are presented in an annual exhibition presided over by Margaret Harris and often opened by such notables as Sir John Gielgud or, until her death, Dame Peggy Ashcroft. Established theatre artists flock to it—interested in seeing the work of the latest Motley group. In no crass way, it also serves as an informal hiring fair, both for the graduates and for those who come to see and renew ties. For two weeks or ten days in July, with Margaret Harris greeting her old friends and students, one has a glimpse of that collegial warmth that must have infused the Motley studio in St. Martin's Lane many years ago.

There is a personal dimension to this instruction that forges close ties among all who have studied with Margaret Harris. Each student has a different, but equally personal story. Mitsuru Ishii, once Motley's student, is now a prominent designer working in Japan, the United States, and England in the theatre and television. He set aside a degree in law from Tokyo University to come to London and study set and costume design at the Central School. Once in England, he realized that his funds would not support a three-year course of study. He called upon Margaret Harris. Recognizing his extraordinary talent, she created an extra space for him in that year's course. He perfected his English working in a Kentucky Fried Chicken restaurant. Since 1975, when he returned to Tokyo, his designs have blended Japanese and Western motifs—most recently in a production of Mozart's *Magic Flute* produced by NHK, the Japanese national television company. When former students come through London, they stop by to visit and to reinforce that worldwide network of theatre artists with ties through Motley. Once, when asked by an impertinent interviewer if she wished she had married and had had children, Margaret Harris smiled and said, "Why should I? I have *hundreds* of children, most of them grown up, thank God, as it is."

Motley's influence has spread also through the preservation of their designs for study by scholars and theatre artists and by an exhibition that presented their work to audiences numbering three million in the United States and England.

"How in the world," one puzzled English actor asked me in the Royal National Theatre green-room, "did Motley's designs end up in an American library amidst the Illinois cornfields?" There is no simple answer to that question, for some rather extraordinary serendipity brought together the Motley designers, the nation's third largest university library, and the National Endowment for the Humanities. In 1976, *Macbeth Onstage* was published, a book reconstructing the 1955 Laurence Olivier–Vivien Leigh *Macbeth* directed by Glen Byam Shaw in Stratford-upon-Avon. In 1977, as that book's creator, I sought out Margaret Harris to interview her about her Shakespeare designs. From that first meeting came a plan to gather and preserve all of Motley's designs that could be found. Margaret Harris hoped that they might be kept in an English museum or library, but that hope grew dim. The subsidy supporting Motley's Design Course at the English National Opera had been canceled by the British government's budget cuts; the same cuts barred purchase or even proper storage of the designs by an English institution. By 1980 they had been gathered together in her Smith Square atelier where, Margaret Harris said, "a young woman from Sotheby's" was preparing an inventory with prices. The famed auction house obviously took the matter seriously. Sotheby's advised sales in lots to art dealers, who would frame and sell individual pieces. The threat of the designs being separated and sold as unique works of art spurred to action the University of Illinois Library, where the value of preserving the collection as a whole was recognized. The University purchased the collection for its own Rare Book Library.

In September 1981, Harriet Jump (née Devine), Sophia Harris's daughter, came to the University of Illinois with two steamer trunks containing all the designs belonging to Motley. After the initial excitement faded, library personnel faced the large tasks of sorting, cataloguing, and storing the 5,500 pieces in acid-free folders and boxes. Over the next two years, slide copies were made as added insurance against deterioration and as an aid for research and teaching. Before the designs could form a useful research collection, however, research needed to establish their origins. What shows were they made for? Who were the directors, the actors, and other designers on each production? What were the designers' intentions? How did the critics react? Files of reviews for each of the three hundred-odd Motley productions were compiled. These drew

on the resources of the University of Illinois Library, the Harvard Theatre Collection, the Raymond Manders and Joe Mitchenson Theatre Collection, the Theatre Museum (the last two both in London), the Shakespeare Centre Library (Stratford-upon-Avon), and John Gielgud's personal scrapbooks. Extensive tape-recorded interviews with Elizabeth Montgomery and Margaret Harris elucidated the designers' intentions. Edited transcriptions were added to the archive, now named the Motley Collection of Set and Theatre Designs.

By 1985, the "Motley project" had acquired an office, a "Motley crew" of research assistants, and a permanent home in the Rare Book Library. In 1986–1990, grants from the National Endowment for the Humanities funded *Design by Motley,* an interpretive exhibition that toured the United States. The American tour took the exhibition to the Los Angeles Theatre Center; the Ashland, Oregon, Shakespeare Festival; the Seattle Public Library, the Boston Public Library; the University of Texas Performing Arts Center (Austin); the Kennedy Center (Washington, D.C.); Lincoln Center (New York); the Florida Center for the Book (Fort Lauderdale); and the 1800 North Clybourn Center (Chicago). The exhibition subsequently transferred to the Royal National Theatre, London. Since then, Motley's classic book *Designing and Making Costumes for the Stage* has been revised, *Costume and Set Designs by Motley,* a selection of slides and a monograph on Motley has been published, and the entire design collection has been put onto color microfiche, thereby making it accessible at major research libraries.[3]

Paramount to these unusual events has been the strong working partnership between theatre artists, humanists, and librarians. Few people who see a play or ballet think, nor should they, of the complex process by which the script or musical score has become living art. One recognizes the actors and the directors and, to some extent, the designers. But mostly, one remembers the play as an intense, moving experience. In the best productions, the audience lives the play along with its performers, and it becomes part of their individual lives. Thanks to the partnership between artists, scholars, and librarians, in Motley's designs one may glimpse present and past worlds from the very special perspective shared by Motley and the theatre-and filmgoers exposed to their art. Many of those visions, embedded deeply in contemporary culture, have become landmarks. *South Pacific* transformed the American experience of World War II and the Far East into a bittersweet fable, cloaking themes of women's independence—"I'm Gonna Wash That Man Right Outa My Hair"—and racial prejudice—"You've Got to Be Taught"—themes that years later would rip through American society like a scythe through long grass. Motley's swifter rhythms and more appealing costumes also awakened a respect in audiences—many of them Americans—for Shakespeare, who they learned to appreciate more as a contemporary playwright than as a literary artifact.

This then, has been the Motley legacy, a rich contribution to the cultural life of the United States and Great Britain during the central decades of the twentieth century. Their contribution lives on in the memories of those many hundreds of thousands, perhaps millions who saw plays, films, operas, and ballets designed by Motley. Their work has taken on a second life as designs that are the primary research materials for theatre artists and scholars. And, as Margaret Harris rightly observed, through the work of Motley's many "children," an artistic legacy has passed from its creators to artists and audiences throughout the world.

Appendix
Motley's Students

Where are the graduates of the Motley Design Course now? A listing of some of Motley's students gives an idea of the broad scope of their influence. The information below, supplied by the former students, is of course an incomplete listing of their design credits. In parentheses appear the year each completed The Design Course:

Susie Caulcutt (1967)
: Freelance: designer, U.K.

Hayden Griffin (1967)
: Freelance: Royal National Theatre, Royal Ballet, West End, London theatres, BBC television, U.K.; Deutsches Schauspeielhaus, Germany; Australia, Canada, Italy, U.S.A.; also film.

Carol Lawrence (1967)
: BBC costume designer.

Derek Nicholson (1967)
: Former head of theatre design, Sydney University, now freelance designer and lighting designer, Australia.

Elroy Ashmore (1968)
: Freelance: U.K., Belfast, Northern Ireland; Germany; Japan.

David Collis (1968)
: Freelance: English National Opera, lecturer on theatre design; resident designer, Arts Theatre, London.

Michael Holt (1968)
: Freelance: U.K. and Australia;; lecturer on theatre design, Manchester Univeristy; author of two books on design.

Miki von Zwannenberg(1968)
: Freelance: films.

Ruth Dar (1969)
: Camara and Habima Theatre, Tel Aviv, Israel.

Martin Johns (1969)
: Freelance: Me and My Girl, U.K. and U.S.A.

Bronwen Casson (1970)
: Designing and directing, Abbey Theatre, Dublin.

Kim Carpenter (1971)
: Deviser, designer, and teacher at NIDA, Theatre of Image, Sydney, Australia.

David Lay (1971)
: Freelance: designer and scenic artist, U.K.

Andrea Montag (1971)
: Freelance designer and instructor, U.K.

David Reekie (1971)
: Freelance television designer, U.K.

Di Seymour (1971)
: Freelance: U.K. and U.S.A.

David Ultz (1971)
: Freelance: Royal Shakespeare Company, Royal National Theatre, U.K.; Canada; U.S.A.

Edith Del Campo (1972)
: Head of Costume, TV Channel 13; instructor, theatre faculty, University of Chile.

Philip Jung (1972)
: Freelance: New York and U.S.A.; died 1992.

Bob Morse (1972)
: Freelance costumier based in Lincoln; also designs pantomime costumes, U.K.

David Short (1972) — Freelance: Royal Exchange, Manchester; Chichester Festival, U.K.

Timian Alsaker (1973) — Head of Design, Royal National Theatre, Oslo

Phoebe de Gaye (1973) — Freelance: television commercials and film, U.K.

Jamie Leonard (1973) — Freelance film designer *(Fools of Fortune)*.

Etyan Levy (1973) — Film and television in Israel.

John Parkinson (1973) — Freelance: costumes, sets, and props designer and maker, Cumbria, U.K.

Gavin Semple (1973) — Associate Professor, Department of Drama, University Calgary, Canada.

Peter Hartwell (1974) — Freelance: Royal Shakespeare Theatre, Royal Court, London; Mark Taper Forum, Los Angeles; National Arts Centre, Ottawa, Canada.

Gemma Jackson (1974) — Films: *Chicago Joe and the Showgirl, The Miracle.*

Len Birchenall (1975) — Designer, BBC Bristol, U.K.

Mike Bridges (1975) — Film and television, Australia.

Mary Greaves (1975) — BBC set designer, U.K.

Mitsuri Ishii (1975) — Set and costume designer, Tokyo, London, U.S.A.

Shawn Kerwin (1975) — Freelance: set and costume designer, Canada.

Ramon Lopez (1975) — Director, Catholic University Drama School; designer and lighting designer, Santiago, Chile.

Miranda Melville (1975) — Freelance: dance, theatre, and film, Ireland, U.K.

John Otto (1975) — Freelance: Brussels and Amsterdam.

Douglas Robinson (1975) — Freelance: theatre and television designer, Canada.

Nicola Borella (1976) — Head of her own design company, Paris, France.

David Buckingham (1976) — BBC designer, U.K.

Anne Diamond (1976) — Thames Television designer, U.K.

Penny Hadrill (1976) — Fabric designer, dyeing and painting, landscape design, U.K.

Juliet Watkinson (1976) — Head of Design, Gateway Theatre, Chester, U.K.

Sue Willmington (1976) — Freelance: Royal National Theatrer, London; costumes for *Phantom of the Opera*, Melbourne and Toronto; Hong Kong Arts Festival.

Loy Arcenas (1977) — Freelance: U.S.A.

Kandis Cook (1977) — Freelance: Royal Shakespeare Company, Royal Exchange, Manchester, U.K.

Anthony McDonald (1977) — Freelance: Royal National Theatrer, Second Stride, and other dance companies, U.K.; France.

Steve Addison (1977) — Artistic Director, Proteus Company, Basingstoke, U.K.

Man Cheng (1978) — Head of design, television, Singapore.

Carmel Collins (1978) — Film and television, U.K.

Frank Conway (1978) — Gate Theatre, Abbey Theatre, Dublin.

Eamon D'Arcy (1978) — Design consultant, Sydney, Australia.

Gerard Howland (1978) — Royal Shakespeare Company, Sadler's Wells Opera, films, U.K.

Rod Langsford (1978) — Freelance designer, Royal Shakespeare Company, Scottish Opera, Old Vic, U.K.

Peter Peacock (1978) — U. K. Exhibition and tradeshow designer.

John Thompson (1978) — Television director and production designer, U.K.

Eric Chevalier(1979) — Costume and set designer, France.

Alex Byrne (1980) — Freelance: Royal Shakespeare Company, U.K.; Lincoln Center, New York; televison.

Claudia Mayer (1980)   Freelance: opera and drama, U.K.; France and Portugual.
David Roger (1980)   Opera designer, Opera Factory, U.K.; Germany.
Annie Smart (1980)   Sets and costumes, Royal National Theatre, London.
Caroline Amies (1981)   Production designer and art director, films, U.K.
Paul Doran (1981)   Freelance: set designer, propmaker, television, U.K.
Frank Flood (1981)   Freelance: theatre designer, Gaiety, Dublin; Arena, Washington,
                                  D.C.; film, television, rock video.
Brigitte Lambert (1981)   Resident designer, New Victoria Theatre, Stoke-on-Trent; in-
                                  structor, Rose Bruford School, London.
Inez Nordell (1981)   Costume designer, BBC television, Manchester, U.K.
Pip Nash (1981)   Regional theatre, U.K.
Anabel Temple (1981)   Freelance: U.K. film and theatre design; 1989 *Time Out*
Tom Cairns (1982)   Opera designer, English National Opera, U.K; director and de-
                                  signer for theatre, opera, and dance.
Ken Harrison (1982)   Freelance: set and costume designer; Head of Design, Mercury
                                  Theatre, U.K.
Margo Harkin (1982)   Film writer and director, television, Northern Ireland.
John Warden (1982)   Head of Design, Maddermarket Theatre, Norwich, U.K.
Francesca Boyd (1983)   BBC television designer, U.K.
Maria Djurkovic (1983)   Freelance: film, television, and dance designer, U.K.
Paul Ghirardani (1983)   Assistant designer on *Miss Saigon* (New York, 1989).
Ashley Martin-Davis (1983)   Freelance: Royal Shakespeare Theatre, Royal National Theatre;
                                  instructor, Motley Theatre Design Course, London.
Brien Vahey (1983)   Freelance: theatre and television, Ireland; instructor, Motley
                                  Theatre Design Course, London.
Antony Waterman (1983)   Freelance: Royal National Theatre, Royal Shakespeare Theatre,
                                  instructor Motley Theatre Design Course, London.
Lucy Weller (1983)   Freelance: Royal National Theatre, regional theatres, U.K.
Chisato Yoshimi (1983)   Freelance: Abbey Theatre, Gate Theatre, television, films; in-
                                  structor, Trinity College, Dublin.
Paul Brown (1984)   Freelance: Royal Opera House, Covent Garden; BBC television;
                                  France, Italy, Sweden.
Lia Cramer (1984)   Art director for television commercials, U.K.
Marjoke Henrichs (1984)   Freelance: Royal National Theatrer, London; Head of Design,
                                  Wolsey Theatre, Ipswich, U.K.
David Neat (1984)   Schauspielhaus, Hamburg, Germany.
Blaithin Sheerlin (1984)   Freelance: Gate Theatre, Belfast; television, Northern Ireland.
Gary Thorn (1984)   Designer, Stratford Shakespeare Festival, Canada.
Michael Vale (1984)   Freelance: Royal Shakespeare Company, West End theatres, re-
                                  gional theatres, U.K.
Luca Antonucci (1985)   Film, television, and opera, France, Italy, and Switzerland.
Andy Beauchamp (1985)   Computer-aided design (CAD) trade shows, and construction,
                                  U.K.
Gaia Shaw (1985)   Freelance: instructing, workshops, U.K.
Sophie Becher (1985)   Freelance: film and television, U.K.
George Souglides (1985)   Freelance: Edinburgh and Belfast.
Catherine Armstrong (1986)   Freelance: designer, U.K.
John Boundy (1986)   Visual effects, BBC, U.K.
Jeremy Herbert (1986)   Freelance: theatre and dance, U.K.
Nicky Herbert (1986)   Freelance: New York; BBC Scotland.
Andy Hunt (1986)   Freelance: sets and television, U.K.

Nicholas Lundy (1986)   Freelance: U.S.A.
Maggie Douglas (1987)   Freelance: Royal Shakespeare Company, Lyric Hammersmith, London; Opera Comique, France.
Alison Hughes (1987)   Freelance: set and costume designer, Royal Theatre, Northampton, U.K.
Timothy Northam (1987)   Freelance: Royal Shakespeare Company, regional theatre, U.K.; France.
Penny Fitt (1988)   Freelance: Royal National Theatre, London Fringe, Octagon Theatre, Bolton, and regional theatre, U.K.
Mini Grey (1988)   Freelance: London Fringe, Scotland.
Madeline Herbert (1988)   Freelance: London, U.K.
Michael Hoeschen (1988)   Freelance: props, model-making, set design, Canada.
Jenny Jones (1988)   Freelance: Assistant to Timothy O'Brien, Royal Shakespeare Company, U.K.
Anthony Lamble (1988)   Freelance: Royal National Theatre Studio, London, and regional theatres, U.K.
Naomi Wilkinson (1988)   Freelance: theatre and television, U.K.
Eryl Ellis (1989)   Freelance: U.K.
Anna Georgianis (1989)   Freelance: U.K. and Athens, Greece.
Nanako Kume (1989)   Freelance: designer and coordinator for visition theatre companies, Tokyo.
Julie Matthews (1989)   Freelance: designer, founder and artistic director of her own company, Bristol, U.K.
Kenny Maclellan (1989)   Freelance: set designer, London, Winner of the 1989 Linbury Prize for Stage Design; Athens, Greece.
Neil Warmington (1989)   Freelance: West End and Scotland.
Shimon Castile (1990)   Freelance; designer and scenic artist, U.K.
David Howarth (1990)   Resident designer and scenic artist, Salisbury Playhouse, U.K.
Kevin McKeon (1990)   Freelance: designer, U.K.
Charlotte Malik (1990)   Freelance: designer, U.K.
Jose Montero (1990)   Freelance: Barcelona, Spain.
Andrea Blotkamp (1991)   Freelance: Holland.
Fiona Cunningham (1991)   Freelance: designer and instructor, Ireland.
Anne Holloway (1991)   Freelance: designer and instructor, U.K.
Laura Hopkins (1991)   Freelance: U.K.
Megumi Kwaminami (1991)   Freelance: designer, U.K.; coordinator with Japan.
Teresa McCann (1991)   Freelance: film designer and director, U.K.
Paul McCauley (1991)   Freelance: Royal Court, London, U.K., and Ireland.
Emanuela Pischedda (1991)   Freelance: designer, Italy.
Fiona Watt (1991)   Freelance: designer, U.K.
Christopher Woods (1991)   Freelance: theatre, opera, film, and television designer, U.K.
Lily Aharon Ben-Nachson (1992) Freelance: designer, Israel.
Roy Bell (1992)   Freelance: fringe and regional theatre, U.K.
Kate Driver (1992)   Freelance: designer, Wales.
Annie Kelley (1992)   Freelance: regional and fringe theatre, U.K.

At this writing, the Motley Theatre Design Course is headed by Alison Chitty with Margaret Harris and Hayden Griffin as co-directors. Administrative director Christine Rodgers oversees the day-to-day arrangements for guest speakers and projects, thereby allowing Margaret Harris to scale back the amount of time spent on the premises. John Simpson continues as honorary administrator.

Chronology:
Motley Productions and Credits, 1927–1978

Unlike facts about births and deaths, facts about theatre and film can be difficult to ascertain. Newspapers occasionally make mistakes; theatre people can misremember a year—or a title—as easily as can anyone else. The information below is as accurate as diligent research can make it.

Playwrights' names follow play titles. Where Shakespeare is the playwright, I omit his name. Whenever possible, individual credits for sets and costume designs are given; if none appear, the credit for both goes to "Motley" collectively. When no city is named after the theatre, London is assumed. Dates indicate opening nights. Film credits appear as the first entries for a given year. Productions that were transferred, which often involved redesign, are entered as a single production, except where separation in time or place between versions of a production makes it clearer to make two entries. By this accounting, Motley designed 280 productions, or more than 300 separate stagings.

c. 1927

The Nativity Play, anonymous, d. Tom Harrison. St. Martin-in-the-Fields. Costumes only.

1928

Romeo and Juliet, d. Terence Gray, s. George Colouris. Festival Theatre, Cambridge. Sets by Dora Paxton. Costumes by Elizabeth Montgomery.

1930

Cochran's Revues, C. B. Cochran, d. Frank Collins, London Pavilion, 27 March ; 1931 revue by Noel Coward, d. Frank Collins, London Pavilion. Costumes only. Subsequent revues took place at the Trocadero, where Motley designed some numbers.

1931

Much Ado About Nothing, d. John Gielgud, s. Gielgud and Dorothy Green. Sadler's Wells Theatre season. Two costumes only by Elizabeth Montgomery.

1932

Romeo and Juliet, d. John Gielgud, s. George Devine, Peggy Ashcroft, Edith Evans. Oxford University Dramatic Society (O.U.D.S.), February. Sets by Molly McArthur. Costumes by Motley.

Men About the House, Robert York, d. Andre Charlot, s. Ben Webster, Olga Lindo, Cecil Parker, Wallace Douglas. Globe Theatre, 7 June.

Richard of Bordeaux, "Gordon Daviot" [Elizabeth Mackintosh], d. John Gielgud, s. Gielgud, Harcourt Williams, Gwen Ffrangcon-Davies, Anthony Quayle. Two Sunday performances by the Arts Theatre Club, 26 June, preceded its run at the New Theatre, which opened 3 February 1933, with new costumes. It ran for over a year.

A Midsummer Night's Dream, d. Robert Atkins, s. Phyllis Nielson-Terry, Fay Compton, Jessica Tandy, Martita Hunt, John Laurie, Jack Hawkins, and Robert Atkins. Regents Park Open Air Theatre, 7 July; repeated the summer following with some cast changes. Costumes only.

Strange Orchestra, Rodney Ackland, d. John Gielgud, s. Hugh Williams, Laura Cowie, David Hutcheson, Mary Casson, Clifford Bartlett, Jean Forbes-Robertson. St. Martin's Theatre, 27 September.

Merchant of Venice, d. John Gielgud, s. Marius Goring, Peggy Ashcroft, Anthony Quayle, George Devine, Malcolm Keen, Harcourt Williams. Old Vic Theatre, 12 December.

1933

Red Wagon, film, adapted from the novel by Lady Eleanor Smith, d. Paul Stein, P. Walter C. Mycroft, s. Charles Bickford, Raquel Torres, Greta Nissen, Don Alvarado, Anthony Bushell, Paul Graetz. British International Pictures, Elstree. B/W. 97m. Art director (a.d.) John F. Mead. Costumes only.

Ball at the Savoy, Alfred Grunwald and Fritz Lohner-Beda, adapted by Oscar Hammerstein with music composed by Paul Abraham, d. Hammerstein, s. Maurice Evans, Valerie Hobson. Drury Lane Theatre, 8 September. Costumes only.

1934

Brewster's Millions, film, d. Thornton Freeland, p. Herbert Wilcox, s. Jack Buchanan, Lili Damita, Nancy O'Neill, Amy Veness, Sydney Fairbrother, Fred Emney, Sebastian Shaw. British and Dominion Film Corporation, Elstree. A.d. L.P. Williams. Costumes by Motley with Schiaparelli and Norman Hartnell.

Spring 1600, Emlyn Williams, d. John Gielgud, s. Isabel Jeans and Joyce Bland. Shaftesbury Theatre, 31 January.

The Haunted Ballroom, Geoffrey Toye, choreographed by Ninette de Valois, s. Robert Helpmann, Alicia Markova, Margot Fonteyn. Sadler's Wells Theatre, 18 March.

Queen of Scots, Gordon Daviot, d. John Gielgud,

s. Laurence Olivier, Glen Byam Shaw, Gwen Ffrangcon Davies. New Theatre, 8 June. Sets McKnight Kaufer. Women's costumes only.

Sweet Aloes, Jay Mallory, d. Tyrone Guthrie, s. Diana Wynyard, Ernest Trimmingham, Joyce Carey. Wyndham's Theatre, 31 October. Costumes only.

Hamlet, d, John Gielgud, s. Gielgud, Glen Byam Shaw, Jessica Tandy, Anthony Quayle, George Devine, Alec Guinness. New Theatre, 14 December.

1935

The Old Ladies, Hugh Walpole, adapted by Rodney Ackland, d. John Gielgud, s. Edith Evans, Jean Cadell, Mary Jerrold. New Theatre, 3 April.

Noah, Andre Obey, d. Michel Saint-Denis, s. George Devine, John Gielgud, Marius Goring, Alec Guinness, Harry Andrews, Jessica Tandy. New Theatre, 2 July.

Dusty Ermine, Neil Grant, d. A.R. Whatmore, s. Whatmore, Rosalind Atkinson, Morris Harvey. Arts Theatre, 24 September. Costumes only.

Romeo and Juliet, d. John Gielgud, s. Gielgud, Laurence Olivier, Peggy Ashcroft, Glen Byam Shaw, Alec Guinness, Edith Evans, George Devine. New Theatre, 17 October.

Aucassin and Nicolette, Wendy Toye, choreographed by Wendy Toye, s. Anton Dolin, Alicia Markova. Duke of York's Theatre, 23 December. Costumes only.

1936

Bitter Harvest, Catherine Turney, d. Stephen Thomas, s. Martita Hunt, Holland Bennet, Roy Russell. Arts Theatre, 29 January; transferred to St. Martin's Theatre, 12 May. Women's costumes only.

Richard II, d. John Gielgud, Glen Byam Shaw, s. David King-Wood, Vivien Leigh, Florence Kahn. O.U.D.S., New Theatre, Oxford, 17 February.

A Doll's House, Henrik Ibsen, d. Irene Hentschel, s. Lydia Lopokova. Arts Theatre, Cambridge, 17 February; transferred to the Criterion Theatre, London, 2 March.

Rosmersholm, Ibsen, d. Irene Hentschel, s. Jean Forbes-Robertson, John Laurie. Arts Theatre,

Cambridge, 19 February; transferred to the Criterion Theatre, London, 5 March.

Hedda Gabler, Ibsen, d. Irene Hentschel, s. Jean Forbes-Robertson. Arts Theatre, Cambridge, 21 February; transferred to the Criterion Theatre, London, 9 March.

The Master Builder, Ibsen, d. Irene Hentschel, s. Lydia Lopokova, Wilfrid Grantham. Arts Theatre, Cambridge, 20 February; transferred to the Criterion Theatre, London, 12 March.

The Happy Hypocrite, Max Beerbohm, adapted for the stage by Clemence Dane and Richard Addinsell, d. Maurice Colbourne, s. Ivor Novello, Marius Goring, Isabel Jeans, Vivien Leigh. His Majesty's Theatre, 9 April.

Parnell, Elsie T. Schauffler, d. Normal Marshall, s. Margaret Rawlings, Marda Vanne, Toska Bissing, Glen Byam Shaw, Margaret Webster, James Mason. Gate Theatre, 23 April; transferred to the New Theatre, 4 November. Costumes only.

Farewell Performance, Lajos Zilahy, adapted by John L. Balderston, d. Irene Hentschel, s. Griffith Jones, Mary Gaskell, Margaret Rutherford, Mary Ellis. Lyric Theatre, 10 September.

Charles the King, Maurice Colbourne, d. Colbourne, s. Barry Jones, Gwen Ffrangcon-Davies. Lyric Theatre, 8 October.

The Witch of Edmonton, Thomas Dekker, d. Michel Saint-Denis, s. Marius Goring, Alec Guinness, Michael Redgrave, Edith Evans, Hedley Briggs, Beatrix Lehmann. Old Vic Theatre, 8 December.

1937

The London Theatre Studio. Founded by Michel Saint-Denis in 1936, the L.T.S. was a precursor of the Old Vic School. It trained actors, directors, and designers, with Motley in charge of training designers. Not all productions can be assigned certain dates, casts, or theatres, although the designs suggest that they were indeed staged.

A Woman Killed with Kindness, Thomas Heywood, d. Michel Saint-Denis. London Theatre Studio, n.d. 1937.

The Beaux' Stratagem, Richard Brinsley Sheridan, London Theatre Studio, 1937.

Hay Fever, Noel Coward, d. Michel Saint-Denis, s. Peter Whitehead, Merula Salaman, Pierre

Lefevre. London Theatre Studio, 28 June.

L'Occasion, Prosper Merimee, d. Michel Saint-Denis, Vera Poliakoff, Pierre Lefevre. London Theatre Studio, 30 June.

Candida, George Bernard Shaw, d. Irene Hentschel, s. Athene Seyler, Stephen Haggard. Globe Theatre, 10 February.

Henry V, d. Tyrone Guthrie, s. Laurence Olivier, Alec Guinness, Marius Goring, Harcourt Williams, Jessica Tandy. Old Vic Theatre, 6 April.

He Was Born Gay, Emlyn Williams, d. Williams, s. Williams, John Gielgud, Gwen Ffrangcon-Davies, Glen Byam Shaw. Queen's Theatre, 26 May.

The Great Romancer, Jules Eckert Goodman, s. Carol Goodner, Robert Morley, Peter Coke, Charles Lefeaux, Vivienne Bennett, Marie Dorval. New Theatre, 16 June.

Richard II, d. John Gielgud, Glen Byam Shaw, s. Peggy Ashcroft, John Gielgud, Michael Redgrave, Glen Byam Shaw, George Devine, Anthony Quayle, Alec Guinness, Harcourt Williams, Leon Quartermaine, Harry Andrews, Pardoe Woodman. Queen's Theatre, 6 September.

The School for Scandal, Richard Brinsley Sheridan, d. Tyrone Guthrie, s. Peggy Ashcroft, John Gielgud, Michael Redgrave, Glen Byam Shaw, Harcourt Williams, George Devine, Leon Quartermaine, Harry Andrews. Queen's Theatre, 25 November.

Macbeth, d. Michel Saint-Denis, s. Laurence Olivier, Judith Anderson. Old Vic Theatre. 26 November.

1938

Marigold, film, based on the play of the same name by L. Allen Harker and F. R. Pryor, d. Thomas Bentley, p. Walter C. Mycroft, s. Sophie Stewart, Patrick Barr, Phyllis Dare, Edward Chapman, Nicholas Hannen, Hugh Dempster, Elliot Mason, Katie Johnson, James Hayter. Associated British Picture Corporation, Elstree. A.d. John F. Mead. Costumes by Sophia Harris.

The Top of the Ladder, a project undertaken for Judy Guthrie and never staged.

The Three Sisters, Chekhov, d. Michel Saint-Denis, s. Gielgud, Peggy Ashcroft, Glen Byam Shaw, Michael Redgrave, George Devine, Alec

Guinness, Gwen Ffrangcon-Davies, Carol Goodner, Angela Baddeley. Queen's Theatre, 28 January.

The Merchant of Venice, d. John Gielgud, Glen Byam Shaw, s. Gielgud, Glen Byam Shaw, Peggy Ashcroft, Richard Ainley, Angela Baddeley, George Devine. Queen's Theatre, 21 April.

Ariadne, Gabriel Marcel, d. Michel Saint-Denis. London Theatre Studio, 6 May.

Electra, Sophocles, d. Michel Saint-Denis, s. Noel Willman, Lalage Lewis, Laura Dyas, Francis Crowdy. London Theatre Studio, 7 May.

Judith and Holofernes, Jean Giraudoux, d. Michel Saint-Denis. London Theatre Studio, 8 May.

Dear Octopus, Dodie Smith, d. Glen Byam Shaw, s. Marie Tempest, Valerie Taylor, Angela Baddeley, Kate Cutler, Nan Munro, John Gielgud, Leon Quartermaine. Queen's Theatre, 14 September.

1939

I Met a Murderer, film, d. Roy Kellino, p. Roy Kellino, Pamela Kellino, James Mason, s. James Mason, Pamela Kellino, Sylvia Coleridge, William Devlin, Peter Coke, Esme Cannon, James Harcourt, Sheila Morgan. Gamma Films. Costumes by Sophia Harris.

Weep for the Spring (or *House in Silesia*), Stephen Haggard, d. Michel Saint-Denis, s. Stephen Haggard, Peggy Ashcroft. U.K. tour.

Marriage of Blood, Federico Garcia Lorca, d. Michel Saint-Denis, s. Martita Hunt, Vera Lindsay. Savoy Theatre, 19 March.

Twelfth Night, d. Irene Hentschel, s. Jay Laurier, John Laurie, Alec Clunes, Joyce Bland. Shakespeare Memorial Theatre, Stratford-upon-Avon, 13 April.

Scandal in Assyria, Alex Kjellstrom, adapted by Gerald Bullett, d. John Gielgud, s. Francis Sullivan, Ernest Thesiger, Jack Hawkins. Globe Theatre, 30 April. Costumes only.

The Confederacy, John Vanbrugh, d. Michel Saint-Denis, s. Peter Hicks, Peter Ustinov, Noel Willman. London Theatre Studio, 22 May.

Rhondda Roundabout, Jack Jones, d. Glen Byam Shaw, s. Mervyn Johns, Hugh Griffith, Kay Bannerman, George Devine. Globe Theatre, 31 May.

Hamlet, d. John Gielgud, s. Gielgud, Faye Compton, Jack Hawkins, Laura Cowie. Kronborg Castle, Elsinore, Denmark, 6 July.

The Importance of Being Earnest, Oscar Wilde, d. John Gielgud, s. Gielgud, Peggy Ashcroft, Edith Evans, Margaret Rutherford, Gwen Ffrangcon-Davies. Globe Theatre, 16 August. The production was revived at least four times during World War II, and transferred to New York in 1947.

Great Expectations, Charles Dickens, adapted by Alec Guinness, d. George Devine, s. Marius Goring, Martita Hunt, Vera Lindsay, Merula Salaman, Alec Guinness. Rudolph Steiner Hall, 7 December.

1940

The Beggar's Opera, John Gay, d. John Gielgud, s. Michael Redgrave, Roy Henderson, Constance Willis, Audrey Mildmay, Irene Eisinger. Glyndebourne Opera Company production that toured before coming into the Haymarket Theatre, 5 March. Set and costumes by Sophia Harris.

Romeo and Juliet, d. Laurence Olivier, s. Laurence Olivier, Vivien Leigh, Fifty-First Street Theatre, New York, 9 May. Opened in San Francisco and played in Chicago before coming to New York. Sets and costumes by Margaret Harris and Elizabeth Montgomery.

1941

Three Virgins and a Devil, Agnes de Mille with Lucia Chase, choreogrraphed by Agnes de Mille, s. Agnes de Mille, Sybil Shearer, Lucia Chase, Annabel Lyon, Eugene Loring, Jerome Robbins (debut). Majestic Theatre, New York, 11 February. Set by Arne Lundborg ("after sketches by Miss [Margaret] Harris [Motley]"). Costumes by Margaret Harris and Elizabeth Montgomery.

The Cherry Orchard, Anton Chekhov, d. Tyrone Guthrie, s. Athene Seyler, Nicholas Hannen, James Dale, Walter Hudd, Rosalind Atkinson, Stanford Holm. New Theatre, 28 August. Costumes by Sophia Harris.

1942

I Married an Angel, film, based on the Rodgers

and Hart musical (1938), d. W. S. Van Dyke II, p. Metro-Goldwyn-Mayer, s. Nelson Eddy, Jeanette MacDonald, Edward Everett Horton, Binnie Barnes, Reginald Owen, Douglass Dumbrille. MGM. MGM bought the rights for J. M., then deferred production. Costumes by Margaret Harris and Elizabeth Montgomery with Robert Kalloch.

The Doctor's Dilemma, George Bernard Shaw, d. Irene Hentschel, s. Vivien Leigh, Frank Allenby, Peter Glenville, Cyril Cusack. Haymarket Theatre, 4 March. Sets by Michael Relph. Costumes by Sophia Harris.

The Doctor's Dilemma, George Bernard Shaw, d. Guthrie McClintic, s. Katharine Cornell, Vivien Leigh, Cyril Cusak. Shubert Theatre, New York, 11 March. Set by Donald Oenslager. Costumes by Margaret Harris and Elizabeth Montgomery.

Watch on the Rhine, Lillian Hellman, d. Emlyn Williams, s. Diana Wynyard, Anton Walbrook, Charles Goldner, Athene Seyler. Aldwych Theatre, 22 April. Sets by Michael Relph. Costumes by Sophia Harris.

The Importance of Being Earnest, Oscar Wilde, d. John Gielgud, s. Gielgud, Gwen Ffrangcon-Davies, Cyril Ritchard, Jean Cadell, Peggy Ashcroft, Edith Evans. Phoenix Theatre, 14 October. Costumes by Sophia Harris. A revival of the earlier production, with a somewhat different cast. The production was revived at least three more times during World War II.

Rodeo, Agnes de Mille, music by Aaron Copland, choreographed by Agnes de Mille, s. de Mille, John Kriza, Casimir Kokitch, Jennie Workman. Metropolitan Opera House , New York, 16 October. Sets by Oliver Smith. Costumes by Elizabeth Montgomery [credited to Kermit Love in some sources].

The Three Sisters, Chekhov, d. Guthrie McClintic, s. Judith Anderson, Katharine Cornell, Ruth Gordon, Alexander Knox. Ethel Barrymore Theatre, New York, 21 December. Sets by Margaret Harris. Costumes by Elizabeth Montgomery.

1943

A Month in the Country, Turgenev, adapted by Emlyn Williams, d. Emlyn Williams, s. Valerie Taylor, Michael Redgrave, Ronald Squire. St. James's Theatre, 11 February. Costumes by Sophia Harris.

Richard III, d. George Coulouris, s. Coulouris, Philip Bourneuf, Mildred Dunnock, Norma Chambers, John Ireland, Herbert Ratner, Randolph Echols. Forrest Theatre, New York, 26 March. Sets by Margaret Harris. Costumes by Elizabeth Montgomery.

Dim Lustre, Anthony Tudor, choreographed by Anthony Tudor. Metropolitan Opera House, New York, 8 May. Sets by Margaret Harris. Costumes by Elizabeth Montgomery.

Lovers and Friends, Dodie Smith, d. Guthrie McClintic, s. Raymond Massey, Katharine Cornell, Henry Daniell, Carol Goodner. Plymouth Theatre, New York, 28 November. Sets by Margaret Harris. Costumes by Elizabeth Montgomery.

1944

The Cherry Orchard, Chekhov, d. Margaret Webster, Eva Le Gallienne, s. Le Gallienne, Stefan Schnabel, Joseph Schildkraut. National Theatre, New York, 25 January. Sets by Margaret Harris. Costumes by Elizabeth Montgomery.

Tally-Ho, or *The Frail Quarry,* Agnes de Mille, choreographed by Agnes de Mille, s. Agnes de Mille, Lucia Chase. Metropolitan Opera House and American tour, 11 April. Sets and costumes by Elizabeth Montgomery.

Highland Fling, Margaret Curtis, d. George Abbot, s. Margaret Curtis, Ralph Forbes, John Ireland, Karl Swenson, Ivan Miller. Plymouth Theatre, New York, 28 April. Sets by John Root. Costumes by Margaret Harris and Elizabeth Montgomery.

The Last of Mrs. Cheyney, Frederick Lonsdale, d. Tyrone Guthrie, s. Athene Seyler, Coral Browne. Savoy Theatre, 15 June. Costumes by Sophia Harris.

Sadie Thompson, Howard Dietz and Rouben Mamoulian, music by Vernon Duke, d. Mamoulian, s. June Havoc, Beatrice Kraft, Doris Patston, Walter Burke, Lansing Hatfield. Alvin Theatre, New York, 16 November. Sets by Boris Aronson. Costumes by Elizabeth Montgomery.

A Bell for Adano, Paul Osborn, adapted from John Hersey's novel, d. H. C. Porter, s. Fredric March, Albert Raymo, Charles Mayer, J. Scott Smart, Margo [sic]. Cort Theatre, New York, 6

December. Sets by Margaret Harris. Costumes by Elizabeth Montgomery.

1945

The Tempest, d. Margaret Webster, Eva Le Gallienne, s. Arnold Moss, Frances Heflin, Canada Lee, Vera Zorina. Alvin Theatre, New York, 25 January. Sets by Margaret Harris. Costumes by Elizabeth Montgomery.

Hope for the Best, William McCleery, d. Marc Connelly, s. Franchot Tone, Jane Wyatt, Leo Bulgakov. Fulton Theatre, New York, 7 February. Sets by Margaret Harris. Costumes by Elizabeth Montgomery.

The Wind of Heaven, Emlyn Williams, d. Williams, s. Williams, Diana Wynyard. St. James's Theatre, 12 April. Costumes by Sophia Harris.

Sigh No More, Noel Coward, d. Coward, s. Cyril Ritchard, Joyce Grenfell. Piccadilly Theatre, 28 August. Costumes by Sophia Harris.

You Touched Me! Tennessee Williams and Donald Windham, adapted from D. H. Lawrence's short story, d. Guthrie McClintic, s. Montgomery Clift, Neil Fitzgerald, Edmund Gwenn, Catherine Willard, Marianne Stewart. Booth Theatre, New York, 25 September. Sets by Margaret Harris. Costumes by Elizabeth Montgomery.

Carib Song, William Archibald, music by Baldwin Bergersen, d. Mary Hunter, s. Katherine Dunham, Avon Long. Adelphi Theatre, New York, 27 September. Sets by Jo Mielziner. Costumes by Elizabeth Montgomery.

Skydrift, Harry Kliner, d. Roy Hargrave, s. Eli Wallach, Elliott Sullivan, Paul Crabtree. Belasco Theatre, New York, 13 November. Sets by Margaret Harris. Costumes by Elizabeth Montgomery.

Pygmalion, George Bernard Shaw, d. Cedric Hardwicke, s. Gertrude Lawrence, Raymond Massey, Melville Cooper. Ethel Barrymore Theatre, New York, 26 December. Sets by Donald Oenslager. Costumes by Elizabeth Montgomery.

1946

Great Expectations, film, adapted from Charles Dickens's novel, d. David Lean, p. Ronald Neame and Anthony Havelock-Allan, s. John Mills, Jean Simmons, Valerie Hobson, Bernard Miles, Francis L. Sullivan, Martita Hunt, Alec Guinness, Anthony Wager, Finlay Currie. Cineguild (U.K.). B/W. 118m. Production designer (p.d.) John Bryan. A.d. Wilfrid Shingleton. Independent Producers. Costumes by Sophia Harris with Margaret Furse.

He Who Gets Slapped, Leonid Andreyev, adapted by Judith Guthrie, d. Tyrone Guthrie, s. Dennis King, Stella Adler. Theatre Guild at the Booth Theatre, New York, 20 March. Sets and costumes by Elizabeth Montgomery.

Second Best Bed, N. Richard Nash, d. Ruth Chatterton and Nash, s. Chatterton, Barry Thomas, Richard Dyer-Bennet. Ethel Barrymore Theatre, New York, 3 June. Sets by Margaret Harris. Costumes by Elizabeth Montgomery.

The Dancer, Milton Lewis and Julian Funt, d. Everett Sloane, music by Paul Bowles, s. Edgar Kent, Anton Dolin. Biltmore Theatre, New York, 5 June. Sets and costumes by Elizabeth Montgomery.

Antony and Cleopatra, d. Glen Byam Shaw, s. Godfrey Tearle, Edith Evans, Anthony Quayle, Michael Goodliffe. Piccadilly Theatre, 20 December. Sets and costumes by Margaret Harris.

The King Stag, Carlo Gozzi, adapted by Carl Wildman, d. George Devine, s. Stuart Burge, Jean Wilson, Joan Hopkins, Maurice Browning. Young Vic, Lyric, Hammersmith, 26 December; subsequently toured England. Sets by Margaret Harris. Costumes by Sophia Harris.

1947

Blanche Fury, film, adapted by Audrey Erskine Lindop, Hugh Mills, and Cecil McGovern from the novel by Joseph Shearing, d. Marc Allegret, p. Anthony Havelock-Allan, s. Stewart Granger, Valerie Hobson, Walter Fitzgerald, Michael Gough, Maurice Denham. Independent Producers/Cineguild, released in 1948. P.d. John Bryan. A.d. Wilfrid Shingleton. Costumes by Sophia Harris with Margaret Furse.

Captain Boycott, film, d. Frank Launder, p. Frank Launder and Sidney Gilliat, s. Stewart Granger, Kathleen Ryan, Cecil Parker, Robert Donat, Alastair Sim, Mervyn Johns, Noel Purcell, Niall McGinnis, Eddie Byrne, Liam Gaffney, Liam Redmond. Independent Producers/Individual Pictures.

A.d. Edward Carrick. Costumes by Sophia Harris.

The Shoemaker's Holiday, Thomas Dekker, d. Nevill Coghill, s. Robert Hardy, William Patrick, John Schlesinger, Heather Couper, Norman Painting. Young Vic, n.d.; Oxford Playhouse, 2 March 1948; transferred to the Toynbee Hall Theatre, East London, 22 March. Sets by Margaret Harris. Costumes by Sophia Harris.

The Courtneys of Curzon Street (The Courtney Affair, U.S.A.), film, d. Herbert Wilcox, p. Wilcox, s. Anna Neagle, Michael Wilding, Gladys Young, Coral Browne, Jack Watling, Michael Medwin, Edward Rigby, Helen Cherry, Bernard Lee, Thora Hird, Nicholas Phipps. Imperadio Pictures. A.d. William C. Andrews. Dresses by Sophia Harris.

The Importance of Being Earnest, Oscar Wilde, d. John Gielgud, s. Gielgud, Margaret Rutherford, Royale Theatre, New York, 3 March. Sets by Margaret Harris. Costumes by Sophia Harris and Elizabeth Montgomery.

The Snow Queen, Hans Christian Andersen, adapted by Suria Magito and Rudolph Weil, d. Magito, Michel Saint-Denis, s. Young Vic Company. Old Vic Theatre, 23 December; subsequently toured England; revived the next year at the Old Vic Theatre, 20 December. Sets by Margaret Harris. Costumes by Elizabeth Montgomery.

1948

So Evil My Love, film, d. Lewis Allen, p. Hal B. Wallis, s. Ray Milland, Ann Todd, Geraldine Fitzgerald, Leo G. Carroll, Raymond Huntley, Martita Hunt, Moira Lister, Raymond Lovell, Muriel Aked, Finlay Currie, Ivor Barnard, Hugh Griffith, Eliot Makeham. Paramount British. A.d. Tom Morahan. Costumes by Sophia Harris with Edith Head.

The Wedding, Anton Chekhov, d. George Devine, s. Young Vic Company. Old Vic Theatre, 30 May. Sets and costumes by Margaret Harris.

The Winter's Tale, d. Anthony Quayle, s. Esmond Knight, Paul Scofield, Diana Wynyard, Claire Bloom. Shakespeare Memorial Theatre, Stratford-upon-Avon, 3 June. Sets by Margaret Harris. Costumes by Elizabeth Montgomery.

Troilus and Cressida, d. Anthony Quayle, s.

Quayle, Paul Scofield, Heather Stannard. Shakespeare Memorial Theatre, Stratford-upon-Avon, 2 July. Sets by Margaret Harris. Costumes by Elizabeth Montgomery.

Anne of a Thousand Days, Maxwell Anderson, d. H. C. Potter, s. Joyce Redman, Rex Harrison, Percy Waram, Charles Francis, John Williams, Wendell Phillips, Russell Gaige, Harry Irvine. Shubert Theatre, New York, 8 December. Sets by Jo Mielziner. Costumes by Elizabeth Montgomery.

1949

Billy the Kid, Lincoln Kirstein, with music by Aaron Copland. Metropolitan Opera House, January. Sets and costumes by Elizabeth Montgomery.

As You Like It, d. Glen Byam Shaw, s. Jeanne Wilson, Pierre Lefevre, Young Vic Company. Old Vic Theatre, 3 January. Sets and costumes by Margaret Harris.

The Heiress, adapted from Henry James's *Washington Square* by Ruth and Augustus Goetz, d. John Gielgud, s. Ralph Richardson, Peggy Ashcroft, replaced by Godfrey Tearle and Wendy Hiller [February, 1950]. Haymarket Theatre, 1 February. Sets and costumes by Margaret Harris and Sophia Harris, a redesign of the New York production.

Antigone, Sophocles, adapted by Jean Anouilh, translated by Lewis Galantiere, d. Laurence Olivier, s. Olivier, Vivien Leigh, George Relph. New Theatre, 10 February. Costumes by Sophia Harris.

South Pacific, Richard Rodgers and Oscar Hammerstein, d. Joshua Logan, s. Mary Martin, Ezio Pinza, Juanita Hall, Myron McCormick, William Tabbert, Betta St. John. Majestic Theatre, New York, 7 April. Sets by Jo Mielziner. Costumes by Motley. Toured and revived extensively in the United States and England.

Marriage Story, Jacques Deval, d. Michael Macowan, s. Angela Baddeley, Percy Fitzgerald. Strand Theatre, 4 May. Costumes by Sophia Harris.

Miss Liberty, Robert E. Sherwood and Irving Berlin, d. Moss Hart, s. Mary McCarty, Allyn McLerie, Imperial Theatre, New York, 15 July. Sets by Oliver Smith. Costumes by Elizabeth Montgomery.

1950

Happy as Larry, Donagh MacDonagh, d. Burgess Meredith, s. Meredith, Marguerite Piazza, Barbara Perry, Gene Barry. Coronet Theatre, New York, 6 January. Sets and costumes by Elizabeth Montgomery.

The Innocents, William Archibald, d. Peter Glenville, s. Beatrice Straight. Playhouse Theatre, New York, 1 February; Glenville directed a different production, with a different cast, at Her Majesty's Theatre, London, in September, 1952. Sets by Jo Mielziner. Costumes by Elizabeth Montgomery.

Peter Pan, James M. Barrie, music by Leonard Bernstein, d. John Burrell and choreographed by Wendy Toye, s. Boris Karloff, Marcia Henderson. Imperial Theatre, New York, 24 April. Sets by Ralph Alswang. Costumes by Elizabeth Montgomery.

The Liar, Carlo Goldoni, adapted by Edward Eager and Alfred Drake, music by John Mundy, d. Drake, s. William Eythe, Melville Cooper. Broadhurst Theatre, New York, 18 May. Sets by Donald Oenslager. Costumes by Elizabeth Montgomery.

Hamlet, d. Hugh Hunt, s. Mark Dignam, Michael Redgrave, Walter Hudd, Yvonne Mitchell. Kronborg Castle, Elsinore, 7 June; an earlier production directed by Hugh Hunt opened at the New Theatre, 2 February; Motley did not design it. Sets for Elsinore by Margaret Harris.

For Love or Money, Jordan Lawrence, d. Willard Stoker, s. Hermione Baddeley, Tod Slaughter, Frank Tickle. Ambassador's Theatre, 24 August. Sets by Margaret Harris. Costumes by Sophia Harris.

Bartholomew Fair, Ben Jonson, d. George Devine, s. Alec Clunes, Ursula Jeans, Robert Eddison, Roger Livesey, Young Vic Company. Edinburgh Festival, 21 August; subsequently transferred to the Old Vic, London, 18 December. Sets and costumes by Margaret Harris.

Captain Carvallo, Denis Cannan, d. Guthrie McClintic, s. Katharine Cornell. Erlanger Theatre, Buffalo, N.Y., 6 December. Sets by Rolf Gerard. Costumes by Elizabeth Montgomery. Closed 23 December, before coming into New York City.

1951

Henry V, d. Glen Byam Shaw, s. Alec Clunes, Richard Pasco, Mark Dignam, Paul Rogers, Dorothy Tutin. Old Vic Theatre, 30 January.

The Wedding, Anton Chekhov, d. George Devine, s. Dorothy Tutin, Sheila Ballantine, Leo McKern, Paul Rogers, Pierre Lefevre, Lee Montague. Old Vic Theatre, 13 March. (Revival of 1948 Young Vic production). Sets and costumes by Margaret Harris.

Hassan, James Elroy Flecker, d. Basil Dean, s. Andre Huguenet, Elizabeth Sellars, Hilda Simms, Arthur Lowe, Laurence Harvey. Cambridge Theatre, 9 May. Sets by Margaret Harris. Costumes by Sophia Harris.

Two on the Aisle, Betty Comden and Adolph Green, d. Abe Burrows, s. Bert Lahr, Dolores Gray, Elliot Reid, Collette Marchand. Mark Hellinger Theatre, New York, 19 July. Costumes by Elizabeth Montgomery.

Othello, d. Orson Welles, s. Welles, Peter Finch, Gudrun Ure, Maxine Audley. St. James's Theatre, London, 18 October. Sets and costumes by Margaret Harris.

Paint Your Wagon, Alan Jay Lerner and Frederick Lowe, d. Daniel Mann, Agnes de Mille, s. Bert Matthews, Olga San Juan, Ralph Baker, Shubert Theatre, New York, 12 November. Sets by Oliver Smith. Costumes by Elizabeth Montgomery. Subsequently transferred to London, where Sophia Harris reworked Elizabeth Montgomery's designs.

The Grand Tour, Elmer Rice, d. Rice, s. Richard Derr, Beatrice Straight, Martin Beck Theatre, New York, 10 December. Sets by Howard Bay. Costumes by Elizabeth Montgomery.

Colombe, Jean Anouilh, d. Peter Brook, s. Yvonne Arnaud, Michael Gough, John Stratton, Joyce Redman, Laurence Naismith. New Theatre, 13 December. Costumes by Sophia Harris. Elizabeth Montgomery designed the New York production, entitled *Mademoiselle Colombe,* directed by Harold Clurman, s. Julie Harris, Edna Best, Longacre Theatre, New York, 6 January 1954 (see below).

1952

The Card (The Promoter, U.S.A.), film, Arnold

Bennet, adapted by Eric Amber, d. Ronald Neame, p. John Bryan, s. Alec Guinness, Glynis Johns, Valerie Hobson, Petula Clark, Edward Chapman, George Devine, Frank Pettingell, Michael Hordern, Wilfrid Hyde-White. British Film Makers. A.d. Tim Hopewell Ash. Costumes by Sophia Harris.

The Happy Time, Samuel Taylor based on the novel by Robert Fontaine, d. George Devine, s. Rachel Kempson, Genevieve Page, George Devine, Peter Finch. St. James's Theatre, 30 January. Sets by Vivienne Kernot. Costumes by Sophia Harris.

Coriolanus, d. Glen Byam Shaw, s. Anthony Quayle, Laurence Harvey. Mary Ellis, Michael Hordern, Siobhan McKenna. Shakespeare Memorial Theatre, Stratford-upon-Avon, 13 March. Sets and costumes by Margaret Harris.

Candida, George Bernard Shaw, d. Herman Shumlin, s. Olivia de Havilland, Terrence Kilburn. National Theatre, New York, 22 April. Sets by Donald Oenslager. Costumes by Elizabeth Montgomery.

To Be Continued, William Marchant, d. Guthrie McClintic, s. Neil Hamilton, Mary Gildea, Dorothy Stickney, Luella Gear, Grace Kelly. Booth Theatre, 23 April. Sets by Donald Oenslager. Costumes by Elizabeth Montgomery.

As You Like It, d. Glen Byam Shaw, s. Margaret Leighton, Laurence Harvey, Michael Bates, Siobhan McKenna, Michael Hordern. Vanessa Redgrave, Keith Michell. Shakespeare Memorial Theatre, Stratford-upon-Avon, 29 April; with changes in the cast, it subsequently toured to Australia in 1953. Sets and costumes by Margaret Harris.

Eugene Onegin, Peter Illych Tchaikovsky, d. George Devine, cond. James Robertson, s. Amy Shuard, Elisabeth Robinson, Rowland Jones, Frederick Sharp, Olwen Price. Sadler's Wells Opera, Sadler's Wells Theatre, 22 May; revived several times. Sets by Margaret Harris. Costumes by Sophia Harris.

The Innocents, adapted by William Archibald from the novel by Henry James, d. Peter Glenville, s. Flora Robson, Barbara Everest. His Majesty's Theatre, 3 July; a re-staging of the New York production with a different cast. Sets by Jo Mielziner. Costumes by Sophia Harris.

The River Line, Charles Morgan, d. Michael MacOwan, s. John Westbook, Paul Scofield, Pamela Brown, Virginia McKenna. Lyric, Hammersmith, 2 September; transferred to the Strand Theatre, 28 October. Sets by Alan Tagg. Costumes by Sophia Harris.

1953

Ballad, Agnes de Mille, choreographed by Agnes de Mille. Agnes de Mille Dance Theatre Company. U.S. tour, 126 theatres. Sets and costumes by Elizabeth Montgomery.

Conversations Pleasant and Unpleasant, Agnes de Mille, choreographed by Agnes de Mille. Agnes de Mille Dance Theatre Company. U.S. tour, 126 theatres. Sets and costumes by Elizabeth Montgomery.

Dances of Elegance: 1860–1928, Agnes de Mille, choreographed by Agnes de Mille. Agnes de Mille Dance Theatre Company. U.S. tour, 126 theatres. Sets and costumes by Elizabeth Montgomery.

Hell on Wheels, Agnes de Mille, choreographed by Agnes de Mille. Agnes de Mille Dance Theatre Company. U.S. tour, 126 theatres. Sets and costumes by Elizabeth Montgomery.

Legends, Agnes de Mille, choreographed by Agnes de Mille. Agnes de Mille Dance Theatre Company. U.S. tour, 126 theatres. Sets and costumes by Elizabeth Montgomery.

Mid-Summer, Vina Delmar, d. Paul Crabtree, s. Geraldine Page, Suzanne Caubage. Vanderbilt Theatre, New York, 21 January. Costumes by Elizabeth Montgomery.

Paint Your Wagon, Alan Jay Lerner and Frederick Loewe, d. Daniel Mann, dances by Agnes de Mille, s. Desmond Ainsworth, Sally Ann Howes, Ken Cantril. Her Majesty's Theatre, 11 February (transfer from New York). Sets by Oliver Smith. Costumes by Elizabeth Montgomery and Sophia Harris.

Richard III, d. Glen Byam Shaw, s. Marius Goring, Harry Andrews, Basil Hoskins, Yvonne Mitchell. Shakespeare Memorial Theatre, Stratford-upon-Avon, 24 March. Sets and costumes by Margaret Harris.

Antony and Cleopatra, d. Glen Byam Shaw, s. Peggy Ashcroft, Michael Redgrave, Harry Andrews, Marius Goring. Shakespeare Memorial Theatre, Stratford-upon-Avon, 28 April; subsequently played at the Prince's Theatre, 10 January 1954, and on a European tour. Sets and costumes by Margaret Harris.

Can-Can, Cole Porter and Abe Burrows, d. Burrows, Michael Kidd, s. Gwen Verdon, Peter Cookson, Hans Conreid. Shubert Theatre, New York, 7 May. Sets by Jo Mielziner. Costumes by Elizabeth Montgomery. It transferred to the London Coliseum, opening 14 October; and was revived at the National Theatre, Washington, D. C., 12 June 1955.

King John, d. George Devine, s. Michael Hordern, Richard Burton, John Neville. Old Vic Theatre, 27 October. Permanent surround by James Bailey. Sets and costumes by Margaret Harris.

1954

Mademoiselle Colombe, Jean Anouilh, d. Harold Clurman, s. Julie Harris, Edna Best, Eli Wallach, Sam Jaffe. Longacre Theatre, New York, 6 January. Sets by Boris Aronson. Costumes by Elizabeth Montgomery. Not to be confused with the 1951 London production, d. by Peter Brook, entitled *Colombe,* which was also designed by Motley (Sophia Harris).

The Immoralist, Ruth and Augustus Goetz, adapted from the book by Andre Gide, d. Daniel Mann, s. Geraldine Page, John Heldabrand, Charles Dingle, Louis Jourdan, James Dean. Royale Theatre, New York, 8 February 1954. Sets by George Jenkins. Costumes by Elizabeth Montgomery.

Charley's Aunt, Brandon Thomas, d. John Gielgud, s. John Mills, Simon Lack, Gwen Ffrangcon-Davies. New Theatre, 10 February. Sets by Margaret Harris. Costumes by Sophia Harris.

I Capture the Castle, Dodie Smith, d. Murray MacDonald, s. George Relph, Virginia McKenna, Cyril Luckham, Roger Moore, Yvonne Furneaux. Aldwych Theatre, 4 March. Sets by Paul Sherif. Costumes by Sophia Harris.

A Midsummer Night's Dream, d. George Devine, s. Anthony Quayle, Powys Thomas, Basil Hoskins, Zena Walker, Keith Michell, Tony Britton, Leo McKern. Shakespeare Memorial Theatre, Stratford-upon-Avon, 23 March 1954. Sets and costumes by Margaret Harris.

Wedding in Paris, Vera Caspary, music by Hans May, lyrics by Sonny Miller, d. Charles Hickman, s. Brian Leslie, Maidie Andrews, Evelyn Laye, Anton Walbrook. Hippodrome, 3 April. Sets by Thea Neu. Costumes by Sophia Harris.

Romeo and Juliet, d. Glen Byam Shaw, s. Laurence Harvey, Zena Walker. Shakespeare Memorial Theatre, Stratford-upon-Avon, 27 April. Sets and costumes by Margaret Harris.

Hedda Gabler, Henrik Ibsen adapted by Max Faber, d. Peter Ashmore, George Devine, s. Peggy Ashcroft, George Devine, Rachel Kempson, Michael MacLiammoir, Alan Badel. Lyric, Hammersmith, 8 September; transferred to the Westminster Theatre, 29 November. Sets by Margaret Harris. Costumes by Sophia Harris.

Nelson, Lennox Berkeley and Alan Pryce-Jones, d. George Devine, cond. Vilem Tausky, s. Robert Thomas, Anna Pollak, Sheila Rex, Victoria Elliott, Arnold Matters, David Ward, Stanley Clarkson. Sadler's Wells Opera, Sadler's Wells Theatre, 22 September. Sets by Felix Kelly. Costumes by Sophia Harris.

Can-Can, Cole Porter and Abe Burrows, d. Jerome Whyte, s. Gillian Lynne, Irene Hilda, Edmund Hockridge, Alfred Marks. London Coliseum, 14 October; transfer from New York. Sets by Jo Mielziner. Costumes by Elizabeth Montgomery and Sophia Harris.

Peter Pan, James M. Barrie with music by Mark Charlap and lyrics by Carolyn Leigh et al., d. Jerome Robbins, s. Mary Martin, Cyril Ritchard, Kathy Nolan, Margalo Gillmore, Sondra Lee. Winter Garden Theatre, New York, 20 October. Sets by Peter Larkin.

1955

Oklahoma!, film, based on the Richard Rodgers and Oscar Hammerstein III musical (1943), d. Fred Zinnemann, choreography by Agnes de Mille, s. Gordon MacRae, Shirley Jones, Rod Steiger, Gloria Grahame, James Whitmore, Marc Platt, Gene Nelson, Charlotte Greenwood, Eddie Albert, Bambi Lynn, Jennie Workman, James Mitchell. Magna Theatres/Todd-AO. 145 m. 10 October 1955. A.d. Joseph C. Wright. Costumes by Elizabeth Montgomery and Orry-Kelly. Although the credits read "Costume design by Motley," Elizabeth Montgomery did not supervise their construction.

The Magic Flute, Wolfgang Amadeus Mozart and Emanuel Schikaneder, d. George Devine, cond. Rudolf Schwartz, s. Thomas Round, Denis Dowling, Marion Studholme, June Bronhill, Patricia Howard, Ereach Riley, Stanley Clarkson, David Ward. Sadler's Wells Opera, Sadler's Wells Theatre, 24 February; revived in 1957, 1962. Sets and costumes by Margaret Harris.

The Honeys, Roald Dahl, d. Frank Corsaro, s. Dorothy Stickney, Jessica Tandy, Hume Cronyn. Longacre Theatre, New York, 28 April (closed 28 May 1955). Sets by Ben Edwards. Costumes by Elizabeth Montgomery.

The Merry Wives of Windsor, d. Glen Byam Shaw, s. Angela Baddeley, Joyce Redman, Keith Michell, Anthony Quayle. Shakespeare Memorial Theatre, Stratford-upon-Avon, 12 July. Sets by Margaret Harris. Costumes by Sophia Harris.

The Young and the Beautiful, Sally Benson, based on short stories by F. Scott Fitzgerald, d. Marshall Jamison, s. Douglas Watson, Lois Smith, Peter Brandon, James Hickman. Longacre Theatre, New York, 1 October. Sets by Eldon Elder. Costumes by Elizabeth Montgomery.

The Island of Goats, Ugo Betti, d. Peter Glenville, s. Laurence Harvey, Uta Hagen, Ruth Ford, Tani Seitz. Fulton Theatre, New York, 4 October. Sets by Jo Mielziner. Costumes by Elizabeth Montgomery.

1956

The Middle of the Night, Paddy Chayefsky, d. Joshua Logan, s. Edward G. Robinson, Gena Rowlands. ANTA Theatre, New York, 8 February. Sets by Jo Mielziner. Costumes by Elizabeth Montgomery.

A Likely Tale, Gerald Savory, d. Peter Ashmore, s. Robert Morley, Violet Farebrother, Margaret Rutherford, Judy Parfitt, Richard Pearson. Globe Theatre, 22 March. Sets by Margaret Harris. Costumes by Sophia Harris.

The Mulberry Bush, Angus Wilson, d. George Devine, s. Rachel Kempson, Gwen Ffrangcon-Davies, Alan Bates. Royal Court Theatre, 2 April. Sets by Margaret Harris. Costumes by Sophia Harris.

The Crucible, Arthur Miller, d. George Devine, s. Mary Ure, Rachel Kempson, Joan Plowright, Michael Gwynn, Alan Bates, Devine. Royal Court Theatre, 9 April. Sets by Stephen Doncaster. Costumes by Sophia Harris.

The Chalk Garden, Enid Bagnold, d. John Gielgud, s. Peggy Ashcroft, George Rose, Edith Evans, Felix Aylmer. Haymarket Theatre, 11 April. Sets by Reece Pemberton. Costumes by Sophia Harris.

The Most Happy Fella, Frank Loesser, adapted from Sidney Howard's play *They Knew What They Wanted,* d. Joseph Anthony, dances by Dania Krupska, s. Robert Weede, Jo Sullivan, Shorty Long, Art Lund, Susan Johnson. Imperial Theatre, New York, 3 May (closed 30 June 1956). Sets by Jo Mielziner. Costumes by Elizabeth Montgomery.

Look Back in Anger, John Osborne, d. Tony Richardson, s. Alan Bates, Mary Ure, Kenneth Haigh. Royal Court Theatre, 8 May; transferred with Richard Pasco, Alan Bates, and Doreen Aris to the Lyric, Hammersmith, 5 November; transferred with Heather Sears back to the Royal Court, 11 March 1957; transferred with a different cast to the Lyceum Theatre, New York, 1 October 1957. Sets by Alan Tagg. Costumes by Sophia Harris.

Othello, d. Glen Byam Shaw, s. Harry Andrews, Emlyn Williams, Margaret Johnston, Diana Churchill, Toby Robertson, Mark Dignam. Shakespeare Memorial Theatre, Stratford-upon-Avon, 29 May. Sets and costumes by Margaret Harris.

Cards of Identity, Nigel Dennis, d. Tony Richardson, s. Nigel Davenport, Kenneth Haigh, Peter Duguid, Rachel Kempson, John Osborne, Alan Bates, Joan Plowright, George Devine. Royal Court Theatre, 2 June. Sets by Alan Tagg. Costumes by Sophia Harris.

The Seagull, Anton Chekhov, translated by David Magarshack, d. Michael MacOwan, s. Diana Wynyard, Jill Bennett, Hugh Williams, Lyndon Brook, George Relph. Saville Theatre, 2 August. Sets by Margaret Harris. Costumes by Sophia Harris.

Long Day's Journey into Night, Eugene O'Neill, d. Jose Quintero, s. Katharine Hepburn, Jason Robards, Frederick March. Helen Hayes Theatre, New York, 7 November. Sets by David Hays. Costumes by Elizabeth Montgomery.

The Country Wife, William Wycherly, d. George

Devine, s. Laurence Harvey, Nigel Davenport, Alan Bates, Joan Plowright, Esme Percy, Diana Churchill, Devine. Royal Court Theatre, 12 December; transferred to the Adelphi Theatre, New York, 4 February 1957. Sets by Margaret Harris. Costumes by Sophia Harris.

1957

As You Like It, d. Glen Byam Shaw, s. Richard Johnson, Peggy Ashcroft, Mark Dignam, Cyril Luckham, Robert Harris. Shakespeare Memorial Theatre, Stratford-upon-Avon, 2 April. Sets and costumes by Margaret Harris.

Shinbone Alley, Joe Arion, Mel Brooks, and George Kleinsinger, based on Don Marquis's "archy and mehitabel" stories, d. Peter Lawrence, Rod Alexander, s. Ertha Kitt. Broadway Theatre, 14 April. Sets by Eldon Elder. Costumes by Elizabeth Montgomery.

The First Gentleman, Norman Ginsbury, d. Tyrone Guthrie, s. Inga Swenson, Walter Slezak, Helen Burns, Peter Donat. Belasco Theatre, New York, 25 April. Sets by Ralph Alswang. Costumes by Elizabeth Montgomery. Motley (Sophia Harris) also designed the costumes for the London production, starring Robert Morley.

Julius Caesar, d. Glen Byam Shaw, s. Cyril Luckham, Alec Clunes, Clive Revill, Patrick Wymark, Julian Glover. Shakespeare Memorial Theatre, Stratford-upon-Avon, 28 May. Sets and costumes by Margaret Harris.

Merchant of Venice, d. Jack Landau, s. Katharine Hepburn, Morris Carnovsky, Richard Waring. American Shakespeare Festival, Connecticut, 10 July. Sets by Rouben Ter-Arutunian. Costumes by Elizabeth Montgomery.

Mike Todd's Birthday Party, Madison Square Garden, New York, 17 October. Elizabeth Taylor's husband the film producer Mike Todd threw a gala birthday party for *Around the World in Eighty Days,* inviting the stars to come in costume and offering tickets for sale to the general public. It was on national television for ninety minutes. Elizabeth Montgomery designed the costumes.

Requiem for a Nun, William Faulkner, d. Tony Richardson, s. Ruth Ford, Zachary Scott, Royal Court Theatre, 26 November; transferred, with changes in the supporting cast to the John Golden Theatre, New York, 30 January 1959. Sets by Margaret Harris. Costumes by Sophia Harris.

Look Homeward, Angel, Ketti Frings, based on the novel by Thomas Wolfe, d. George Roy Hill, s. Anthony Perkins, Jo Van Fleet, Hugh Griffith, Bibi Osterwald. Ethel Barrymore Theatre, New York, 28 November. Sets by Jo Mielziner. Costumes by Elizabeth Montgomery.

1958

Lady at the Wheel, Frederic Raphael and Lucienne Hill, words and music by Leslie Bricusse and Rodney Beaumont, d. Wendy Toye, Tommy Linden, s. Kenneth McClellan, Vivienne Bennett, Henry Longhurst, Frederick Schiller, Maggie Fitzgibbon. Lyric, Hammersmith, 23 January; transferred to Westminster Theatre, 19 February. Sets by Richard Negri. Costumes by Sophia Harris.

Asmodee, Francois Mauriac, translated by Beverly Thurman, d. John O'Shaughnessy, s. Joyce Ebert, Michael Ebert, Taylor Graves. Theatre 74, New York, 25 March. Sets by Elizabeth Montgomery. Costumes by Ballou.

Romeo and Juliet, d. Glen Byam Shaw, s. Richard Johnson, Dorothy Tutin. Shakespeare Memorial Theatre, Stratford-upon-Avon, 8 April. Subsequently toured to Leningrad and Moscow. Sets by Margaret Harris. Costumes by Sophia Harris.

Love Me Little, John G. Fuller, adapted from the novel by Amanda Vail, d. Alfred Drake, s. Joan Bennett, Donald Cook. Helen Hayes Theatre, New York, 14 April. Sets by Ralph Alswang. Costumes by Elizabeth Montgomery.

Jane Eyre, Huntington Hartford, adapted from the novel by Charlotte Bronte, d. Demetrios Vilan, s. Jan Brooks, Blanche Yurka, Eric Portman. Belasco Theatre, New York, 1 May. Sets by Ben Edwards. Costumes by Elizabeth Montgomery.

Hamlet, d. Glen Byam Shaw, s. Michael Redgrave, Dorothy Tutin, Mark Dignam, Googie Withers, Ron Haddrick, Cyril Luckham, Ian Holm. Shakespeare Memorial Theatre, Stratford-upon-Avon, 3 June; subsequently toured to Leningrad and Moscow. Sets and costumes by Margaret Harris.

Much Ado About Nothing, d. Douglas Seale, s. Cyril Luckham, Michael Redgrave, Ian Holm, Zoe Caldwell, Richard Johnson, Julian Glover,

Googie Withers. Shakespeare Memorial Theatre, Stratford-upon-Avon, 26 August. Sets by Tanya Moiseiwitsch. Costumes by Sophia Harris.

Major Barbara, George Bernard Shaw, d. George Devine, s. Vanessa Redgrave, Joan Plowright, Alan Dobie, Alan Webb, Frances Rowe, Simon Carter. Royal Court Theatre, 28 August. Sets by Margaret Harris. Costumes by Sophia Harris.

The Cold Wind and the Warm, S. N. Behrman, d. Harold Clurman, s. Eli Wallach, Maureen Stapleton, Morris Carnovsky, Suzanne Pleshette. Morosco Theatre, New York, 8 December. Sets by Boris Aronson. Costumes by Elizabeth Montgomery.

1959

The Rivalry, Norman Corwin, d. Corwin, s. Nancy Kelly, Richard Boone. Bijou Theatre, New York, 7 February. Sets by David Hays. Costumes by Elizabeth Montgomery.

A Majority of One, Leonard Spigelgass, d. Dore Schary, s. Cedric Hardwicke, Gertrude Berg. Shubert Theatre, New York, 16 February. Sets by Donald Oenslager. Costumes by Elizabeth Montgomery.

The Magistrate, Arthur Wing Pinero, d. Douglas Seale, s. Michael Hordern, Barrie Ingham, Silvia Francis, Pauline Jameson. Old Vic Theatre, 19 March. Sets by Margaret Harris. Costumes by Sophia Harris.

The Merry Wives of Windsor, d. John Houseman, Jack Landau, s. Will Geer, Ed Asner, Larry Gates, Nancy Marchand, Sada Thompson. American Shakespeare Festival, Stratford, Connecticut, 8 July. Sets by Will Steven Armstrong. Costumes by Elizabeth Montgomery.

The Aspern Papers, Henry James, adapted by Michael Redgrave, d. Basil Dean, s. Redgrave, Pauline Jameson, Beatrix Lehmann, Flora Robson. Queen's Theatre, 12 August. Sets by Paul Mayo. Costumes by Sophia Harris.

King Lear, d. Glen Byam Shaw, s. Charles Laughton, Cyril Luckham, Zoe Caldwell, Albert Finney, Ian Holm, Angela Baddeley, Stephanie Bidmead, Robert Hardy, Julian Glover, Roy Dotrice. Shakespeare Memorial Theatre, Stratford-upon-Avon, 18 August. Sets and costumes by Margaret Harris.

Il Trovatore, Giuseppe Verdi, d. Fausto Cleva,

Herbert Graf, s. Antoinette Stella, Carlo Bergonzi. Metropolitan Opera House, New York, 26 October. Sets and costumes by Elizabeth Montgomery. Revived several times, notably on 28 January 1961, when Leontyne Price made her debut.

Rosmersholm, Henrik Ibsen, translated by Ann Jellicoe, d. George Devine, s. Peggy Ashcroft, Mark Dignam, Eric Porter, John Blatchley. Royal Court Theatre, 18 November; transferred to the Comedy Theatre, 5 January 1960. Sets by Margaret Harris. Costumes by Sophia Harris.

Tannhäuser, Richard Wagner, d. Antony Besch, cond. Colin Davis, s. Marie Collier, Joan Stuart, Ronald Dowd, Raimund Herincx, David Ward. Sadler's Wells Opera, Sadler's Wells Theatre, 9 December; revived several times. Sets by Margaret Harris. Costumes by Sophia Harris.

1960

Simon Boccanegra, Giuseppe Verdi, d. Dimitri Mitropoulos, Margaret Webster. s. Richard Tucker, Renate Tebaldi, Anselmo Colzani. Metropolitan Opera House, New York, 23 March; subsequently revived with a different cast. Sets by Frederick Fox. Costumes by Elizabeth Montgomery.

The Naming of Murderer's Rock, Frederick Bland, d. John Bird, s. Kenneth Macintosh, Colin Blakely, Nicholas Selby. Royal Court Theatre, 30 March; previously produced 22 November 1959 "without decor." Sets by Margaret Harris. Costumes by Sophia Harris.

Ross, Terence Rattigan, d. Glen Byam Shaw, s. Peter Bayliss, Alec Guinness, Harry Andrews, Robert Arnold, Mark Dignam. Haymarket Theatre, 12 May; with John Mills in the title role, transferred to the Eugene O'Neill Theatre, New York, 26 December. Sets and costumes by Margaret Harris.

A Man for All Seasons, Robert Bolt, d. Noel Willman, s. Paul Scofield, Leo McKern, Carole Goodner, Keith Baxter. Globe Theatre, 1 July; transferred to the ANTA Theatre, New York, 12 November (closed 1 June 1963; 637 performances). Sets by Margaret Harris. Costumes by Sophia Harris.

Waiting in the Wings, Noel Coward, d. Margaret Webster, s. Mary Clare, Lewis Casson, Sybil Thorndike, Edith Day, Norah Blaney, Maidie Andrews, Marie Lohr, Maureen Delaney, William Hutt. Duke of York's Theatre, 7 September. Sets by Margaret Harris. Costumes by Sophia Harris.

Becket, Jean Anouilh, d. Peter Glenville, s. Anthony Quinn, Laurence Olivier. St. James's Theatre, New York, 5 October. Sets by Oliver Smith. Costumes by Elizabeth Montgomery.

You in Your Small Corner, Barry Reckord, d. John Bird, s. Pearl Numez, Gordon Woolford, Neville Munroe, Jeanne Hepple, Margery Withers, Allan Mitchell, Rachel Herbert. Royal Court Theatre, 23 October; revived at the Royal Court, 21 March 1961. Sets by Margaret Harris. Costumes by Sophia Harris.

The Complaisant Lover, Graham Greene, d. Glen Byam Shaw, s. Michael Redgrave, Sandy Dennis, Richard Johnson, Gene Wilder, Ethel Barrymore Theatre, New York, 1 November. Sets by Margaret Harris. Costumes by Elizabeth Montgomery.

Toys in the Attic, Lillian Hellman, d. John Dexter, s. Wendy Hiller, Diana Wynyard, George Webb, Coral Browne, Ian Bannen, Judith Stott. Piccadilly Theatre, 10 November. Sets by Howard Bay. Costumes by Sophia Harris.

Song in the Theatre, Dudley Moore, d. Bernard Shaktman, s. Freda Jackson, Zoe Caldwell. Royal Court Theatre, 18 December. No sets. Costumes by Sophia Harris.

1961

The Innocents, film, based on *The Turn of the Screw* by Henry James, adapted from the play *The Innocents* by William Archibald, screenplay by Truman Capote and John Mortimer, d. Jack Clayton, p. Clayton, s. Deborah Kerr, Michael Redgrave, Peter Wyngarde, Megs Jenkins, Pamela Franklin, Martin Stephens, Clytie Jessop. Achilles/Twentieth Century-Fox. B/W 99m. A.d. Wilfrid Shingleton. Costumes by Sophia Harris.

A Taste of Honey, Shelagh Delaney and Tony Richardson, d. Tony Richardson, p. Richardson, s. Rita Tushingham, Dora Bryan, Murray Melvin, Robert Stephens, Paul Danquah. Woodfall Films. B/W. 100 m. A.d. Ralph Brinton. Costumes Sophia Harris.

Martha, Freidrich von Flotow and Ann Ronell, d. Carl Ebert, Nino Verchi, s. Richard Tucker, Rosalind Elias. Metropolitan Opera House, New York, 26 January. Sets by Oliver Smith. Costumes

by Elizabeth Montgomery.

The Lady From the Sea, Henrik Ibsen, d. Glen Byam Shaw, s. Margaret Leighton, Richard Pasco, Andrew Cruikshank, Esmond Knight, Vanessa Redgrave, John Neville, Queen's Theatre, 15 March. Sets by Margaret Harris. Costumes by Sophia Harris.

Dazzling Prospect, M. J. Farrell and John Perry, d. John Gielgud, s. Margaret Rutherford, Joyce Carey, Hazel Hughes. Globe Theatre, 1 June. Sets by Margaret Harris. Costumes by Sophia Harris.

As You Like It, d. Word Baker, s. Will Geer, Kim Hunter, Donald Harron. American Shakespeare Festival, Stratford, Connecticut, 16 June. Sets by Robert O'Hearn. Costumes by Elizabeth Montgomery.

Macbeth, d. Jack Landau, s. Pat Hingle, Jessica Tandy, Will Geer. American Shakespeare Festival, Stratford, Connecticut, 28 June. Sets by Robert O'Hearn. Costumes by Elizabeth Montgomery.

Troilus and Cressida, d. Jack Landau, s. Hiram Sherman, Carrie Nye. American Shakespeare Festival, Stratford, Connecticut, 23 July. Sets by Robert O'Hearn. Costumes by Elizabeth Montgomery.

Kwamina, Robert Alan Arthur and Richard Adler, d. Robert Lewis, Agnes de Mille, s. Will Steven Armstrong, Brock Peters, Norman Barrs. Fifty-Fourth Street Theatre, New York, 23 October. Sets by Will Steven Armstrong. Costumes by Elizabeth Montgomery.

1962

Long Day's Journey Into Night, film, based on the play by Eugene O'Neill, d. Sidney Lumet, p. Ely Landau, Jack J. Dreyfus, Jr., s. Katharine Hepburn, Ralph Richardson, Jason Robards, Jr., Dean Stockwell, Jeanne Barr. Embassy Pictures. B/W. 174m. A.d. Richard Sylbert. Costumes by Sophia Harris, adapting those of Elizabeth Montgomery, who designed the costumes for the 1956 premiere in New York.

The Loneliness of the Long Distance Runner (also known as *Rebel With a Cause*), film, based on Alan Sillitoe's story, d. Tony Richardson, p. Richardson, s. Tom Courtenay, Michael Redgrave, Avis Bunnage, Peter Madden, James Bolam, Julia Foster. Woodfall-Bryanston-Seven Arts. B/W. 104 m. P.d. Ralph Brinton. A.d. Ted Marshall. Costumes by Sophia Harris.

Night of the Eagle (Burn, Witch, Burn! in U.S.A.; working title *Conjure Wife),* film, d. Sidney Hayers, p. Albert Fennell, Julian Wintle-Leslie Parkyn, s. Janet Blair, Peter Wyngarde, Margaret Johnston, Anthony Nicholls, Colin Gordon, Kathleen Byron, Reginald Beckwith. Independent Artists. A.d. Jack Shampan. Costumes by Sophia Harris.

Latin Quarter, Liberace. A nightclub act designed by Elizabeth Montgomery. Played in New York. n.d.

The Rake's Progress, Igor Stravinsky, W. H. Auden, and Chester Kullman, d. Glen Byam Shaw, cond. Colin Davis, s. Elsie Morison, Alexander Young, Don Garrard, Raimund Heinicx, Kevin Miller, Ann Robson, Edith Coates. Sadler's Wells Opera, Sadler's Wells Theatre, 2 February; often revived, in 1965 it toured Europe. Sets by Margaret Harris. Costumes by Sophia Harris.

We Take the Town, Felice Bauer and Matt Dubey, adapted from the screenplay *Viva Villa!,* lyrics by Matt Dubey, music by Harold Carr, d. Alex Segal, s. Robert Preston, Mike Kellim, Carmen Alvarez. Shubert Theatre, New Haven, 19 February; later transferred to New York. Sets by Peter Larkin. Costumes by Elizabeth Montgomery.

Richard II, d. Allen Fletcher, s. Richard Basehart, Hal Holbrook, Philip Bosco. American Shakespeare Festival, Stratford, Connecticut. 17 June. Sets by Eldon Elder. Costumes by Montgomery.

Henry IV Part One, d. Douglas Seale, s. Eric Berry, James Ray, Will Geer, Hal Holbrook, Sada Thompson. American Shakespeare Festival, Stratford, Connecticut, 17 June. Sets by Eldon Elder. Costumes by Elizabeth Montgomery.

Playing with Fire, August Strindberg, d. John Blatchley, s. Sheila Allen, Michael Hordern, Kenneth Haigh. Aldwych Theatre, 18 June. Sets by John Bury. Costumes by Sophia Harris.

Idomeneo, Wolfgang Amadeus Mozart and Giambattista Varesco, d. Glen Byam Shaw, cond. Colin Davis, s. John Wakefield, Elsie Morison, Donald McIntyre, Ronald Dowd, William McAlpine, Rae Woodland, John Kentish, John Hauxvell. Sadler's Wells Opera, Sadler's Wells Theatre, 11 October; frequently revived. Sets and costumes by Margaret Harris.

Vanity Fair, musical based on Thackeray's novel, book by Robin Miller and Alan Pryce-Jones, music by Julian Slade, d. Lionel Harris, s. Joyce Carey, Sybil Thorndike, Frances Cuka, George Baker. Queen's Theatre, 27 November. Sets by Tom Lingwood. Costumes by Sophia Harris.

The Tulip Tree, N. C. Hunter, d. Glen Byam Shaw, s. George Benson, Lynn Redgrave, Celia Johnson, Nan Munro, John Clements. Haymarket Theatre, 29 November. Sets by Margaret Harris. Costumes by Sophia Harris.

1963

This Sporting Life, film, based on the novel by David Storey, d. Lindsay Anderson, p. Albert Fennell, Karel Reisz, Julian Wintle-Leslie Parkyn, s. Richard Harris, Rachel Roberts, Alan Badel, William Hartnell, Colin Blakely, Arthur Lowe, Leonard Rossiter. Independent Artists. A.d. Alan Withy. Costumes by Sophia Harris.

Night Must Fall, film, based upon the play by Emlyn Williams, adapted by Clive Exton, d. Karel Reisz, p. Albert Finney, Karel Reisz, s. Albert Finney, Mona Washbourne, Susan Hampshire, Sheila Hancock, Michael Medwin. MGM British (released January 1964). P.d. Timothy O'Brien. A.d. Lionel Couch. Costumes Sophia Harris.

Lorenzo, Jack Richardson, d. Arthur Penn, s. Alfred Drake, Robert Drivas, Carmen Mathews. Plymouth Theatre, New York, 14 February; closed after 4 performances. Sets by David Hays. Costumes by Elizabeth Montgomery.

Tovarich, David Shaw, Lee Pockriss, and Anne Croswell, d. Peter Glenville, Herbert Ross, Rolf Gerrard, s. Vivien Leigh, Byron Mitchell. Broadway Theatre, New York, 18 March. Sets by Rolf Gerard. Costumes by Elizabeth Montgomery.

Così fan Tutte, Wolfgang Amadeus Mozart and da Ponte, d. Glen Byam Shaw, cond. Colin Davis, s. John Wakefield, Donald McIntyne, Thomas Hemsley, Heather McMillan, Catherine Wilson, Iris Kells. Sadler's Wells Opera, Sadler's Wells Theatre, 22 March. Sets by Margaret Harris. Costumes by Sophia Harris.

Mother Courage and Her Children, Bertholt Brecht, d. Jerome Robbins, Ming Cho Lee, s. Anne Bancroft, Gene Wilder, Barbara Harns. Martin Beck Theatre, New York, 26 March. Sets by Ming Cho Lee. Costumes by Elizabeth Montgomery.

The Doctor's Dilemma, George Bernard Shaw, d.

Donald McWhinnie, s. Anna Massey, Philip Grout, Peter Howell, Brian Bedford. Haymarket Theatre, 23 May. Sets by Margaret Harris. Costumes by Sophia Harris.

Where Angels Fear to Tread, Elizabeth Hart, based on the novel by E.M.Forster, d. Glen Byam Shaw, s. Mary Williams, Nan Munro, Michael Denison, Dulcie Gray, Keith Baxter. New Arts Theatre, 6 June; transferred to St. Martin's Theatre, 9 July. Sets by Margaret Harris. Costumes by Sophia Harris.

Der Freischütz, Carl Maria von Weber and Friedrich Kind, d. Glen Byam Shaw, Colin Davis, s. Donald McIntyre, Frank Olegario, Elizabeth Robeson, Ava June, Norman Lumsden, Alberto Remedios, Julian Moyle, Diana Chadwick. New Theatre, Oxford, 19 August; Sadler's Wells, London, 12 September. Sets and costumes by Margaret Harris.

110 in the Shade, N. Richard Nash, Tom Jones, and Harvey Schmidt, d. Joseph Anthony , choreography by Agnes de Mille, s. Will Geer, Inga Swenson. Broadhurst Theatre, New York, 24 October; re-staged, d. Charles Blackwell, s. Pamela Dyer, Michael Hyatt, at the Palace Theatre, London, 8 February 1967. Sets by Oliver Smith. Costumes by Elizabeth Montgomery.

1964

The Pumpkin Eater, Harold Pinter, adapted from the novel by Penelope Mortimer, d. Jack Clayton, p. James Woolf, s. Anne Bancroft, Peter Finch, James Mason, Cedric Hardwicke, Richard Johnson, Anthony Nicholls, Maggie Smith, Eric Porter, Cyril Luckham. Romulus Films. 118 m. A.d. Edward Marshall. Costumes by Sophia Harris.

Hobson's Choice, Harold Brighouse, d. John Dexter, s. Joan Plowright, Michael Redgrave, Frank Finlay. National Theatre at the Old Vic, Old Vic Theatre, 7 January; revived at the same theatre, 9 March 1965. Sets by Margaret Harris. Costumes by Sophia Harris.

The Makropulos Case, Leos Janacek and Karel Capek, d. John Blatchley, Charles Mackerras, s. Marie Collier, Raimund Heinicx, Eric Shilling, Stanley Bevan, Gregory Dempsey, John Chorley, Jenny Hill, Joan Davies, Margaret Gale, Michael Maurel. Sadler's Wells Opera, Sadler's Wells Theatre, 12 February. Sets by Margaret Harris. Costumes by Sophia Harris.

The Right Honourable Gentleman, M. Bradley-Dyne, d. Glen Byam Shaw, s. Colin Redgrave, Anthony Quayle, Jack Gwillim, Anna Massey, Coral Brown. Her Majesty's Theatre, 28 May. Sets by Margaret Harris. Costumes by Sophia Harris.

Faust, Charles Gounod, d. Glen Byam Shaw, cond. Colin Davis, s. Donald McIntyre, Wendy Baldwin, Alberto Remedios, Mary Gilmore, John Hauxvell, Kelvin Jones. Opera House, Manchester, 7 September; Sadler's Wells Theatre, London, 16 September. Sets and costumes by Margaret Harris.

A Cuckoo in the Nest, Ben Travers, d. Anthony Page, s. Nan Munro, Nicol Williamson, Beatrix Lehmann, John Osborne. Royal Court Theatre, 22 October. Sets by Alan Tagg. Costumes by Sophia Harris.

Ben Franklin in Paris, Sidney Michaels, Mark Sandrich, Jr., d. Jack Brow, choreographed by Michael Kidd, s. Robert Preston. Lunt-Fontaine Theatre, New York, 27 October. Sets by Oliver Smith. Costumes by Elizabeth Montgomery.

Hay Fever, Noel Coward, d. Coward, s. Derek Jacobi, Edith Evans, Maggie Smith, Lynn Redgrave. Old Vic Theatre, 27 October. Revived, d. Murray MacDonald, s. Celia Johnson, Lucy Fleming, Roland Culver, Prunella Scales. Duke of York's Theatre, 14 February 1968. Sets by Margaret Harris. Costumes by Sophia Harris.

1965

The Spy Who Came in From the Cold, film, adapted from John Le Carré's novel by Paul Dehn and Guy Trosper; d. Martin Ritt, p. Ritt, s. Richard Burton, Claire Bloom, Sam Wanamaker, Oskar Werner, Peter Van Eyck, George Voskovec, Rupert Davies, Cyril Cusak, Michael Hordern, Beatrix Lehmann, Esmond Knight, Robert Hardy, Bernard Lee, Warren Mitchell. Salem Films, for Paramount. B/W. 112m. A.d. Edward Marshall. Costumes by Sophia Harris.

Fog (A Study in Terror in the U.S.A., *Sherlock Holmes Grosster Fall* in Germany), film, based on Sir Arthur Conan Doyle's characters with script and screenplay by Donald and Derek Ford, d. James Hill, p. Herman Cohen, s. John Neville,

Donald Houston, Anthony Quayle, Robert Morley, Frank Finlay, Judi Dench, Cecil Parker, Barry Jones, John Fraser, Barbara Windsor, Adrienne Corri, Georgia Brown. Compton-Tekli-Sir Nigel-Planet for Columbia. 95m. A.d. Alec Vetchinsky. Costumes by Sophia Harris.

A Masked Ball, Giuseppi Verdi and Antonio Somma, d. Glen Byam Shaw, cond. Colin Davis, s. Stafford Dean, Gerwyn Morgan, Diane Todd, Donald Smith, Robert Bickerstaff, Tadea Pylko, Kelvin Jones, Elizabeth Fretwell. Sadler's Wells Opera, Sadler's Wells Theatre, 27 January. Sets by Margaret Harris. Costumes by Margaret Harris and Sophia Harris.

Baker Street, Jerome Coopersmith, music and lyrics by Marion Grudeff and Raymond Jessel, d. Harold Prince, choreographed by Lee Becker Theodore, s. Fritz Weaver, Peter Sallis, Daniel Keyes, Inga Swenson. Broadway Theatre, New York, 16 February. Sets by Oliver Smith. Costumes by Elizabeth Montgomery.

Spring Awakening, Frank Wedekind, translated by Desmond O'Donovan, d. Desmond O'Donvavan, s. Nicol Williamson, Ann Holloway, Vanessa Forsyth. Royal Court Theatre, 19 April. Sets by Dacre Punt. Costumes by Sophia Harris. 27 CD. The play was first produced, with a different cast, at the Royal Court on 21 April 1963, as a low-budget "production without decor."

The Devils, John Whiting, d. Michael Cacoyannis, s. James Coco, Jason Robards, Anne Bancroft. Broadway Theatre, New York, 16 November. Sets by Rouben Ter-Artunian. Costumes by Elizabeth Montgomery.

Trelawny of the "Wells," Arthur Wing Pinero, d. Desmond O'Donovan, s. Graham Crowden, Michael York, Ian McKellan, Ronald Pickup, Louise Rurnell, Robert Stephens. Chichester Festival, Chichester; Prospect Theatre Company, Old Vic Theatre, 17 November. Sets by Alan Tagg (Chichester) and Sophia Harris (London). Costumes by Sophia Harris.

1966

Dance of the Vampires (The Fearless Vampire Killers in the U.S.A.), film, d. Roman Polanski, p. Martin Ransohoff, Roman Polanski, s. Jack MacGowran, Roman Polanski, Alfie Bass, Jessie Robins, Sharon Tate, Ferdy Mayne, Fiona Lewis. Cadre Films-Filmways, for MGM. P.d. Wilfrid Shingleton. A.d. Fred Carter. Costumes by Sophia Harris ("Sophie Devine" in the credits).

You Never Can Tell, George Bernard Shaw, d. Glen Byam Shaw, s. Keith Baxter, Cyril Luckham, Ralph Richardson, Angela Thorne, Harry Andrews. Haymarket Theatre, 12 January. Sets by Margaret Harris. Costumes by Sophia Harris.

La Bohème, Giacomo Puccini and Murger, d. John Blatchley, cond. Mario Bernardi, s. Ann Howard, Robert Bickerstaff, Heather Thomson, John Wakefield, Derek Hammond Stroud, Noel Mangin, David Bowman, Eric Shilling, Neville Griffiths. Sadler's Wells Opera, Sadler's Wells Theatre, 2 March; subsequently revived for years at Sadler's Wells, the London Coliseum, and Opera North. Sets by Margaret Harris. Costumes by Sophia Harris; after the original costumes were burned in a fire, Margaret Harris redesigned them for a later revival.

The Clandestine Marriage, George Colman and David Garrick, d. Desmond O'Donovan, s. Sarah Badel, Clive Swift, Margaret Rutherford, Bill Fraser. Chichester Festival Theatre, 1 June. Sets by Alan Tagg. Costumes by Sophia Harris.

The Fighting Cock, Jean Anouilh, d. Norman Marshall, s. John Clements, Sarah Badel, Zena Walker, Clive Swift. Chichester Festival Theatre, 7 June. Sets by Alan Tagg. Costumes by Tagg and Sophia Harris.

The Rivals, Richard Brinsley Sheridan, d. Glen Byam Shaw, s. Ralph Richardson, Keith Baxter, Margaret Rutherford, Angela Thorne. Haymarket Theatre, 6 October. Sets by Margaret Harris. Costumes by Anthony Powell.

Don't Drink the Water, Woody Allen, d. Stanley Prager, s. Kay Medford, Lou Jacobs, Anita Gillette. Morosco Theatre, New York, 17 November. Sets Jo Mielziner. Costumes by Montgomery.

1967

The Dance of Death, August Strindberg, d. Glen Byam Shaw, s. Laurence Olivier, Kate Lansbury, Geraldine McEwan, Robert Stephens, Carolyn Jones. National Theatre at the Old Vic, Old Vic Theatre, 21 February. Sets and costumes by Margaret Harris.

The Unknown Soldier and His Wife, Peter Ustinov, d. John Dexter, s. Brian Bedford, W. B. Brydon, Howard da Silva. Vivian Beaumont Theatre, New York, 6 July; transferred to the George Abbott Theatre, New York, 18 September; transferred, with a different cast, to the Chichester Festival, England, 22 May 1968; re-staged in Lyons with Ustinov directing a French cast; and re-staged once again, s. Bedford, Ustinov, Peter Abbot, at the New London Theatre, January 1973. Sets and costumes by Elizabeth Montgomery. Margaret Harris designed the sets for London.

The Merchant of Venice, d. Glen Byam Shaw, s. Jack Gwillim, Ralph Richardson, Angela Thorne, Malcolm Reid. Haymarket Theatre, 7 September. Sets by Margaret Harris. Costumes by Elizabeth Montgomery.

Wise Child, Simon Gray, d. John Dexter, s. Alec Guinness, Gordon Jackson, Cleo Sylvestre, Simon Ward. Wyndham's Theatre, 10 October. Sets by Margaret Harris. Costumes by Elizabeth Montgomery.

1968

The Bells, Leopold Lewis, d. Marius Goring, s. Goring, Marian Foster. Vaudeville Theatre, 24 January. Sets by Margaret Harris. Costumes by Elizabeth Montgomery.

The Mastersingers of Nuremberg, Richard Wagner, d. Glen Byam Shaw, John Blatchley, cond. Reginald Goodall, s. Norman Bailey, Noel Mangin, David Kane, Julian Moyle, Derek Hammond Stroud, David Bowman, John Brecknock, David Morton-Gray, Louis Browne, James Singleton, Gerwyn Morgan, Eric Stannard, Alberto Remedios, Gregory Depsey, Margaret Curphey, Ann Robson, Stafford Dean. Sadler's Wells Opera, Sadler's Wells Theatre, 31 January; transferred to the London Coliseum, 26 August; frequently revived. Sets by Elizabeth Montgomery and Margaret Harris. Costumes by David Walker. Margaret Harris re-did the costumes after a fire in the early 1970s damaged the originals.

1969

Trio [three one-act plays]: *The Will, Village Wooing, Ways and Means,* J. M. Barrie, George Bernard Shaw, Noel Coward, d. Michael Denison, s. Michael Denison, Dulcie Gray. Yvonne Arnaud Theatre, Guildford. Sets and costumes by Margaret Harris.

1970

Three [one-act plays]: *(1) How He Lied to Her Husband, (2) Village Wooing, (3) Press Cuttings,* George Bernard Shaw; (1) d. Michael Denison, s. Clive Francis, June Barry, Robert Fleming; (2) d. Nigel Patrick, s. Dulcie Gray, Michael Denison; (3) d. Ray Cooney, s. Michael Denison, Clive Francis, Connie Merigold. Fortune Theatre, 26 January. Sets and costumes for all three plays by Margaret Harris and Elizabeth Montgomery.

The Heretic, Morris West, d. West with Joseph O'Connor, s. Douglas Rain, Francesca Annis. Duke of York's Theatre, 16 July. Sets by Don Ashton. Costumes by Elizabeth Montgomery.

The Wild Duck, Henrik Ibsen, d. Glen Byam Shaw, s. Michael Denison, Dulcie Gray, Hayley Mills, Paul Hardwick. Criterion Theatre, 10 November. Sets by Margaret Harris. Costumes by Elizabeth Montgomery.

1972

War and Peace, Serge Prokofiev's opera based on Tolstoy's novel, d. Colin Graham, cond. David Lloyd-Jones, s. Norman Bailey, Raymond Myers, Kenneth Woollam, John Brecknock, Josephine Barstow, Tom McDonnell, Denis Dowling, Gregory Dempsey, Anne Collins, Ann Hood, Eric Shilling, Malcolm Rivers, Norman Welsby. Sadler's Wells Opera, London Coliseum, 11 October; it remained in the repertory throughout into the 1980s. Sets and costumes by Margaret Harris.

1975

A Family and a Fortune, Julian Mitchell, d. Alan Strachan, s. Alec Guinness, Margaret Leighton.

Apollo Theatre, 10 April. Sets and costumes by Margaret Harris.

1976

Tosca, Giacomo Puccini, d. John Blatchley, cond. Roderick Brydon, s. Anne Evans, Keith Erwin, Norman Bailey, John Tomlinson, Eric Shilling, Edward Byles, John Kitchiner. English National Opera, London Coliseum, 4 February; subsequently revived at the English National Opera and Opera North. Sets and costumes by Margaret Harris.

Paul Bunyan, Benjamin Britten and W. H. Auden, d. Colin Graham, cond. Steuart Bedford, s. Phillip Doghan, Neil Jenkins, Russell Smythe, Paul Maxwell, Iris Saunders, Donald Stephenson, Nigel Rogers. English Musical Theatre, Snape Maltings, Aldeburgh Festival, 4 June; Sadler's Wells Theatre, London, 9 September. Sets and costumes by Margaret Harris.

1978

The Consul, Gian Carlo Menotti, d. David Ritch, cond. Howard Williams, s. Stuart Kale, Ann Howard, Ava June, Patrick Wheatley, Geoffrey Chard, Marie McLaughlin, Anna Gomez. English National Opera, London Coliseum, London, 12 August. Sets and costumes by Margaret Harris.

Notes

Chapter 1. Childhood and Youth (1900–1930)

1. Walter Richard Sickert (1866–1942) began his career working as a scene painter for Henry Irving and Madge Kendal at Sadler's Wells Theatre. He subsequently worked with Whistler at his Tite Street Studio. "Apart from architecture and portraits, his chief interest was in the theatre, especially the stage and the auditorium of London's music halls," notes the *Dictionary of National Biography*, 1941–1950. A member of the Royal Academy, he resigned in protest in 1935 over the destruction of statues by Jacob Epstein on a building in the Strand, as reported in Sidney C. Hutchinson's *The History of the Royal Academy* (London: Chapman and Hall, 1968), 177–78.

Chapter 2. Foundations and Beginnings (1927–1932)

1. Ronald Hayman, *John Gielgud* (New York: Random House, 1971), 73, confirms that "he bought some [designs] to give to his mother and friends and helped the girls, who assumed the collective name of Motley, to arrange an exhibition of their work."

2. For an excellent account of the changes underway in English theatre in the period leading up to World War I, see Cary M. Mazer, *Shakespeare Refashioned: Elizabethan Plays on Edwardian Stages* (Ann Arbor, Mich.: UMI Research Press, 1981), especially his chapter "Shakespeare and the New Stagecraft," 85–121. For a good account of continental theatre design, contemporary with the formation of Motley, see James Laver, "Continental Designers in the Theatre," in George Sheringham and James Laver, *Design in the Theatre* (London: The Studio, 1927) 17–29.

3. For a vivid account of the Old Vic at this time, see Harcourt Williams, *Four Years at the Old Vic: 1929–1933* (London: Putnam, 1935).

4. A part of the Frank Benson legend I have often heard repeated in Stratford, but which I have not been able to find in the public record.

5. For an overview with good illustrations see James Laver, *Costume in the Theatre* (London: Harrap, 1964), 186–219.

6. Theodore Komisarjevsky, *Myself and the Theatre* (London: Dutton, 1930), provides an account of his career in Russia, Paris, London, New York, and elsewhere.

7. Of course their aims were different. The theatre interested Barry Jackson mainly as an arena for experimentation; he eschewed the commercial and traditional. Although experimental in their approach, Motley were firmly allied to the theatrical establishment.

8. The definitive account of Messel's work is Charles Castle's *Oliver Messel: A Biography* (London: Thames and Hudson, 1986). Oliver Messel, *Stage Designs and Costumes* (London: John Lane at the Bodley Head, 1933), gives a sample of his work at that time. See also George Sheringham and James Laver et al., *Design in the Theatre* (London: The Studio, 1927), for a selection of representative drawings by contemporary designers with essays on the state of the art.

9. Founded in 1885, the O.U.D.S. (pronounced to rhyme with "clouds") was disbanded during World War I and revived afterwards. It barred women members until 1947.

10. Christopher Hassal (1912–63) later became a librettist. George Devine (1910–66) became an actor and director. William Devlin (b. 1911) became an actor. Hugh Hunt (b. 1911) became a director. Terence Rattigan (b. 1911) became a playwright.

11. For a full account of the production and the ins and outs of Devine's involvement with the O.U.D.S., see Irving Wardle, *The Theatres of George Devine* (London: Eyre Methuen, 1978), 11–24.

12. See Billington's *Peggy Ashcroft* (London: Murray, 1988), 48–51, for an account of the production from her point of view.

Chapter 3. An Emergent Style (1932–1935)

1. John Gielgud, *Early Stages* (London: Falcon Press, 1939), 210–11.

2. J. C. Trewin, *The Theatre Since 1900* (London: Andrew Dakers, 1951), 224.

3. Gielgud, *Early Stages*, 231.

4. Anthony Quayle, *A Time to Speak* (London: Barrie & Jenkins, 1990), 162.

5. Harold Hobson, *Theatre in Britain* (Oxford: Phaidon, 1984), 54.

6. Audrey Williamson, *Theatre of Two Decades* (New York: Macmillan, 1951), 36–40.

7. Wardle, *The Theatres of George Devine*, 38

8. His remarks appear in Ronald Harwood's *The Ages of Gielgud: An Actor at Eighty* (London: Hodder and Stoughton, 1985), 25–26.

9. Gielgud, *Early Stages*, 231–32, 241.

10. James Agate, *Red Letter Nights* (London: Jonathan Cape, 1944), 310–13.

11. Michael Billington, *Peggy Ashcroft* (London: Murray, 1988), 66.

12. In an interview with the author, August 1988.

13. Richard Findlater, *These Our Actors* (London: Elm Tree Books, 1983), 55.

14. Gielgud, *Early Stages*, 218, remembered his attempts to cast Mrs. Pat Campbell, rather than Motley's witty set.

15. Harcourt Williams, *The Old Vic Saga* (London: Winchester Publication Ltd., 1939), 124.

16. Quoted in Billington, *Peggy Ashcroft*, 62.

17. Quayle, *A Time to Speak*, 166.

18. Billington, *Peggy Ashcroft*, 62

19. Quoted in Trewin, *Shakespeare on the English Stage: 1900–1964* (London: Barrie and Rockliff, 1964), 141.

20. Wardle, *Theatres of George Devine*, 37.

21. Quayle, *A Time to Speak*, 181.

22. For further details of Motley's studio and early business arrangements, see Wardle, *Theatres of George Devine*, 31–32, 35.

23. They were incorporated as Motley, Ltd., in 1935.

24. Gielgud, *Early Stages*, 246.

25. Agate, *Red Letter Nights* 314–16.

26. While Kurt Ganzl's authoritative *British Musical Theatre* (London: Macmillan, 1986), II: 1,214, credits "Cockie" with dozens of musicals, there is no specific mention of the revues.

27. Rosenfeld, *A Short History of Scene Design in Great Britain*, 174–175, notes that Cochran's use of modern artists—Rex Whistler among them—"ensured high artistic quality." For the Motley women, it also must have reinforced a painterly approach to design.

28. The "Samoiloff effect," which Motley admired, was invented by Adrian Samoiloff, who became famous for color lighting stunts in the early 1920s. Using colored gels and stage lighting instruments, the Samoiloff effect rendered one color invisible by illuminating it with light of its opposite, complementary color. For a full explanation of how the effect worked, see Frederick Bentham, *The Art of Stage Lighting* (London: Pitman House, 1980), 102–3, 105.

29. P. W. Manchester, *The Vic-Wells Ballet* (London: Gollancz, 1942), 47.

30. Laurence Olivier, *Confessions of an Actor* (London: Weidenfield and Nicolson, 1982),73–74.

31. *Designing and Making Stage Costumes*, 2d ed. rev. with an introduction by Michael Mullin (London: Herbert Press, 1992), 24.

32. Williamson, *Theatre of Two Decades*, 40–44.

33. Trewin, *Shakespeare on the English Stage*, 150.

34. Reported in Alec Guinness, *Blessings in Disguise* (London: Hamish Hamilton, 1985), 66–69.

35. For a full account, with illustrations, see *Play Pictorial* (August 1935): 3–10. Irving Wardle, *The Theatres of George Devine*, 44–50, describes the events that led Saint-Denis to move from France to England.

36. The costumes must have been very well made. In 1940 Anthony Quayle, then in the Navy, used them to put on *Noah* in Gibraltar: "I tracked down the animals' costumes from the original production in London, and a visiting destroyer brought them out." *A Time to Speak*, 222.

37. Geoffrey Whitworth, *Theatre in Action* (New York: Studio Publications, n.d. but likely late 1930s), 84.

38. Williamson, *Theatre of Two Decades*, 44.

39. Ibid., 50.

40. Trewin, *Shakespeare on the English Stage*, 152.

41. Billington, *Peggy Ashcroft*, 76.

42. In itself, the use of period paintings for set and costume design was a standard practice dating back at least to Charles Kean's "archaeological" revivals of Shakespeare early in the nineteenth century. Motley's innovation was to stress character, mood, and artistic unity over exact replication. For a contemporary reference on the subject, see Frances M. Kelly, *Shakespearian Costume for the Stage and Screen* (London: Adam and Charles Black, 1938).

43. Elmer Edgar Stoll's pioneering work in the 1920s had of course drawn attention to Shakespeare's dramaturgy; yet most academic criticism focused on the thematic or philosophical dimensions of the plays, rather than their stagecraft, an approach that has since become almost doctrinaire through the writings of John Russell Brown, John Styan, and more recently, Jean E. Howard in her *Shakespeare's Art of Orchestration: Stage Technique and Audience Response* (Urbana: University of Illinois Press, 1984).

44. Brook's remarks referred specifically to his approach to filming *King Lear*, released in 1969; *The Shifting Point* (New York: Harper & Row, 1987), 203–4.

Chapter 4. Motley's the Only Wear (1936–1940)

1. "I feel very strongly still that young theatre artists need to work in a professional environment in which they can develop their talents and skills," she concluded in an interview with the author, August 1988. For further details on the Motley Design Course, see chapter 14.

2. The Eames chair, a prototype for all sorts of molded furniture, came later. Motley were involved in its early conception at the Eames's studio in California.

3. For more information on these "basic costumes," see Motley's *Designing and Making Costumes for the Stage*, 85–86.

4. For a full description of the L.T.S. from George Devine's point of view, see Wardle, *Theatres of George Devine*, 51–75.

5. Williamson, *Theatre of Two Decades* (New York: Macmillan, 1951), 50.

6. These productions are described more fully in chapter 2. For detailed descriptions and analyses of them, please see the author's "Strange Images of Death: Sir Herbert Beerbohm Tree's *Macbeth*, His Majesty's Theatre, 1911," *Theatre Survey* 17 (1976): 125–42; "*Macbeth* in Modern Dress: Royal Court Theatre, 1928," *Theatre Journal* 30 (1978): 176–85; and "Augures and Understood Relations: Theodore Komisarjevsky's *Macbeth*," *Theatre Journal* 26 (1974): 20–30.

7. Quoted in Wardle, *Theatres of George Devine*, 75.

8. Robert Speaight, *Shakespeare on the Stage*, 92, 157. The "Bradley" he mentions is A. C. Bradley, whose Oxford lectures on Shakespeare, first published in 1904, had become accepted as a near-definitive reading of the plays.

9. Olivier, *Confessions of an Actor*, 81.

10. For more information on this production, please see *"Macbeth" Onstage: An Annotated Facsimile of Glen Byam Shaw's Promptbook*, ed. Michael Mullin (Columbia: University of Missouri Press, 1976) and the author's "Rhythm, Pace, and Movement: *Macbeth* at Stratford-upon-Avon, 1955," *Shakespeare Studies* 9 (1976): 269–82.

11. Ibid 53–54; he also comments on *Richard II*, as quoted below.

12. Ibid 56.

13. For further comment on the production, see Patrick Miles, *Chekhov on the English Stage* (London: Cambridge University Press, 1993), especially Gordon McVay, "Peggy Ashcroft and Chekhov," 85–93.

14. In *Designing and Making Costumes for the Stage*, 42, Motley discuss further the means by which they made small variations in uniforms to suggest differences among the soldiers.

15. Williamson, *Theatre of Two Decades*, 58–60.

16. Quoted in Billington, *Peggy Ashcroft*, 93.

17. Williamson, *Theatre of Two Decades*, 60–61.

18. Ibid., 60.

19. Ibid.

20. Ibid., 96.

21. Trewin, *The Theatre Since 1900*, 219. Dodie Smith was best known for her very successful *Autumn Crocus*, another comfortable play about middle-class English life.

22. See Guinness, *Blessings in Disguise*, 58, 160–61, 218.

23. Hayman, *John Gielgud*, 119.

Chapter 5. Motley Takes the Town: New York (1940–1945)

1. Ethan Mordden, *American Theatre* (New York: Oxford University Press, 1981), 190.

2. Olivier, *Confessions of an Actor*, 88.

3. For an interesting and extended treatment of the subject, see Mordden's *American Theatre*, which follows the fortunes of American theatre with particular attention to its relationship to British theatre from the beginnings to the 1970s. His observations are more in the form of an extended essay reflecting the consensus—rather than a revisionist treatment.

4. For a full account of his career, see Richard Huggett, *Binkie Beaumont: Eminence Grise of the West End Theatre, 1933–1973* (London: Hodder & Stoughton, 1989). Huggett mentions Motley only in passing.

5. For an account of American theatre practice from the designer's point of view, see Orville K. Larson, *Scene Design in the American Theatre from 1915 to 1960* (Fayetteville and London: University of Arkansas Press, 1989), 48–130. United Scenic Artists Local 829 in 1941 counted among its members 137 designers, 213 scenic artists, 29 studio operators, 13 make-up artists, 62 costume designers, 60

mural artists, and 375 diorama, display artists, and model makers (127).

Although Larson mentions Motley as "a unique phenomenon among American scenic artists" (142) and notes two Motley-designed New York productions, his chronology lists only seventeen of their New York shows, ending with *Happy as Larry* in 1950.

6. For a vivid recollection of the process of rehearsal and tryouts for a dance production, see Agnes de Mille, *And Promenade Home* (Boston: Little, Brown, and Company, 1956), 95–114.

7. Agnes de Mille, *Dance to the Piper* (Boston: Little, Brown, and Company, 1952), 262–63.

8. Grace Roberts, *The Borzoi Book of Ballets* (New York: Alfred A. Knopf, 1949), 337. The piece had evolved through several transformations, beginning in London in 1934, as Grace Roberts reports.

9. See Margaret Speaker-Yuan, *Agnes de Mille* (New York: Chelsea House Publishers, 1990), 76, for a photograph of Anton Dolin and Lucia Chase in the leading parts.

10. Robert Speaight, *Shakespeare on the Stage* (Boston: Little, Brown & Company, 1973), 232.

Chapter 6. Elizabeth Montgomery in New York (1946–1966)

1. Reprinted in *First Nights and Footlights* (London: Hutchinson, 1955), 177.

2. Readers wishing to know more about the musicals designed by Motley—details of plot and song titles, information on what else was playing during a given season—should turn to Gerald Bordman's authoritative *American Musical Theatre: A Chronicle* (New York: Oxford University Press, 1978).

3. *Designing and Making Stage Costumes*, 20.

4. In an interview with the author, April 1993.

5. Richard Rodgers tells some charming anecdotes about the genesis of the musical in his *Musical Stages* (New York: Random House, 1975), 258–64; 266–68. Ebullient with confidence in the show, on opening night he tempted fate by throwing a party and ordering two hundred copies of the Times for the guests. He was right, of course, and enjoyed basking in Brooks Atkinson's praise. In a season that included Arthur Miller's *Death of a Salesman*, *South Pacific* won eight Tony and nine Donaldson awards, the Pulitzer Prize for drama, and a gold record for Columbia's cast recording. Only *Oklahoma!* and *My Fair Lady* ran longer on Broadway.

6. *Designing and Making Stage Costumes*, 12.

7. Fred Fehl, *On Broadway*, 139.

8. The facts and figures appear in Barry Rivadue, *Mary Martin: A Bio-Bibliography* (Westport, Conn., and London: Greenwood Press, 1991), 45.

9. Quoted in Fehl, *On Broadway*, 234.

10. The influence of the Old Vic on Broadway is reported by Ethan Mordden, *The American Theatre*, 202–3.

11. *Designing and Making Stage Costumes*, 8–12.

12. Quoted in Fehl, *On Broadway*, 241.

13. *Designing and Making Stage Costumes*, 11.

14. Elizabeth Montgomery's remarks appeared in "Modern Dress—Fun or Frustration: by Motley," *Players Magazine*, 39–40 (1963), 202, 206. See also *Designing and Making Stage Costumes*, 13.

15. Clifton Fadiman's appreciation of the accomplishments of the Metropolitan Opera Guild (*Opera News*, 8 October 1960) featured Elizabeth Montgomery's costume sketches for Sir Tristram, Nancy, and Lionel. "On opening night for this rarely produced opera, the horse Matilda, on stage to pull a carriage, took off in the wrong direction, heading straight for the orchestra; a groom and stagehands were needed to bring her around," reported Harold Schonberg (*Times*, 27 January 1962).

"For *Martha* I had to work with Oliver Smith, who did the sets," recalled Elizabeth Montgomery. "He was a real terror, awfully difficult to work with, because we had completely opposite ideas about color. We just like different colors, and they didn't go together." None of the critics seems to have agreed with her low opinion of the results.

16. *Designing and Making Stage Costumes*, 33.

17. Ibid., 12.

18. Fehl, *On Broadway*, 367.

19. *Designing and Making Stage Costumes*, 37.

20. Ibid., 26.

21. Hal Prince, *Contradictions: Notes on Twenty-Six Years in the Theatre* (Cornwall, N.Y.: Cornwall Press, 1974), 113–16.

Chapter 7. Motley in London (1940–1947)

1. Wardle, *Theatres of George Devine*, 90.

2. Harold Hobson, *Theatre in Britain* (Oxford: Phaidon, 1984), 120.

3. After the Old Vic was bombed in the spring of 1941, the Council for the Encouragement of Music and the Arts (C.E.M.A.), a wartime forerunner of the present-day Arts Council, made the Old Vic and other theatre companies peripatetic, bringing theatre to some 160 provincial towns that had been theatreless for years, as reported by J. C. Trewin, *The Theatre Since 1900*, 265–66.

4. For these and other details about Sophia Harris I am indebted to her daughter Harriet Jump.

5. 12th ed., 901.

6. The incident is reported in Colin Wilson, *Bernard Shaw: A Reassessment* (New York: Atheneum, 1969), 198. Wilson argues that *The Doctor's Dilemma* marked the high point of Shaw's achievement as a playwright, after which his public persona "G.B.S." began to come before Bernard Shaw the artist. The play is, of course, a minor modern classic; Motley designed a post-War revival as well (see chapter 12). For reviews of the original 1906 production and its revival with a different cast in 1914, see Desmond McCarthy, *Shaw's Plays in Review* (New York: Thames and Hudson, 1951), 66–76.

7. From contemporary reviews in the Manders and Mitchenson Collection, London. The cuttings lacked reviewers' names, newspapers, and dates.

8. This version of the story varies a bit from the incident as described by Gielgud in the foreword to this book.

Chapter 8. The Old Vic, the Young Vic, and the Old Vic School (1947–1953)

1. See Wardle's *Theatres of George Devine*, 96–142, for a comprehensive and detailed account of the Old Vic work. Throughout the pages following, I draw upon his masterful explanation of the politics and aspirations involved in that brave attempt to weld together divergent artistic and commercial interests.

2. Ibid., 114.

3. Trewin, *The Theatre Since 1900*, 298–99.

4. Frances Tenguen, *The Curious History of "Bartholomew Fair"* (London and Toronto: Associated University Presses, 1985), 120–23.

5. Wardle, *Theatres of George Devine*, 137.

6. *Shakespeare Quarterly* 2 (1951): 338.

7. Ibid., 339.

8. For these and other details of the staging I am indebted not only to interviews with Margaret Harris but also to Glen Byam Shaw's promptbook and notes, which he lent me.

9. He subsequently founded the Centre Nationale Dramatique de l'Est at Strasbourg.

Chapter 9. The English Stage Company and The Royal Court Theatre (1954–1966)

1. See Irving Wardle's account, understandably told from Devine's point of view, in *Theatres of George Devine*, 157–59. What is not clear from this account, other than the fact that he notes Devine's

discomfort with his role as father to young Harriet and his wife's being ten years older than himself, is how their emotional shift influenced (or did not influence) their work in the theatre. To the designers Peter Gill and Reg Hanson I am indebted for first-hand accounts of these times in interviews with the author, March 1987 and August 1992, respectively.

2. In interviews with the author, as noted above.

3. Hobson, *Theatre in Britain*, 183.

4. Billington, *Peggy Ashcroft*, 153.

5. Ibid., 153, 156.

6. In an interview with the author, August 1988.

7. Wardle, *Theatres of George Devine*, 172.

8. Hobson, *Theatre in Britain*, 183.

9. John Russell Taylor, *Anger and After* (London: Methuen, 1962), 33, reported that the show netted a profit of £10,000. His detailed study of the "Angry Young Men" makes the salient point that *Look Back in Anger* had been preceded by a number of forerunners—among them Brecht, Anouilh, Ugo Betti, and Beckett—and that its initial reception was by no means the utter critical disaster others remember, Margaret Harris among them. A brief excerpt on television seems to have given the box office a boost, but the real impetus came from a public who were devoted to the English Stage Company's ideals. His historical, literary approach has little to say about production or design; he does not mention Sophia Harris's contributions.

10. In an interview with the author, March 1987.

Chapter 10. The Shakespeare Memorial Theatre (1948–1958)

1. For an informed and affectionate account of their work together in Stratford, see Anthony Quayle's *A Time to Speak*, 325–41.

2. Leech's thoughtful review of record appeared in *Shakespeare Quarterly* 4 (1953): 465–66.

3. Billington, *Peggy Ashcroft*, 148.

4. *Shakespeare Survey* 7 (1954): 125–26.

5. Billington, *Peggy Ashcroft*, 151–52.

6. *Shakespeare Quarterly* 5 (1954): 388.

7. For an account of Motley's designs for *A Midsummer Night's Dream*, see "A 'Purge on Prettiness': Motley's Costumes for *A Midsummer Night's Dream*, Shakespeare Memorial Theatre, Stratford-upon-Avon, 1954," *Shakespeare Studies* (Japan) 27 (1988–89): 65–77 (with David McGuire).

8. *Shakespeare Quarterly* 7 (1956): 408.

9. *Shakespeare Quarterly* 8 (1957): 401 ff. Her remarks on *As You Like It*, quoted below, appear in the same article.

10. Billington, *Peggy Ashcroft*, 169.

11. *Shakespeare Quarterly* 9 (1958): 134.

12. Ibid., 132–34.

13. Besides her work in London, Tanya Moiseiwitsch had established herself as the principal designer for the Stratford, Ontario, Shakespeare Festival.

14. *Shakespeare Quarterly* 11 (1960): 189–206.

Chapter 11. The Sadler's Wells Opera and the English National Opera (1952–1978)

1. I am grateful to Edmund Tracey, opera critic and a former director of the English National Opera, for clarifying the distinction between the two opera companies and for providing other background information not to be found in printed sources.

2. The company traced its origins back to Lilian Baylis's coming to the Old Vic in 1898 at the invitation of her aunt Emma Cons. By 1931 a public appeal allowed the company to buy and refurbish the theatre at Sadler's Wells, where for a few years opera, ballet, and Shakespeare alternated between the two theatres. Artistic standards in set and costume design were impaired by scarce funds. During the War, Sadler's Wells Opera toured the country, with occasional stints in London. After the War, they enlarged their repertory and, despite competition from the glitzier Covent Garden and Glyndebourne companies, they came to thrive as a major opera company, moving from Sadler's Wells to the London Coliseum in 1970. See Richard Jarman, *A History of Sadler's Wells Opera* (London: Fast Print, Ltd., 1975).

3. In Pushkin's libretto the action moves from the Garden to Tatiana's bedroom (the "letter scene"), back to the Garden, to her birthday party, to the duel next to a mill, to the Prince's ball, and then to the room where Tatiana finally leaves Onegin to his grief.

4. For an account of these two Motley-designed operas at Sadler's Wells, see Wardle, *Theatres of George Devine*, 143–45.

5. The opera's fantastical plot seems to have put unusual demands on the designer's invention. The set designs for two other productions of the opera the next season also came in for sharp criticism. John Piper's sets at Covent Garden were deplored as "the underneath of a gate-legged table" by Philip Hope-Wallace (*Manchester Guardian*, 21 January 1956). Although an improvement, Oliver Messel's design for Glyndebourne "over encumbered" the stage with "fussy detail," said Peter Heyworth (*The Observer*, 29 July 1956).

In 1962, with John Blatchley directing and Colin Davis conducting, Sadler's Wells Opera restaged *The Magic Flute*, using Motley's 1955 sets and costumes. Amidst praise for the production, the design was again faulted by the critics.

6. "A director from the dramatic theatre has been brought into the service of opera, and Glen Byam Shaw shows himself to be musically most sensitive," *Plays and Players* (March 1962) pronounced authoritatively.

7. Reported in a profile on Byam Shaw by Frank Granville Barker in *Music and Musicians*, September, 1963. In fact, Byam Shaw and Colin Davis's appointments as director of productions and musical director were related to larger plans to re-site and re-finance the Sadler's Wells Opera. Two companies—one in London, one on tour—were formed, with the end in view that they would amalgamate in London for larger operas during the regular season. In the end, after attempts at relocation that included incorporation in the then putative South Bank performing arts complex, the company relocated at the London Coliseum in St. Martin's Lane in 1968 and was given the title of the English National Opera by the British Government in 1975. It continues there to this day.

8. Reported by J. Roger Baker, the opera critic, in *The Tatler*, 7 November 1962.

9. As explained in an earlier chapter, for Cochran's revues at the Trocadero nightclub in the 1930s, Motley used this special lighting effect to make some parts of a costume invisible while other parts remained visible.

10. I follow the spelling used by the opera company and the British reviewers. The spelling in the United States is usually Makropoulos.

11. The term "toytown" appeared in the reviews in the *Financial Times* (1 February 1968) and was echoed in the *Tribune's* review (16 February 1968).

12. William Mann, *Times*, 13 October 1972.

13. For an account of the music and history of the piece, see Peter Evans, *The Music of Benjamin Britten* (Minneapolis: University of Minnesota Press, 1979), 95–103. Alan Kendall, *Benjamin Britten* (London: Macmillan, 1973), 25–26, in his illustrated biography makes passing mention of Paul Bunyan in relation to Britten's better known *Billy Budd, Peter Grimes*, and *The Rape of Lucretia*.

Chapter 12. In the West End (1946–1975)

1. Trewin, *The Theatre Since 1900* (London: Andrew Dakers, 1951), 285.

2. Hobson, *Theatre in Britain* (Oxford: Phaidon, 1984), 142–44.

3. Nathan, *Costumes by Nathan* (London: Newnes, 1960), 104.

4. Quoted in Billington, *Peggy Ashcroft*, 161.

5. Ibid., 162.

6. Milton Levin, *Noel Coward* (New York: Twayne Publishers, 1968), omits mention of the play entirely.

7. Strong, *British Theatre Design: The Modern Age* (London: Weidenfield and Nicolson, 1989), 18.

Chapter 13. Film (1933–1966)

1. For her expert assistance on Motley's design for film, I am grateful to Catherine Surowiec, Designs Collection researcher for the British Film Institute. Information about film credits comes from the American Film Institute Catalogue.

2. *The Motion Picture Guide,* 2570, credits Paula Newman for the costumes.

3. For an intelligent account by an author who was part of the industry, see Paul Rotha, *The Film Till Now: A Survey of World Cinema* (New York: Funk & Wagnalls, 1951, rev. ed.), especially the preface (15–61), "The British Film" (313–322) and "The British Film" (544–60). Rotha suggests that the vigor of British film during the War came from patriotism and a "new faith in native film production" (36).

4. Ibid., 360.

5. Ibid., 36.

6. It was titled *Burn, Witch Burn!* in the United States; the working title had been *Conjure Wife.*

7. Directed by Richard Thorpe, it starred Robert Montgomery, Rosalind Russell, and Dame May Whitty.

8. It was titled *A Study in Terror* in the United States, *Sherlock Holmes Grosster Fall* in Germany.

Chapter 14. The Motley Legacy (1966–   )

1. At this writing, the Motley Theatre Design Course is headed by Alison Chitty with Margaret Harris and Hayden Griffin as co-directors. Administrative director Christine Rodgers oversees the day-to-day arrangements for guest speakers and projects, thereby allowing Margaret Harris to scale back the amount of time spent on the premises. John Simpson continues as honorary administrator.

2. *Designing and Making Costumes for the Stage,* with an introduction and edited by Michael Mullin (London: Herbert Press; and New York: Routledge, 1992).

3. Ibid.; *Costume and Set Designs by Motley* (Glendale and London: KaiDib International 1988), 125 pp. with 210 slides; *The Motley Collection of Set and Costume Designs:* Color Microfiche, with an introduction by Michael Mullin (Haslemere, Surrey: Emmet Publishing, 1933).

List of Works Consulted

Adburgham, Alison. *Shops and Shopping, 1800–1914: Where, and in What Manner The Well-dressed Englishwoman Bought Her Clothes.* 2d ed. London: Allen and Unwin, 1981.

Agate, James. *First Nights.* London: Nicholson & Watson, 1934.

———. *Red Letter Nights.* London: Jonathan Cape, 1944.

Anthony, Pegaret, and Arnold, Janet. *Costume: A General Bibliography.* Rev. and enlarged ed., London: Costume Society, V & A Museum, 1977.

Anthony, Gordon. *John Gielgud.* London: Geoffrey Bales, 1938.

Appelbaum, Stanley, ed. *The New York Stage.* New York: Dover, 1976.

Arnold, Janet. *Patterns of Fashion: Englishwomen's Dresses and Their Construction, c. 1860–1940.* London: Wace, 1966.

———. *Patterns of Fashion: Englishwomen's Dresses and Their Construction, c. 1660–1840.* London: Macmillan, 1972.

———. *Patterns of Fashion: The Cut and Construction of Clothes for Men and Women, c. 1560–1620.* London: Macmillan, 1985.

Aronson, Arnold. *American Set Design.* New York: Theatre Communications Group, 1985.

Arranca, Bonnie, and Dasgupta, Gautam. *American Playwrights: A Critical Survey.* New York: Drama Book Specialists, 1981.

Arundell, Dennis. *The Story of Sadler's Wells, 1683–1964.* New York: Theatre Arts, 1965.

Atkinson, Brooks. *Sean O'Casey: From Times Past.* New York: Barnes and Noble, 1982.

———. *Broadway Scrapbook.* New York: Theatre Arts, Inc., 1947.

———. *Broadway.* New York: Macmillan, 1974.

Baines, Barbara Burman. *Fashion Revivals from the Elizabethan Age to the Present Day.* New York: Drama Book Publishers, 1981.

Baker, Blanch M. *Theatre and Allied Arts: A Guide to Books Dealing with the History, Criticism, and Technic of the Drama and Theatre.* New York: H. W. Wilson Company, 1952.

Balcon, Michael; Ernest Lindgren; Roger Manvell; and Forsyth Hardy. *Twenty Years of British Films: (1925–1947).* London: Falcon Press, 1948.

Barker, Felix. *Laurence Olivier.* New York: Hippocrene Books, 1984.

Baxter, Beverley. *First Nights and Footlights.* London: Hutchinson, 1955.

Baygan, Lee. *Makeup for Theatre, Film, and Television.* New York: Drama Book Publishers, 1982.

Behl, Dennis. *Tanya Moiseiwitch: Her Contribution to Theatre Arts from 1935–1980.* Ann Arbor, Mich.: University Microfilms International, 1981.

Bentham, Frederick. *The Art of Stage Lighting.* 3d ed., London: Pitman House, 1980.

Bernheim, Alfred L. *The Business of the Theatre: An Economic History of the American Theatre, 1750–1932.* New York: Benjamin Blom, 1932. Rpt. 1964.

Billington, Michael. *Peggy Ashcroft*. London: Murray, 1988.

Black, Kitty. *Upper Circle: A Theatrical Chronicle*. London: Methuen, 1984.

Blau, Herbert. *Take Up the Bodies-Theatre at the Vanishing Point*. Urbana: University of Illinois Press, 1982.

Boehn, Max von. *Die Mode: Menschen und Moden vom Beginn unsrer Zeitrechnung bus zum Ende des neunzehnten Jahrhunderts nach Bildern und Kupfern der Zeit*. 8 vols. Munich: Bruckmann, 1904.

———. *Modes and Manners: Ornaments*. London: J. M. Dent & Sons, 1929.

Bordman, Gerald. *American Musical Theatre, A Chronicle*. New York: Oxford University Press, 1978.

Bossert, Helmuth *Folk Art of Europe*. New York: Praeger, 1953. 2d printing, 1964.

Boucher, Francois. *20,000 Years of Fashion: The History of Costume and Personal Adornment*. Expanded edition. New York: Harry N. Abrams, 1965.

Bragg, Melvyn. *Laurence Olivier*. London: Hutchinson, 1984.

Breitman, Ellen. *Art and the Stage*. Bloomington: Indiana University Press, 1981.

Broby-Johansen, R. *Body and Clothes*. New York: Reinhold, 1968.

Brook, Peter. *The Shifting Point*. New York: Harper & Row, 1987.

Bruder, Karl C. *Properties and Dressing the Stage*. New York: Richard Rosen Press, 1969.

Bruhn, Wolfgang, and Tilke Max. *A Pictorial History of Costume: A Survey of Costume of All Periods and Peoples from Antiquity to Modern Times including National Costume in Europe and Non-European Countries*. New York: Frederick A. Praeger, 1955.

Bryde, Penelope. *The Male Image, Men's Fashion in Britain 1300–1970*. London: Batsford, 1979.

Carrick, Edward. *Art and Design in the British Film, A Pictorial Directory of British Art Directors and Their Work*. London: Dennis Dobson, 1948.

———. *Designing for Motion Picures*. London: Studio Publications, 1941.

Castle, Charles. *Oliver Messel: A Biography*. London: Thames and Hudson, 1986.

Cavanagh, John. *British Theatre: Bibliography, 1901 to 1985*. Mottisfont, U.K.: Motley Press, 1989.

Christgau, Patricia. "Motley behind the scenes: Liz Montgomery," *American Artist* 38. 384–389. (November 1974): 65–69, 104–105.

Cochran, Charles B. *The Secrets of a Showman*. London: Heinemann, 1925.

Colas, Rene. *Bibliographie Generale du Costume et de la Mode*. 2 vols. Paris: Librairie Rene Colas, 1933.

Contini, Mila. *Fashion: From Ancient Egypt to the Present Day*. New York: Odyssey Press, 1965.

Corey, Irene. *The Mask of Reality: An Approach to Design for Theatre*. Anchorage, Kentucky: Anchorage Press, 1968.

Corson, Richard. *Stage Makeup*. 7th ed. Englwood Cliffs, N.J.: Prentice-Hall, 1986.

Craig, Edward. *Gordon Craig: The Story of His Life*. New York: Knopf, 1968.

Craig, Edward Gordon. *On the Art of the Theatre*. New York: Theatre Arts, 1911.

———. *Scene*. London: Humphrey Milford, 1923.

———. *Index to the Story of My Days*. New York: Viking Press, 1957.

Cunnington, Phillis. *The History of Underclothes*. London: Faber and Faber, 1981. Rev. ed. by Susan Luckham and Valerie Mansfield.

———. *Costume in Pictures*. London: Studio Vista, 1964. Rept. 1969.

Darlington, W.A. *Laurence Olivier*. London: Morgan Grampian, 1968.

Davenport, Millia. *The Book of Costume*. 2 vols. New York: Crown, 1948.

de Marly, Diana. *Costume on the Stage: 1600–1940*. London: Batsford, 1982.

———. *Working Dress: A History of Occupational Clothing*. London: Batsford, 1986.

de Mille, Agnes. *And Promenade Home*. Boston: Little, Brown & Co., 1958.

———. *The Book of Dance*. New York: Golden Press, 1963.

————. *Dance to the Piper*. Boston: Little, Brown & Co., 1952.

————. *Lizzie Borden*. Boston: Little, Brown & Co., 1968.

————. *Reprieve*. New York: Doubleday & Company, 1981.

————. *Speak to Me. Dance with Me*. Boston: Little, Brown & Co., 1973.

————. *To a Young Dancer*. London: Putnam, 1960.

de Valois, Ninette. *Invitation to the Ballet*. New York: Oxford University Press, 1938.

Dean, Basil. *Seven Ages*. London: Hutchinson & Co., 1970.

Diesel, Leota. "Liz Montgomery of Motley: One Third of a Team," *Theatre Arts* 35 (November 1951): 38–41, 68.

Downs, Harold. *The Critic in the Theatre*. London: Pitman & Sons, 1953.

Earle, Alice Morse. *Two Centuries of Costume in America*. 2 vols. New York: Benjamin Blom, 1903. Reissued 1968.

Edson, Doris. *Period Patterns*. Boston: Walter H. Baker Company, 1942.

Elsom, John. *Post-War British Theatre*. London: Routledge & Kegan Paul, 1976.

Emery, Joy Spanabel. *Stage Costume Techniques*. Englewood Cliffs, N.J.: Prentice-Hall, 1981.

Evans, Mary. *How to Make Historic American Costumes*. New York: Barnes & Co., 1942. Rept. Detroit: Gale, 1976.

Evans, Peter. *The Music of Benjamin Britten*. Minneapolis: University of Minnesota Press, 1979.

Ewing, Elizabeth. *Everyday Dress, 1650–1900*. London: Batsford, 1984.

————. *History of Twentieth Century Fashion*. London: Batsford, 1974.

Fehl, Fred. *Stars of the Broadway Stage: 1940–1967*. In *Performance Photographs*. New York: Dover Publications, 1983.

————. *On Broadway: Performance Photographs*. Text by William and Jane Stott. Austin: University of Texas Press, 1974.

Findlater, Richard. *These Our Actors: Peggy Ashcroft, John Gielgud, Laurence Olivier, Ralph Richardson*. London: Elm Tree Books, 1983.

————. *Emlyn Williams*. London: Rockliff, 1956.

Foster, Vanda. *Bags and Purses*. New York: Drama Book Publishers, 1982.

Fuerst, Walter Rene, and Hume, Samuel J. *Twentieth-Century Stage Decoration*. 2 vols. New York: Benjamin Blom, 1967. First published by New York: Knopf, 1929.

Ganzl, Kurt. *The British Musical Theatre*. New York: Macmillan, 1986.

————. *British Musical Theatre: 1915–1984*. London: Macmillan, 1986.

Geen, Michael. *Theatrical Costume and the Amateur Stage*. London: Arco, 1968.

George, Kathleen. *Rhythm in Drama*. Pittsburgh: University of Pittsburgh Press, 1980.

Gielgud, John. *Early Stages*. London: Falcon Press, 1939.

————. *Stage Directions*. New York: Random House, 1963.

Goodwin, John. *British Theatre Design, The Modern Age*. London: Weidenfeld & Nicolson, 1989.

————, ed. *Royal Shakespeare Theatre Company: 1960–63*. London: Max Reinhardt, 1964.

Guinness, Alec. *Blessings in Disguise*. London: Hamish Hamilton, 1985.

Guthrie, Tyrone. *A Life in the Theatre*. New York: McGraw-Hill, 1959.

Hainaux, Rene. *Stage Design throughout the World Since 1935*. New York: Theatre Arts, 1955.

————. *Stage Design throughout the World Since 1950*. New York: Theatre Arts, 1964.

Hale, Lionel. *The Old Vic: 1949–50*. London: Evans Brothers, 1950.

Hansen, Henny Harald. *Costumes and Styles*. New York: E. P. Dutton, 1956. Reissued 1972.

Hartley, Dorothy, and Margaret M. Elliot. *Life and Work of the People of England*. 6 vols. London: Batsford, 1925.

Harwood, Ronald, ed. *The Ages of Gielgud: An Actor at Eighty*. London: Hodder and Stoughton, 1985.

Hayman, Ronald. *John Gielgud*. New York: Random House, 1971.

Henderson, Mary C. *Theatre in America, 200 Years of Plays, Players, and Productions*. New York: Harry N. Abrams, 1986.

Hewison, Robert. *Under Siege: Literary Life in London, 1939–45.* New York: Oxford University Press, 1977.

Hiler, Hilaire and Meyer. *Bibliography of Costume.* New York: Benjamin Blom, 1939. Reissued 1967.

Hobson, Harold. *Theatre in Britain: A Personal View.* Oxford: Phaidon, 1984.

Hodge, Francis, ed. *Innovations in Stage and Theatre Design: Papers of the Sixth Congress, International Federation for Theatre Research.* American Society for Theatre Research, 1972.

Houseman, John. *Run-through.* New York: Simon and Schuster, 1972.

Howard, Diana. *London Theatres and Music Halls, 1850–1950.* London: The Library Association, 1970.

Howard, Jean E. *Shakespeare's Art of Orchestration.* Urbana: University of Illinois Press, 1984.

Howard, John T., Jr. *A Bibliography of Theatre Technology: Acoustics and Sound, Lighting, Properties, and Scenery.* Westport, Conn.: Greenwood Press, 1982.

Howgego, James L. *London in the Twenties and Thirties.* London: B.T. Batsford, Ltd., 1978.

Huggett, Richard. *Binkie Beaumont: Eminence Grise of the West End Theatre, 1933–1973.* London: Hodder & Stoughton, 1989

Hutchinson, Sidney C. *The History of the Royal Academy 1768–1968.* London: Chapman's Hall, 1968.

Ingham, Rosemary, and Covey, Liz. *The Costume Designer's Handbook: A Complete Guide for Amateur and Professional Costume Designers.* Englewood Cliffs, N.J.: Prentice-Hall, 1983.

Jackson, Sheila. *Costumes for the Stage.* New York: E. P. Dutton, 1978.

Jacobson, Robert. *Magnificence: Onstage at the Met.* London: Thames and Hudson, 1985.

Jarman, Richard. *A History of Sadler's Wells Opera.* London: Fast Print, Ltd., 1975.

Jefferys, James B. *Retail Trading in Britain, 1850–1950.* Cambridge: Cambridge University Press, 1954..

Kaye, Phyllis Johnson. *National Playwrights Directory.* New York: Drama Book Specialists, 1977.

Kelly, Frances M. *Shakespearian Costume for the Stage and Screen.* London: Adam & Charles Black, 1938.

Kendall, Alan. *Benjamin Britten.* London: Macmillan, 1973.

Keown, Eric. *Peggy Ashcroft.* London: Rockliff, 1955.

Kiernan, Thomas. *Sir Larry: The Life of Laurence Olivier.* New York: Times Books, 1981.

Koehler, Carl. *A History of Costume.* Ed. & augmented by Emma von Sichart. Philadelphia: David McKay, n.d.

Komisarjevsky, Theodore. *Myself and the Theatre.* London: Dutton, 1930.

———. *The Theatre and a Changing Civilisation.* London: Bodley Head, 1935.

Larson, Orville K. *Scene Design in the American Theatre from 1915 to 1960.* Fayetteville and London: University of Arkansas Press, 1989.

Lauts, Jan. *Carpaccio: Paintings and Drawings.* London: Phaidon, 1962.

Laver, James. *The Concise History of Costume and Fashion.* New York: Charles Scribner's Sons, 1969.

———. *Costume.* New York: Hawthorn, 1963.

———. *Costume in the Theatre.* London: Harrap, 1964.

———. *Costume through the Ages.* New York: Simon and Schuster, 1963.

———. *Drama: Its Costume and Decor.* London: Studio Publications, 1951.

Leiter, Samuel L. *From Belasco to Brook: Representative Directors of the English-Speaking Stage.* New York and London: Greenwood Press, 1991.

Lester, Katherine Morris, and Oerke, Bess Viola. *Accessories of Dress: An Illustrated History of Those Frills and Furbellows of Fashion Which Have Come to be Known as.* Peoria: Manual Arts Press, 1940.

Leese, Elizabeth. *Costume Design in the Movies.* London: BCW, 1976; New York: Frederick Ungar, 1977. (Subsequent reissue by Dover, New York: 1991 deletes Motley and adds film credits through 1987.)

Levin, Milton. *Noel Coward.* New York: Twayne Publishers, 1968.

Linthicum, M. Channing. *Costume in the Drama of Shakespeare and his Contemporaries.* New York: Hacker Art Books, 1972.

Manchester, P. W. *The Vic-Wells Ballet: A Progress.* London: Gollancz, 1942.

Marchant, William. *To Be Continued, A Play in Three Acts.* New York: Dramatists Play Service, 1952.

Mates, Julian. *America's Musical Stage: Two Hundred Years of Musical Theatre.* Westport, Conn.: Greenwood Press, 1985.

May, Robin. *A Companion to the Theatre: The Anglo-American Stage from 1920.* New York: Hippocrene Books, 1973.

Mazer, Cary M. *Shakespeare Refashioned: Elizabethan Plays on Edward Ian Stages.* Ann Arbor, Mich.: UMI Research Press, 1981.

McCarthy, Desmond. *Shaw's Plays in Review.* New York: Thames and Hudson, 1951, 66–76.

McClellan, Elisabeth. *Historic Dress in America, 1607–1870.* New York: Arno Press, 1977. First published 1904–1910.

McClintic, Guthrie. *Me and Kit.* Boston: Little, Brown and Company, 1955.

McMullan, Frank. *Directing Shakespeare in the Contemporary Theatre.* New York: Richard Rosen, 1974.

Messel, Oliver. *Stage Designs and Costumes.* London: John Lane the Bodley Head, 1933.

Miles, Patrick, ed. *Chekhov on the British Stage.* London: Cambridge University Press, 1993.

Montgomery, Elizabeth. "Lilian Bayliss and The Old Vic," *Players Magazine,* December 1963, 90.

Mordden, Ethan. *The American Theatre.* New York: Oxford University Press, 1981.

———. *Rodgers and Hammerstein.* New York: Harry N. Abrams, 1992.

Morse, H. K. *Elizabethan Pageantry: A Pictorial Survey of Costume and its Commentators from c. 1560–1620.* London: The Studio, Ltd., 1934.

Motley. "Modern Dress-Fun or Frustration?" *Players Magazine* 39–40 (April 1963): 202–206.

———. *Designing and Making Stage Costumes.* Studio Vista, London: 1964. 2d ed. revised and with an introduction by Michael Mullin, London: Herbert Press, 1992.

———. *Theatre Props.* New York: Drama Book Specialists, 1975.

Mullin, Michael, ed. *"Macbeth" Onstage: An Annotated Facimile of Glen Byam Shaw's Promptbook.* Columbia: University of Missouri Press, 1976.

Myerscough-Walker, R. *Stage and Film Decor.* London: Pitman & Sons, 1939 (?).

Nathan, Archie. *Costumes by Nathan.* London: Newnes, 1960.

Noble, Peter. *British Theatre.* London: British Yearbooks, 1946.

Norris, Herbert. *Costume and Fashion.* 2 vols. J. M. Dent, London: 1940. First published 1927.

Oenslager, Donald. *Stage Design: Four Centuries of Scenic Invention.* New York: Viking, 1975.

Olivier, Laurence. *Confessions of an Actor.* London: Weidenfeld and Nicolson, 1982.

Onions, C. T., et al. *Shakespeare's England: An Account of the Life and Manners of His Age.* 2 vols. Oxford: Clarendon Press, 1916.

Owen, Bobbi. *Scenic Design on Broadway: Designers and Their Credits, 1915–1990.* New York: Greenwood Press, 1991.

Payne, Blanche. *History of Costume from the Ancient Egyptians to the Twentieth Century.* New York: Harper & Row, 1965.

Pepper, Terence. *Howard Coster's Celebrity Portraits.* National Portrait Gallery, London, in association with New York: Dover Publications, Inc., 1985.

Pilbrow, Richard. *Stage Lighting.* New York: Drama Book Specialists, 1970, 1979.

Planché, James Robinson. *A Cyclopaedia of Costume or Dictionary of Dress.* 2 vols. London: Chatto and Windus, 1876.

———. *A History of British Costume.* London: Bell and Sons, 1913.

Poggi, Jack. *Theatre in America: The Impact of Economic Forces, 1870–1967.* Ithaca: Cornell University Press, 1968.

Poole, Austin Lane, ed. *Medieval England.* 2 vols. Oxford: Oxford University Press, 1958.

Poynter, Sir Edward J., ed. *The National Gallery.* London: Cassell & Company, 1899.

Prince, Hal. *Contradictions: Notes on Twenty-Six Fears in the Theatre*. Cornwall, N.Y.: Cornwall Press, 1974.

Prisk, Berneice. *Stage Costume Handbook*. New York: Harper & Row, 1966.

Prisk, Berneice, and Byers, Jack A. *Costuming*. New York: Richards Rosen, 1970.

Quayle, Anthony. *A Time to Speak*. London: Barrie & Jenkins, 1990.

Racinet, Albert. *The Historical Encyclopedia of Costumes*. New York and Oxford: Facts on File Publications, 1988.

Redgrave, Michael. *Mask or Face, Reflections in an Actor's Mirror*. New York: Theatre Arts, 1958.

Reid, Francis. *The Stage Lighting Handbook*. New York: Theatre Arts, 1976.

Rivadue, Barry. *Mary Martin: A Bio-Bibliography*. New York: Greenwood Press, 1991.

Roberts, Grace. *The Borzoi Book of Ballets*. New York: Alfred A. Knopf, 1949.

Rodgers, Richard. *Musical Stages: An Autobiography*. New York: Random House, 1975.

Roose-Evans, James. *London Theatre from the Globe to the National*. Oxford: Phaidon, 1977.

Rosenfeld, Sybil. *A Short History of Scene Design in Great Britain*. Oxford: Basil Blackwell, 1973.

Rotha, Paul. *The Film Till Now*. New York: Funk & Wagnalls, 1951.

Russell, Douglas A. *Costume History and Style*. Englewood Cliffs, N.J.: Prentice-Hall, 1983.

Saint-Denis, Michel. *Theatre: The Rediscovery of Style*. New York: Theatre Arts, 1960.

Sanderson, Michael. *From Irving to Olivier: A Social History of the Acting Profession in England, 1880–1963*. New York: St Martin's Press, 1984.

Schouvaloff, Alexander. *Theatre on Paper*. London: Sotheby's, 1990.

Sheringham, George, et. al. *Design in the Theatre*. London: The Studio, 1927.

Short, Ernest. *Fifty Years of Vaudeville*. Westport, CT: Greenwood Press, 1978.

Simon, John. "Play Reviews." *Theatre Arts* 46, (February 1962): 10–11.

Smith, C. Ray, ed. *The Theatre Crafts Book of Make-up, Masks, and Wigs*. Emmaus, Pa.: Rodale Press, 1974.

Snowden, James. *The Folk Dress of Europe*. New York: Mayflower Books, Inc., 1979.

Speaight, Robert. *Shakespeare on the Stage*. Boston: Little, Brown & Company, 1973.

———. *William Poel and the Elizabethan Revival*. Melbourne, London, Toronto: William Heinemann, Ltd., London, 1954.

Speaker-Yuan, Margaret. *Agnes de Mille*. New York: Chelsea House Publishers, 1990.

Stevenson, Isabelle. *The Tony Award: A Complete Listing with a History of the American Theatre Wing*. New York: Arno Press: 1975.

Stott, William with Jane Stott. *On Broadway*. Austin: University of Texas Press, 1978.

Strong, Roy. *British Theatre Design: The Modern Age*. London: Weidenfeld and Nicolson, 1989.

Tanitch, Robert. *Ashcroft*. London: Hutchinson, 1987.

Taylor, John Russell. *Anger and After*. London: Methuen, 1962.

Teague, Frances. *The Curious History of "Bartholomew Fair."* London and Toronto: Associated University Presses, 1985.

Thomas, Beverly Jane. *A Practical Approach to Costume Design and Construction*. 2 vols. Boston: Allyn and Bacon, 1982.

Thorndike, Sybil. *Lilian Baylis: As I Knew Her*. London: Chapman & Hall, n.d.

Tilke, Max. *Costume Patterns and Designs: A Survey of Costume Patterns and Designs of All Periods and Nations from Antiquity to Modern Times*. New York: Frederick A. Praeger, 1955.

Tomkins, Julia. *Easy-to-Make Costumes for Stage and School*. Boston: Plays, Inc., 1976.

———. *Stage Costumes and How to Make Them*. Boston: Plays, Inc., 1969.

Trewin, J. C. *Shakespeare on the English Stage: 1900–1964*. London: Barrie and Rockliff, 1964.

———. *The Theatre Since 1900*. London: Andrew Dakers, 1951.

———. *The Turbulent Thirties: A Further Decade of the Theatre*. London: Macdonald, 1960.

Trewin, J.C.; Mander, Raymond; and Joe Mitchenson. *The Gay Twenties, A Decade of the Theatre*. London: MacDonald, 1958.

Tynan, Kenneth. *He That Plays the King*. London: Longmans, Green and Co., Ltd., 1950.

Veaner, Daniel. *Scene Painting: Tools and Techniques*. Englewood Cliffs, N.J.: Prentice-Hall, 1984.

Vickers, John. *The Old Vic in Photographs*. London: Saturn Press, 1947.

Walton, J. Michael. *Craig on Theatre*. London: Methuen, 1983.

Wardle, Irving. *The Theatres of George Devine*. London: Eyre Methuen, 1978.

Warner, Marina. *The Crack in the Teacup: Britain in the 20th Century*. New York: Houghton Mifflin, 1979.

Waugh, Norah. *Corsets and Crinolines*. New York: Theatre Arts Books, 1954. 2d printing 1970.

———. *The Cut of Men's Clothes: 1600–1900*. New York: Theatre Arts, 1964.

———. *The Cut of Women's Clothes: 1600–1930*. New York: Theatre Arts, 1968.

Whitworth, Geoffrey. *Theatre in Action*. New York: Studio Publications, n.d. (late 1930s).

Willett, C., and Cunnington, Phillis. *A Picture History of English Costume*. New York: Macmillan, 1960.

Williams, Emlyn. *Emlyn: An Early Autobiography, 1927–1935*. London: Bodley Head, 1973.

———. *George: An Early Autobiography*. New York: Random House, London: 1961.

Williams, Harcourt. *Four Years at the Old Vic, 1929–1933*. London: Putnam, 1935.

———. *The Old Vic Saga*. London: Winchester Publications Limited, 1939.

Williams, John T. *Costumes and Settings for Shakespeare's Plays*. London: Batsford, 1982.

Williamson, Audrey. *Old Vic Drama: A Twelve Year's Study of Plays and Players*. London: Rockliff, 1948.

———. *Theatre of Two Decades*. New York: Macmillan, 1951.

Wilson, Colin. *Bernard Shaw: A Reassessment*. New York: Atheneum, 1969.

Zinkeisen, Doris. *Designing for the Stage*. London and New York: Studio, n.d.

Index

This index covers items in the body of the text; it does not cover items in the appendices or notes. **Boldface** page numbers indicate illustrations.

Abbott, George, 82
Abraham, Paul, 40
Actors Company, 73, 199
Adler, Richard, 103
Albery, Bronson, 32, 34, 39, 40, 44, 47
Allen, Lewis, 201
Allen, Woody, 106–7
Almeida Theatre, 207
Alswang, Ralph, 100
American Ballet Theatre, 78–79
American Shakespeare Festival, 97–101
Amram, David, 100
Anderson, Judith, 63–65
Anderson, Lindsay, 125, 203, 204
Anderson, Maxwell, 94–95
Andrews, Harry, **45, 46, 67, 68,** 138–40, 145–48, 189
Angel, Maurice, 66
Anne of a Thousand Days, 94–95
Anouilh, Jean, 95–96, 102, 176, 188–89
Antigone, 173
Antony and Cleopatra: Byam Shaw (1946), 112, 139; Byam Shaw (Shakespeare Memorial Theatre, 1953), 138–40; Olivier (1951), 139
Archibald, William, 83, 95
Arden, John, 125
Argle, Duchess of, 109
Ariadne, 61
Arlen, Stephen, 156
Aronson, Boris, 95–96, 100
Around the World in Eighty Days, 99
Arthur, Jean, 91
Arthur, Robert Alan, 103
As You Like It: 13; Lovat Fraser (1920), 28; Baker (1961), 102; Byam Shaw (Young Vic, 1949), 118–19; Byam Shaw (Shakespeare Memorial Theatre, 1952), 137–38; Byam Shaw (Australian tour, 1953), 136; Byam Shaw (Shakespeare Memorial Theatre, 1957), 148–49
Asche, Oscar, 145
Ash, Tim Hopewell, 201
Ashcroft, Peggy, 14, 15, 31–33, 48–51, 65–66, 68–69, **68, 69,** 70, 74, 110, 125, **125,** 132–33, **132,** 137, 138–40, 173, 177, 209
Ashmore, Peter, 125, 177

Asmodee, 100
Aspern Papers, The, 178
Atkins, Robert, 28, 36
Atkinson, Rosaline, 144
Auber, Maurice, 164
Aucassin and Nicolette, 51–52
Auden, W. H., 170
Audley, Maxine, 14
Aumont, Jean Pierre, 105

Babes in Arms, 80
Baddeley, Angela, **68,** 70, 137, 142, 144
Badel, Alan, 126
Baily, James, 123
Baker Street, 106
Baker, Word, 102
Bakst, Leon, 29
Balanchine, George, 79, 80, 101
Balcon, Michael, 196
Ball at the Savoy, 40
Ballantyne, Sheila, 118
Ballet Russe, 29–30, 40
Ballet Russe de Monte Carlo, 79
Bamford, Freda, 40
Bancroft, Anne, 105, 106
Barker, Harley Granville. *See* Granville Barker, Harley
Barr, Jeanne, 203
Barrie, James M., 91, 192
Bartholomew Fair, 119–21, **120**
Basehart, Richard, 105
Baster, Beverly, 110
Baxter, Keith, 103, 186, 189
Baylis, Lilian, 28, 29, 40, 58, 65
Bayne, Peter, 61
BBC Radio, 41
Beaton, Cecil, 193, 195
Beaumont, Cyril W., 51–52
Beaumont, Hugh "Binkie," 57, 65–70, 109, 112, 174
Beckett, 102
Beerbohm, Max, 55, 56–57
Beerbohm Tree, Sir Herbert, 27–28
Beggars' Opera: Lovat Fraser (1920), 28; Gielgud (1939), 74, 155

Bell for Adano, A, 82
Bells, The, 191–92
Ben Franklin in Paris, 106
Bennet, Arnold, 201
Bennett, Joan, 100
Bennett, Vivien, 177
Benois, Alexandre, 29
Benson, Frank, 29
Benson, George, 186
Benson, Sally, 96
Benthall, Michael, 123
Berg, Gertrude, 100–101
Bergersen, Baldwin, 83
Bergonzi, Carlo, 101
Berkeley, Lennox, 157
Berman, S. M., 100
Bernardi, Mario, 165
Berry, Eric, 105
Besch, Anthony, 158
Betti, Ugo, 96
Bickford, Charles, 197
Billington, Michael, 32, 37, 51, 70, 139, 177, 191, 207
Bird, John, 133
Birmingham Repertory Theatre, 30
Bitter Harvest, 55
Blair, Janet, 204
Blakely, Colin, 204
Blanche Fury, 200
Bland, Frederick, 133
Blaney, Norah, 183
Blatchley, John, 163, 165, 166, 186, 206
Blithe Spirit, 197
Blood Wedding, 72
Bloom, Clair, 205
Bolt, Robert, 104
Bond, Edward, 125, 207
Boone, Richard, 100
Born Free, 205
Bosco, Philip, 105
Botticelli, 48, 49
Boundy, John, 15
Bourgeoise Gentilhomme, Le, L.T.S. (1938), 70
Boyer, Charles, 105
Bracken, Eddy, 93
Bradley-Dyne, M., 186
Brecht, Bertholt, 105
Brenton, 125
Brewer, Marcel, 39, 61
Brewster's Millions, 197
Brief Encounter, 197
Briggs, Hedley, 58
Brighouse, Harold, 186
Brinton, Ralph, 203
British Film Academy award, 205
Britten, Benjamin, 170–71
Britton, Tony, 138–40
Brook, Peter, 47, 54, 145, 151, 154, 176
Brooks, Jan, 100
Brown, Ivor, 56
Browne, Coral, 111, 187
Bryan, Dora, 203
Bryan, John, 195, 199, 200, 201
Buchanan, Jack, 197
Bulgakov, Leo, 83
Burnett, Ivy Compton. *See* Compton-Burnett, Ivy

Burrell, John, 91
Burton, Richard, 122, 205
Bury, John, 186, 194
Byam Shaw, Glen, 14, 15, 20, 40, 41, 48, 51, 52, 55–56, 57, 61, 63, 65–66, **67, 68,** 70, 71–72, 72, 74, 97, 103, 104, 112, 113, 121–22, 183, 186, 187, 189, 190–91, 192, 193–94; Old Vic Centre, 114–23; Sadler's Wells and English National Opera, 155–70; Shakespeare Memorial Theatre, 135–54

Cacoyannis, Michael, 106
Cadell, Jean, 110
Caesar and Cleopatra, 139
Callas, Maria, 101
Can-Can, 92, **92,** 176–77
Candida, 95
Captain Boycott, 200–201
Captain Carvallo, 95
Card, The, 175, 201
Cards of Identify, 129
Carey, Joyce, 183
Carey, Kathleen, 21
Carib Song, 83, 88, 95
Carnovsky, Morris, 99, 100, 101
Carousel, 87
Carpaccio, 48
Carrick, Edward, 201
Carroll, Leo G., 201
Carter, Terry, 103
Caspary, Vera, 177
Chalk Garden, The, 177
Chapman, Edward, 197
Charles the King, 57
Charliy's Aunt, 176
Charlot, Andre, 33
Chase, Lucia, 76
Chayefsky, Paddy, 96
Chekhov, Anton, 68, 118, 177
Cherry Orchard, The: L.T.S. (1938), 70; Saint-Denis (1939), 74, 110; Webster (1944), 81
Chichester Festival, 188, 194
Chitty, Alison, 207
Christie, John, 74
Church, Diana, **131**
Church, Esme, 56
Clandestine Marriage, 188–89
Clare, Mary, 183
Clark, Petula, 201
Clayton, Jack, 202, 204
Clift, Montgomery, 83
Clunes, Alec, 121
Clurman, Harold, 100
Cochran's Revues, 28, 41
Cochran, Charles B., 41
Cohen, Alexander H., 106
Colbert, Claudette, 105
Colbourne, Maurice, 56
Cold Wind and the Warm, The, 100
Collier, Marie, 163
Colman, George, 188
Colombe, 176
Compagnie des Quinze, 9, 44–45, 58, 126
Complaisant Lover, The, 84, 103–4
Compton-Burnett, Ivy, 193
Confederacy, The, **60,** 61
Cons, Emma, 28

Consul, The, 171–72
Cook, Donald, 100
Cooper, Melville, 84
Copeau, Jaques, 44
Copland, Aaron, 79–80
Corbett, Marta [Mrs. William Montgomery], 23, **24**
Coriolanus, 137
Cornell, Katharine ("Kit"), 79, **79,** 80–81, 84, 95
Corwin, Norman, 100
Così fan Tutte, 160–62, **161**
Coulouris, George, 81
Country Wife, The: American transfer (1957), 99; Devine (Royal Court, 1956), 129–30, **130, 131**
Courtenay, Tom, 203–4
Courting at Burnt Ranch. See Rodeo
Courtneys of Curzon Street, The, 201
Coward, Noel, 33, 111, 182–83, 188, 192
Cowie, Laura, 36
Craig, Edward Gordon, 20, 29, 31, 54
Cranach, Lucas, 42, 73
Critics Circle Award, 97
Cronyn, Hume, 77, 96
Crucible, The, 126–27
Crutchley, Rosalie, 126–27
Cuckoo in the Nest, A, 133
Cuickshank, Andrew, 183
Cukor, George, 199
Curtis, Margaret, 82
Cusak, Cyril, 205

Dahl, Roald, 96
Dance of the Vampires, 205
Dancer, The, 94
Dane, Clemence, 56
Daniels, Maurice, 14, 15
Danquah, Paul, 203
Dare, Phyllis, 197
Davies, Rupert, 205
Daviot, Gordon [Elizabeth Mackintosh], 33, 40, 41
Davis, Colin, 156, 158, 161, 162, 164, 165
Davis, Joe, 52
Day, Edith, 183
Dazzling Prospect, 183–84
de Havilland, Olivia, 95
de Mille, Agnes, 76, 78–80, 83, 85, 87, 91, 105
de Nobili, Lila, 145, 193
de Valoise, Ninette, 40
Dean, Basil, 174
Dean, James, 96
Dear Octopus, 71–72, **71**
Dekker, Thomas, 57
Delmar, Vina, 95
Dench, Judi, 205
Denison, Michael, 186, 192
Dennis, Nigel, 129
Der Freischütz, 162–63
Design for the Ballet, 51–52
Deval, Jacques, 105, 174
Devils of Loudun, The, 106
Devils, The, 106
Devine, George: 9, 13, 31–32, 39, 44–48, 51, 54, 58–61, 64–65, **68,** 70, 72, 73, 74, 99, 108, 111, 122, 123, 126–27, 129–30, 133, 135, 156, 157, 176, 199, 201; Old Vic Centre, 114–23; English Stage Company, 124–34; English Stage Society, 130–31

Devlin, William, 32, 41, 144
Dexter, John, 107, 125, 131, 183, 188, 191
Diaghilev, Serge, 29, 40, 54
Diamond, David, 82
Dickens, Charles, 73, 74
Dietz, Howard, 82
Dignam, Mark, 121, 132–33
Dillman, Bradford, 97
Dim Lustre, 81
Dixon, Jean, 95
Doctor's Dilemma, The: McClintic (New York, 1942), 79, **79;** Hentschel (London, 1942), 110; McWhinnie (London, 1963), 186
Dolin, Anton, 51, 81
Doll's House, A, 5
Don't Drink the Water, 106–7
Donald, James, 173–74
Donat, Peter, 97
Doncaster, Stephen, 115
Doyle, Arthur Conan, 205
Drake, Alfred, 91, 100
Drury Lane Theatre, 207
Duke, Vernon, 82
DuMaurier, 197
Dunham, Joanna, 183

Eager, Edward, 91
Eaton, Andrew, 14, 15
Eddy, Nelson, 195, 199
Edwards, Ben, 96, 100
Elder, Eldon, 93, 96, 105
Eldridge, Florence, 97
Electra, **60,** 61
Elizabeth II, Queen, 138
Elizabethan Stage Society, 30
Ellis, Mary, 137
English National Opera, 13, 155–70, 206
English Stage Company, 123, 124–34
English Stage Society, 130–31
Eugene Onegin, **156,** 157
Evans, Edith, 30, 48, 58, **58, 73,** 74, 110, 112, 188

Family and a Fortune, A, 193
Fantasticks, The, 105
Farrah, Abdul, 194
Farrell, M. J., 183
Faulkner, William, 100, 131–32
Faust, 164
Fearless Vampire Killers, The, 205
Feder, Abe, 96
Fennell, Albert, 204
Ffrangcon-Davies, Gwen, **34, 40,** 57, **68, 73,** 110
Fighting Cock, The, 189
Finch, Peter, 176, 204–5
Finlay, Frank, 205
Finney, Albert, 153
Firth, Tazzena, 194
Fitzgerald, F. Scott, 96
Flare Path, 85
Fletcher, Allen, 105
Flower, Fordham, 138
Flynn, Erroll, 100
Fontaine, Robert, 176
For Love or Money, 174
Fog, 205

Forbes-Robertson, Jean, 56
Ford, Ruth, 96, 131–32
Forster, E. M., 186
Fraser, Claude Lovat, 28, 54, 74
Freeland, Thornton, 197
Frings, Ketti, 99–100
Furse, Roger, 122, 199

Gabel, Martin, 100
Garcia Lorca, Federico, 72
Garrick, David, 188–89
Gaskill, William, 125
Gates, Larry, 101
Gautier, Madeline, 44, 45–46
Geer, Will, 101, 102
Gibbons, Cedric, 199
Gide, Andre, 96
Gielgud, John, **10**, 15, 20, 25, 27, 28, 31–33, 33–44, 47, 48–51,
    52, 54, 55–56, 61, 63, 66–70, **67, 68, 71,** 72, **73,** 74, 94, 110,
    113, 173–74, 176, 183–84, 209
Gilbert and Sullivan, 106
Gilette, Anita, 106–7
Gill, Peter, 14, 15, 124, 133, 203, 207
Gilliat, Sidney, 200–201
Glenville, Peter, 102
Globe Season, 72
Glyndebourne Opera Company, 74, 155
Goetz, Augustus, 96, 173–74
Goetz, Ruth, 96, 173–74
Good Companions, The, 32
Goodall, Reginald, 166
Goodner, Carol, **68,** 103
Goring, Marius, 56–57, **56,** 57–58, 70, 74, 138–40, 191
Gothard, David, 14, 207
Gounod, Charles, 164
Gozzi, Carlo, 115–16
Graham, Colin, 168
Graham, Martha, 87
Grand Tour, The, 95
Granger, Stewart, 195, **300**
Granville-Barker, Harley, 28, 30, 72
Gray, Dulcie, 186, 192
Gray, Simon, 191
Great Expectations, 73, 196, **198**
Green Grow the Lilacs, 87
Greene, Graham, 103
Grenfell, Joyce, 111
Griffin, Hayden, 14, 15, 194, 206, 207
Griffith, Hugh, 99–100
Grunwald, Alfred, 40
Guiness, Alec, 28, 45, 47, 48, 52, 61, **68,** 70, 73, 175, 191,
    193, 199, **200,** 201
Guthrie, Tyrone, 28, 30, 42, 56, 61–63, 66, 97, 110–11, 119,
    122
Gwynn, Michael, 126–27

Haffenden, Elizabeth, 195
Hagen, Uta, 96
Haggard, Piers, 186
Haggard, Stephen, 186
Haigh, Kenneth, 127–28, **128**
Hall, Natalie, 40, 191
Hall, Peter, 145, 153, 186, 194
Hamlet: 30; Byam Shaw (1959), 41; Gordon Craig (1912), 29;
    Gielgud (1934), 33, 41–44, **41;** Gielgud (1939), 72, 73–74;

Guthrie (1937), 61; Hunt (1950), 119; Barry Jackson (1928);
    Byam Shaw (Shakespeare Memorial Theatre, 1958), 151–52
Hammer horror films, 204, 205
Hammerstein, Oscar, 39, 88
Hancock, 164
Hands, Trevor, 194
Hanson, Reg, 15, 124, 133, 162
Happy as Larry, 91
Happy Hypocrite, 56–57, **56**
Happy Time, The, 176
Hardwicke, Cedric, 84, 100–101, 205
Hardy, Robert, 153
Hare, David, 125
Hargrave, Roy, 83
Harris, Dale, 15
Harris, Julie, 95–96, 99, 130
Harris, Kathleen, **22**
Harris, Margaret: evolution of theatre design, 194; personal
    matters, 9, 13, 15, 19, **20,** 21–23, 74–75, 111–13. *See also*
    entries under Motley
Harris, Richard, 204
Harris, Robert, 148–49
Harris, Sophia: design for film, 195–205; personal matters, 9,
    11, 13, 19, **20,** 21–23, 74, 107, 108, 124, 133–34, **134,** 189,
    201; "Sophia Devine," 205; wartime experience, 108–13.
    See also entries under Motley
Harris, William, 19, **22**
Harrison, Rex, 94–95
Harrison, Tom, 46
Harron, Donald, 102
Hart, Elizabeth, 186
Hartnell, Norman, 197
Hartnell, William, 204
Harvey, Laurence, 96, 99, 129–30, 137–38, 141–42
Hassan, 174
Hassel, Christopher, 31
Haunted Ballroom, The, 40, 51–52
Havoc, June, 82
Hay Fever, 188
Hays, David, 97, 100
Hayward, Leland, 88
He Was Born Gay, 63
He Who Gets Slapped, 93
Head, Edith, 201
Hedda Gabler: Hentschel (1936), 56; Devine (1954), 125–26,
    125
Heiress, The, 96, 173
Hellman, Lillian, 110, 183
Helpmann, Robert, 40
Henby, Harry, 46
Henderson, Marcia, 91
Henry IV, Part One, 104–5
Henry V: Byam Shaw (Old Vic, 1950), 119, 121–22; Guthrie
    (1937), 61–63, **62, 63,** 76; Olivier (film), 122, 197, 199
Henry VIII. See Private Life of Henry VIII, The
Hentschel, Irene, 55, 56, 135
Hepburn, Katharine, 97, 99, 203
Herbert, Jocelyn, 58, 126, 203
Heretic, The, 192
Highland Fling, 82
Hill, George Roy, 99–100
Hill, James, 205
Hiller, Wendy, 183
Hines, Patrick, 102
Hingle, Pat, 102

Hitchcock, Alfred, 197
Hobson, Valerie, 109, 199, **200,** 201
Hobson's Choice, 186–87, **187**
Holbrook, Hal, 105
Holm, Ian, 153
Honeys, The, 96
Hope for the Best, 83
Hordern, Michael, 122, 137, 205
Horner, Harry, 101
Houston, Donald, 205
How He Lied to Her Husband, 192
Howard, Edwin, 97
Howe, George, 48
Howells, Roger, 14
Howes, Sally Ann, 103
Hughes, Hazel, 183
Hunt, Hugh, 32, 119, 122
Hunt, Martita, 73, **198,** 199, 201
Hunter, Kim, 102
Huntley, Raymond, 72
Hurok, Sol, 81
Hurry, Leslie, 193
Huxley, Aldous, 106
Hyde-White, Wilfrid, 201

I Married an Angel, 195, 197–98
I Met a Murderer, 197
Ibsen Cycle, 56
Idomeneo, 159–60, **160**
Il Trovatore, 101–2, 155
Illinois, University of, Library, 13–14
Immoralist, The, 96
Importance of Being Earnest, The, 72–73, **73,** 74, 94, 110
Innocents, The, 95, 176, 196, 202
Irving, Henry, 28, 44, 191
Irving, Laurence, 195, 200
Ishii, Mitsuru, 14, 209
Island of Goats, 96
It Happened in September, 110

Jackson, Barry, 30, 31, 72
Jacobi, Lou, 106–7
James, Henry, 95, 96, 176, 178
Janacek, Leos, 163
Jane Eyre, 100
Jeans, Isabel, 56, **56**
Jenkins, Fred, 136, 149
Jenkins, George, 96
Jenkins, Megs, 202
Johns, Glynis, 201
Johnson, Celia, 186
Johnson, Richard, 103, 148–49, 151, 205
Johnston, Margaret, 204
Johnstone, Alex, 56
Jones, Alan Pryce. *See* Pryce-Jones, Alan
Jones, Barry, 57
Jones, David Jones. *See* Lloyd Jones, David
Jones, Jack, 72
Jones, Robert Edmond, 30, 76
Jones, Tom, 105
Jourdan, Louis, 96
Judith and Holofernes, 61
Julius Caesar, 149–51, **150**
Jump, Harriet, 14, 15, 111, 113, 130, 133–34, **134,** 210

Kahn, Florence, 55–56
Karloff, Boris, 91
Kauffer, McKnight, 40
Kean, Charles, 28
Keen, Malcolm, **37**
Kellino, Pamela, 197
Kellino, Roy, 197
Kelly, Felix, 157
Kelly, Grace, 95
Kempson, Rachel, 126, 176
Kern, Jerome, 87
Kerr, Deborah, 109, 202
Key, Peter, 188
Keynes, Maynard, 56
King John, 122
King Lear, 152–53
King Stag, The, 115–16, **116**
Kiss Me Kate, 91
Kitt, Eartha, 93
Klee, Paul, 140
Kliner, Harry, 83
Knight, Esmond, 135, 183, 205
Komisarjevsky, Theodore, 30, 31, 66, 72
Korda, Alexander, 196
Kronborg Castle, Elsinore, 73
Kulukundis, Eddie, 192
Kwamina, 102–3, **103**

La Bohème, 165–66
Lady at the Wheel, 177
Lady from the Sea, 183, **184, 185**
Landau, Ely, 203
Landau, Jack, 99, 102
Langley, John, 15
Langner, Lawrence, 97
Last of Mrs. Cheyney, The, 110–11
Laughton, Charles, 152–53, 196–97
Launder, Frank, 200–201
Laurie, John, 56
Lawes, David, 192
Lawrence of Arabia, 182
Lawrence, Carol, 14
Lawrence, D. H., 83
Lawrence, Gertrude, 84
Lawrence, Jordan, 174
Laye, Evelyn, 177
Le Carré, John, 205
Le Gallienne, Eva, 81, 82
Lean, David, 73, 197, 199, 200
Lee, Canada, 82–83
Lee, Ming Cho, 47, 105
Lee, Robert E., 102
Lee, Sondra, 92–93
Lehmann, Beatrix, 205
Leigh, Vivien, 55–56, 56–57, **56,** 65, 74, 76–77, 105, 110, 139
Leighton, Margaret, 137–38, 183, 193
Lend-lease productions from London, 93
Lerner, Alan Jay, 91–92
Lewis, Leopold, 191
Liar, The, 91
Liberty's of London, 91
Life and Death of Colonel Blimp, The, 197
Life with Father, 85
Likely Tale, A, 177
Liliom, 87

Lindsay, Vera, 73
Littler, Emile, 187
Lloyd, Frederick, **68**
Lloyd Jones, David, 168
Lockwood, Margaret, 195
Loesser, Frank, 93
Loewe, Frederick, 91–92
Logan, Joshua, 88
Lohner-Beda, Fritz, 40
Lohr, Mary, 183
London Calling, 33
London Theatre Museum, 14
London Theatre Studio (L.T.S.), 47–48, 53, 54, 56, 58–61, 70, 72, 73, 112, 206
Loneliness of the Long Distance Runner, The, 196, 203–4
Long Day's Journey into Night: drama, 97; film, 97, 196, 203
Longhurst, Henry, 177
Lonsdale, Frederick, 110–11
Look Back in Anger: American transfer (1957), 99, 100; film, 203; Royal Court (1956), 128–29, **128**
Look Homeward, Angel, 99–100
Lopokova, Lydia, 56
Lorca, Federico Garcia. *See* Garcia Lorca, Federico
Lorenzo, 105
Love Me Little, 100
Love, Kermit, 79
Lovers and Friends, 81
Lowe, Arthur, 204
Luckham, Cyril, 189, 205

Macbeth Onstage, 210
Macbeth: American Shakespeare Festival (1961), 102; Beerbohm Tree (1911), 28, 64; Byam Shaw (1955), 65; Barry Jackson (1928), 64; Komisarjevsky (1933), 64; Saint-Denis (1937), 63–65, **64**
MacDonald, Jeanette, 195, 199
MacLiammoir, Michael, 126
MacOwan, Michael, 177
Madamoiselle Colombe, 95–96
Magarshack, David, 177
Magic Flute, The, 157–58, 209
Magistrate, The, 178
Magito, Suria, 111, 116–18
Major Barbara, 132
Majority of One, A, 100–101
Makropulos Case, The, 163–64, **163**
Mallory, Jay, 41
Mamoulian, Rouben, 82
Man For All Seasons, A, 103, 104, 182
Manders and Mitchenson Theatre Collection, 14, 15
Mangan, Richard, 15
March, Frederic, 97
Marchant, William, 95
Marigold, 197; Thomas Bentley, 197
Markova, Alicia, 40, 51
Marks, Joe E., 92–93
Marriage of Blood [*Blood Wedding*], 72
Marriage Story, 174
Marshall, Edward, 205
Martha, 101, 102
Martin, Betty, 175
Martin, Mary, 88–90, 92–93
Marty, 96
Masked Ball, A, 164–65

Mason, James, 195, 197, 205
Massey, Anna, 187
Massey, Raymond, 84
Master Builder, The, 56
Mastersingers of Nuremberg, The, 85, 166–67
Matter of Life and Death, A, 197
Mauriac, Francois, 100
McArthur, Molly, 31, 33, 55
McBean, Angus, 35
McClintic, Guthrie, 79, 80–81, 83, 84, 95
McCormack, Reverend "Pat," 25
McEwan, Geraldine, 190
McKern, Leo, 182
McWhinnie, Douglas, 186
Medford, Kay, 106–7
Melvin, Murray, 203
Men About the House, 33
Mendleson, Anthony, 205
Menotti, Gian Carlo, 156, 171–72
Merchant of Venice, The: Byam Shaw (1967), 190–91; Gielgud (1932), 37–39, **38**; Gielgud and Byam Shaw (1938), 70; Landau (1956), 99
Meredith, Burgess, 91
Merry Wives of Windsor, The: American Shakespeare Festival (1959), 101; Byam Shaw (Shakespeare Memorial Theatre, 1955), 143–45, **142, 143, 144, 145, 146**
Messel, Oliver, 30, 38, 195
Michell, Keith, 115, 141, 144
Michener, James, 88
Mid-Summer, 95
Middle of the Night, 96
Midsummer Night's Dream, A: Atkins (1932), 36, 39; Beerbohm Tree (1900), 28; Brook (1970), 154; Devine (Shakespeare Memorial Theatre, 1954), 140–41; Granville-Barker (1914), 28
Mielziner, Jo, 91, 94, 96, 97, 100, 106–7
Mildmay, Audrey, 74
Miles, Bernard, 199
Milhaud, Darius, 64
Military service: by Motley's close friends, 108–9
Milland, Ray, 201
Miller, Arthur, 126–27
Mills, Hayley, 192
Mills, John, 104, 176, 199, **200**
Miss Liberty, 91
Mitchell, Byron, 105
Mitchell, Julian, 193
Mitchell, Yvonne, 61, 73, 138–40
Mitchenson. *See* Manders and Mitchenson Theatre Collection
Moiseiwitsch, Tanya, 145, 152, 193
Montague, Lee, 115
Montgomery, Elizabeth, **94**; American Shakespeare Festival, 97–99, 101–2, 104–5; New York hits, 86; New York collaborators, 86; New York musicals, 87–93; New York opera; 101–2; personal matters, 9, 13, 15, **23**, 23–24, **26**, 74–75, 85, 86, 97, 102, 107; "straight plays" in New York, 93–113. *See also* entries under Motley
Montgomery, William, 23, **24**
Month in the Country, 110
Moore, Dudley, 133
Morahan, Tom, 201
Morgan, Charles, 176
Morgan, Joanna, 15
Morley, Robert, 177, 205
Mortimer, Penelope, 204–5

Most Happy Fella, The, 93
Mother Courage and Her Children, 105
Motley: couturier, 39, 109–10, **109;** studio workshops, 9, 34–35, 36, 38–39, 44, 111, 113; Design Course, 61, 154, 206–11; designs for films, 195–205; principles of design, 53–54; retrospective London exhibition, 190; Sophia Harris's death, 189; West End hits, 173; West End career, 193–94
Mozart, Wolfgang Amadeus, 157, 159, 160–62
Much Ado About Nothing: Old Vic (1930), 27; Stratford Memorial Theatre, (1958), 152
Mulberry Bush, The, 126
Mullin, Margaret Mary, 15
Munday, John, 91
Music Man, The, 106
Musser, Tharon, 97

Naming of Murderer's Rock, The, 133
Napier, John, 194
National Endowment for the Humanities, 210
Nativity Play (1927), 25–26
Neagle, Anna, 201
Neame, Ronald, 73, 201
Negri, Richard, 115
Nelson, 157
Neville, John, 122, 183, 205
Nicholls, Anthony, 204, 205
Nielson-Terry, Phyllis, 37
Night Must Fall, 204
Night of the Eagle, 204
Nissen, Greta, 197
Niven, David, 197
Noah, 34, 45–48, 59, 115
Nolan, Kathy, 92–93
Novello, Ivor, 56–57, **56**
Nunn, Trevor, 194
Nutting, Anthony, 178
Nye, Carrie, 102

O'Brien, Tim, 194
O'Donovan, Desmond, 188
O'Hearn, Robert, 102
O'Toole, Peter, 182
Obey, Andre, 44
Oenslager, Donald, 79, 91, 95, 100
Oklahoma!, 79, 87, 93, 196, 201–2
Old Ladies, The, 44
Old Vic Centre, 114–23, 178, 206
Old Vic School, 61, 113, 114–23
Old Vic Theatre: costume balls, 27; history of, 28–29, 36–37, 53, 57–58, 65, 76–77, 177–78
Olivier, Laurence, 11, 28, 40, 48, 51, 52, 63–65, 70, 74, 102, 119, 122, 139, 174, 188, 190, 197
110 in the Shade, 105–6
Orry-Kelly, 201–2, **202**
Osborn, Paul, 82
Osborne, John, 99, 125, 128–29
Othello: Byam Shaw (Shakespeare Memorial Theatre, 1956), 145–48, **147,** Webster (1943), 81; Welles (1951), 174–75
Oxford University Dramatic Society (O.U.D.S.), 9, 13, 29, 31–33, 48

Page, Geraldine, 95, 96
Paint Your Wagon, 91–92, 176, 196
Parfitt, Judy, 177
Parker, Cecil, 205

Parkyn, Leslie, 204
Parnell, 57
Pasco, Richard, 121, 183
Patience, 106
Patrick, Nigel, 192
Paul Bunyan, 170–71, **171**
Pears, Peter, 170
Perkins, Anthony, 99–100
Perry, John, 183
Peter Pan: Bernstein (1950), 91; Robbins (1954), 91, 92–93
Pettingell, Frank, 201
Phillip, Prince, 138
Phipps, John T., 15
Pinero, Arthur Wing, 188
Pinza, Ezio, 88
Playfair, Giles, 111
Playfair, Nigel, 28, 30
Playing with Fire, 186
Pleshette, Suzanne, 100
Plowright, Joan, 129, 132, 186–87, 190
Poel, William, 30, 31
Polanski, Roman, 205
Poliakoff, Vera, 59
Porter, Cole, 92
Porter, Eric, 132–33, 205
Portman, Eric, 100
Potter, H. C., 82
Press Cuttings, 192
Preston, Robert, 104, 106
Price, Leontyne, 101–2
Pride, Malcolm, 115
Prince Hal, 106
Pringle, Marian, 15
Private Life of Henry VIII, The, 196–97
Prokofiev, Sergei, 156, 168–70
Promoter, The, 201
Pryce-Jones, Alan, 157
Puccini, Giacomo, 165, 170
Pulitzer Prize, 97
Pumpkin Eater, The, 204–5
Pygmalion, 84

Quartermaine, Leon, 65–66, **68**
Quayle, Anthony, 34, 41, 65–66, 112, 135–37, 141, 144, 187, 205
Queen of Scots, 40
Queen's Season, 65
Quinn, Anthony, 102
Quintero, Jose, 97

Rainmaker, The, 105
Rake's Progress, The, 158–59
Rattigan, Terence, 32, 104, 178
Reader, Hilda, 26–27, 40, 109
Rebel with a Cause, 203–4
Reckord, Barry, 133
Red Wagon, The, 72, 197
Redgrave, Lynn, 186, 188
Redgrave, Michael, 41, 65–66, 67, **67, 68,** 70, 74, 103, 110, 138–40, 151–52, 186–87, 202, 203–4
Redgrave, Vanessa, 141, 183
Redman, Joyce, 94–95, **94**
Reinhardt, Max, 37
Reisz, Karel, 204
Relph, Michael, 110

Requiem for a Nun: American transfer (1959) 100; Richardson (Royal Court, 1957), 131–32

Rhondda Roundabout, 72

Rice, Elmer, 95

Richard II: Old Vic (1929), **26;** O.U.D.S. (1935), 55–56; Queen's (1937), 65–66, **66;** American Shakespeare Festival (1962), 104–5

Richard III: Coulouris (1943), 81; Byam Shaw (Shakespeare Memorial Theatre, 1953), 138–39

Richard of Bordeaux, 9, **10,** 33–36, **34,** 39, 55, 118

Richardson, Ralph, 28, 70, 173–74, 189, 190, 203

Richardson, Tony, 126–27, 128–29, 131–32, 203

Rickards, Jocelyn, 203

Right Honourable Gentleman, The, 186–87

Ritch, David, 171–72

Ritchard, Cyril, 92–93, 110, 111

Ritt, Martin, 205

Rivalry, The, 100

Rivals, The, 189–90

River Line, The, 176

Riverside Studios, 207

Robards, Jason, Jr., 97, 106

Robbins, Jerome, 92–93, 105

Roberts, Anthony, 106–7

Roberts, Rachel, 204

Robinson, Edward G., 97

Rodeo or *The Courting at Burnt Ranch,* 79–80, **80**

Rodgers, Chris, 15

Rodgers, Richard, 88

Rogers, Paul, 121

Romberg, Sigmund, 87

Romeo and Juliet: Brook (1947), 151; Byam Shaw (Shakespeare Memorial Theatre, 1954), 140–42; Byam Shaw (Shakespeare Memorial Theatre, 1958), 151; Gielgud (1935), 33, 47–51, 151; Terence Gray (1928), 27; Olivier (1940), 11, 74, 76–77; O.U.D.S. (1932), 9, 13, 27, 31–33, **32,** 34, 48

Rosmersholm: Hentschel (1936), 56; Devine (1959), 132–33

Ross, 103, 104, 178–82, **179**

Rossiter, Leonard, 204

Rousseau, Henri Douanier, 115

Royal Ballet, 41

Royal Court Theatre, 13, 123, 126–27, **127**

Royal National Theatre, 53, 70, 123, 153–54, 207

Royal Shakespeare Company, 53, 70, 106, 123, 153–54

Rutherford, Margaret, 177, 183, 189–90

Sadie Thompson, 82, 88

Sadler's Wells Ballet, 41

Sadler's Wells Opera; 155–70; move to London Coliseum, 168, 170, 206

Saint-Denis, Blaise, 44

Saint-Denis, Michel: 9, 44–48, 54, 56, 57–61, 63–65, 66–70, 72, 74, 80, 111, 113, 126, 156, 207; Old Vic Centre, 114–23

Salaman, Merula, 46

Salaman, Susan, 45

Samoiloff lighting, 40

Saturday Night and Sunday Morning, 204

Savory, Gerald, 177

Scandal in Assyria, 72

Schiaparelli, 197

Schiller, Frederick, 177

Schleis, Thomas, 15

Schmidt, Harvey, 105

School for Scandal, 66, **67**

Schwartz, Rudolf, 157–58

Schweitzer, Albert, 23

Scofield, Paul, 103, 104, 135, 182

Scott, Zachary, 131–32

Scribe, Eugène, 164

Seagull, The, 177

Seale, Doublas, 105, 152, 178

Second Best Bed, 93–94

Seitz, Tani, 96

Selznick, Irene, 103

Seyler, Athene, 110, 111

Seymour, Barbara, 47

Shakespeare Centre Library, 14

Shakespeare Memorial Theatre, 13, 53, 123, 135–54; traditions, 29, 136–37, 142–43, 153–54

Shaw, George Bernard, 28, 79, **79,** 84, 95, 110, 132, 139, 189, 192

Shaw, Glen Byam. *See* Byam Shaw, Glen

Sheridan, Richard Brinsley, 189–90

Sherringham, James, 28

Sherwood, Robert, 105

Shinbone Alley, 93

Shingleton, Wilfred, 195, 199, 200, 202, 205

Shoemaker's Holiday, The, 116–18, **117, 118**

Showboat, 87

Sickert, Walter, 23

Sigh No More, 111

Simionato, Giuletta, 101

Simmons, Jean, 199

Simon Boccanegra, 101–2

Skydrift, 83–84

Slezak, Walter, 97

Smith, Dodie, 71, 81

Smith, Maggie, 188, 205

Smith, Oliver, 79, 85, 105, 106

Snow Queen, The, 116–18

So Evil My Love, 201

Song in the Theatre, 133

Sonrel, Pierre, 121

South Pacific, 88–91, **88, 89, 90,** 211

Spanish Writers' Relief Agency, 72

Spiegelgass, Leonard, 100–101

Spring 1600, 39–40

Spring Awakening, 133

Spy Who Came in From the Cold, The, 205

Squires, Ronald, 74

Stannard, Heather, 135

Stapleton, Maureen, 100

Stella, Antoinette, 101

Stephens, Robert, 190

Stewart, David J., 96

Stewart, Sophie, 197

Stickney, Dorothy, 95

Stockwell, Dean, 203

Storey, David, 204

Strange Orchestra, 37

Strindberg, August, 186, 190, **191**

Student Prince, The, 87

Sullivan, Francis L., 199

Summer and Smoke, 95

Suroweic, Catherine, 15

Sweet Aloes, 41, 61

Swenson, Inga, 97, 106

Swinford, Susan, 177

Tagg, Alan, 115, 188

Tales of the South Pacific. See *South Pacific*
Tally-Ho or *The Frail Quarry,* 81, 85
Tandy, Jessica, 36, 41, 51, 63, 96, 102
Tannhäuser, 158
Taste of Honey, A, 203
Tate, Sharon, 205
Tausky, Villem, 157
Taylor, Elizabeth, 99
Taylor, Valerie, 110
Tchaikovsky, Peter Ilyich, 157
Tearle, Godfrey, 112
Tempest, Marie, 71, **71**
Tempest, The, 82–83
Ter-Arturian, Rouben, 99, 106
Terry, Ellen, 20
Terry, Phyllis Nielsen. *See* Nielsen-Terry, Phyllis
Thackeray, William Makepeace, 186
Theatre Guild, 30
Theatre Museum, London, 14
Theatre practices: American different from English, 76–78, 84–85, 86–87, 103; wartime London, 108–12
This Sporting Life, 204
Thomas, Powys, 118
Thompson, Sada, 101
Thorndike, Sybil, 110, 183
Thorne, Angela, 189, 190–91
Three, 192
Three Sisters: Komisarjevsky (1928), 66; McClintic (1942), 80–81; Saint-Denis (1938) 66–70
Three Virgins and the Devil, 78–79
Tickle, Frank, 73
Titus Andronicus, 154
To Be Continued, 95
Todd, Ann, 201
Todd, Mike, 99
Tom Jones, 203, 204
Toms, Carl, 115
Tone, Franchot, 83
Tony Award, 102
Torres, Raquel, 197
Tosca, 170
Tovarich, 105
Toye, Geoffrey, 41
Toye, Wendy, 51, 91, 111
Toys in the Attic, **182,** 183
Tracey, Edmund, 15
Travers, Ben, 133
Trelawny of the Wells, 188
Trio, 192
Trocadero, 41
Troilus and Cressida: American Shakespeare Association (1961); 102; Quayle (Shakespeare Memorial Theatre, 1948), 135–56
Truce of the Bear, The, 86
Tucker, Norman, 156
Tudor, Anthony, 81
Tulip Tree, The, 186
Turn of the Screw, The, 95, 176
Tushingham, Rita, 203
Tutin, Dorothy, 121, 151–52
Twelfth Night: L.T.S. (1938), 70; Hentschel (1939), 72, 135

Uncle Vanya, L.T.S. (1938), 70
University of Illinois Library, 13–14
Unknown Soldier and His Wife, The, 107, 192–93

Ure, Mary, 126–27, 128–29, **128**
Ustinov, Peter, 61, 107, 192–93

Vail, Amanda, 100
Van Eyck, Peter, 205
Van Fleet, Jo, 99–100
Vanity Fair, 186
Verdi, Giuseppe, 164–65
Verdon, Gwen, 92
Vic-Wells Ballet, 41
Vilan, Demetrios, 100
Village Wooing, 192
von Weber, Carl Maria, 162
Voskovec, George, 205
Vosper, Frank, **41,** 43

Wagner, Richard, 158, 166
Waiting in the Wings, 182–83
Walbrook, Anton, 177
Walker, David, 85, 166
Walker, Zena, 141–42
Wallach, Eli, 95–96, 100
Wallis, Hal B., 201
Wanamaker, Sam, 205
War and Peace, 156, 168–70
Ward, Simon, 191
Warren, Jeff, 177
Warren, Leonard, 101
Washbourne, Mona, 204
Washington Square, 96
Watch on the Rhine, 110
Watts, Margaret, 39, 199
Ways and Means, 192
We Take the Town, 104
Weaver, Fritz, 106
Webb, Alan, 132
Webster, Margaret, 40, 81, 81–83, 183
Wedding in Paris, 176–77
Wedding, The, 118
Wedekind, Frank, 133
Werner, Oskar, 205
Wesker, Arnold, 125
West, Morris, 192
Where Angels Fear to Tread, 186
White, Wilfrid Hyde. *See* Hyde-White, Wilfrid
Wilcox, Herbert, 197, 201
Wild Duck, The: Byam Shaw (1970), 192; L.T.S. (1938), 70
Wilder, Gene, 105
Wilding, Michael, 201
Will, The, 192
Williams, Emlyn, 39–40, 59, 63, 110, 111, 145–48, 204
Williams, Esther, 97
Williams, Harcourt, 37
Williams, Howard, 172
Williams, Hugh, 177
Williams, Tennessee, 83, 95
Williamson, Nicol, 133
Willman, Noel, 61, 104, 182
Wilmot, John, 169
Wilmot, Patrick, 85, 86
Wilson, Angus, 126
Wilson, Jean, 141
Wind of Heaven, The, 111
Windham, Donald, 83
Winter's Tale, A: Granville-Barker (1912), 28; Quayle (Shake-

speare Memorial Theatre, 1948), 135
Wintle, Julian, 204
Wise Child, 191
Witch of Edmonton, The, 57–58
Withers, Googie, 103
Wolfe, Thomas, 99
Woodman, Pardoe, **67**
Wright, Marie, **68**
Wyatt, Jane, 83
Wycherley, William, 99, 129–30
Wyngarde, Peter, 202, 204
Wynyard, Diana, 41, 110, 177, 183

York, Robert, 33
You in Your Small Corner, 133
You Never Can Tell, 189
You Touched Me, 83
Young and the Beautiful, The, 96
Young Vic, The, 114–15

Zeffirelli, Franco, 193
Zimmerman telegram, 23
Zinkeisen, Doris, 28
Zorina, Vera, 82